RAND McNALLY ILLUSTRATED
Dictionary of Sports

RAND McNALLY ILLUSTRATED
Dictionary of Sports

Graeme Wright

Rand McNally & Company
CHICAGO   NEW YORK   SAN FRANCISCO

Contents

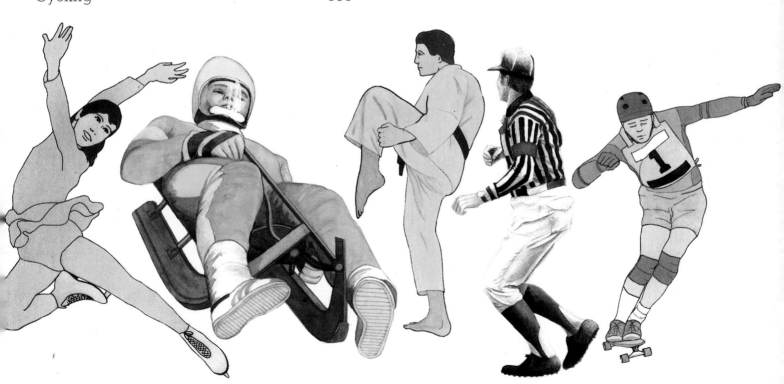

Introduction

Ideas, however transitory, have a strange way of returning in concrete form. So it was when **Dictionary of Sports** was suggested to me. I had long thought that there was a need for a glossary of sporting terms to help the armchair sports fan understand the jargon beloved by so many commentators. This editorial idea was more adventurous, and also more useful than my original one. This book, illustrated throughout in full color, enables the reader to see in visual form what words often express inadequately. I feel sure the reader's knowledge of sports and their terminology will be increased enormously, and that this book will bring a new dimension to his or her sports-viewing . . . be it at an actual event or in front of the television.

To those readers whose sport is not included, or whose favorite terms I have omitted, my apologies. With the increasing interest in sports of all kinds it would have been impossible to include every one. Because sports are international, and as the book is designed for an international readership, I have consciously tried to take the international point of view, rather than a national one. For this reason, too, measurements are generally somewhat mixed. The metric system has been used for truly international sports and most Olympic sports. The U.S. standard has been used for American sports such as football and in certain instances when metric measurements would not be meaningful to most U.S. readers.

No book of this nature can be the work of one or two people, and although my name appears below I consider myself merely as the spokesman for the many people involved in the project: the illustrators, designers, editors and researchers. Appropriately, for a book on sports, it is very much a team effort.

My special thanks go to my former colleague Andy Wilson, not only for writing certain aquatic articles, but also for his assistance at a time when personal circumstances dictated that I was unavailable.

Graeme Wright

Altitude Sports

Gliding

Few sports allow man to experience such a communion with nature as gliding. Powered flight could almost be said to violate nature; but to remain airborne, gain lift and travel long distances in a heavier-than-air machine without an engine require both a dependence on and an understanding of the elements. Only for the launch is the glider dependent on mechanically powered forces such as a plane, car, or winch—and for the absolute purist there is always the bungey launch. The principles of gliding are governed by the science—some would say art—of soaring by means of thermals, slope and wave lifts. These allow the pilot to climb the glider to a certain height before utilizing the force of gravity to glide quickly down towards an area where another up-current will provide more lift. By such means—soaring and gliding—the glider can travel long distances across country.

The smooth silence of unpowered flight has attracted man from the earliest days of aviation, but it was only with the discovery in the 1920s of thermal lift that gliding really developed as a sporting pastime. Today, new materials and techniques have given the glider an aerodynamic efficiency undreamed of in pioneering days. With their streamlined fiberglass-bodied gliders and their advanced soaring expertise, the best of modern pilots can fly distances of 600mi given the right conditions. Pilots are graded through a series of national and international proficiency awards up to the three diamonds and the 1000km diploma. In championships points are awarded for speed along a given route, a triangular or out-and-return course, or occasionally around a number of turning points.

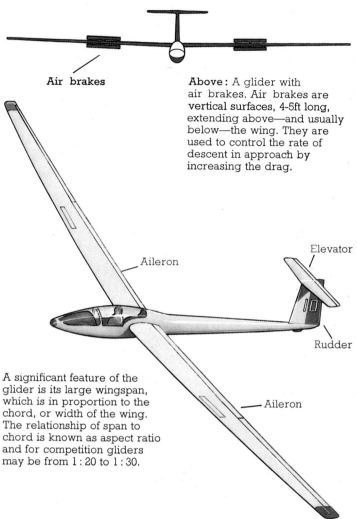

Air brakes

Above: A glider with air brakes. Air brakes are vertical surfaces, 4-5ft long, extending above—and usually below—the wing. They are used to control the rate of descent in approach by increasing the drag.

Elevator

Aileron

Rudder

Aileron

A significant feature of the glider is its large wingspan, which is in proportion to the chord, or width of the wing. The relationship of span to chord is known as aspect ratio and for competition gliders may be from 1:20 to 1:30.

absolute altitude A record category for heights achieved.

ailerons The control surfaces on the trailing edges of a glider's wings to control its lateral balance and angle of bank.

air brakes Plates which can be extended vertically above and/or below the wings to allow a pilot to control his rate of descent by steepening his glide path when landing.

airplane tow The launching method in which a light plane is used to tow a glider into the air on the end of a synthetic fiber rope. At above 1600ft the glider pilot releases the rope.

airspeed indicator The flight instrument which gives the speed at which a glider is flying through the air. Correct at sea level, it can under-read progressively with increasing altitudes and can be adversely affected by large angles of yaw (*qv*).

altimeter The flight instrument which shows the height at which a glider is flying. As it is, in effect, a barometer measuring

the change in pressure in terms of height, the heights given are above the level at which the instrument was set at zero, ie at sea level, or at ground level on the airfield.

artificial horizon A cloud-flying instrument which gives the attitude (*qv*) of a glider without its pilot having to make visual reference to the natural horizon.

ASI Airspeed indicator.

attitude A glider's position in relation to the ground. The term is also used to refer to the pilot's view of the horizon in relationship to the nose of his glider.

B badge A national proficiency award for a pilot who has made three solo flights and proved an ability to take off, land and turn in both directions.

barograph A barometer which records pressure changes in terms of height and also records the length of a flight. It is an essential instrument when records and proficiency badge flights are made.

bronze C A proficiency badge,

awarded in Britain only, to a pilot who has achieved two soaring (*qv*) flights of 30 minutes (60min if airplane towed), satisfied an instructor of his or her competence, and passed examinations in navigation and airmanship, meteorology, principles of flight and air law. It is equivalent to a national license and qualifies a pilot to try for the international badges.

bungey launch A manual method of launching a glider by catapulting it from a hilltop with a rubber rope stretched out in a 'V' shape. Five or six people may be needed on either side of the 'V'.

C badge A national proficiency award for a pilot who has completed his first soaring flight.

calculator A circular slide rule used to work out the height needed to glide a certain distance, or alternatively the distance of glide from a specific height. It is calibrated specially for the type of glider in which it is used.

car-tow The method of launching a glider by towing it into the

wind behind a car traveling at around 50mph. The principle is similar to that of launching a kite, the glider rising into the air as its speed increases. At the top of the launch, the pilot releases the cable.

chord The width of the wing in a fore and aft direction.

CIVV Commission Internationale Vol à Voile, the world controlling body for gliding under the aegis of the FAI (*qv*).

climb rate The speed in feet per second at which a glider ascends.

diamonds The highest international proficiency badges, of which there are three. They are awarded for: (1) a distance flight of 500km; (2) a triangular course flight of 300km; (3) a gain of height of 5000m.

distance to a declared goal The record category for a distance flight to a point determined before departure.

distance to a turn point and back to a starting place The record category for an out-and-return

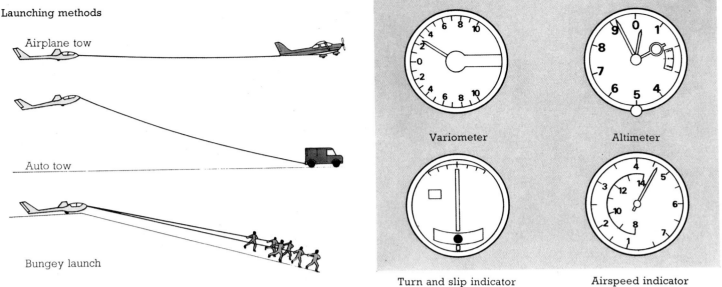

Launching methods

Airplane tow

Auto tow

Bungey launch

Variometer

Altimeter

Turn and slip indicator

Airspeed indicator

Above: The instrument panel of a glider. The instruments show that the plane is flying at almost 2000ft, or 610m, (see altimeter) and climbing at a rate of 3 knots (variometer). It has an airspeed of just over 45 knots. The needle of the turn and slip indicator shows that the craft is on a straight course ahead. The ball of the instrument shows that the glider is in balanced flight. The 'off' flag disappears when the instrument is functioning properly. The turn and slip indicator is fundamental to instrument flying. The small figures showing through the window in the altimeter are atmospheric pressure settings (in millibars).

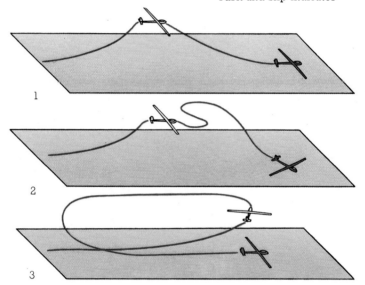

Right: Landing after a failed launch, which may have been due to a cable break, the most common cause. (1) Straight ahead; (2) across the field if the glider is too far up the field. This requires a turn to one side—the downwind side, if there is any crosswind—and then another turn before landing. If this is not possible, the pilot turns once more to make an abbreviated circuit or a 360° turn (3), depending upon the height available, before making a landing.

distance or speed flight. Photographic evidence of reaching the previously declared turn point must be produced.

drag Resistance to movement through the air.

elevator The flap on the trailing edge of the tailplane to control pitching (*qv*).

FAI Fédération Aéronautique Internationale, the world governing body for flying sports.

gain of height The height climbed after release. It is also a record category.

gold C The international proficiency badge awarded to a pilot who has made a flight of five hours' duration, flown 300km across country, and made a gain of height of 3000m.

lift The upward force from the wing which acts at right-angles to the relative air flow.

MacCready ring The circular scale on some variometers (*qv*) which gives a pilot the best speed at which to fly between thermals, taking into account the strength of the available lift.

1000km diploma The international award to pilots who have accomplished a distance flight of 1000km or 621⅖ mi.

outlanding A landing made elsewhere than the point of launch.

pitch The upwards and downwards movement of a glider's nose. It is controlled by the elevator (*qv*).

pure distance The category for a distance flight in any direction. The distance is measured as a great circle course between the starting point and the place of landing.

roll A tilting movement off the lateral balance to the left or right so that the glider banks.

rudder The control surface on the trailing edge of the fin to control yaw (*qv*).

silver C The international proficiency badge awarded to a pilot who has made a flight of five hours' duration, flown 50km across country, and made a gain of height of 1000m.

sink rate The speed, measured in feet per second, at which

a glider makes its descent.

slope lift Soaring (*qv*) on upcurrents produced by the wind blowing against and over the face of hills or mountains.

soaring Finding and using upward currents of air to gain height (*qv*).

solo Flying alone. In Britain, the minimum age for solo flights is 16; in the United States and some other countries it is 14.

speed over a triangular course The category in which a glider's flight is timed from when it crosses the starting line to when it crosses the finishing line. Pilots must produce evidence of reaching the declared turning point.

standard class A competition class of glider in which the wing span is limited to 49ft 2in and other restrictions are applied to keep costs to a minimum. The other class is *open*.

thermals Rising bubbles of air resulting from the sun's heating of the ground. Damp or cool areas do not produce good thermals.

trim Balance of the glider in the fore and aft sense. A small control surface called a *trim tab* is attached to the elevator.

tug The aircraft which effects an airplane tow launch.

turn and slip indicator A cloud-flying instrument which serves a similar purpose to an artificial (*qv*) horizon.

variometer A pressure instrument which indicates the climb (*qv*) and sink (*qv*) rates of a glider.

wave lift Soaring on the upcurrents caused by air which has been forced over the top of hills or mountains and which, when flowing down on the lee side, rebounds in a series of waves.

winch-launch The method of launching a glider by pulling it into the wind with a steel cable being wound around an engine-driven drum. The principle of launch is similar to that of the car-tow (*qv*).

yaw The lateral (sideways) deviation of a glider's nose from the line of flight.

Hang-gliding

Although it was over 80 years ago that pioneer hang-glider Otto Lilienthal made some 200 flights from his specially-built hill in Germany, the discovery of the Wright brothers and the advent of power flight spelled the death of low-speed ultralight aircraft until the mid-1960s. Then Professor Francis Rogallo developed a flexible wing parachute for steering space re-entry vehicles back to earth. It formed the basis of the foot-launched 'rogallo'-type hang-glider.

The original rogallo has undergone many modifications since the early 1970s and the modern version is a complex design of aerodynamics, sail cutting and structural engineering. But the concept has remained the same and the most common type of hang-glider is still basically a Dacron sail, supported on an aluminum frame. The pilot is suspended from the latter in a hammock-like harness, usually nowadays in a prone position, though the earlier sitting position is still maintained by some trainee flyers.

A hang-glider flies by the same principles that apply to any other aircraft. The sail fills during flight to form an airfoil section through the chord of the wing. Airflow round the airfoil section creates lift on the upper surface of the wing. The lift over the flying surface does not defy gravity, but merely delays it. The glider still floats to earth, but at a much slower sinking speed than, for example, a parachute. By flying in upcurrents of air, the hang-glider pilot can remain airborne for long periods of time, executing turns and other aerobatics. More sophisticated hang-gliders, with slower sinking speeds, can now exploit thermals or converging masses of air. With these same gliders, cross country flights and height gains of many feet are now becoming commonplace among expert pilots.

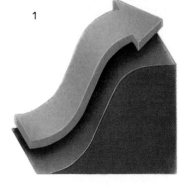

Top left: The flow of the wind over different contours. 1 An ideal ridge forms a smooth air flow. 2 A spine forms dangerous rotors on the leeward side. 3 Rotors at the base and behind the lip of a cliff.

Below: A thermal flight path. Hills, towns and plowed fields spawn thermals. Forest and lakes create sink.

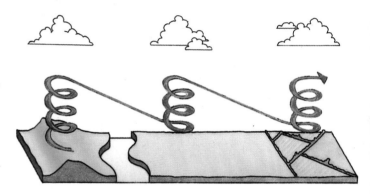

airfoil The curved section through the chord (qv) of the sail upon which a great deal of the aerodynamic features of that sail hinge.

airframe The triangular frame to which the lower rigging wires (qv) are attached and onto which the pilot holds as a lever to shift his bodyweight.

airspeed The speed of the hang-glider relative to the air flowing past the glider.

angle of attack The angle between the chord line of the wing and the airflow which strikes the wing. The angle of attack is governed by the forward and backward movement of the pilot's body. By increasing the angle the speed is reduced.

aspect ratio The ratio of the wingspan to width (chord) of the wing. A high-aspect ratio wing is narrower than a low-aspect ratio wing.

batten Fibreglass or wooden stiffeners used to support, shape and smooth a sail.

billow The fullness of each half

of the glider wing. This is calculated by measuring the nose angle (qv) of the sail laid flat on the floor minus the nose angle of the airframe.

chord The width of the wing measured from the leading edge (qv) to the trailing edge (qv).

convergence Two converging masses of air (for example a ruling wind and an opposing sea breeze) which can be used for height gain in a hang-glider.

deflexor A metal outrigger used in conjunction with wing wires to bend the leading edges thus giving the sail better aerodynamic qualities.

flare out The maneuver carried out in the landing sequence. The angle of attack (qv) is progressively increased as the pilot approaches the ground. This slows the airspeed of the glider. Just prior to touchdown the nose is raised quickly, effectively stalling the glider.

glide ratio or glide angle The ratio between the distance flown and the height lost. A glide ratio

of 6:1 means a hang-glider will theoretically fly 590½ft from a 98ft 5in hill. This is usually quoted as a measure of glider performance.

ground loop A situation where the nose of the glider is raised too high while the pilot is still on the ground causing the kite and the pilot to be flipped over backwards by the strength of the wind.

groundspeed The speed of the glider relative to the ground.

harness The hammock-like sling in which the pilot lies while flying. It can also be a swing seat arrangement with a lap strap.

keel The center boom of the airframe.

kingpost A tubular support for the upper rigging wires.

leading edge one of the two booms which form the forward edge of the kite.

luff A luff occurs when the sail deflates. This can either happen when the kite is put into a steep dive so that the airflow strikes the top of the sail instead of the

underneath, or, momentarily, in turbulence (sometimes called a sail deflation).

nose angle The angle subtended by the two leading edges.

pitch The change in attitude of a glider in flight. This can be visualized as a rotation about the crossboom: to pitch up means the nose goes up, to pitch down means the nose goes down.

reflex A slight upwards curve of the airfoil along a section of the wing parallel to the keel. Reflex gives a kite stability in pitch making it want to pull out of a dive.

ridge lift The lift caused by a wind flowing up the side of a hill, ridge or cliff, etc.

rigging wires All the wires which brace the glider, holding the airframe rigid.

roach tip A larger area of sail which overhangs the trailing edge and is supported by battens (qv). Washout, an important stabilizer, is located at the tips and by roaching the tips a larger area of washed out sail

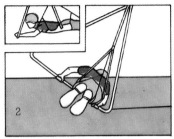

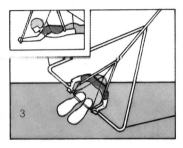

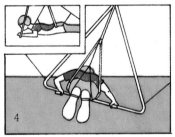

Left: This series of diagrams shows how a glider is turned. 1 The pilot, flying straight and level, slightly increases his speed by pulling his weight forward. 2 The pilot rolls the glider by moving his body to one side of the A frame. He then begins to push out, causing the nose of the glider to pitch up, sweeping it round the turn. 3 The pilot moves back to the center of the A frame to prevent the glider side-slipping, but still pushes out. The glider stays banked in the turn. 4 The pilot moves his weight to the opposite side of the A frame and pulls his weight forward. The glider rolls out of the turn and assumes normal flying speed.

Top right: The silhouettes show how the hang-glider has evolved through the shape of its wing. 1 a rogallo; 2 a second generation kite; 3 a third or fourth generation kite; 4 a monoplane configuration with a tail; 5 a biplane with no tail.

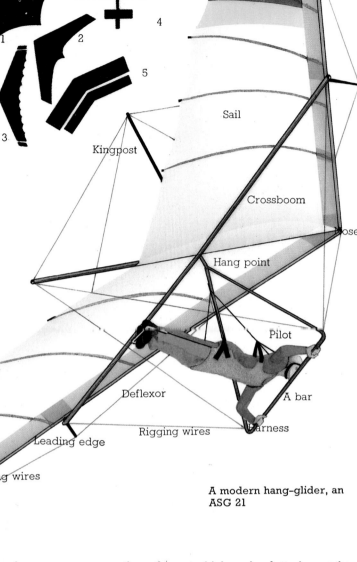

Sail

Kingpost

Crossboom

Nose

Hang point

Pilot

Deflexor

A bar

Harness

Rigging wires

Trailing edge

Battens

Leading edge

Wing wires

A modern hang-glider, an ASG 21

can be obtained giving better stability under certain conditions.

rogallo The general name given to the original delta-shaped hang-gliders which were based on the designs of Francis Rogallo for a space re-entry vehicle parachute.

roll The change in attitude of the glider in flight, visualized as the rotation about the keel. The movement as one wing goes up and the other goes down. During a turn the glider is initially rolled and then pitch is applied to bank it round the turn.

rotor A turbulent area 'of wind found in the lee of any obstruction in a wind. Behind the edge of a sharp-edged cliff the wind will curl over into the sheltered area and blow in the opposite direction to the main wind.

sail deflation See luff.

second-generation kite A derivative of the standard rogallo. The billow of the sail has been reduced, the aspect ratio increased, and other changes, such as the addition of wing

wires, may have been made. Further developments of these gliders are sometimes called third- or fourth-generation gliders.

sink Any mass of air which is descending relative to the ground.

sink rate The rate of descent of a glider usually measured in feet per second. Often quoted in performance data.

soaring Keeping the glider airborne in areas of lift. This may mean tacking back and forth close to the brow of a hill when there is little wind and a narrow lift band.

stall The point where a glider is traveling so slowly that the air flow over the upper surface of the sail breaks up, causing the glider to lose airspeed and lift. The glider will drop suddenly but will soon pick up enough airspeed to re-establish the airflow.

thermal A rising bubble of warm air. Thermals are formed when the lower parts of the atmo-

sphere are warmer than the upper parts, usually caused by the sun warming the ground. Gliders can circle in the rising pockets of air, which can sometimes attain a vertical speed of over 984ft per minute.

tipdraggers Fins located on the tips of some hang-gliders, which are deflected in flight causing air drag to be exerted in one direction thus turning the glider. A similar principle to a ship's rudder.

trailing edge The loose edge of the sail at the rear of the kite.

turnbuckles Bottle screws which can be used to tension rigging wires affording a useful method for 'tuning' a glider.

Venturi effect The speeding up of the air as it is drawn through a confined space. This is most noticeable when attempting to cross a gully in a hillside while flying.

washout An area of the sail which during normal flight has no aerodynamic lifting power but which, when the glider is flown

at a high angle of attack near the stall, will start giving lift, thus maintaining the glider on a level keel. The washed out areas are located near to the tips so that near the stall speed, or during a stall, stability is provided by the tips.

wind gradient With an increase in altitude the windspeed increases, because the wind, like any fluid or gas flowing over a surface, tends to stick to the surface, in this case the hillside or ground.

wingover An aerobatic maneuver where the pilot banks the glider to such a degree that the wing can be perpendicular to the ground.

wing wires Wires which are used in conjunction with outriggers to flex the leading edges in such a way that the shape of the sail is pulled into a better configuration.

yaw A skidding or sideways movement when it is not flying through the air in the direction it is pointed.

Mountaineering

Put in the simplest of terms, mountaineering is the sport or pastime of climbing mountains. But such a simplification fails to encapsulate the many facets that make people climb—not only mountains but also rock faces. It is a sport of ethics, of philosophies, of science, of fitness and fortitude. Mountaineers, contrary to the popular cliché, do not climb a mountain or rock just because it's there, although there have been and always will be exceptions. The majority view the climb as a challenge to their skills, techniques and courage; even to their intellect. And this challenge is what makes mountaineering a sport. It is a competition between the climber and the elements; at times between man and himself as he tests his own judgment and nerve. At the same time, mountaineering is not just about one climber. Many climbs require a team effort, with each climber placing his trust in the ability and selflessness of those about him. On major expeditions, success is dependent on each member of the party fulfilling his role efficiently.

The primary aim of the climber is not simply to reach the summit. There are other goals for which he can strive. One is to climb by more difficult routes, and perhaps the ultimate is to reduce the number of aids—such as pitons, chocks, or steps—and protection on these more difficult routes. Because route-finding is an essential ingredient of the sport, navigation becomes an important skill; more so as the major peaks are conquered and modern aids and techniques lead to the climbing of the more difficult rock faces. Rock climbing techniques are as essential to the all-round mountaineer as are snow and ice techniques, and for many rock climbing is a sport in itself. As such, it takes three basic forms: outcrop climbs, crag climbs and 'big wall' climbs in mountain regions.

Above: A high altitude 'winter' boot fitted with a front-point crampon.

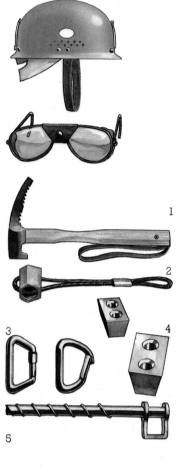

Left: Helmet and goggles. In a sport where serious accidents are always possible, wearing a helmet has been a major cause in reducing the number of head injuries.
1 A hammer-axe, which incorporates features of the ice-axe and the peg hammer.
2 The Chouinard hexentric, a six-sided artificial chock with a permanent wire sling.
3 Two types of karabiner. In the version far left, the gate, or spring clip, is locked by a screw collar.
4 Examples of artificial chocks.
5 An ice screw, which is used for belays and runners on steep ice-climbs. The enclosed ring is for fitting karabiners.
6 Climbing rope, which is made of nylon and is either hawser laid or kernmantel. It comes in a variety of thicknesses and breaking loads according to required uses.

abseil A method of making a rapid descent by sliding down a doubled rope hanging from a natural or artificial protrusion. Also known as a *rope down* or *en rappel*.

à cheval A method of climbing an angled rib (*qv*) by placing one foot on either side, gripping the crest, and 'hopping' up.

artificial climbing Using man-made implements such as pitons (*qv*), bolts (*qv*), or étriers (*qv*) to assist in climbing otherwise very difficult or even blank rock.

backing up A method of climbing a chimney by placing the back on one side and the feet or knees against the other, then pushing up with the hands against the back wall.

belay An anchoring procedure to protect a party of climbers should a fall occur. One or more of the stationary climbers secures himself to the face or slope by passing the climbing rope over an anchor point while the climber ahead advances.

bergschrund A crevasse separating the upper slopes of a glacier from the upper snows of the mountain.

bolts Expansion bolts screwed into a hole drilled in the rock face to provide purchase. They are considered unethical by most schools of climbers.

bottoming When a piton reaches the back of a crack before its blade is properly secured.

bridging Method of climbing a wide chimney or groove, using the right hand and foot on one wall and the left hand and foot on the opposite side.

cagoule A long hooded smock, windproof and waterproof, worn as an outer garment.

chimney A narrow and vertical opening in a rock face; wide enough for a man to enter.

chockstone A stone which is jammed firmly into a crack or chimney and so can be used as the anchor point for a belay or runner (*qv*).

climb The route taken.

col A dip in a ridge between two peaks. Also called a *saddle*.

cornice A bank of consolidated snow, formed by prevailing winds and projecting over the edge of a ridge.

couloir A furrow or gully caused by erosion. It may be rock, ice, or snow.

crack A narrow opening in the rock face used for holds and inserting artificial aids.

crag A steep rockface.

crampon A metal frame with steel spikes. Fitted to the sole of a boot, and held on by straps, it is used for climbing on ice and snow.

crevasse A crack or cleft in the surface of a glacier.

dead man A flat metal plate fitted with a wire loop which is embedded in snow to create a belay. Also called a *snow anchor*.

duvet A down-filled jacket.

étrier Portable stirrup or step which can be clipped to a piton or hooked to a sky hook so that the climber can stand on it.

fixed ropes Permanent ropes, chains, or hawsers on a popular climb; also ropes fixed by an

expedition so that its party is able to move more quickly up and down the mountain.

free climb One in which artificial aids are not used.

front-pointing An ice-climbing technique in which the climber stabs two ice-axes (or an axe and dagger) and the front prongs of his crampons into the ice to obtain four-point contact.

gangway An inclined ledge on a rock face.

gardening The removal of vegetation from a rock climb.

glissading Controlled sliding down a snow slope using the ice-axe as a brake.

grading A system of assessing the difficulty of climbs using either numerals or words.

hammer-axe A short ice-axe with a hammer head replacing the blade and a specially curved pick for front-pointing.

hand traverse A sideways crossing of a rock face with most of the weight on the hands owing to the lack of footholds.

high altitude Generally applied

Above: A figure eight knot used by climbers for tying on the main rope.
Below: A figure eight knot with a stopper knot.

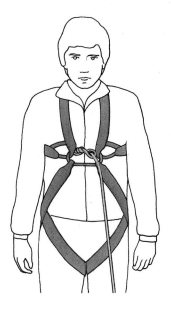

Above right: A combination chest and thigh harness. In Britain and the United States, the waist harness is preferred.
Right: The original, or 'classic' abseil.
Below: A figure eight descendeur, a special friction device used when abseiling with a harness around each leg.

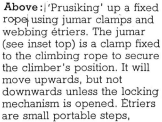

Above: 'Prusiking' up a fixed rope using jumar clamps and webbing étriers. The jumar (see inset top) is a clamp fixed to the climbing rope to secure the climber's position. It will move upwards, but not downwards unless the locking mechanism is opened. Étriers are small portable steps, available in webbing or with alloy steps fitted to rope. Prusiking derives from the practice of the Austrian climber Dr Prusik, who would secure himself by a rope that was tied to the main rope with a knot which would move up, but would not slide down when pressure was applied.

to climbs in ranges exceeding 17,000 ft.

hold A crack or unevenness in or on which a climber can place his hands or feet during a climb. On ice they may have to be cut.

ice screws Metal tube pitons, threaded so that they can be screwed into ice for belays and runners.

jamming Rock climbing technique in which the hand or foot is wedged into a crack, the climber relying on the friction of the 'jam' for purchase.

jumar A clamp which, when attached to a rope, moves freely up the rope but locks when downward pressure is applied.

karabiner An oval or D-shaped spring-loaded clip for attaching to ropes, slings, screws, or pitons for belays, runners, or abseils.

layback A rock-climbing technique applied to corner cracks. Both feet are placed against the outer edge while the hands grip the nearer edge, progress being made by moving the hands and feet alternately along the crack.

mantelshelf A rock-climbing technique in which the palms of the hands are placed on the hold and the body is pulled up until one foot can be raised to the same hold. The climber then stands upright.

mixed climbing Climbing that involves both rock and ice/snow climbing.

on sight Said of a climb which the leader has never previously inspected.

outcrop climbs Small climbs on rock faces normally no more than one pitch long.

outside route One either behind or over the front of a chockstone blocking a chimney.

overhang A rock face leaning out beyond a vertical plane; also a sudden protuberance of rock on a face.

peel Traditional slang for a fall. More common expressions include a plop, lob, bone, or pine box (*qv*).

pied d'éléphant A short sleeping bag covering legs and hips.

pillar A tall, narrow column of rock jutting out from a mountain.

pine box A fatal fall.

pitch The actual distance a climber has to travel from one belay to the next.

piton A metal spike hammered into rock cracks or ice where there are no holds. Karabiners (*qv*) are clipped to them to establish a belay, runner, or abseil. Also called a *peg*.

protection The protection a climber is able to provide for himself by safeguarding his position. The most common form is a belay or runner.

rib A ridge or a steep edge.

ridge Where the two opposing faces of a mountain or crag meet; the 'spine' of a mountain.

roof The underside of an overhang.

runner A method used by a climber to ensure protection as he advances. He secures a sling on the face or slope and clips it to a karabiner through which he clips the climbing rope. Also called a *running belay*.

run-out The length of rope between the leader and the second man on a climb.

scree Fragments of rock that have fallen from a crag to the slopes below.

siege tactics Method of achieving a summit by repeated efforts interspersed with returns to base camp. Fixed ropes are left.

sky hook A metal hook to which an étrier (*qv*) can be attached and which itself can be hooked on to a small natural projection. It saves using pitons or bolts.

stance A place where a climber is able to halt at the top of a pitch to secure a belay (*qv*).

terrordactyle A specially curved ice-axe with the pick at 55° to the shaft, so that it holds firmly in place when dug into the ice.

traverse To move sideways across a face rather than upwards; also to climb a mountain by one route and descend by another.

verglas A thin coating of ice over rocks; it adds to the difficulty of a climb.

Parachuting

As a sport, parachuting owes its origins not simply to the parachute, which is by no means a recent innovation: the first successful parachute descent was in 1797, over Paris. It was as much the invention of the ripcord, at the beginning of the twentieth century, which set the parachutist free of dependence on static line devices and allowed him to experience the sensation of free falling, or skydiving as it is often known. Two further developments were the discovery that, by movements of the head, body and limbs, the skydiver could, to some degree, control his flight and perform acrobatic maneuvers; and the introduction of the steerable canopy with blank gores and steering windows to give the parachutist control of the flow of air through the canopy and, consequently, of his horizontal movement.

Competition jumping, for men and women, comprises accuracy, style and relative work. Accuracy, for individual and group jumps, involves landing on a central disc on the target: 0.00 points are scored for a DC landing; 0.1 of a point is added for every centimeter the parachutist lands from the disc. Jumps are from 600-800m. Style, for individuals only, requires the skydiver to perform a schedule of loops and turns against the clock. Scoring is on the average time over four jumps, these being from 1800-2000m (about 5900-6600ft) with the free fall periods of 25-30 seconds, according to the height. In relative work, a team of jumpers combine during the free fall period to complete a predetermined group of formations—diamond, caterpillar, etc. One point is scored for each formation completed correctly within the working time, which commences when the first jumper has visible separation from the aircraft.

Above: A parachutist in the spread stable position, with his legs spreadeagled and slightly bent, and the arms outstretched. The back is arched and the head bent back with the force of the uprushing air.

Above: A three-man star, one of the standards of relative work. Relative work is one of the joys of jumping in tandem or with a group. In order to achieve this standard, the parachutist has learned to maneuver himself horizontally and to judge his distance and speed so that, in approaching the other jumpers, he does not collide. Each jumper's glide path is just off to one side of the other during the approach. Other formations include diamonds, caterpillars, snowflakes and Ys—all aspects of hand and foot holds.

AOD Automatic opening device; most types use the changes in barometric pressure to trigger the mechanism which opens the pack (*qv*).
apex The hole at the top of the canopy (*qv*).
attack point In accuracy jumping, an imaginary point over which the jumper should be positioned at a height of 100m.
back loop A backward somersault during a free (*qv*) fall.
back-to-earth stable The position in which a jumper free falls with his/her back (and pack) facing the ground. It is the reverse of the basic stable (*qv*) position.
barrel roll A 360° left or right movement around a horizontal axis during a free fall.
bridle line A nylon cord connecting the pilot (*qv*) 'chute to the sleeve (*qv*).
bungees Colloquial name for the elastic opening bands that run across the back of the pack.
canopy The nylon or silk part of the parachute which fills with air on opening to slow down the

jumper's speed of fall.
Capewell release A method of connecting, or disconnecting, the main part of the parachute to, or from, the body harness. It consists of male and female sections, the former attached to each of the four risers (*qv*), the latter to the harness.
CIP Commission Internationale de Parachutism, the controlling committee for international parachuting.
connector links The four metal links that connect the rigging (*qv*) lines to the four risers; seven to each riser.
DC The dead center of the target for accuracy jumps.
deep Being upwind, during free fall, of the opening point required for landing in the DZ.
delta position A free fall position in which the skydiver has his/her legs straight some 30° apart and the arms swept back at an angle roughly equivalent to that of the legs.
drogue Another name for the pilot 'chute.

dropping zone (DZ) The area of ground on to which parachutists may be safely dropped.
elastics Another name for the pack opening bands.
extractor Another name for the pilot 'chute.
forward loop A forward somersault during a free fall.
free fall A descent to a certain altitude before opening the parachute. During this time, the skydiver is able to perform maneuvers by movements of the arms, hands, legs and feet.
frog position An adaptation of the stable (*qv*) free fall position. The back is not so prominently arched, the arms bent at right-angles from the elbow so that the hands point forward in line with the head, and the legs are slightly bent at the knees.
full cross The ground (*qv*) signal that conditions are safe for parachuting.
gore The wedge-shaped piece of the canopy between two rigging lines.
ground signals Used by the DZ

controller to advise the jumpmaster (*qv*) on the suitability of conditions for jumping. Made with colored panels in red, orange, yellow, or white, they comprise a full cross and the letters T, I and L.
group jump An accuracy team event in which four jumpers leave the aircraft almost simultaneously.
high In group jumping, the last jumper to open his/her parachute.
I The ground signal that all parachuting is temporarily suspended.
jumpmaster The person in charge of all jumps from an aircraft; usually an instructor, or in advanced jumping the most experienced parachutist.
L The ground signal that all parachuting has been suspended and that the aircraft must land.
lift The number of parachutists jumping from an aircraft during a flight.
lo-po A low-porosity canopy; one that allows less air to pass

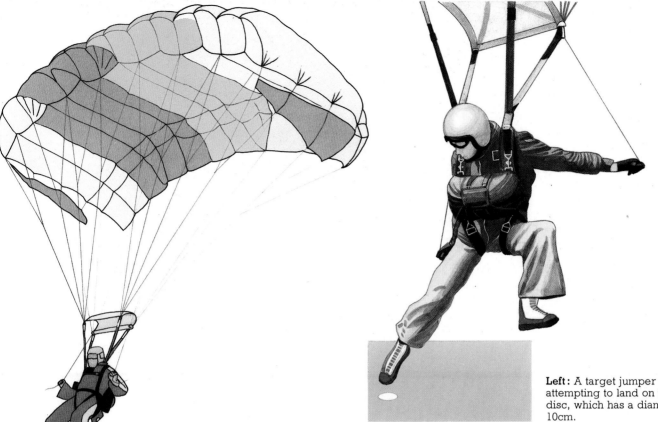

Left: For years, round parachutes reigned supreme—great white and colored jellyfish in an azure sky. But today, although there are still many popular round varieties, square-shaped 'chutes are taking precedence. Known as Ram-Air models, these multi-colored canopies have lower rates of descent and higher forward speeds.

Right: Bird's-eye view of the whole target area used in accuracy jumps. It has a diameter of 50m, while the distance from the inside end of the arms of the cross to the center of the central disc is 5m. Points are awarded according to the closeness of the landing to the disc.

Left: A target jumper attempting to land on the central disc, which has a diameter of 10cm.

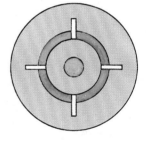

through it than a canopy of high porosity.

low In group jumping, the first jumper to open his/her parachute.

mouth lock A flap of fabric on the bottom of the sleeve (*qv*) to prevent any suction from dragging the canopy from the sleeve before the rigging lines are clear.

pack The container in which the pilot 'chute, rigging lines and sleeve are kept intact until it is time for the parachute to be opened.

para-ascending An event in which a person wearing a deployed parachute is towed aloft on a long line attached to his/her harness and pulled by a motor vehicle or a powerboat.

piggyback rig A system in which the reserve parachute is mounted above the pack of the main 'chute.

pilot 'chute A small parachute which is deployed immediately the pack is opened, its purpose being to pull the sleeve and rigging lines from the pack.

reserve 'chute A smaller para-chute worn as a safeguard against malfunctioning of the main 'chute.

rigger A person who specializes in the maintenance of parachutes and related equipment.

rigging lines The nylon lines joining the canopy to the harness by means of the connector links and risers. They are also known as *suspension lines*.

ripcord A braided stainless steel cable with a handle on one end for the parachutist to pull, and on the other a series of pins which lock the pack together. When operated, it releases the pins and the opening bands spring the pack open to release the pilot 'chute.

risers The nylon-webbing straps running from the harness to the connector links.

short Being downwind during free fall of the opening point required for landing in the DZ.

skydiving Free (*qv*) falling.

sleeve The long, windsock-like container in the pack (*qv*) in which the parachute canopy and the rigging lines are stored.

spiral A turn (*qv*).

spotting Choosing the correct moment to jump from the aircraft in order to land in the target area, taking into account the wind conditions and the rate and angle of descent while free falling and under canopy.

stable position The basic exit position adopted by a jumper after leaving the aircraft. The body is horizontal to the ground, back uppermost, with the arms fully extended at 90° to the body and the legs, slightly bent at the knees, spread at approximately 45°. It is also known as the *full-spread stable position*.

static line A length of webbing used to open a pack without a rip-cord, one end of the line being attached to a point in the aircraft and the other to a nylon line attached to the pins holding the pack together. The weight of the jumper's body pulls the static line taut and the nylon ties remove the pins to open the pack.

stick Colloquial name for a lift.

streamer Colloquial name for the wind drift indicator.

T The ground signal that jumping conditions are safe only for experienced parachutists.

target A cross of white, red, yellow, or orange material on the dropping zone.

terminal velocity The maximum speed at which a skydiver travels during free fall.

toggle The left- or right-hand steering line attached to the appropriate rear riser. When pulled, it steers the parachute.

tracking Covering ground in a horizontal direction during a free fall.

turn A 360° movement to the left or right around a vertical axis. Also known as a spiral.

WDI Wind drift indicator; a weighted rod with a strip of colored paper attached. It is thrown from the aircraft at a height suitable for assessing the wind speed and direction para-chutists will encounter under canopy.

17

Athletics

Track and Field

Track and Field includes a variety of events where the three basic disciplines of running, jumping and throwing are practiced. Such activities have been popular throughout the ages and were featured in the sports of the ancient Greek games. Organized athletics, amateur form, is of modern origin, dating from nineteenth-century England. It evolved primarily from the private schools and Oxford and Cambridge universities, spread nationally with the formation of clubs and then internationally, and inevitably to the first modern Olympic Games in 1896. It remains the major sport of the Olympic Games and seen within the Olympic stadium or major championships is divided into 'track and field' events; generally cross-country running, long-distance running on a track or public roads (eg the marathon), and race walking are included in the track events.

Track and field athletics consists of, essentially, 21 championship events for men and 14 for women. The track events are the 100m, 200m and 400m sprints; the middle-distance races over 800m, 1500m, 5000m (men) and 10,000m (men); the 100m (women), 110m (men) and 400m (men) hurdles; a 3000m steeplechase (men); and relay events for four-man teams over 400m and 1600m. The field events are the long jump, high jump, pole vault (men), and triple jump (men), throwing the discus, putting the shot, throwing the javelin and throwing the hammer (men). Two all-round events are the pentathlon, for women, and the decathlon, for men.

At the international level and in most championships, races are run over metric distances. However, such distances as the mile retain their magic. The IAAF is the world controlling body for athletics and most countries have their own governing associations.

Running

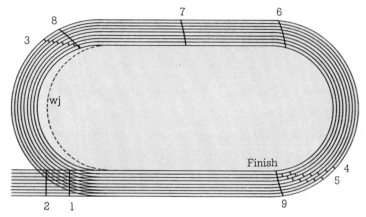

Above: 'On your marks! Set!' and with the report of the gun the runner is off and into his stride. The 'two-positions' start is used for all sprint and hurdles races up to and including 800m, although some 800m runners prefer to adopt the starting position shown on the left. This is also used by other middle-distance and long-distance runners.

A standard 400m track, showing the starts for the different races. They all finish at the same point. 1 100m and 100m hurdles; 2 110m hurdles; 3 200m; 4 400m and 400m hurdles; 5 800m; 6 1500m; 7 3000m steeplechase; 8 5000m; 9 10,000m; wj marks the area where the water jump is placed, the steeplechasers following the dotted line.

age groups Because these have not been standardized by the IAAF (qv), age categories vary with national associations. For the purposes of international competition, it is generally accepted that a junior is one who is not 20 years of age during the year of the competition.

all-weather tracks Those on which a resilient synthetic surface has been laid. Such surfaces are used for field events' approaches as well as running tracks (qv).

amateur A competitor who, by IAAF definition, competes for the love of sport and as a means of recreation, without any financial motive.

anabolic steroids Synthetic male hormones used to increase weight by encouraging protein formation in the body. They are banned by the IAAF.

anemometer A gauge used to determine the speed of the wind in distance per second and resolve the wind assistance (qv).

bend The curve of the running track; more especially the final curve before the finish. Runners are said to come 'off the bend' into the final straight.

championship A meeting held under the auspices of a regional, national or international association.

check or cue mark A scratch on the surface of the track or perhaps a sprinkling of powder to guide a competitor in a jumping event, at the steeplechase water jump, or at a relay exchange. No solid object may be placed on the track or runway, and any relay check mark must be within the runner's own lane.

cinder track A track surfaced with cinders, clay, clay and cinders, or a mixture of other natural materials.

coach Person responsible for the guidance, development, preparation and motivation of an athlete.

cross-country running A race over natural terrain including obstacles. Races may be held on race-courses with man-made

hurdles. Principally a winter pursuit, it comprises team and individual classes. Distances vary, but races are approximately $7\frac{1}{2}$-$8\frac{3}{4}$mi for senior men and $1\frac{1}{2}$-3mi for women.

decathlon An all-round event of track and field events, contested over two days by men. Day one features, in running order, 100m, long jump, shot, high jump and 400m; day two 110m hurdles, discus, pole vault, javelin and 1500m. Points are awarded on an IAAF table of performance.

fartlek A method of training; literally 'speed-play'. It involves a mixture of unmeasured and untimed short sprints, fast strides and jogging.

fell running A form of running practiced mostly in the high regions of England and Scotland over distances up to 40mi.

final The last round of an event at a meeting or championship. In track events, finalists emerge from heats (qv) while competitors in field events qualify for the six final rounds by attaining a

qualifying distance.

heats Qualifying rounds in a running event to produce the required number of runners for the final (qv).

IAAF (International Amateur Athletic Federation) The governing body of athletics. All international competitions must be held under its rules through the jurisdiction of an affiliated national body. It is responsible for ratifying world records (qv).

indoor athletics Held during the winter months in specially built arenas. The banked tracks, usually 200m to a lap, are of board or synthetic surfaces on which the runners wear short needle spikes (qv). Sprints are usually up to 60m, while in the 400m and above runners are not confined to lanes. All field events except the hammer, javelin and discus are contested. Best performances are recorded in place of records (qv).

interval running A method of training involving sprinting a set time or distance with a predeter-

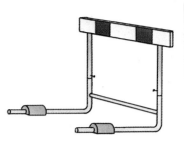

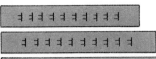

A representative diagram contrasting the distances of the three championship hurdle events: women's 100m, men's 110m, and men's 400m. In each race there are 10 barriers.

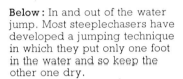

Above: The standard international hurdle with counterbalance weights so that it topples over readily if an athlete comes into contact with it. The hurdle shown is set at 2ft 9in for the women's 100m hurdles, but it is adjustable so that it can easily be raised to 3ft for the men's 400m hurdles and to 3½ft for the men's 110m hurdles.

Below: The walker, who races on either road or track, practices one of the most disciplined of track events. Throughout his race, he must maintain unbroken contact with the ground, having to ground his advancing foot

before taking his rear foot off the ground. Additionally he must momentarily straighten the leg of the grounded foot each step.

Above: Hurdling has been described as 'rhythm sprinting', and never is this description more apt than in the 110m, or 'high hurdles' as the event is known. The first four figures (right to left) depict the approach to the hurdle; the fifth shows the lead leg clearing the hurdle; and the last three relate to the clearance of the hurdle.

Below: In and out of the water jump. Most steeplechasers have developed a jumping technique in which they put only one foot in the water and so keep the other one dry.

mined recovery phase of jogging, walking, or resting alternating with each timed run.

isometrics A method of training which involves tension but no movement by opposing one muscle to another, or to a resistant object.

judges A number of judges are allotted to each field event to ensure that the athlete remains within the rules of the event.

lane A marked subdivision of the running track. There must be six to eight lanes of uniform width for a major meet. In events up to and including 400m, runners must remain in their lanes throughout the race; in the 800m the runners must remain in their lanes around the first bend. Runners draw lots for lanes.

lap One circuit of a track (*qv*).

long-distance running Events, run on a track or on roads, over 10,000m or 6⅛mi.

marathon A road race standardized for championship purposes at 26⅛mi. Because of varying conditions only world best performances, and not world records, are recognized.

orienteering A running event for individuals and teams across rough terrain. The competitor passes through a number of control points before completing the course. At each point the runner is given a map reference and next objective—he then decides his own route.

pain barrier Term used to describe a physical and/or psychological pain which an athlete may have to overcome during training or competition if he is to produce maximum effort.

peak To strike top form at a certain stage of the season, eg for a major championship.

pentathlon An all-round event of track and field events, contested over two days by women. Day one consists of 100m hurdles, shot, and high jump; day two of the long jump and 800m. Points are awarded on an IAAF table of performance.

race walking A road and track event in which 'progression is

by steps so taken that unbroken contact with the ground is maintained; ie the advancing foot must make contact with the ground before the rear foot leaves the ground'. The leg must be straightened for at least one moment. Championships are most frequently contested on road routes at 12½mi and 31mi.

record The best performance by an amateur in an outdoor event. For a world record the performance must have taken place in genuine competition in conditions according to IAAF regulations, been approved by the national association where the performance took place, and then been ratified by the IAAF. Only fully automatic electrical times are now recognized for 100-400m records at national level upwards.

resistance running A training method, often used out of season, to build up stamina and strength. The runner trains on surfaces or in conditions that handicap his progress, eg on

loose sand or wearing a harness attached to a heavy object.

scratch line The marker line at the end of the javelin, long jump and triple jump approach runways. Also denotes the starting line of a race.

sex tests Introduced in 1966 to prove that female athletes are, medically, female.

spikes Colloquial name given to spiked running shoes. On spiked shoes, a maximum of six spikes is allowed on the sole and two on the heel. These must not project further than 1in

stadium A structure with spectator stands at which there are facilities for all track and field events.

Tartan track Trade name of an all-weather synthetic resin surface used on running tracks and the approach runs for field events.

tension A term used to describe unnecessary tightening of the muscles during competition, which adversely affects an athlete's performance.

timekeeping Times of runners

21

Jumping

Left: The long jump showing the hitch-kick technique practiced by most long jumpers. The hitch-kick does little to improve the length of the jump but rather is a balancing action. More important are a firm takeoff and a correct landing.

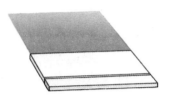

Left: The takeoff board and Plasticine indicator for the long jump and triple jump. It is set into the ground so that the board is level with the runway. The board measures 7⅞in from the end of the runway to the scratch or takeoff line; the Plasticine indicator, used to detect over-stepping, is an additional 4in from the takeoff line.

Right: Since the success of its innovator at the 1968 Olympics, the Beamon landing method is used by many top jumpers.

Left: The runway and landing area for the long jump (top) and triple jump (bottom). Both events use a sand-filled landing area. In the long jump, the take-off line is 3ft 3in from the front of the area; in the triple jump it is 42ft 8in away. The runway is 4ft wide.

Below: The hop, step and jump technique of the triple jumper.

are recorded either manually by stopwatch, or electronically by the photo-finish camera which is activated by the starter's pistol and produces times to 100th of a second up to and including the 400m. These are then adjusted to a tenth of a second for events up to and including 1500m and to a fifth for those over. Where watches are used, three time-keepers are normally allotted to each finisher. When two of the three watches agree, their time is taken; when all three disagree the middle time is taken.

track A circuit, usually 400m in length and divided into six or eight lanes. The track for the 100m and for the 100m hurdles and 110m hurdles is straight. As the finish line is fixed, races start at various points around the track depending on their distance.

training The process of preparation for an event. The athlete, helped by his coach (qv), tries to improve or sharpen his skill, strength, stamina and speed and to develop a positive mental approach to his event. As well as various forms of running such as fartlek (qv), interval (qv), and resistance (qv) running, training involves weightlifting and other exercises and demands strict adherence to a correct life-style.

walking See race walking.

wind-assisted An athlete benefiting from a following wind of more than 2m per second in sprinting and hurdling events up to 200m and in the horizontal jumps is said to be wind-assisted and his performance cannot be considered for acceptance as a record.

Track events

alternate method A method of baton (qv) changing in which the carrier transfers the baton into the opposite hand of the outgoing runner.

anchor leg The last leg of a relay (qv).

barging Making physical contact with another runner. It occurs mostly in middle-distance events where runners are not confined to a lane. It can result in disqualification.

baton In relay (qv), a hollow tube made of a rigid material, between 11-11⅘in long, 4¾in in circumference, and weighing at least 1¾oz. In non-championship events, a wooden baton may be used.

bell Rung to signify that a runner has commenced the last lap of a race.

blocks See starting blocks.

boxed in A situation in which a runner is surrounded by other runners and so is unable to adjust his tactical position without changing his running rhythm.

break Used in distance running to describe an attempt by one or more runners to move away from the main group of runners.

change-over zone See take-over zone.

chopping Shortening the length of stride (qv) in order to conform to a set rhythm; especially in hurdling.

dip finish Breasting the tape by thrusting forward with the chest as the runner takes a final stride.

down-sweep A method of baton change in which the incoming runner places the baton into the upturned palm of the outgoing runner.

fading Slowing down towards the finish of a race.

free distance The space between the incoming and out-going runners at a baton take-over. It represents time gained.

front-running A middle-distance tactic in which a runner dictates the pace of the race from the front.

gun A pistol or similar weapon fired by the starter to commence a race.

hurdles Sprint events in which the runners have to clear ten hurdles, the height of which varies according to the length of the race. The hurdler is required to clear the hurdle with both legs, and must not deliberately knock down a hurdle.

The straddle

The western roll

The Fosbury flop

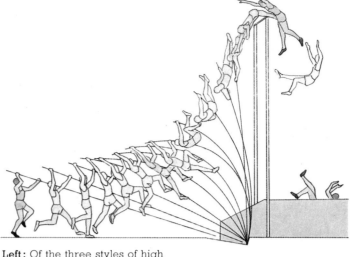

Left: Of the three styles of high jumping illustrated, the western roll is rarely practiced today, the favored methods being the straddle and the flop. The flop, named after Dick Fosbury who used this technique to win the 1968 Olympic gold medal, owes much of its popularity to its flexibility, its exponents adapting the basic technique according to their own strengths and weaknesses. The straddle, on the other hand, is a more disciplined technique, and for the purist it is the more aesthetically pleasing of the two.

Above and below: Pole vaulting has developed dramatically with the advent of the fiberglass pole. Today's vaulter plants his pole in the sunken box, bends it back, and allows himself to be catapulted upwards. His predecessors, with the rigid bamboo and later metal poles, were merely levered up.

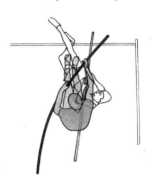

100m hurdles Raced by women. The hurdles, 2ft 9in high, are spaced at 8.5m with a 13m approach to the first hurdle and a 10.5m run-in to the finish line.

110m hurdles Known as the high hurdles. The hurdles, 3½ft high, are spaced at 9.14m with a 13.72m approach and a 14.02m run-in.

400m hurdles These are the intermediate hurdles, 3ft high and spaced at 35m with a 45m approach and a 40m run-in.

lead leg/arm Used in hurdling to describe the leg/arm the hurdler puts over the hurdle first.

leg The distance run by one runner in a relay race.

leg speed Term used in sprinting to denote the rate at which the runner moves his legs.

middle-distance running Track events from 800m up to and including 10,000m or non-metric equivalents.

'on your marks' The first instruction given to runners by the starter (qv), telling them to take their positions on the starting line.

race An event over a determined distance in which the first runner to reach the near edge of the finish line with any part of his or her torso is the winner.

relay An event in which a team of runners covers an apportioned distance (leg) in sequence. The most common relays are the two track events of 4 × 100m, in which each of four runners covers 100m, and 4 × 400m. The runners carry a baton which is transferred from the incoming runner to the outgoing runner in the take-over zone (qv). The baton must change hands, as opposed to being thrown, and if dropped must be retrieved by the runner who dropped it before the outgoing runner continues.

'set' The second instruction given to runners by the starter after 'on your marks' (qv). It is given only in races up to 400m in which the runners use the sprint start.

sitting in Term used to describe the position and tactics of a distance runner running slightly behind and outside the shoulder of another runner.

split to the ears Term used to describe hurdlers with disproportionately long legs.

sprinting Running at or close to top speed for the length of a race. Events up to 400m are considered sprints.

staggered starts Used in races up to and including 800m in which runners have to remain in their lanes (qv) while running round bends. The stagger, or echelon, ensures that runners in all lanes run the same distance.

starter The official who gets races under way. He instructs the runners and when he considers they are all ready fires his gun.

starting blocks Aids used by runners in events up to and including 400m and in 4 × 100m and 4 × 400m sprint relays. A part of each foot must be touch-

ing the ground when the runner is in the 'set' (qv) position.

steeplechase A 3000m event for men in which the runners have to clear solid hurdles 3ft high and a water jump faced by a hurdle. The water has a maximum depth of 2ft 4in with a spread of 12ft. The runners cover the first part-lap without obstacles and then have to clear four hurdles and the water jump for seven full laps. The obstacles can be spaced at varying intervals—the water jump can be inside or outside the track.

stride The distance covered from the time one foot touches the ground until the other foot touches the ground. A sprinter's stride is considered to be some 20-40 per cent more than his or her height.

stride pattern The number of strides taken by a hurdler between hurdles.

surging A distance-running tactic with which the front-runner, by quickening the pace and then slowing it again once

Throwing

There are four throwing field events: the discus, hammer, and javelin throws and the shot put. Women do not compete in the hammer throw.

The implements for the four throwing events: the javelin, discus, shot and hammer. There are five sizes of javelin: men's, women's, under 15, 17 and 19. The men's javelin is 8ft 6¼in – 8ft 10¼in long and weighs 1lb 12¼oz the women's is 7ft 2½in–7ft 6½in long and weighs 1lb 5¼oz. There are also five sizes of discus. The men's has an overall diameter of 8⅝-8¹¹⁄₁₆in and weighs 4lb 6⅔oz: the women's has a diameter of 7³⁄₃₂-7⁵⁄₃₂in and weighs 2lb 3¼oz. The men's shot weighs 16lb and has a diameter of 4⅝-5⅛in: the women's weighs 8lb 13oz and has a diameter of 3¾-4⅜in. The hammer, which consists of the handle, a single length of spring-steel wire, and the spherical ball (diam. 4-4¾in), has an overall length of 3ft 10¼-3ft 11¾in and an overall weight of 16lb.

Right: Putting the shot.

Below: Throwing the javelin.

Javelin   Discus   Hammer   Shot put

---

the field has reacted to his move, disrupts the rhythm and pattern of the other runners.

take-over zone An area of 20m within which the baton (*qv*) must be transferred in a relay race. In races up to 4 × 200m, the outgoing runner may start his run from 10m outside the take-over zone.

tape A line stretched at breast height across the front edge of the finish line to indicate to the judges the vertical plane of that edge. The runners are placed in the order in which any part of their torso reaches the tape.

up-sweep A method of baton change in which the incoming runner brings the baton up into the palm of the outgoing runner.

Field events—jumps

broad jump *See* long jump.
countback System used to determine a tied place in the high jump and pole vault. Taken into consideration first are the failures at the height at which the tie occurred: the competitor with

fewer failures wins. If this does not produce a result, all failures during the competition are counted and the one with fewest failures is awarded the place. If this does not resolve the tie, the one with the least number of jumps is placed higher. A tie for first place is resolved by extra jumps.

hang A long jump technique, less popular than the hitch-kick, in which the athlete arches back with arms raised and legs lowered behind the trunk.

high jump An event for men and women who attempt to jump over a bar supported between two uprights. Takeoff must be from one foot only. If the bar is dislodged, that attempt counts as a failure, and after three consecutive failures, the competitor is eliminated. The crossbar is raised after each round.

hitch-kick A long jump technique in which the athlete in mid-flight continues to move his or her legs as if he or she were running.

horizontal jumps Term used to describe the long jump (*qv*) and triple jump (*qv*).

long jump An event for men and women who, after a sprint approach, jump from a takeoff board into a sand landing area. The distance is measured from the front of the takeoff board to the nearest mark made by any part of the body in the sand. If the jumper oversteps the takeoff board, that attempt is a no jump (*qv*). Flags are used to indicate whether a jump is fair (white) or a no jump (red). Each contestant has three jumps and it is usual for the best six or eight competitors to have three more. The one with the longest jump is the winner.

no jump An illegal long jump or triple jump. A Plasticine indicator is usually placed on the landing area side of the takeoff board to help the judge decide whether or not the competitor overstepped the board.

plant To place the pole in the sunken box prior to vaulting in

the pole vault (*qv*).

pole vault An event for men in which the athlete uses a flexible pole to help him vault a crossbar supported between two uprights. If his pole touches beyond the sunken box below the crossbar, his hands climb up the pole, or he dislodges or fails to clear the crossbar, that attempt counts as a failure. After three consecutive failures he is eliminated. The crossbar is raised after each round.

triple jump An event for men in which the athlete, after a sprint approach to the takeoff board, performs a hop, steps off the same foot, and jumps off the other foot into the sand landing area. Similar rules apply to takeoff and landing as for the long jump (*qv*).

Field events—throws

angle of release The angle at which an implement should be released to gain maximum performance. It is related to the speed of release (*qv*).

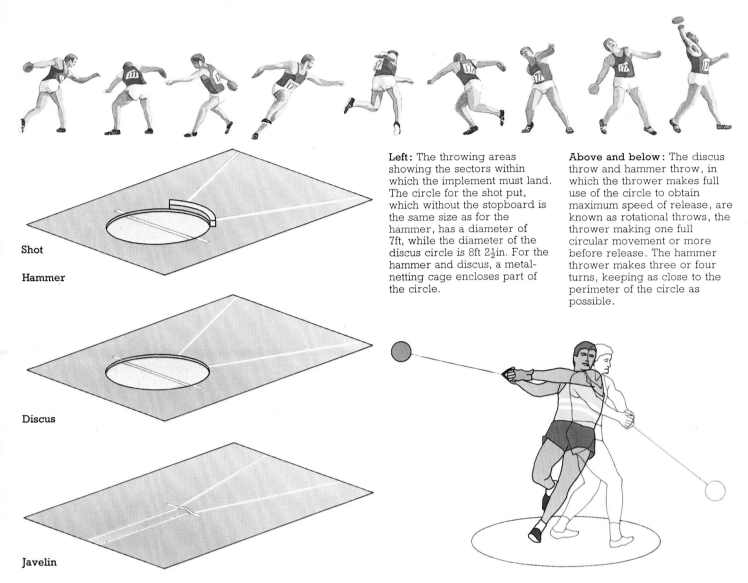

Shot

Hammer

Discus

Javelin

Left: The throwing areas showing the sectors within which the implement must land. The circle for the shot put, which without the stopboard is the same size as for the hammer, has a diameter of 7ft, while the diameter of the discus circle is 8ft 2½in. For the hammer and discus, a metal-netting cage encloses part of the circle.

Above and below: The discus throw and hammer throw, in which the thrower makes full use of the circle to obtain maximum speed of release, are known as rotational throws, the thrower making one full circular movement or more before release. The hammer thrower makes three or four turns, keeping as close to the perimeter of the circle as possible.

discus An event for men and women in which a discus is thrown from within the confines of a caged circle to land within a marked sector. Each thrower has three throws, and then the leading six or eight have three more. The one achieving the furthest distance wins. If the thrower touches the top of the ring bounding the circle or steps beyond it, that throw is considered a foul.

hammer An event for men in which a hammer is thrown from the confines of a caged circle to land within a marked sector. Each thrower has six or eight throws, unless eliminated after three, and the one achieving the furthest distance wins. If the thrower touches the top of the ring bounding the circle or steps beyond it, that throw is a foul.

in the bucket Term used to describe the position of a shot putter's front foot if it is too much to his or her left (right-hand putter) or right (left-hand putter) at the moment of release.

javelin An event for men and women in which the javelin is thrown from behind an arc at the end of a runway to land point first within a marked sector. Each thrower has three throws, and then the leading six or eight have three more. The one achieving the furthest distance wins. If the thrower touches the arc or the scratch line, or steps beyond these, that throw is considered a foul.

lift The upward movement of the rear leg at the moment of releasing the shot.

lift force That which offsets the pull of gravity on an implement after release. Speed of release (qv) is a lift force.

O'Brien glide A method of shift (qv) used by shot putters and developed by the American Parry O'Brien.

put The act of releasing the shot. It must not be a throw but be an extension of the arm from the position in which the shot is held close in to the neck.

reverse The process of recovery by which the putter remains within the circle after releasing the shot.

running rotation The technique used by a discus thrower to build up speed prior to releasing the discus.

shift Backwards movement across a throwing circle prior to release.

shot An event for men and women in which the shot is put (qv) from within the confines of a circle to land within a marked sector. Each thrower has three throws, and then the leading six or eight have three more. The one achieving the furthest distance wins. A put is considered foul if the putting hand is dropped below its starting position, if the shot goes behind the line of the shoulders, or if the putter touches the top of the stopboard or steps beyond it. He may, however, touch the inside of the stopboard.

speed of release The force with which a thrower releases his or her implement. The development of throwing techniques has been directed towards obtaining maximum velocity at the moment of throwing.

T-position Used by some shot putters seeking an increased range of movement within the circle. The putter stands on the rear leg in order to lean back beyond the rear of the circle before going into the shift (qv).

transition The movement in hammer throwing when the thrower, after the second of his wind-ups (qv), moves on to his front foot to commence his first turn (qv).

turn The complete movement through 360° by the hammer thrower. Throwers make three or four turns prior to release.

wind-up Term used for the build-up of torque by a discus thrower.

wind-ups The preliminary swings by a hammer thrower while he is in a stationary position.

Combat Games

Boxing

The art, some would say science, of fighting with gloved fists in a square, roped-off 'ring', boxing flourishes in both its amateur and professional forms. In its amateur form it is a major sport at the Olympic Games, and for some a stepping-stone to a professional career. For the majority who practice boxing, professional or amateur, it is a fast-moving, skillful and aggressive sport in which the aim is to better the opposing fighter by amassing more points than him or by knocking him down for the count of ten.

Modern boxing has come a long way from the bare-knuckle prize-fights of eighteenth-century England. Then there were no weight divisions, wrestling and unsavory tactics were allowed, and a round continued until one man went down. In 1743, John Broughton's rules put a stop to hitting below the belt or hitting a man while he was down, and they gave the man on the ground 30 seconds to recover and return to the mark. Not until the Queensberry rules of 1866 did boxing develop a modern aspect. Rounds were to last three minutes, with a minute between when the boxers could rest in their corners; the ten seconds count was introduced, as were gloves 'to be fair-sized . . . of the best quality, and new'. About this time, too, 'middleweight' and 'lightweight' divisions came into being.

The Queensberry rules, with revisions and additions, have provided the basis for today's rules. Properly enforced — a boxer may be disqualified from a bout for infringing them — they ensure that the sport is contested to the strictest, fairest and safest standards. Critics will always argue that boxing is never safe. But as Mr Justice Grantham advised an Old Bailey jury in 1901: '. . . much better for a man to use weapons God has given him, namely his fists. . . .'

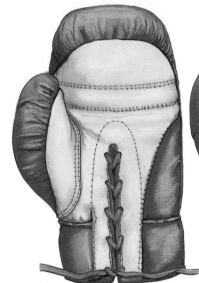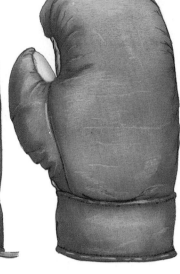

Above: Gloves vary in weight according to the status and weight of the boxer. Amateurs wear 8oz gloves, as do professionals above welterweight. Welterweights and below wear 6oz gloves The laces are always tied at the back of the glove.

Left: The bandages must not cover the knuckles.

ABA The Amateur Boxing Association, founded in 1880 to develop and control amateur boxing in Britain.

AIBA Association Internationale de Boxe Amateur, formed in 1946 to replace the existing controlling body of amateur boxing.

amateur A boxer who does not compete for financial reward. Amateur bouts are limited to three rounds of two or three minutes according to age and ability. Amateurs use 8oz gloves and fight wearing jerseys and identification sashes.

back peddle To move backwards out of range of an opponent's punches.

bandages Wrapping of soft bandage and/or adhesive tape worn by boxers under their gloves. The bandages must not cover the knuckles and must be approved by an official before the gloves are put on.

bantamweight A weight division. Professionals must not exceed 118lb, amateurs under AIBA championship rules must be above 112lb 7oz and not exceed 119lb.

BBBC The British Boxing Board of Control. It is responsible for professional boxing in Britain.

bell Sounded by the timekeeper at the beginning and end of each round. Both boxers must stop fighting as soon as the bell signifies the end of the round.

below the belt A foul punch delivered below an imaginary line across the body from the top of the hip bones.

bolo An uppercut (qv) which begins its upward swing from as low as possible.

bout A boxing contest.

box on Command to the boxers by the referee after an interruption to the fighting, eg after a knock-down (qv).

break Command to the boxers by the referee when they are in a clinch. Both boxers must draw apart and step back. Failure to do so, or throwing a punch after the command, can warrant disqualification.

butting Use of the head, which is illegal, against an opponent's face or head.

canvas, on the Said of a boxer who has been knocked to the floor of the ring.

catchweight A bout in which both boxers agree to box at any weight. Such contests are not allowed by the BBBC.

caution Given to a boxer by the referee for infringing the rules of boxing. Repeated infringements can lead to a formal warning and disqualification.

contender A boxer who is rated as a challenger for a title.

contest The official designation for a boxing fight.

corner The two boxers occupy a corner, diagonally opposite each other, where they sit between rounds accompanied by their seconds.

count An audible count by the referee and the timekeeper when a boxer is knocked down, the timekeeper taking his time from a stopwatch as soon as the boxer goes down and his

opponent retires to a neutral corner (qv). If not on his feet by the count of ten, the boxer is 'counted out' and has lost on a knock-out (qv). Except at the end of the last round, the count continues after the bell until the contestant rises to his feet or is counted out.

distance The full number of rounds to a bout.

EBU The European Boxing Union, which controls professional boxing in Europe.

featherweight A weight division. Professionals must not exceed 126lb; amateurs under AIBA championship rules must be above 119lb and not exceed 125lb 11oz.

fixed Said of a fight when the result has been prearranged.

flyweight The lightest professional weight division with a limit at 112lb. Amateurs under AIBA championship rules must be above 105lb 13oz and not exceed 112lb 7oz.

foul A punch or act that infringes the rules and could lead to

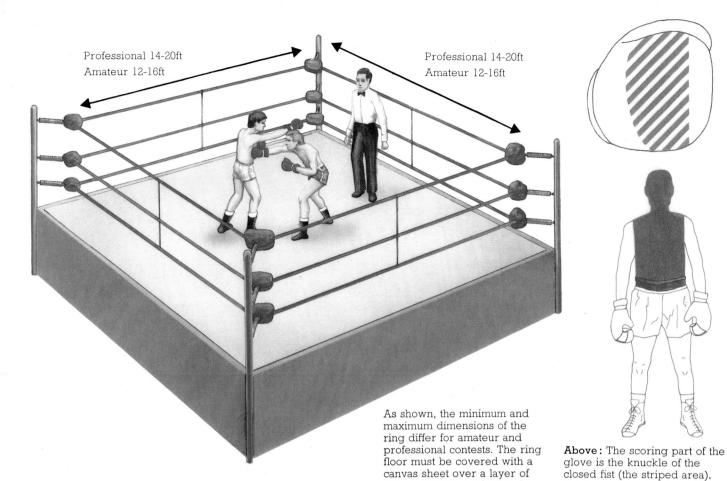

Professional 14-20ft
Amateur 12-16ft

Professional 14-20ft
Amateur 12-16ft

Left: The fist is made by clenching the hand so that the lower parts of the fingers are almost at right-angles to the back of the hand and the tops are tucked underneath with the thumb laid along the fingernails.

As shown, the minimum and maximum dimensions of the ring differ for amateur and professional contests. The ring floor must be covered with a canvas sheet over a layer of felt or rubber and fastened securely. In addition, as the ring is usually elevated, there must be a minimum of $1\frac{1}{2}$ft of ring floor extending outside the ropes. Most bouts are fought in a three-roped ring, but some contests are held in a four-roped ring.

Above: The scoring part of the glove is the knuckle of the closed fist (the striped area). Points are awarded for clean hits to the front and side of the head and body above the belt (the area illustrated in red).

disqualification. Among the fouls listed are hitting on the back of the head or neck, hitting with an open glove, using the pivot blow, ungentlemanly conduct, persistent ducking below the waistline, not trying, intentionally falling without being hit, holding an opponent and hitting him, and hitting an opponent as he is falling or is on the canvas.

foul-proof protector An abdominal protector compulsory for all boxers.

Golden Gloves A famous American tournament for amateurs. Champions win a gold medal and the diamond-studded Golden Gloves trophy.

gum-shield A mouth guard worn by boxers.

heavyweight The heaviest weight division. Professionals may be any weight; amateurs under AIBA championship rules must be above 178lb 9oz.

hook A close-quarters punch made with either hand, though a hook to the head with the right hand (or a southpaw's (*qv*) left)

is usually a right (or left) cross. Essentially, the hook is a lead (*qv*) shortened to a jab with the elbow at right angles and the wrist turned on impact so that the blow is delivered with the knuckle part of the hand.

in-fighting Boxing at close quarters, using hooks and uppercuts to pummel the body and the opponent's guard to get an opening to his head.

jab A punch delivered with more speed and purpose and at a closer range than a normal lead (*qv*).

junior-lightweight A professional weight division with a limit of 130lb.

junior-middleweight A professional weight division with a limit of 154lb.

junior-welterweight A professional weight division with a limit of 140lb.

kidney punch An illegal blow delivered to the kidneys.

knock-down A boxer's falling to the canvas from an opponent's blow, as opposed to slipping.

He is still considered down even if he is on one or both feet if another part of his body is touching the canvas, or if he is still rising.

knock-out When a boxer fails to get to his feet by the count of ten. Officially known as a *count out* or *being counted out*.

lead The punch with which a boxer begins his attack. It is usually a straight left (*qv*); or a right for a southpaw.

license Issued to everyone connected with professional boxing and renewable annually. No amateur boxer can be given a professional license until he is 18, but may be granted an apprentice license at 17.

lightweight A weight division. Professionals must not exceed 135lb; amateurs under AIBA championship rules must be above 125lb 11oz and not exceed 132lb 15oz.

light-flyweight The lightest amateur weight division with a limit of 105lb 13oz.

light-heavyweight A weight divi-

sion. Professionals must not exceed 175lb; amateurs under AIBA championship rules must be above 165lb 6oz and not exceed 178lb 9oz.

light-middleweight An amateur weight division above 147lb 11oz and not exceeding $156\frac{1}{2}$lb under AIBA championship rules.

light-welterweight An amateur weight division above 132lb 5oz and not exceeding 140lb under AIBA rules.

Lonsdale belt Awarded by the BBBC to the winner of a British title. Any boxer winning three titles in the same division wins his belt outright.

Master of ceremonies The official who introduces the contestants at the beginning of a bout and publicly announces the official results of all contests.

middleweight A weight division. Professionals must not exceed 160lb; amateurs under AIBA championship rules must be above $156\frac{1}{2}$lb and not exceed 165lb 6oz.

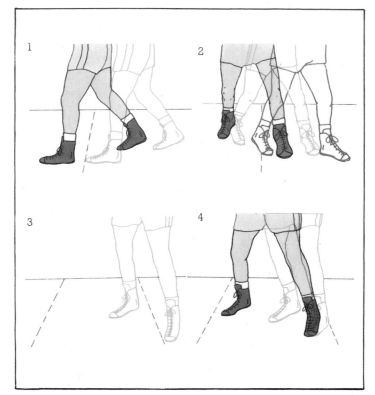

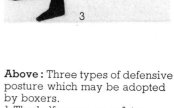

Above: The classic stance adopted by orthodox boxers. Although an attacking boxer is generally more spectacular to watch, it should be remembered that boxing is the art of self-defense and that the so-called classic stance is based on defense more than attack. No matter how aggressive a boxer appears, he cannot score points if his opponent's defense prevents him from landing blows to the correct scoring areas. In adopting the classic stance, the boxer keeps his hands well up with the elbows tucked in. The left hand is slightly extended to keep the opponent at a safe distance and to protect the face; the right hand guards the other side of the head but is always poised to attack.

Above: From the classic stance, the boxer advances (1) by moving his left foot forward and then bringing up his right foot. He retreats (2) by first drawing his right foot back, the left foot following in a straight line to maintain a balanced stance. Figures 3 and 4 depict the shift, or sidestep, to the right from a stationary stance.

Above: Three types of defensive posture which may be adopted by boxers.
1 The half-cover, or safety, guard.
2 The American cross-arm guard.
3 The Continental-style double-arm guard.

neutral corner Either of the two corners not used by the contestants and their seconds. In the event of a knock-down, the boxer still standing must retire to a neutral corner until instructed to box on.

no-foul rule Introduced in 1930 by the NYSAC to stop boxers from throwing (*qv*) a fight by hitting below the belt and thus being automatically disqualified. However, contestants can still be disqualified for other offenses.

NYSAC The New York State Athletic Commission. Its boxing department was set up in 1920 to enforce the state laws regarding boxing, and under those laws it may have no allegiance to any other controlling body. It does, however, have a working arrangement with the BBBC and the WBC (*qv*).

one-two A left lead followed in rapid succession by a right cross to the jaw.

points The means of arriving at a decision when both contestants go the distance. In amateur boxing, points are awarded by a panel of five judges who give 20 points a round to the more skilful boxer and proportionately fewer to his opponent. In professional boxing, ten points are awarded to the better contestant and a proportion to his opponent. In Britain, where the referee is the sole judge, he awards whole points only. Points are awarded for clean hits with the knuckle of the closed glove to the front and side of the head above the belt and to the body above the belt, and for skilful defensive boxing.

prize-fighting Boxing with bare knuckles. It is illegal.

promoter The person responsible for staging a boxing program. In addition to notifying the controlling body of his program, he must deposit with it a bond to cover his maximum costs.

punch A blow delivered with a clenched fist.

punchbag A hard-stuffed canvas or leather sack suspended from a pulley or ceiling to help a boxer in training develop and correct his punching.

punchball Ball fixed to a spring attached to a solid base at floor level.

purse The amount of money put up by the promoter for a professional bout. It is split between the two fighters: 60-40 in favor of the champion if it is a title bout, or 50-50 if a vacant title is at stake.

Queensberry rules These rules, drawn up in the mid-1860s by the Marquess of Queensberry, Lord Lonsdale and Arthur Chambers, heralded the end of prize-fighting and are the basis of the modern rules.

rabbit punch An illegal blow to the back of the head.

reach The distance from fingertip to fingertip when a boxer's arms are outstretched sideways.

referee The official who controls a bout. Under BBBC rules he is the sole adjudicator of points, but in other countries he is assisted by two judges, the majority verdict deciding the result. In amateur contests the referee takes no part in awarding points.

right cross A right-hand hook to the head, often made over an opponent's left-hand lead.

ring The roped area within which a bout is contested. The name is thought to derive from the games ring instituted in London's Hyde Park in 1723 by order of George I. Padding the floor beneath the canvas covering with foam rubber or felt to protect a contestant's head was an innovation of the early 1890s. The corner posts, too, must be padded.

roadwork Running a certain number of miles in training to lose weight and gain stamina.

round The duration of boxing before a compulsory rest period. It begins and ends with the bell. Rounds are of two or three minutes according to age and experience, novice professionals beginning with six two-minute round bouts before being upgraded to three-minute

Right: Four punches which should form part of a boxer's repertoire. 1 The hook. The wrist should be turned on impact so that the blow is delivered with the back of the knuckles. 2 The uppercut. 3 The straight right. 4 The left jab, or lead. The hook and uppercut may be delivered with either hand.

Left and below: Defensive moves and counter-punches. In each of the figures, the boxer in the white shorts is defending and in some instances counter-attacking.
5 Blocking the left jab and countering with a left jab.

6 Parrying the left jab with the right guard and countering with a left jab.
7 Slipping the punch by ducking inside it. The fighter is now in a good position to develop a two-fisted attack on his opponent's body and head with

short hooks and uppercuts.
8 The elbow or forearm block to protect the body from a left hook.
9 Rolling under the right cross and countering with a straight right to the unguarded side of the opponent's body.

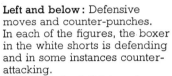

bouts. Title fights should be 15 rounds, although in some countries this is reduced to 12 or even 10.

roundhouse A long-distance punch with either hand that comes round on to the opponent's head or body.

RSC Referee stopped contest; the verdict when the referee ends a bout inside the distance because he considers a boxer unfit to continue.

saved by the bell Said of a boxer who is prevented from being counted out by the sounding of the bell at the end of a contest.

score-card Used by the referee and/or judges to record points awarded to the contestants.

seconds Those who assist a boxer in his corner between rounds. The number varies with local rules. An official second is appointed for each corner by the promoter to look after any boxer without his own second, to assist as required, and to make sure there is clean water available.

seconds out The timekeeper's

command telling the seconds to vacate the ring before the start of each round.

shadow boxing Fighting an imaginary opponent. It is used in training to quicken timing.

slip a punch To avoid a punch by moving away from or inside it.

solar plexus The nerve center at the central point below the ribs.

southpaw A boxer who takes up a stance with his right arm leading and his right foot forward.

spar To box in training, often against a partner of similar build and style to a forthcoming opponent. Sparring brings a boxer to fighting pitch.

speedball An inflated ball suspended under a platform to help a boxer in training perfect his speed, timing and co-ordination.

standing count An enforced break to the count of eight after a knock-down. It is enforced in amateur contests and by many professional bodies. The BBBC is a notable exception.

straight left Usually a boxer's

leading punch and a valuable points' scorer. It should be delivered straight from the shoulder with the full weight of the body going in behind it.

throw a fight To lose intentionally.

throw in the towel To retire from a contest. A boxer's second throws his towel into the ring to indicate to the referee that he wants to save his fighter from further punishment.

timekeeper The official responsible for timing the rounds, the interval between rounds, and the count in the event of a knockdown.

TKO Technical knock-out; an American verdict in the event of the referee stopping the fight because he considers a boxer is unfit to continue.

uppercut A punch delivered with either hand in an upward swinging movement to the head or body.

warning A formal reprimand to a boxer for infringing the rules. In amateur bouts, a boxer

receiving three warnings is automatically disqualified.

WBA The World Boxing Association. Originally formed as the National Boxing Association in the United States in opposition to the NYSAC, it proclaims its own world champions, often in conflict with the WBC.

WBC The World Boxing Council. Set up as a counter to the WBA in 1963, it comprises most national and international governing bodies and receives the support of the NYSAC. It has its own world champions.

weigh-in Before amateur contests, boxers weigh in on the first morning of a competition and have only one attempt at making the limit. Professionals are given a limited period of time, usually an hour, to make the weight.

welterweight A weight division. Professionals must not exceed 147lb; amateurs under AIBA championship rules must be above 140lb and not exceed 147lb 11oz.

Fencing

Mask

An international sport which has enjoyed Olympic status since 1896, fencing is the use of swords by two contestants for offense and defense. Such a simplification, however, does no justice to a sport whose traditions have given it conventions and techniques that require keen mental and physical agility.

Fencing is practiced with four weapons: men's and women's foils, épée, and sabre. The foil is the one with which fencing should be learned, for its rules and conventions teach an appreciation of fencing time, measure and phrase. The principle of the conventions, which are similar for sabre, is that the initial attack has the right to proceed until parried, when the right of attack passes to the opponent's riposte. If this is parried, the first attacker's counter-riposte has the right of way, the phrase so continuing until either lands a hit. Epée, being the duelling sword, is not bound by conventions.

For all four weapons, a bout lasts until one fencer has scored five hits, or for six minutes' actual fencing. If the time expires, the fencer who has scored the most hits wins. If, in foil and sabre, hits are equal, the bout continues until a deciding hit is landed. If, in épée, hits reach 5-5 with a double hit and with time remaining, the bout continues until a deciding hit is landed, but if hits are equal when time expires the result is a double defeat. Hits with the electric foil and épée are recorded on special apparatus, but hits and cuts in sabre have to be observed by the jury. In foil, the president has to analyze the phrase to ensure that a hit has been made in keeping with the rules and conventions of the sport.

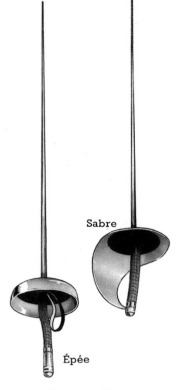

Sabre

Épée

Above: The mask for the foil and the épée consists of wire mesh. A reinforced canvas bib extends under the chin. For sabre, the mesh sections along the sides and top can be replaced with leather.

Left: Both the épée and the sabre are usually taken up after the student has acquired some training in the foil. The épée has a triangular, fluted blade. The bell-guard is larger than the foil's. The sabre is a lighter, cut-and-thrust weapon—points can be scored with edge and point. The sabreur thus has a more varied repertoire of attacks and parries.

Below: All competitive épée is now judged with electrical apparatus. A spring-loaded electric point registers each hit.

absence of blade When the blades are not engaged.

advance To step forward. The leading foot is carried forward a step, and then the rear foot is brought up an equal distance by lifting as opposed to sliding.

aids The last three fingers of the sword hand (not including the index finger). They are used to steady the handle.

angulation Angling the wrist when making a hit, the intention being to have the point at right angles to the target.

à pied ferme An attacking movement or movements made without moving the feet.

assault A bout.

attack An offensive movement made with the object of landing a hit on the opponent's target. It may be either a simple (qv) or a compound (qv) attack.

attack on preparation An attack launched while an opponent makes a preparation of attack.

attack on the blade A preparation (qv) of attack by beat (qv), froissement (qv), or pressure (qv). It is made to deflect the opponent's blade to force an opening for a direct attack, or to obtain an opening in another line as a result of his reaction.

balestra A short jump forward from the soles of both feet as part of an attack.

barrage A tie or fight-off.

beat A preparation of attack made by delivering a sharp blow on an opponent's blade. There is a *direct beat* and a *change beat*, the latter preceded by a change of engagement (qv).

bind A *prise de fer* (qv) in which the fencer carries his opponent's blade in a diagonal from a high line to a low line (qv) on the opposite side of the target, or from a low to a high line.

breaking ground Taking a step backwards. The movement is the reverse of the advance (qv).

cadence The rhythm in which a sequence of movements is made.

ceding parry A parry (qv) made by giving way to an opponent who is preparing for an attack by a *prise de fer* (qv).

change of engagement Crossing an opponent's blade into a new line by passing under the blade.

circular parry A parry in which the defender describes a circle with his blade to gather the attacker's blade and return it to the original line of engagement. Also called *counter-parry*.

compound attack A combination of simple attacks with one or more feints (qv) in an attempt to draw a premature parry before making the final thrust.

compound riposte A riposte (qv) made with one or more feints.

coquille The bell-shaped guard of the épée and foil.

corps à corps When two fencers are so close together that neither is able to use his sword correctly. When they are in a similar position but still able to use their swords they are said to be at *close quarters*.

coulé A thrust which remains in contact with an opponent's blade.

counter-attack Made as soon as an opponent launches his attack. It is either a stop hit (qv) or a stop hit with opposition (qv).

counter-disengagement An indirect attack made to deceive an opponent's change of engagement or his circular parry.

counter-parry *See* circular parry.

counter-riposte An offensive action made by a fencer after he has parried a riposte or counter-riposte.

counter-time A premeditated attack against an opponent with a penchant for launching a counter-attack as soon as he sees a preparation of attack. It consists of inducing a stop hit or stop hit with opposition, parrying it, and scoring with a riposte. It is also called a *second intention attack*.

covered The position of the sword and sword hand when they close the line of engagement against a direct thrust.

croisé A *prise de fer* in which the fencer carries his opponent's blade from a high line to a low line on the same side of the target as the engagement.

cut A hit in sabre with the front

Right: The foil is the basic weapon for the practice of fencing The quadrilateral foil blade should be light and flexible. Its balance depends on the weight of the pommel in relation to the length of the blade. This is a matter of personal preference for each fencer, though usually the point of balance is situated one to two inches along the blade from the guard. In competitions judged by electrical apparatus, the weapon is fitted with a spring-loaded 'barrel' tip enclosing an electrical contact.

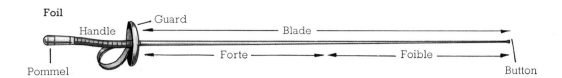

Foil

Handle — Guard — Blade

Pommel — Forte — Foible

Button

Target areas

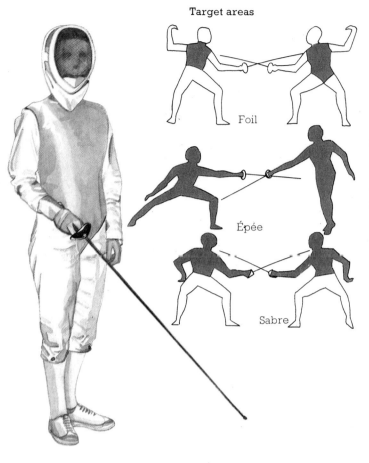

Foil

Épée

Sabre

Above: The ancestors of the sabre include the eastern sabre, the English broadsword, and the cavalry sabre. It was refined by the Italians into a light fencing and duelling sword. The Italian style, however, has generally given way to the Hungarian style, whose grip is shown here. Only the ball of the thumb rests on the back of the handle, the main weight resting on the heel of the hand.

Left: Of the three weapons, the target area for the foil is the most restricted. It includes only the trunk to the V-shaped bounds of the groin in front and to the hip bones in the back. However, if a limb is used to deflect a hit or a move is made to receive it on another part of the body, it is counted as a hit.

Left: The target area for the épée is the most extensive. The entire body, clothing and equipment is game. Since there is no right-of-way as in foil and sabre, whoever hits first, wherever, scores.

Left: The target area for the sabre consists of the body from the waist up. Thrusts are usually directed at the torso; cuts are to the head, cheeks, sword arm, thighs and chest.

Far left: The swordsman dressed for an engagement. Jackets and breeches are traditionally made of strong white canvas. The jacket can either cover the entire trunk or can be a waist-length version. Gloves are of chamois or soft hide for foil and sabre, of stronger doeskin for épée. Light-soled shoes have rawhide or rubber soles.

---

edge or with the first third of the back edge of the sword.
cut-over A simple attack in which the attacker's blade passes over that of his opponent.
cutting the lines Circular parries which are not made in the line of engagement.
delayed attack/riposte One made after a pause.
dérobement The action with which a fencer, while his arm is extended and the point of his sword threatens his opponent's target, evades his opponent's attempt either to take or make an attack on the blade.
detached parry One in which the defender removes his blade from his opponent's as soon as he has deflected it.
development and return to guard The lunge (*qv*) and the recovery from it.
direct attack/riposte One made in the line of engagement.
disengagement An attack where a fencer passes his blade under his opponent's to move into an opposite line of engagement.

doigté Finger play (*qv*).
doublé A disengagement followed by a counter-disengagement. The blade goes through a complete circle in order to deceive the opponent's circular parry.
double hit Recorded by the electric apparatus in épée when a fencer's hit arrives less than $\frac{1}{25}$th of a second after his opponent's hit. A hit is awarded to each fencer.
engagement The crossing of blades.
en marchant Taking one or more steps forward.
envelopment A *prise de fer* in which a fencer engages his opponent's threatening blade and describes a circle, without losing the contact of blades, to return to the line of engagement.
épéeist A man who fences with the épée, the duelling sword.
false attack One in which the attacker does not intend to score a hit.
feint A movement which resembles an attack. It is made to draw

some response from an opponent.
fencing positions Those in which the sword arm and the sword are placed so that they cover the lines of the target.
fencing time That needed to make one simple fencing movement. It is also called a period of fencing time.
finger play The method of controlling and directing the sword with the fingers rather than the wrist or the arm.
flèche A running attack, as opposed to a lunge or movements *en marchant*. It depends on speed and surprise for success.
foible The half of the blade nearer the point.
foilist A man or woman who fences with the foil.
forte The half of the blade nearer the guard.
froissement A preparation of attack which deflects an opponent's blade by grazing it with a strong, sharp movement. It is also called the *graze*.

gaining ground Taking a step forwards.
gaining on the lunge Bringing the rear foot up to the leading foot before making a lunge.
graze *See froissement.*
ground judges The two judges who, when the electric apparatus is in use for foil and épée, watch for hits made on the ground.
guard The part of the sword between the handle and the blade, or partly encompassing the handle, to protect the sword hand.
high lines The parts of a fencer's target visible above his sword hand when he is on guard.
hit Contact made with the point, plus an edge in sabre, on an opponent. To score, it must be landed on the target area.
indirect attack/riposte One made by a simple disengagement or cutover to the opposite line, or by a counter-disengagement (*qv*).
in quartata An attack made while at the same time sidestepping out of line.

Above: The 'on-guard' position for the foil. Note the half-extended arm, the slightly upraised foil following the line of the forearm. The front foot extends roughly two foot lengths in front of the back foot, while the body 'sits' balanced between the two. The other arm is raised so that the upper arm is level with the shoulder and the hand is held in a relaxed position slightly above the head. The trunk is bent slightly forward, following the direction of the eyes and sword toward the opponent. This position is assumed after every disengagement. The Italian variation of this basic French stance places the trunk at a more sideways position vis-à-vis the opponent.

Above: The standard 'on-guard' position for the épée. It is rather similar to that for the foil, but the knees are slightly less bent and apart. The rear shoulder is held further back, thus effacing the trunk by turning it sideways. The épée is held with the point slightly lower than the hilt, giving the sword arm maximum protection.

Left: The Hungarian 'on-guard' position which has become standard practice for the sabre. It, too, is more upright than the foil stance with the blade at a 45° angle and pointing toward the opponent's head across the sabreur's body. It is left to the fencer's discretion whether his non-sword hand grips the waist or lightly rests, closed, on his hip.

inside lines The parts of the target farthest from the sword arm.

invitation Deliberately opening a line to tempt an opponent to make an attacking movement at the exposed target area.

jury The president and four judges who control and judge a fencing bout.

la belle The deciding hit during a bout.

line of engagement The position of a fencer's sword hand in relation to his target.

lines The imaginary parts of the target related to the positions in which a fencer may place his sword hand when on guard. In addition to the high, low, inside and outside lines, there are the theoretical lines named after the parries designed to protect them. In foil and épée, there are eight: two for each quarter of the target; in sabre there are five.

low lines The parts of a fencer's target visible below his sword hand when he is on guard.

lunge The rapid extension of the sword arm, body, and legs from the on guard position to land a hit on an opponent.

manipulators The thumb and index finger of the sword hand.

martingale The strap attached to the handle of the foil and épée to prevent the weapon from flying out of the hand.

measure, or fencing measure The distance maintained between two fencers during a bout so that it would require a lunge to land a hit.

metallic over-jacket Worn over the target area in foil so that valid hits are registered by a colored light on the electric apparatus.

metallic piste Used when electric apparatus is employed for foil and épée.

molinello A circular cut at the head in sabre. It is a riposte from the parry position of prime.

mounting The part of the sword from and including the guard to the pommel (*qv*).

on guard The position adopted

by a fencer when he is prepared for a bout.

opposition A movement made without disengaging an opponent's blade.

orthopedic grip A handle moulded to the shape of the hand or the fingers.

outside lines The parts of the target nearest the sword arm.

parry A defensive action in which a fencer deflects an attacker's blade with his own blade.

passata sotto Ducking under an opponent's attacking blade while counter attacking.

phrase A sequence of fencing movements leading up to a hit.

piste The area on which a bout is fenced.

plastron An undergarment comprising a double thickness of hemp cloth. It is worn by fencers under the jacket as a safety precaution.

pointe d'arrêt The cylindrical spring-loaded attachment which is fitted to the point of the electric foil and electric épée so that

a hit will be registered.

pommel The piece of metal screwed into the top of the sword to lock the components together and balance the weapon.

preparation of attack A movement by a fencer prior to an attack. It may be a forwards or backwards movement, an attack on the blade, or a *prise de fer* (*qv*).

president The referee of a fencing bout.

pressure A preparation of attack in which a fencer deflects his opponent's blade by pressing it aside without disengaging the blades.

principle of defense Keeping the forte of the blade in contact with the foible of an opponent's blade in a parry.

prise de fer A preparation of attack in which a fencer takes his opponent's threatening blade and dominates it until his own attack is completed. *Prises de fer* include the bind, *croise*, and envelopment.

progressive attack Continuously

Above: Attack in épée. The two fencers have engaged and the fencer on the left makes a lunge toward his opponent, scoring a hit on the upper arm. The fencer on the right has made an ineffectual attempt at a parry, but has left his right side open. The fact that the entire body acts as a target means that épée fencing can provide more of the sensation of a real fight. Jacket fastenings, whether buttons or zips, must be on the side opposite the sword arm.

Left: The flèche attack demonstrated by a sabreur. Because the distance between two fencers is greater in sabre than in foil, it is more often used as an alternative to the lunge in this form of swordplay.

approaching an opponent's target area while developing a compound attack; as opposed to remaining *à pied ferme*.

pronation The position of the sword hand when the fingernails are pointing downwards. In foil and épée, the high lines of *prime* and *tierce* and the low lines of *seconde* and *quinte* are taken with the sword hand in pronation.

rassemblement Bringing the front foot back to the rear foot while at the same time standing to full height.

rédoublement A renewed attack made while still on the lunge and immediately after the original attack has been parried or avoided.

remise An immediately renewed attack, made while still on the lunge and in the same line as the original attack without withdrawing the sword arm.

renewed attack The renewal of an attack which has been parried or avoided.

reprise A renewed attack which is preceded by a momentary

return to guard, either backwards in the usual return to guard, or forwards by bringing up the rear foot and thus gaining distance.

retire To step backwards.

return to guard Recovering to the on guard position after a lunge.

reverse beat A change beat (*q v*). At sabre, it is a beat made with the back of the blade.

riposte The offensive movement by a fencer after he has successfully parried an attack.

sabreur A man who fences with the sabre, the cut-and-thrust weapon.

Salle d'armes The building in which a fencing bout takes place, or where fencing is practiced.

second intention Any movement made by a fencer to draw a response when he intends to overcome.

semicircular parry A parry in which the defender describes a half-circle with his blade from a high to a low line, or from a low to a high line.

sentiment du fer Feeling an opponent's reactions through the contact of the two blades.

simple attack One made directly by a thrust or a *coule*, or indirectly by a disengagement, a cut-over, or a counter-disengagement.

sitting The bent-knees stance of a fencer when on guard.

stance The position of a fencer's feet and legs when he or she is in the on guard position.

stop hit A counter-attack designed to stop the development of an opponent's attack.

stop hit with opposition A counter-attack made by anticipating the line in which an opponent's attack will finish and closing that line by parrying the opponent's blade while making the stop hit. It is also known as a *time hit*.

successive parries A series of parries until contact is made with the attacker's blade.

supination The position of the sword hand when the fingernails are pointing upwards. In foil and

épée, the high lines of *quarte* and *sixte* and the low lines of *septime* and *octave* are taken with the sword hand in supination or half-supination.

taking the blade See *prise de fer*.

tang The end portion of the blade which passes through the handle and into which is screwed the pommel.

thrust A simple and direct attacking movement.

touché The word exclaimed to acknowledge a hit.

trompement Avoiding by deception an opponent's attempt to parry an attack.

two-time A movement made in two periods of fencing time.

uncovered The position of the sword hand and blade in which the line of engagement is not closed.

valid hits Those which arrive on the target area for the weapon being fenced.

warning lines Lines drawn on the *piste* so that the fencers can be warned when they are approaching the rear limit.

Judo

A sport that can be as aesthetically satisfying as it is violent, the martial art of judo emerged in Japan from ju-jitsu, a method of unarmed combat which flowered from the seventeenth to the nineteenth centuries. Its founder was Dr Jigoro Kano, who opened his first dojo in 1882 at the age of 21 and took the more outstanding skills of ju-jitsu to develop what he called Kodokan judo. Literally judo means the 'gentle way', but Kano interpreted it as 'maximum efficiency', seeing it as 'the elevation of an art to a principle'. Not until after World War II, however, did judo become a competitive sport as it is known today. In 1948 the All-Japan championships were first contested, and the European Judo Union (plus the British Federation) was founded. The International Judo Federation was formed in 1951 and staged its first world championships in 1956. Olympic recognition in 1964 led to the introduction of light-, middle-, and heavyweight categories, in addition to the traditional open class, and in 1967 welterweight and light-heavyweight categories were added.

A judo match lasts until one fighter has scored the maximum 10-point ippon or until the end of allotted time, when the result is determined by the two judges, and referee if needed, on points scored, penalties incurred, or aggressiveness. The primary aim, however, is to end the contest by scoring an ippon.

Judo is a very formal sport, with judoka bowing to each other before and after their match, and even in training. There is a grade of seniority (kyu and dan) gained by fighting ability, technical knowledge, learning, and — above 5th dan — contribution to the sport. The terminology, despite the sport's international appeal, remains Japanese.

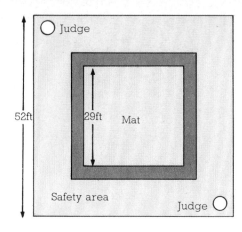

Judo shiai, or contests, are held on a 29ft square mat with a surrounding red danger zone of 1yd. The mat is made of a number of 2 x 1yd tatami held tightly together by a wooden frame within the 52ft square competition area. Two judges sit at opposite corners of the safety area while the referee controls the bout from the mat.

A judoka wearing the judogi, the loose-fitting judo suit. The sleeves of the jacket must cover more than half the forearm, while the jacket itself has to cover the hips. It is, however, slit up each side. To withstand the pressure of grips on the jacket, the lapels and the stitching at the armpits and below the waistline are strengthened. The trousers must cover half the lower leg, while the belt, the color of which denotes a judoka's standard, should be long enough to encompass the body twice. The feet are always bare.

aite Opponent, partner.

ashi Leg/foot.

ashi-barai A sweeping ankle throw.

ashi-garami A leg lock.

ashi-no-ko The instep of the foot.

ashi-no-ura The sole of the foot.

ashi-waza Foot or leg throwing technique.

ashi-yube The toes.

atama The head.

atemi Blows aimed at vital points of the body. *Ate* is a hit.

butsukari See uchi-kome.

chui An official caution from the referee for an infringement of the rules. It costs five penalty points.

dan A degree of attainment in the art of judo. There are 12 stages of dan, though the highest ever awarded is 10th dan. 1st to 5th dans wear a black belt; 6th to 8th a red and white belt; 9th to 11th a red belt; 12th a white belt.

de-ashi-barai An advancing foot sweep throw.

dojo The place where judo training takes place.

eri The collar or lapel of a garment.

eri-jime Strangulation by use of the collar.

fusegi Defense.

fusen Losing by default.

gyaku A reverse technique for throws, locks and holds.

hadaka-jime Strangulation by means other than clothing.

hajime The referee's instruction to begin a contest.

hana The nose.

hane-goshi A spring-hip throw.

hansoku-make A major infringement of the rules. It carries ten penalty points and brings automatic disqualification.

hantei The referee's request to the judges for a decision when no points have been scored.

hara The stomach.

harai A sweeping technique for throwing.

hi dari The left-hand side.

hiji The elbow.

hiki-otoshi A pulling drop throw.

hitai The forehead.

hiza The knee.

hiza-guruma A knee wheel throw, in which the opponent is wheeled over the outstretched left leg.

ippon A full point. Worth ten points when an opponent is thrown on to his back with force, or is trapped in a stranglehold, or has submitted from an armlock or choke-lock, or has been held down on his back for 30 seconds.

jigotai Adopting a defensive stance.

jikan The referee's call for a time-out period.

ju Literally gentle.

judogi The costume worn for judo.

judoka A person who practises judo. In Japan, a very senior player.

juji-jime A basic crossed-arm stranglehold.

juno-kata One of the forms of kata.(*qv*).

kaeshi-waza Counter-throwing techniques.

kake The point of the maximum power of a throw.

kami-shiho-gatame An upper four quarters hold-down, in which the opponent is held down with the greater part of his back on the ground.

kanibasami A scissors throw.

kansetsu-waza An armlock technique.

kao The face.

karu To reap, or to sweep an opponent's leg from under him with part of one's own leg, usually the thigh.

kata A series of formal movements in seven forms. They are now performed mainly for demonstrations and in training, although kata competitions are held with points awarded for technique and fluency of movement. Kata also means the shoulder.

katame-waza Groundwork technique.

katsu A method of resuscitation.

kenshusei Special research students' section at the Kodokan.

keikoku An official warning from the referee for an infringement of the rules. It costs seven penalty points.

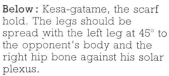

Above: Koshi-guruma, the hip wheel throwing technique.
Below: Okuri-eri-jime, the sliding collar lock. One of the basic strangleholds, it is applied from behind the opponent.

Below: Kesa-gatame, the scarf hold. The legs should be spread with the left leg at 45° to the opponent's body and the right hip bone against his solar plexus.

Above: De-ashi-barai, the advancing foot sweep. One of the most common of the ankle sweeping techniques, it requires little force if performed correctly. The sweep should come just as the opponent, in stepping forward, is off balance and should be assisted by downward pressure on the arm corresponding to the ankle being swept aside.

Below: Ude-garami, the entangled armlock. By turning both his wrists towards the ground, the attacking judoka twists his opponent's arm at the shoulder socket. And by exerting pressure on his opponent's chest, he prevents him from escaping.

kesa-gatame A scarf hold.
kiken Withdrawal from a contest.
kinsa A small advantage to one contestant from a throw or a hold. It is worth three points.
Kodokan The principal dojo (*qv*) of judo. It is situated in Tokyo.
koka A score, almost a yuko (*qv*), with a value of three points.
koshi The hip.
koshi-waza The technique of hip throws.
kubi The neck.
kubi-nage A neck throw.
kuzushi To force an opponent to lose his balance.
kyu One of the grades of judo pupil, beginning with 9th kyu (yellow belt) outside Japan, 5th kyu (white belt) in Japan, and up to 1st kyu (brown belt)
maki-komi A winding technique. The opponent is wound around the body before being thrown to the ground.
mata The inside of the thigh.
matte The referee's command for the contestants to break.
me The eye.
migi The right-hand side.

morote Two hands.
mune The chest.
nage A throwing action.
nage waza A throwing technique. The basic throws are built around hand throws, leg throws, shoulder throws and sacrifice throws.
newaza Groundwork, which is made up of moves, counter-moves and feints to gain an ippon from a stranglehold, armlock, or hold-down.
nuki-shiai A team contest in which the winner stays on the mat until he is beaten.
obi A belt.
obi-otoshi A belt drop throw.
o-goshi A hip throw.
osae-komi Holding; it is called by the referee when one contestant has his opponent in a hold-down.
osae-komiwaza Holding techniques.
o-soto-gake A major outer drop throw.
o-soto-gari A major outer reaping throw.
o-uchi-gari A major interior

reaping throwing technique.
randori Free practice, without the intensity of competition, in which the judoka tries out his techniques against partners of various weights and builds.
rei The bow made on entering the dojo.
renraku-waza Combination techniques.
seio-nage A shoulder throw.
sensei A teacher.
shiai A contest.
shiai-jo The area in which a contest is conducted.
shihan A master, or the highest grade in judo.
shime-waza Strangulation and choking techniques.
sode A sleeve.
sono mama The referee's command to the contestants not to move.
sore-made Literally 'that is all'; the referee's command to the contestants to end the contest.
sutemi-waza Sacrifice throws.
tatami The mats on which the contest is conducted.
tekubi The wrist.

te-awaza Hand throw techniques.
toketa Broken. It is shouted by a contestant when he has escaped from an osae-komi (*qv*).
tskuri-komi Getting an opponent off balance prior to attempting to throw him.
uchi-kome Practicing throwing techniques without actually completing the throw. Also called *butsukari*.
ude The arm.
ude-garami An arm entanglement.
ukemi A break-fall; a method used to cushion the effect of a throw.
ura-nage A rear throw.
waza A technique.
waza-ari Almost an ippon (*qv*), and worth seven points.
waza-ari-ni-chikai waza A near throw and worth seven points.
yoshi The referee's command to carry on with the contest.
yuko A score, almost a waza-ari, with a value of five points.
yusei gachi A decisive score in favor of one contestant which wins him the contest.

Karate

To the casual observer, karate — literally 'empty hand' — appears as a violent form of unarmed combat in which the arms, hands, legs, feet and even head are used at bewildering speed to defeat an opponent. Or he may think that karate is all about smashing tiles, rocks, wood, or similar solid objects with the hands or feet. Such endeavors are merely the physical expressions of a development of mind and body in pursuit of the martial way of life. Paramount to that development is the Zen Buddhist concept of emptiness of mind from dishonourable thoughts, emotions and worries relating to tactics. To assist this, much importance is put on correct and controlled breathing techniques that produce a calming effect as well as building up the muscular strength of the abdomen. Therefore although karate is one of the more modern Oriental martial arts, its philosophies and severe physical demands have their roots in far more ancient times; in fact, well before the birth of Christ.

As a competitive combat sport, karate is by necessity non-contact, apart from sweeping techniques of the leg to throw an opponent to the ground. Bouts are of two or three minutes duration, and are controlled by a referee, four judges who sit one at each corner of the 26ft square match area, and a controller or arbiter. Points are scored by delivering recognized competition hits, thrusts, or kicks in focus (within 2in of the prescribed target areas) from a proper posture and distance. As in judo, an ippon (one point contest) or sanbon (three ippon) win a bout, but if there are no points scored, the decision may be awarded by the referee and judges on superiority throughout the bout. Similarly, karateka are graded within a system of kyu and dan, and the terminology of the art has remained Japanese.

Some of the attacking weapons used by a karateka. The red areas denote the contact points.
1 Tegatana; the handsword.
2 Hira-hasami; the flat scissors or knife hand.
3 The back of the hand used for haishu, the slapping technique to the side of the head.
4 Hizagashira; the knee-cap.
5 Ash-kubi; the ankle.
6 The ball of the foot, which is to foot techniques what the fist is to hand techniques.
7 The bottom of the heel, used for stepping down powerfully on an opponent's instep, and the back of the heel, which is used for ushirogeri, the rear kick.
8 Ashigatana; the footsword.

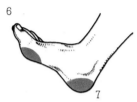
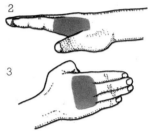

agetsuki A blow delivered in an upwards manner; an uppercut.

ashi-barai A leg sweep.

ashi-kubi The ankle, or kicks delivered with the front of the ankle.

ashi-no-tachi-kata The ways of planting the feet to adopt an attacking or defensive posture.

ashi-waza Leg and foot techniques used for kicking.

chokutsuki A direct thrust or blow.

chudan Mid section of the body.

chusoku The ball of the foot.

empi Literally outstretched arm, but taken to mean elbow attacks on the solar plexus, chest and abdomen. Also known as *hijiate*.

engisen The demonstration line taken by a karateka when practicing kata (*qv*).

fudotachi An immobile posture, with the karateka sideways on, feet wide apart and both legs bent.

fumikiri Step out; a kicking technique so called because of the stepping out action of the leg.

fumiuchi A step blow, made by placing the base of the foot on the opponent's instep and applying total body pressure.

gargu-kamae A posture known as the 'reclining dragon'. The front of the body is turned away from the opponent so that protection is afforded to vital parts of the body.

gedan Lower part of the trunk.

gedan barai Lower sweeping block.

gyaku A reverse action; applied to ways of holding and delivering blows.

hachijitachi A figure-eight posture or stance. In soto-hachijitachi, or outer figure-eight, the heels face inwards with the toes spread out; in uchi-hachijitachi, or inner figure-eight, the heels are spaced about a shoulders-width apart with the toes turning inwards.

haraite Sweeping hand; a method of defense against a hand or leg attack.

heisoku The instep.

hiraken The flat, or level, fist, with the fingers clasped so that the second joints protrude to the front and the thumb presses down on the index finger. The contact points are the second joints of the index finger and middle finger.

hitosashiyubi-ipponken A forefinger fist with the knuckle of the index finger thrust forward as the contact point.

hiza The knee.

hizagashira The knee-cap.

hiza-geri Knee used to attack opponent.

hizatsui A knee hammer; a blow to vital parts of the body with the knee-cap.

jiu-kumite Freestyle fighting, as opposed to demonstrations of techniques.

jodan Head section.

kakato The heel.

kakato-geri Kick with heel.

kaketebiki A special apparatus to help the karateka develop hand and elbow techniques. It consists of a see-saw arrangement on a post some 4ft high

kakiwake A defensive hand technique of thrusting aside with the wrist an opponent's blow.

karate-gi The tunic worn by a karateka. It consists of loose-fitting white trousers and jacket fastened with an obi (colored belt) indicating the grade of the karateka.

karateka A person who practices karate.

kata Arranged sequence of movements to demonstrate methods of attack, defense, and counterattack. It takes the form of imaginary fighting against opponents attacking from several directions.

kekomi Thrusting type of kick.

keriage An upward kick using the sole of the foot or the front of the ankle.

kerihanashi A kick release. Once the kick has been made, using the bottom of the foot, the attacking foot is withdrawn and the initial posture resumed before the opponent has a chance to counterattack.

kerikomi A kick-in; the attacking foot, having delivered a blow on the opponent, then steps against

Right: A high kick to the head of an opponent. The contact point is the ball of the foot.

Left: Two of the basic stances used by the karateka in kata. Far left is zenkutsutachi; the inclined or forward-leaning stance. The downward block of the forward arm should be achieved at the same time as the stance is adopted. Left is kokutsodachi, the retroflex or back-leaning stance with a higher proportion of weight distributed over the rear leg.

Right: Tobigeri; the spectacular jumping kick which may incorporate one of the forward, side, roundhouse, or back kicks. As the object of this kick is to surprise the opponent, it must be performed quickly and nimbly.

Left: Seiken-chudan-tsuki; a thrust punch delivered with a clenched fist to the throat. As he delivers the blow the karateka utters the kiai.

the knee joint to dislocate it.

keriwaza Kicking techniques.

kiai The shout emitted by a karateka as he makes contact with a target. It must come from the lower diaphragm and is forced out by the muscles to help produce a total commitment and generate maximum power to the punch.

kihon A basic training in defensive blocking, thrusts and kicks.

kokutsodachi Back-stance with feet at a 90° angle to each other; weight distribution 75% rear leg, 25% front leg.

kote The forearm.

kumite A contest, or fight.

maegeri Front kick.

makiwara A wooden post padded with straw to assist in the perfecting of punches and kicks, to toughen contact points and to strengthen the joints.

mawashigeri Roundhouse or turning kick.

naifu-anchi-tachi The anti-knife posture. It is also known as *kibadachi* (equestrian posture). The karateka stands facing his

attacker, legs apart with the toes pointing slightly inwards.

nakayubi-ipponken Middle-finger fist; the second joint of the middle finger is projected as the contact point.

neko-ashi-dachi The cat-foot posture; most of the bodyweight is on the rear leg so that the front leg can be poised for kicking.

renketsu-renshuho The coupling method of training in which all the methods of renzoku-renshuho are linked together.

sagi-ashitachi The heron-leg posture in which one foot is lifted to approximately knee height. It is called a front or rear heron leg posture in relation to the position of the raised foot to the knee of the standing leg.

sankakutobi A triangular jump, used in the event of a simultaneous attack by three opponents. The exponent, in a mid-air position with his body parallel to the ground, kicks one adversary with one foot, another with the other foot, and uses his fist and head against the third.

seiken A normal fist, either with the fingers outstretched and the thumb away from the palm, or with the fingertips pressed into the top of the palm and the thumb raised just above the palm.

semete An attacker in kata.

sempai Senior grade below sensei (*qv*).

sensei Honorable teacher.

shihan Honorable professor; a title bestowed on karateka above eighth dan.

sukuite Scooping hand; a defensive hand technique with which the defender grasps his opponent's hand, leg, or foot and attempts to throw him.

tameshiwara Wood breaking.

te The hand.

tegatana The handsword technique in which the thumb is bent into the palm, the fingers are extended and the bottom edge of the palm is used as the contact point.

tekubi The wrist.

tetsui A hammer fist, with the lower part of the lower edge of

the hand forming the contact point.

tewaza Hand techniques.

tobigeri A jumping kick with which the karateka leaps at his opponent with both feet and can kick him with either foot.

tori *See* semete.

tsuki A thrust or blow made with the hand.

uchite Striking with the hand in defense or in attack.

ude The arm.

uke Defense or block.

ukete The karateka 'receiving' the attack in kata. Also means the defensive hand.

uraken The back, or inverted, fist. It is clenched, with the root of the middle finger forming the contact point.

ushirogeri A rear kick, made by kicking back with the rear of the heel.

yokogeri Side kick.

zenkutsutachi The inclined posture, with the karateka slightly sideways on to his opponent. The knee of the advanced leg is bent and the rear leg is fully extended.

Wrestling

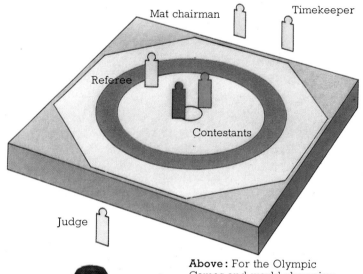

More strictly entertainment than sport in some professional forms, wrestling nonetheless commands worldwide appeal as an individual combat sport. Its different styles, many unique to countries or even regions, are as varied as the throwing and holding techniques employed to achieve the basic aim of wrestlers everywhere: to throw the opponent to the ground and there, if required by the rules, pin him down to register a fall. Only two styles, however, are contested at Olympic Games and at world championships under FILA rules: freestyle and Graeco-Roman, each having the same ten bodyweight classes. These are light-flyweight, flyweight, bantamweight, featherweight, lightweight, welterweight, middleweight, light-heavyweight, heavyweight and heavyweight plus. In each style the object is to win on a fall, but the awarding of points from one to four for successful aggressive and defensive moves ensures a result if there is none.

An amateur bout takes place between two men on a mat, wearing tight-fitting, one-piece costumes called leotards. One wears a red leotard, the other blue. Competitions employ a complicated but fair elimination process rather than a knockout system. Contestants are drawn to meet a number of opponents and remain in the competition until eliminated by the receipt of six penalty points. These are awarded on a scale of zero to four according to the result of each bout. When three or fewer contestants remain with fewer than six penalty points, they contest the final round on a round-robin basis, except that finalists who have met earlier in the competition do not meet again. Instead their points from their previous round are brought forward. The winner is the finalist with the least penalty points.

Above: For the Olympic Games and world championships, the mat must be 8 x 8m. It is usually square, but in recent Olympic events it has been octagonal. Free spaces are left around the edge and the centre is marked with a circle. The referee signals the points by raising the color of the scoring wrestler and indicating the number with his thumb and first two fingers. In the event of dispute, the mat chairman decides.

Left: A wrestler assuming a fighting stance. Competitors must wear a one-piece leotard which is either red or blue. They can wear either wrestling boots or ordinary gym shoes, and are not allowed to wear buckles or jewelry which might cause injury.

ankle and leg drive A standing throw with which a wrestler gets his opponent off balance by grabbing one leg and pulling him to the mat. It is sometimes called a *leg snap*.

body press The exertion of weight against an opponent lying on his back in order to secure a fall (*qv*).

bout Under FILA rules, three three-minute rounds with a minute's rest period between each. In the event of a fall or disqualification, the bout is ended.

breakdown Bringing an opponent to his side or stomach by removing his hand and/or knee support.

bridge The arched position assumed by a wrestler whose back is to the mat. He keeps his body off the mat by supporting himself on his head and on the balls of his feet.

catch-as-catch-can Name sometimes used for freestyle (*qv*).

caution; or public caution Given by the referee to a wrestler who,

in the opinion of the majority of officials, is guilty of passivity (*qv*), foul holds, lack of discipline, or an infringement of the rules. One point is awarded to his opponent. If cautioned a third time, the offender is disqualified and the bout awarded to his opponent.

cradle A ground hold secured by applying a cross-face (*qv*) hold with one arm while bringing the other through the opponent's crotch.

cross-buttock A standing throw with which an opponent is forced over the hips or lower back. It usually follows a head-hold (*qv*).

cross-face A ground hold secured by placing one arm across the side of an opponent's face and grasping his opposite arm above the elbow.

Cumberland-and-Westmorland A form of wrestling practiced in the Lake District of England. The wrestlers begin their bout standing chest to chest with their arms clasped behind the other's back. The grip must be main-

tained throughout as they attempt to throw each other.

Devon-and-Cornwall A form of wrestling practiced in the West of England with contestants wearing jackets. Backs (*qv*) must be achieved from the standing position.

double A hold secured by both arms, or on two of an opponent's limbs.

double nelson See full nelson.

double-thigh pick-up A standing throw with which a wrestler puts his opponent on the mat by hooking him behind the legs.

escape A technique with which a wrestler moves from an underneath to an uppermost position and so earns a point.

fall Pinning (*qv*) both of an opponent's shoulders on the mat long enough for the referee to count one, or to pronounce mentally the word *tomber* (fall) and strike the mat with his hand. The wrestler achieving the fall is the outright winner of the bout.

fall-back Achieving a take-down (*qv*) by holding an opponent

from behind and falling backwards.

FILA Fédération de Lutte Amateur; the international amateur wrestling federation which was founded in 1921.

flying mare A standing throw for which the wrestler uses his opponent's arm as a lever to hurl him over his back.

freestyle One of the three official FILA styles and probably the most popular. Holds, throws, or trips may be employed against any part of the opponent's body.

full nelson A ground hold secured from a position behind the opponent by placing both arms under his armpits and clasping the hands or wrists on the back of his neck. Permitted in senior amateur wrestling, it must be applied from the side, not downwards, and without any use of the legs on any part of the opponent's body. Also called a double nelson.

glima A form of wrestling practiced in Iceland. Around both thighs the wrestlers wear a

The grip for the left hand

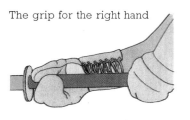

The grip for the right hand

Left: A kendoka in chudan no kamae, the basic posture. The scoring areas, as indicated, are: 1 Men; 2 Migi-men; 3 Hidari-men; 4 Tsuki; 5 Kote or migi-kote; 6 Hidari-kote; 7 Migi-do; 8 Hidari-do. When striking one of these areas, the attacker must call out its name.

Above right: A scoring point with a blow to the migi-do, the kendoka having gone underneath and to the left of his opponent's threatened men attack.
Right: A scoring point with a thrust to the tsuki. Although made here with both hands, the tsuki attack may be one-handed.

Below: A scoring point with a blow to the men.

Below: A scoring point with a blow to the kote.

ponents in succession until defeated, after which the winner continues in the same manner. The outright winner is the kendoka with the most wins.
kamae The basic kendo guard positions.
kata A series of formal movements in which steel-bladed swords may be used.
katana A real sword.
katsugi-waza A shouldering arms technique with which the shinai is swung across the left shoulder at to-ma (*qv*) in an attempt to entice the opponent to relax his defense.
keikogi The jacket worn by kendoka.
keirei A formal salute, in the form of a bow, made slowly from the waist.
kendoka One who practices kendo.
kiai The shout from the kendoka that must accompany a hit.
kissaki The point of the shinai or of a sword.
kote The point just above the wrist which is protected by

gauntlets. It is a scoring area.
kote-ari Called by the referee to announce a successful cut to the kote.
maai The distance between two kendoka after adopting a kamae.
mamoru To protect a scoring area.
men The headguard of steel and padded cloth that protects the head, throat and shoulders. Also a scoring point to the center of the head.
men ari Called by the referee to announce a successful cut to the head.
migi-do The scoring area on the right side of the breastplate.
migi-kote The scoring area on the right wrist.
migi-men The scoring area on the right side of the head just above the ear.
mune The chest.
nihomme Second point; called by the judge after the first point in a multi-point contest has been scored.
nuki-waza Avoidance technique to lure an opponent into making

a stroke, avoiding it, and hitting him at the end of his stroke.
nuku To draw the shinai or a sword.
osu Pushing an opponent, which is an infringement of the rules.
sagaru To retreat.
sandan-waza Attacking a third area when the first and second strokes have been unsuccessful.
sasu To make a forward thrust with the shinai.
shikaki-waza Taking advantage of an opponent being off-guard to attempt a scoring blow.
shinai The practice sword.
shobu Match point; called by the referee when each contestant has landed one hit each.
shobu-ari Match point; called by the referee when one contestant has landed two hits to win the bout.
sonkyo The crouching position in which the kendoka draws his shinai prior to standing up to engage his opponent in the kamae position.
suriage-waza A deflecting technique. The kendoka fends off

his opponent's stroke by sliding his shinai up his opponent's shinai and then takes advantage of his opponent's unbalanced stance to make his own attack.
tare The armor apron worn as a groin protector.
tatsu To stand in position.
to-ma A larger distance between two contestants than issoku-itto no maai (*qv*).
tsuba The guard on the shinai or a sword.
tsuki The throat, which is a scoring area if the blow is a thrust with the point of the shinai.
tsuki-ari Called by the referee to announce a thrust to the throat.
uchiotoshi-waza A warding-off technique in which the opponent's shinai is struck downwards. The kendoka then takes advantage of his opponent's unbalanced stance to make his own attack.
wakigamae Holding the shinai horizontally rearward and extended to either side of the body.
yokomen A blow that lands just above the ear.

Wrestling

More strictly entertainment than sport in some professional forms, wrestling nonetheless commands worldwide appeal as an individual combat sport. Its different styles, many unique to countries or even regions, are as varied as the throwing and holding techniques employed to achieve the basic aim of wrestlers everywhere: to throw the opponent to the ground and there, if required by the rules, pin him down to register a fall. Only two styles, however, are contested at Olympic Games and at world championships under FILA rules: freestyle and Graeco-Roman, each having the same ten bodyweight classes. These are light-flyweight, flyweight, bantamweight, featherweight, lightweight, welterweight, middleweight, light-heavyweight, heavyweight and heavyweight plus. In each style the object is to win on a fall, but the awarding of points from one to four for successful aggressive and defensive moves ensures a result if there is none.

An amateur bout takes place between two men on a mat, wearing tight-fitting, one-piece costumes called leotards. One wears a red leotard, the other blue. Competitions employ a complicated but fair elimination process rather than a knockout system. Contestants are drawn to meet a number of opponents and remain in the competition until eliminated by the receipt of six penalty points. These are awarded on a scale of zero to four according to the result of each bout. When three or fewer contestants remain with fewer than six penalty points, they contest the final round on a round-robin basis, except that finalists who have met earlier in the competition do not meet again. Instead their points from their previous round are brought forward. The winner is the finalist with the least penalty points.

Above: For the Olympic Games and world championships, the mat must be 8 x 8m. It is usually square, but in recent Olympic events it has been octagonal. Free spaces are left around the edge and the centre is marked with a circle. The referee signals the points by raising the color of the scoring wrestler and indicating the number with his thumb and first two fingers. In the event of dispute, the mat chairman decides.

Left: A wrestler assuming a fighting stance. Competitors must wear a one-piece leotard which is either red or blue. They can wear either wrestling boots or ordinary gym shoes, and are not allowed to wear buckles or jewelry which might cause injury.

ankle and leg drive A standing throw with which a wrestler gets his opponent off balance by grabbing one leg and pulling him to the mat. It is sometimes called a *leg snap*.

body press The exertion of weight against an opponent lying on his back in order to secure a fall (*qv*).

bout Under FILA rules, three three-minute rounds with a minute's rest period between each. In the event of a fall or disqualification, the bout is ended.

breakdown Bringing an opponent to his side or stomach by removing his hand and/or knee support.

bridge The arched position assumed by a wrestler whose back is to the mat. He keeps his body off the mat by supporting himself on his head and on the balls of his feet.

catch-as-catch-can Name sometimes used for freestyle (*qv*).

caution; or public caution Given by the referee to a wrestler who,

in the opinion of the majority of officials, is guilty of passivity (*qv*), foul holds, lack of discipline, or an infringement of the rules. One point is awarded to his opponent. If cautioned a third time, the offender is disqualified and the bout awarded to his opponent.

cradle A ground hold secured by applying a cross-face (*qv*) hold with one arm while bringing the other through the opponent's crotch.

cross-buttock A standing throw with which an opponent is forced over the hips or lower back. It usually follows a head-hold (*qv*).

cross-face A ground hold secured by placing one arm across the side of an opponent's face and grasping his opposite arm above the elbow.

Cumberland-and-Westmorland A form of wrestling practiced in the Lake District of England. The wrestlers begin their bout standing chest to chest with their arms clasped behind the other's back. The grip must be maintained throughout as they attempt to throw each other.

Devon-and-Cornwall A form of wrestling practiced in the West of England with contestants wearing jackets. Backs (*qv*) must be achieved from the standing position.

double A hold secured by both arms, or on two of an opponent's limbs.

double nelson See full nelson.

double-thigh pick-up A standing throw with which a wrestler puts his opponent on the mat by hooking him behind the legs.

escape A technique with which a wrestler moves from an underneath to an uppermost position and so earns a point.

fall Pinning (*qv*) both of an opponent's shoulders on the mat long enough for the referee to count one, or to pronounce mentally the word *tomber* (fall) and strike the mat with his hand. The wrestler achieving the fall is the outright winner of the bout.

fall-back Achieving a take-down (*qv*) by holding an opponent

from behind and falling backwards.

FILA Fédération de Lutte Amateur; the international amateur wrestling federation which was founded in 1921.

flying mare A standing throw for which the wrestler uses his opponent's arm as a lever to hurl him over his back.

freestyle One of the three official FILA styles and probably the most popular. Holds, throws, or trips may be employed against any part of the opponent's body.

full nelson A ground hold secured from a position behind the opponent by placing both arms under his armpits and clasping the hands or wrists on the back of his neck. Permitted in senior amateur wrestling, it must be applied from the side, not downwards, and without any use of the legs on any part of the opponent's body. Also called a double nelson.

glima A form of wrestling practiced in Iceland. Around both thighs the wrestlers wear a

Freestyle wrestling throws

Cross-buttock

Standing arm-roll

Quarter-nelson

Half-nelson

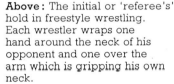

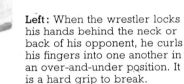

Above: The initial or 'referee's' hold in freestyle wrestling. Each wrestler wraps one hand around the neck of his opponent and one over the arm which is gripping his own neck.

Left: In the ground position it is essential that the palms of the wrestler behind rest only on the shoulder-blades of his opponent.

Left: When the wrestler locks his hands behind the neck or back of his opponent, he curls his fingers into one another in an over-and-under position. It is a hard grip to break.

harness which the opponent must grip throughout the bout. A fall is scored when one contestant is thrown.

Graeco-Roman One of the three official FILA styles. It is contested under the same rules as freestyle except that any form of grasping below the hips or use of the legs to effect a take-down or hold on an opponent is forbidden.

half-nelson A ground hold secured by placing one arm through the opponent's corresponding armpit and around his neck.

head-hold Secured by encircling an opponent's head with one arm. Use of both arms is a foul.

hook To reach around or under an opponent's arm or leg to secure a grasp with the hand or crook of the arm. The term also refers to the placing of the foot or leg behind an opponent's leg to effect a take-down (*qv*).

judge He is equipped with two batons, one red, one blue which he uses to indicate anything missed by the referee. He also

collects the score sheet and gives it to the mat chairman (*qv*).

mat The thick supple surface on which a bout is contested. The wrestling area is circular, of 9m diameter, and is surrounded by a *protection surface* the same thickness as the wrestling surface and 1.20-1.50m wide. The red band inside the circumference is the *passivity zone*.

mat chairman The chief official. He decides on the allocation of points when there is a disagreement between the referee and the judge, co-ordinates the work of the referee and judge, and evaluates the conduct and action of all other officials.

nelson holds *See* full nelson and half-nelson; both ground holds.

passivity A contestant's passive obstruction to the continuity of a bout by obstructing the holds of his more active opponent, by continually lying flat on his stomach, wilfully running off the mat, or holding both of his opponent's hands to prevent him from securing a hold.

pin Securing a fall by holding an opponent's shoulders on the mat.

referee The referee is dressed in white and wears armbands, blue on one arm, red on the other. He is in general charge of the bout – under the direction of the mat chairman – with a number of specific responsibilities: starting, stopping, and interrupting bouts; making the T-sign (*qv*); indicating points scored and inspecting the wrestlers at the beginning of each round.

round Each round lasts three minutes with three rounds in a bout unless one contestant wins the match before the time limit.

sambo One of the three official FILA styles. A blend of Russian styles, it is contested by wrestlers wearing a tight-fitting jacket over a standard costume. The aim is to throw the opponent on his back while the thrower himself remains standing.

slam Lifting an opponent off his feet and slamming him down on the mat. It is illegal in amateur wrestling.

standing arm-roll A standing throw for which the wrestler clasps an opponent's arm and wraps it around his own body so that his opponent is rolled on to the mat.

sumo The traditional Japanese form of wrestling. It permits any hold or throw, the winner being the man who forces his opponent to quit the ring or makes some part of his body (other than his feet) touch the mat.

take-down Any technique used by a wrestler to get his opponent from a standing position on to the mat and there secure a position of advantage.

T-sign Made by the referee with his hands to inform the judges and timekeeper that he is interrupting the round.

warning Given to a wrestler by the referee for an infringement of the rules. If the offence is repeated, a caution (*qv*) is given.

wing The groundwork technique of holding an opponent by locking his arm tightly and rolling him over.

43

Court Games

Badminton

An indoor game played by both sexes, badminton in its original form was played in China, traces of the game being displayed on pottery dated back to around 3500 BC. Army officers played the game in India in the 1860s and brought the game to England where they played it at the Duke of Beaufort's seat, Badminton House, from where the game derives its name. In 1877 the first laws were formulated in India. Not until 1893, however, with the establishment of the Badminton Association (of England), was a uniform set of laws drawn up; and it was 1901 before the court became a proper rectangle.

Today the game is truly international, with more than 70 countries affiliated to the International Badminton Federation (IBF). There are two major international team competitions, the Thomas Cup for men and the Uber Cup for women, and in 1977 the first world championships were held. Until then, the major tournament was the All-England Championship, which still attracts the world's leading players annually.

Matches are played as singles, doubles and mixed doubles. Play commences with a service from the right-hand service court to the service court diagonally opposite and continues with the players hitting the shuttle over the net until one side makes a fault. A fault occurs if the shuttle touches the floor, fails to clear the net, lands outside the court, hits the ceiling, is hit twice, or slung. It is also a fault if the service is not made correctly, if any player feints, balks, or obstructs to gain an unfair advantage, and if any player's person is hit by the shuttle, regardless of whether that player is inside or outside the court. As only the 'in side' may score, a fault by the server results in the loss of serve, not of a point; a fault by the receiving side is a point to the server.

The racket and shuttlecock. The shuttle further from the racket is made of a cork base into which are inserted 14 to 16 goose feathers. The base is usually covered with kid leather. The other shuttle is a nylon variation. The weight must be between 73-85 grains, or about $\frac{1}{5}$ of an ounce.

The grip for the forehand

The grip for the backhand

attacking clear *See* clear.

backhand Strokes played with the reverse side of the racket, the back of the hand facing the shuttle at the moment of contact.

balk A fault (*qv*) if done deliberately to check a player in the act of serving or playing a stroke. It is not considered a balk, however, if a player holds up his racket to protect his face.

bird A colloquialism for the shuttlecock.

block A forehand or backhand stroke used to return a smash. The racket face is angled upwards so that the shuttle bounces off it and lands just over the net.

chassé A movement sideways by transferring weight from one foot to the other without the feet actually crossing over.

clear (1) Defensive: any stroke played overhead which causes the shuttle to fall as nearly vertically as possible on to the opponent's back line thus giving the striker time to re-align himself for the next shot. (2) Attacking: a low stroke played to the back of the opponent's court, just clearing the opponent, who may be positioned too close to the net.

cone A method of defensive positioning used in doubles. It is also called the *triangle* because the defending side makes the base of a triangular or cone shape, the opponent hitting the ball being the apex.

cross shot A return of service to the low service (*qv*). The shuttle is played diagonally across the net to land near the side line on the server's forehand and as close to the net as possible.

Danish swipe A backhand stroke in which the shuttle is hit at about shoulder height to the back of the opposition court. Also known as the side-arm swipe, it is usually played from the back of the court.

defensive clear *See* clear.

double hit A fault called if a player hits the shuttle twice before it crosses the net or if a player and partner both hit it before it crosses the net.

down Used to describe a player who has lost his or her service.

drive An attacking stroke played with the forehand or backhand. The shuttle is hit at shoulder height to skim just over the net and land near the side line about three-quarters of the way to the back boundary line.

drive service A hard-hit service that passes just above the net and is intended to land near the long-service line.

drop A slow, deceptive stroke played overhead so that the shuttle lands just on the other side of the net. The forehand drop is played as a clear or smash, except that the racket is slowed down at the moment of impact; the backhand drop is disguised as a clear.

fault An infringement of the laws. If made by the receiving side, it results in a point to the server; if made by the server, he loses the service.

flick serve A deceptive service used mostly in doubles to clear the receiver. It is played in a similar manner to the low serve except that the wrist unlocks just before hitting the shuttle high enough over the net to clear the striker.

flight The pace and distance of the shuttle through the air, determined by its weight and the atmospheric conditions within the hall.

forehand A stroke played with the front of the racket and with the forearm facing the shuttle at the moment of contact.

game A series of serves and rallies until one player or side reaches a predetermined score. Men's singles and all doubles are played to 15 points, unless the event is a handicap one. Handicaps can be played in games of 11, 15, or 21 points. Ladies' singles are played to 11 points.

hand The advantage of serving. In doubles there are two hands, and each player must lose his or her service before the service passes to the other side. The side serving first, however, has only one hand in its first innings.

46

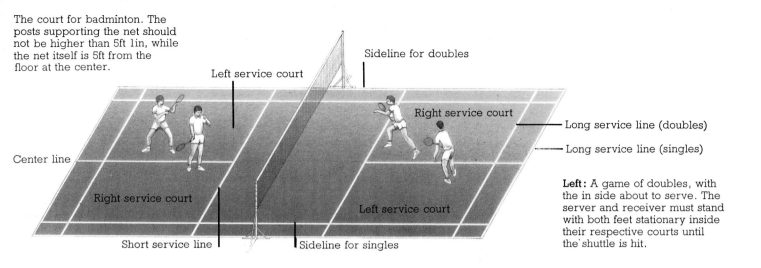

The court for badminton. The posts supporting the net should not be higher than 5ft 1in, while the net itself is 5ft from the floor at the center.

Left service court

Sideline for doubles

Right service court

Long service line (doubles)

Long service line (singles)

Center line

Right service court

Left: A game of doubles, with the in side about to serve. The server and receiver must stand with both feet stationary inside their respective courts until the shuttle is hit.

Left service court

Short service line

Sideline for singles

1 The flight of the fast drop (a) and the smash (b). The drop is played to deceive the opposing player, appearing in its execution like a smash except that the stroke is given less wrist at the moment of impact.

2 The flight of the slow drop (a) and the clear (b). Both are played from the back of the court, and used particularly in defensive positions. For the slow drop, the racket is slowed down at the moment of impact.

Three basic backhand strokes: 1 The underarm clear; 2 The drive; 3 The overhead clear. Underarm strokes are played mostly from a low defensive position, whereas the drive is an attacking stroke played when the shuttle is too low to smash. The overhead clear, an essential stroke in singles, should be played as high and as early as possible.

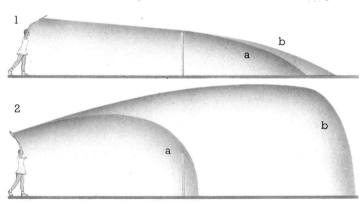

handicap An advantage given to a weaker player or side. The handicap may take the form of a points' start to the weaker player(s), or, in doubles only, the stronger side may be asked to forego one hand every time they win service.

high serve The shuttle is hit as high as possible so that it drops almost vertically near the long-service line.

in play The shuttle is said to be 'in play' from the moment it is hit by the server's racket until either player or side faults.

in side The player or side which has the advantage of serving.

innings One player's or side's turn at serving.

kill To win a rally with a decisive scoring stroke, usually a smash.

let Called by the umpire when an unforeseen incident occurs, such as a shuttle from another court interfering with a rally, or if the shuttle, having crossed the net during a rally, becomes lodged in or on the net. It is not a let if the served shuttle hits the

top of the net. When a let is called, the rally is replayed.

lift An underarm stroke played high from close to the net.

lob An underarm forehand or backhand stroke to the back of the opposition court.

low service The service most used in doubles, played with a locked wrist so that the shuttle skims across the net and lands just inside the service court.

match The best of three games. The players change ends after each game, and halfway through the third game (ie when 8 of 15 or 6 of 11 points have been scored).

net shot A return of service to the low service. The shuttle is angled across the net to land near the side line on the server's backhand and as close to the net as possible.

out side The player or side receiving service.

panhandle A grip used to keep the racket head square on when trying to kill the shuttle at the net.

push A forehand or backhand

stroke used to return a smash. It is similar to the block (qv) except that the racket is moved forward to meet the shuttle and push it back to around 6½-10ft into the opposition court.

rough or smooth Refers to the stringing at the throat, or shaft end, of the racket head. One side of the bottom string runs smoothly across the vertical strings while on the reverse side the stringing is irregular. Players call 'rough' or 'smooth' when the racket is spun at the beginning of a match to determine choice of service or ends.

scoop To sling the shuttle off the racket rather than hitting it cleanly. It is a fault.

setting The decision to extend the length of a game if the scores are level within one or two points of the winning points total. The player or side to reach 13 or 14 (9 to 10) first is given the option of playing to 15 (or 11) or setting the game for a further number of points. When the game is set, the score becomes

love-all and the first to the number set is the winner. The game may still be set should the score become 14-all (10-all). There is no setting in handicap games.

short service Another name for the low service (qv).

shuttle The shuttlecock; the object hit by the racket. It comprises a cork base and goose feathers, although there are also synthetic versions.

skirt The 'feathers' on a nylon or plastic shuttle.

smash An attacking forehand stroke played with the racket overhead. The shuttle should skim over the net and land midway between the short-service and doubles long-service lines.

T The junction of the center line with the short-service line.

toss Another name for the clear.

tramlines The area between the singles and doubles side lines.

wood shot Mis-hitting the shuttle with all or part of the racket frame. It is no longer penalized as a fault.

Basketball

Basketball was actually invented to fulfill a sporting purpose—unlike many sports which have evolved from natural activities or leisure pastimes. And although its rules have undergone changes since January 1892, when the first organized game was played in Springfield, Massachusetts, basketball today retains most of the precepts intended by its innovator, Dr. James Naismith. The aim of the game is simple: to score points by putting the round ball into a goal or basket and to prevent the opposition from scoring. To achieve this, any of the five players on the team may move the ball about the court by passing or dribbling, using the hands only. Advancing more than two steps with the ball in hand is not allowed. The opposing side tries to prevent the offensive team getting within shooting range by a variety of defensive strategies made essential by the rules restricting personal contact. The game consists of two 20-minute halves in college and international play. High schools play four 8-minute quarters, while the professional game consists of four 12-minute quarters. Goals scored during normal play (field goals) are worth two points; goals from free throws are worth one.

It could be said that the game has become dominated by tall players, but while this is so, it is also true that height is not necessarily a substitute for speed on the court or skills at passing, catching, dribbling and shooting. Naismith intended basketball to give equal opportunity to every player, and at many levels this most enjoyable of games does just that. If it did not, there would be little reason for the enormous popularity it enjoys throughout the world.

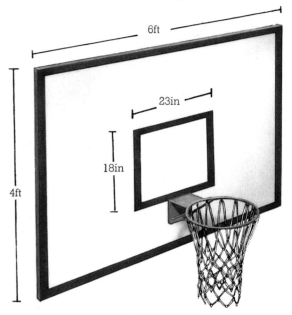

Above: The basket, which forms the goal in basketball, and the backboard. Backboards were originally made of wood, but many modern versions are of unbreakable glass to afford a better view for spectators. The ring of the basket has an inside diameter of ·18in. while the net, which is designed to arrest the ball momentarily as it passes through, is approximately 16in long. Under FIBA rules, teams toss for choice of baskets in the first half, but in some United States' domestic competitions the choice of baskets is the privilege of the visiting team. The teams change baskets for the second half.

---

assist A pass to a team-mate that results in his scoring a basket (qv) immediately.

backboard The piece of white-painted hardwood, or a transparent material of similar firmness, to which the orange metal goal ring is attached. The backboard is suspended from supports so that its lower edge is 2.75m above the floor and 1.20m inside the court from the end line.

back court The half of the court in which a team defends its own (qv) basket.

baseball pass A one-handed pass made with a slinging action similar to that used to throw a baseball or cricket ball.

basket The net of white cord suspended from the goal ring. The term is also used to denote the goal or a goal scored.

basket hanging Said of a player who remains near the opposition's goal to take a long pass out of defence and get a clear shot at goal before the opposition defence forms.

block The tactic of taking up a position to stop an opponent from moving through a certain area or from taking up an advantageous position.

blockout A defensive manoeuvre to prevent the attacking players obtaining the rebound.

blocking Personal contact foul that impedes the progress of an opponent not in possession.

box and one A combination (qv) defence with some players employing zone (qv) defence and others using man-to-man marking.

break To move rapidly to a more attacking position to receive a pass or attempt a shot.

brush-off The action of an offensive player who gets free of the opponent marking him by causing him to 'collide' with another player. Also known as a brush-off screen (qv).

buttonhook Movement by a player who runs in one direction, turns sharply, and doubles back in the opposite direction.

centre The pivot (qv) player.

clear out An offensive strategy against man-to-man marking. The offensive players isolate one offensive player and his guard in an area of the court so that a one-on-one situation occurs when the offensive player is given the ball.

combination defence A defensive system in which both zone and man-to-man defences are employed.

continuity pass A safe pass made when a play breaks down so that another play can begin.

court officials The referee and the umpire who control the game from opposite sidelines. Each has equal jurisdiction during the normal run of play, but the referee is the ultimate authority in case of dispute.

cut To break (qv).

dead ball Occurs when a goal is scored, a violation (qv) or foul (qv) committed, the ball lodges in the basket supports, the first of two or three free throws fails to score, or time expires.

defensive rebound A rebound

(qv) won by the defensive team.

double foul Occurs when two players commit simultaneous personal fouls on each other. The foul is charged against both players and a jump ball (qv) is given instead of any free throw (qv).

diamond and one A combination defence with four players employing a zone defence in a diamond-shaped formation and one playing man-to-man.

double team Term used for two defenders marking one player.

dribble To bounce the ball on the ground while running or walking. A player who receives the ball in a stationary position, or comes to a halt after catching it, must release the ball before lifting his pivot foot if he intends to advance by dribbling. He may not dribble again once he has caught the ball or let it rest in his hand.

drive An offensive player's aggressive dribbling towards the basket in an attempt to score.

dunking Scoring by jumping

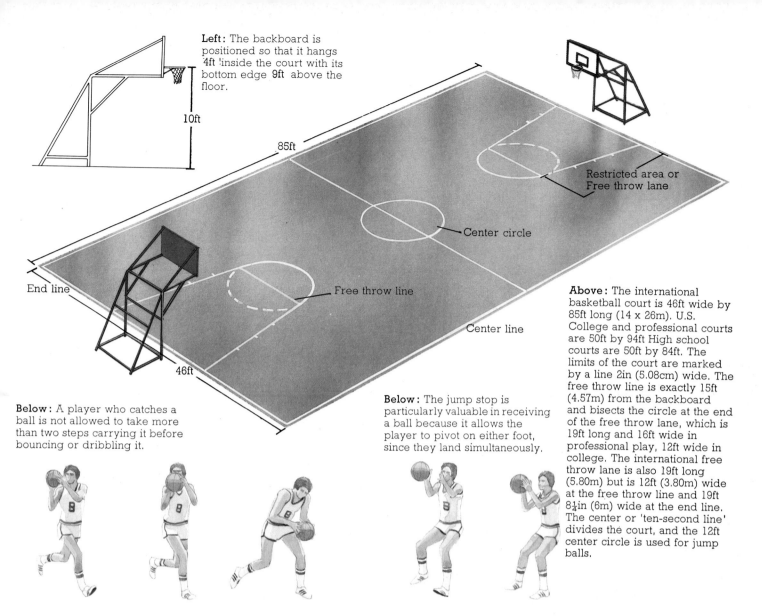

Left: The backboard is positioned so that it hangs 4ft inside the court with its bottom edge 9ft above the floor.

10ft

85ft

Restricted area or Free throw lane

Center circle

End line

Free throw line

Center line

46ft

Below: A player who catches a ball is not allowed to take more than two steps carrying it before bouncing or dribbling it.

Below: The jump stop is particularly valuable in receiving a ball because it allows the player to pivot on either foot, since they land simultaneously.

Above: The international basketball court is 46ft wide by 85ft long (14 x 26m). U.S. College and professional courts are 50ft by 94ft High school courts are 50ft by 84ft. The limits of the court are marked by a line 2in (5.08cm) wide. The free throw line is exactly 15ft (4.57m) from the backboard and bisects the circle at the end of the free throw lane, which is 19ft long and 16ft wide in professional play, 12ft wide in college. The international free throw lane is also 19ft long (5.80m) but is 12ft (3.80m) wide at the free throw line and 19ft 8¼in (6m) wide at the end line. The center or 'ten-second line' divides the court, and the 12ft center circle is used for jump balls.

high enough to push the ball down through goal from above.

fake and drive A fake with which a player feints to shoot over the head of his guard and then, as he jumps to block the shot, goes under and round him, so gaining more time and room for his shot.

faking Feinting with the body or the ball to wrong-foot an opposing player.

fall-away A shot or pass made in one direction while the player moves in another.

fast break Moving straight from defence to attack as soon as the ball is won in order to attempt a shot before the opposition defence has time to group.

FIBA Fédération Internationale de Basketball Amateur; the controlling body of amateur basketball since 1932.

field goal A successful shot into the basket from normal play. It is worth two points.

floating Sideways movement towards the centre of the court of a defender employing a man-to-man defence (*qv*) on the weak

(*qv*) side of the court.

forward One of the playing positions. The forwards, normally the taller players, adopt an offensive position at the side or corners of the front court between the restricted (*qv*) area and the sideline.

foul out To have to leave the game for being charged with five fouls, either personal or technical. The player fouling out is replaced by a substitute.

free throw An unimpeded shot at goal awarded after a technical foul, or a personal foul on a player shooting at goal, or an intentional foul, or after the opponents have committed ten fouls in one half. In all but the first instance, the fouled player must, unless injured, take the throw. One free throw is awarded for technical fouls by a coach, or substitute. Each successful free throw is worth one point.

freeze To maintain possession without attempting to score. Such tactics are limited by the 30-second rule (*qv*).

front court The half of the court in which a team attacks the opposition's basket.

full-court press A press (*qv*) employed over all the court rather than only in the back court.

guard To mark an opponent closely. Also one of the offensive positions, usually played by the shorter players who operate mainly in the mid-court area between the centre line and the free-throw line. He is also known as a *quarterback* or *playmaker*.

half-court press A press employed in the defending team's back court.

held ball Occurs when two opposing players simultaneously have one or both hands on the ball. A jump ball ensues. It may also be considered held ball if a closely guarded player fails to make use of the ball within five seconds.

hook pass A pass with which the player in possession throws the ball back over his head or shoulder to a team-mate standing behind him.

intentional foul A deliberate personal foul. Offenders are liable to disqualification.

jump ball Method used to start play at the beginning of each period and, as in the instance of held ball, to restart play. The referee tosses the ball between two opposing players who jump up and attempt to tap the ball to a team-mate standing outside the circle. Each is allowed only two taps. Jump balls at the start of play take place in the centre circle; after a held ball, in the nearest circle.

key The restricted (*qv*) area, including the circle.

lead pass A pass made into the path of an advancing team-mate rather than directly to him so that he can take the ball on the move without lessening his speed.

live ball The ball becomes live as soon as a player makes contact with it at a jump ball, when it is thrown in, or when a free throw is taken. It ceases to be live when it is dead (*qv*).

loose man-to-man A system of

Left : The lay-up shot
most basic in basketball,
although in the truest sense it
is not a 'shot' at all. It usually
demands some good dribbling
to enable the player to get as
close as possible to the basket,
where, with a final leap, the
ball is either dropped through
the hoop or, if the basket is
approached at an angle,
bounced gently off the
backboard into the basket.

Below : The jump shot is the
most popular shot used today.
The ball is shot at the height
of the jump with a quick snap
of the wrist. The jump shot is
very difficult to defend against.

Below : The hook shot begins
with the player's back to the
basket. He quickly pivots
towards it in a continuous
movement, finally extending
his shooting arm so that his
body remains between any
defender and the ball until he
releases it with a flick of the
wrist and fingers into the
basket.

man-to-man defence in which
the defending team wait until
offensive players are within a
certain distance of the basket
before marking them.

man-to-man defence A defensive
system in which each player is
responsible for marking a particular opponent whenever the
opposition have possession.

moving screen A player creating
a screen (*qv*) while on the move.

multiple foul Occurs when two
or more players simultaneously
commit a personal foul on the
same opponent. Each offending
player is charged with a foul,
and the player fouled receives
two free throws.

offensive The team in possession
of the ball, and therefore attacking the opposition basket.

offensive rebound A rebound
(*qv*) won by the offensive team.

offensive roll The pivoting action
of a player, not in possession,
trying to get free of his defender.

outlet pass The first pass made
after a defensive rebound.

out of bounds The area beyond
the inside edge of the sidelines
and end lines.

overloading Making an attack on
a zone defence by pushing three
or more players up one side of
the court in order to have one
man unmarked if a three on two
or four on three situation develops.

overtime An extra period of five
minutes' play when the score is
tied after full time, or after a tie
after a previous extra period.

own basket/goal That which a
team defends.

pass and cut To pass the ball and
break into an attacking position.
Also known as *give and go*.

passive defence A defensive
system in which the defenders
concentrate on the area around
the basket in an attempt to make
the opposition shoot from a longer range and so risk losing
possession if the basket is not
scored.

personal foul An infringement of
the rules by making personal
contact with an opponent. Personal fouls include pushing,
holding, tripping and unfairly
obstructing a player's progress
(although a player may push past
an opponent who is making no
effort to play a free ball); blocking; taking up a position directly
in the path of a dribbler; or
dribbling between two opponents or an opponent and the
boundary line when contact is
unavoidable. If the foul is committed on a player shooting at
goal, the basket if scored stands
and a free throw is awarded. If
the shot misses, the fouled player
is awarded three attempts to
score two free throws.

pick An offensive manoeuvre to
put a defender off balance and
so allow the player in possession
the chance to shoot. A second
offensive player positions himself to the side or behind the
retreating defender so that he
accidentally bumps into him.

pivot The offensive player who
is positioned near the opposition
basket in an area from the end
line to an imaginary extension of
the free throw line. Also the
action of a player in possession
who, with one foot anchored to
one spot, takes any number of
steps in any direction with the
other foot.

post The offensive player(s) who
takes up a position in the front
court. He may be a centre post
or a side post according to the
area occupied.

press A defence which makes a
positive attempt to regain possession from the moment the opposition wins the ball, or as soon
as they enter a certain part of
the court. It is also called a
pressing defence.

rebound The act of gaining or
attempting to gain possession of
a ball which bounces from the
backboard into the court after a
shot at goal misses. Rebounds
are said to be offensive (*qv*) or
defensive (*qv*) rebounds.

restricted area That part of the
court between the end line and
the free throw line and bounded
by two convergent lines. It is
sometimes referred to as the key
because, with the addition of the

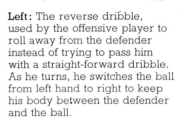

Left: The reverse dribble, used by the offensive player to roll away from the defender instead of trying to pass him with a straight-forward dribble. As he turns, he switches the ball from left hand to right to keep his body between the defender and the ball.

Above: The dribble is one of the basic weapons in attack. The offensive player begins by dribbling on his left; he then switches the ball to his right hand and changes direction to take off on the other side.

Below: Two players decide possession of the ball by means of a jump ball. The referee throws up the ball, and after it has reached its highest point it is tapped by one or both jumpers. It then falls into the hands of one side; the non-jumpers must stay outside the circle until the ball has been touched.

Right: The defending player is never allowed to touch an opponent in order to impede his progress. A personal foul is called for such contact.

outer half of the circle, it bears some resemblance to a keyhole.

safety man An offensive player who plays in the guard position either to defend against an opposition break or to help redevelop an attack if the offensive play breaks down.

screen An offensive manoeuvre in which the attacker directs his play so that his defender 'runs into' some form of obstruction, or in which an offensive team-mate moves into a position to impede the progress of the defender should the attacker cut or drive. In addition, an offensive player standing between a team-mate preparing to shoot and his opponent is said to be screening the shooter.

set play A play planned for use in a certain situation.

set shot A shot taken while standing stationary.

sifting The action of a player who, in an attempt to guard an opponent, moves between a team-mate and his opponent. This technique is usually performed

to overcome a screen.

slow break A controlled attack on a set zone defence.

splitting the post Said of two offensive players when they break at the same time on either side of a post player.

stalling To freeze (*qv*).

steal To take the ball away from an opponent.

strong side The side of the court on which the offensive team has the ball.

substitutions Each team may have up to five substitute players who are allowed to enter the game only when the ball is dead and the clock has been stopped. If this is the result of a violation, the offending team may make a substitution only if their opponents do.

switch The move of two defensive players who exchange the players they are marking, usually to overcome a screen.

table officials The scorer, time-keeper and the 30-seconds operator.

technical foul An infringement

of the rules by unsportsmanlike behaviour or disregard for, or disrespect to, an official. If charged against a player, two free throws are awarded to the opposition; if charged against the coach (or a substitute), one free throw is awarded.

ten-seconds rule Enforces the offensive team to move the ball into the front court within ten seconds of winning possession.

thirty-seconds rule Enforces the offensive team to shoot at goal within 30 seconds of gaining possession on court.

three-seconds rule Limits to three seconds the time an offensive player may stay in the opposition's restricted area while his team has possession. It does not apply during a shot at goal, a rebound, or when the ball is dead.

time out An official suspension of play for a foul, violation, held ball, injury, the end of a 30-seconds period, or undue time spent returning the ball to play. The clock is stopped. If a coach

wishes to stop play while the ball is dead, he may ask for a *charged time out* of one minute.

tip The action of an offensive player who, while still in mid-air, momentarily catches and then pushes the ball back towards the basket from an offensive rebound (*qv*).

tip-off The jump ball at the beginning of each period of play.

transposition Losing possession without making an attempt at a basket.

turnover Running with the ball.

violations Infringements of the rules, but not personal or technical fouls. They are penalized by a throw in to the opposition from the sideline.

weak side The side of the court opposite that in which the offensive team has the ball.

zone defence A defensive system in which each player is allocated an area of the court rather than a certain player to defend. In a *set zone defence* he is responsible for marking the opponent(s) moving into that area.

Squash

Right: A wooden-shafted racket with natural gut stringing and leather grip. In all rackets, the framework of the head is made of wood. The handle shaft may also be made of wood but can be of metal or fiberglass.

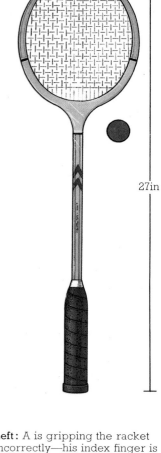

27in

Squash, also known as squash rackets, developed from the game of rackets and is reputed to have begun at Harrow School, England in the mid-nineteenth century. Harrovians, waiting their turn on the rackets court, evolved a knockabout game which, because it was played in a confined area, required a softer ball than the hard one used for rackets. It was from this ball, which could be 'squashed' in the hand, that the name derived, and soon the game took on its own individual form. Courts were built in country houses, large hotels, and even ocean liners. However, the absence of standardized rules before 1922 led to the Americans and Canadians using a smaller court and a harder ball than those now defined in the rules of the International Squash Rackets Federation. This body, when it came into being in 1967, adopted the English rules which were also used in Australia, New Zealand, Pakistan and South Africa.

The aim of squash, primarily a singles game, is to hit the ball on the volley or on the first bounce so that it rebounds off the front wall, either directly into the court or off another wall, in such a way that the opponent is unable to return it correctly. Each player hits the ball alternately, and it must reach the front wall, directly or off another wall, without first touching the floor or going out of court. It must hit the front wall above the board. Under ISRF rules, only the server may win points, the receiver having to win a rally to gain service. Games are to nine points and matches the best of five games. In North America, points may be scored by the receiver as well as the server, and both singles and doubles games go to 15 points.

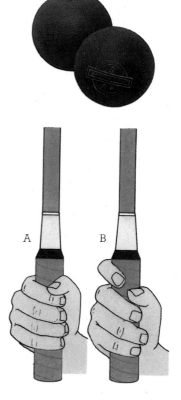

Below: The ball is made of rubber or rubber and butyl and has a matt finish. It weighs 1.05-1.15oz with a diameter of $1\frac{1}{2}-1\frac{3}{4}$in.

A   B

Left: A is gripping the racket incorrectly—his index finger is too close to the middle finger. B has the grip right. B's grip shows the index finger curled as if around a trigger which helps to maintain the balance of the racket.

angle A stroke played so that the ball hits a side wall on its way to the front wall.

appeal A player's request to the referee (*qv*) for a let (*qv*), or to question a decision by the marker (*qv*). It is a player's responsibility to make his own appeals.

backhand A stroke played with the racket arm across the central axis of the body and with the reverse side of the racket. Also that side of the court on which a player hits the ball with a backhand stroke.

board The line or strip of wood on the front wall to mark the upper edge of the tin (*qv*). The top of the board is 19in from the floor.

boast An angle stroke played flat on to the side wall so that the ball draws across the face of the front wall, hits it just above the tin, and rebounds short into the front court or off the side wall. It may be a defensive shot made under pressure, or an attacking one to make an opponent move around the court and lose command of the T-position (*qv*).

court The enclosed four-walled area within which squash is played.

cross-court stroke A drive (*qv*) that makes the ball travel from the striker's side of the court, via the front wall, to the other side.

cut line The line extending across the front wall 6ft above the floor of the court. The ball must be served so that it hits the wall above this line.

drive A firmly hit stroke that travels directly to the front wall and bounces back into the court without being diverted by contact with a side wall.

drop shot A gentle stroke, usually played from in front of the short (*qv*) line to a point on the front wall just above the tin so that the ball merely drops back into the court.

fault A service which hits the wall on or below the cut line, bounces in front of or on the short line, or bounces on the half-court line or in the server's half-court. If the ball goes out (*qv*) the server loses the service.

foot fault A service fault when the server does not stand with at least one foot in the service box when striking the ball.

forehand A stroke played with the forearm facing the ball. Also that side of the court on which a player hits the ball with a forehand stroke.

game A series of serves and rallies until one player scores 9 points with a 2-points advantage. However, if the score reaches 8-8, the receiving player decides whether to play no set (*qv*) or set 2 (*qv*). In North American singles and in ISRF doubles the game is played to 15 points with no set, set 3 (game to 16) or set 5 (game to 18) called at 13-all.

game ball The point in a game when the server needs only win the next rally to win the game.

half-court line The line which extends from the back wall to the short line, dividing the back court into two equal halves: right and left half-court.

hammer A powerful shot played with the racket at or above shoulder height. Used as a service or against a volley.

hand A player's right to serve, either because he won the spin to decide first service or because he won the preceding rally. The server is said to be *hand-in*; the receiver is said to be *hand-out*.

ISRF International Squash Rackets Federation; founded in 1967.

kill An attacking stroke hit fast and low to the front wall and just above the board so that the ball dies on bouncing back into the court.

let An undecided stroke which, at the request of either player or the marker, leads to the point being replayed.

lob A stroke played by bringing the racket up underneath the ball so that it travels in a high arc from the front wall to the back of the court.

marker The official who, from the center of the gallery, con-

Left: The reverse dribble, used by the offensive player to roll away from the defender instead of trying to pass him with a straight-forward dribble. As he turns, he switches the ball from left hand to right to keep his body between the defender and the ball.

Above: The dribble is one of the basic weapons in attack. The offensive player begins by dribbling on his left; he then switches the ball to his right hand and changes direction to take off on the other side.

Right: The defending player is never allowed to touch an opponent in order to impede his progress. A personal foul is called for such contact.

Below: Two players decide possession of the ball by means of a jump ball. The referee throws up the ball, and after it has reached its highest point it is tapped by one or both jumpers. It then falls into the hands of one side; the non-jumpers must stay outside the circle until the ball has been touched.

outer half of the circle, it bears some resemblance to a keyhole.

safety man An offensive player who plays in the guard position either to defend against an opposition break or to help redevelop an attack if the offensive play breaks down.

screen An offensive manoeuvre in which the attacker directs his play so that his defender 'runs into' some form of obstruction, or in which an offensive teammate moves into a position to impede the progress of the defender should the attacker cut or drive. In addition, an offensive player standing between a teammate preparing to shoot and his opponent is said to be screening the shooter.

set play A play planned for use in a certain situation.

set shot A shot taken while standing stationary.

sifting The action of a player who, in an attempt to guard an opponent, moves between a teammate and his opponent. This technique is usually performed

to overcome a screen.

slow break A controlled attack on a set zone defence.

splitting the post Said of two offensive players when they break at the same time on either side of a post player.

stalling To freeze (*qv*).

steal To take the ball away from an opponent.

strong side The side of the court on which the offensive team has the ball.

substitutions Each team may have up to five substitute players who are allowed to enter the game only when the ball is dead and the clock has been stopped. If this is the result of a violation, the offending team may make a substitution only if their opponents do.

switch The move of two defensive players who exchange the players they are marking, usually to overcome a screen.

table officials The scorer, timekeeper and the 30-seconds operator.

technical foul An infringement

of the rules by unsportsmanlike behaviour or disregard for, or disrespect to, an official. If charged against a player, two free throws are awarded to the opposition; if charged against the coach (or a substitute), one free throw is awarded.

ten-seconds rule Enforces the offensive team to move the ball into the front court within ten seconds of winning possession.

thirty-seconds rule Enforces the offensive team to shoot at goal within 30 seconds of gaining possession on court.

three-seconds rule Limits to three seconds the time an offensive player may stay in the opposition's restricted area while his team has possession. It does not apply during a shot at goal, a rebound, or when the ball is dead.

time out An official suspension of play for a foul, violation, held ball, injury, the end of a 30-seconds period, or undue time spent returning the ball to play. The clock is stopped. If a coach

wishes to stop play while the ball is dead, he may ask for a *charged time out* of one minute.

tip The action of an offensive player who, while still in midair, momentarily catches and then pushes the ball back towards the basket from an offensive rebound (*qv*).

tip-off The jump ball at the beginning of each period of play.

transposition Losing possession without making an attempt at a basket.

turnover Running with the ball.

violations Infringements of the rules, but not personal or technical fouls. They are penalized by a throw in to the opposition from the sideline.

weak side The side of the court opposite that in which the offensive team has the ball.

zone defence A defensive system in which each player is allocated an area of the court rather than a certain player to defend. In a *set zone defence* he is responsible for marking the opponent(s) moving into that area.

Handball

Handball, or team handball as it is known in North America, has its roots in antiquity, when a form of the game was played by the ancient Greeks. However, the game as it is known today was developed in Germany from the middle of the nineteenth century, and in 1936 field handball was featured in the Olympic Games in Berlin. Handball is considered to be second only to pelota as the fastest team game in the world, and it is thus an ideal spectator sport. The aim of handball is to score goals, and play is centered almost exclusively around the goal area rather than in midfield. It is a simple and inexpensive game, requiring a minimum of equipment, and is played by men and woman of all ages. The duration of a game depends on the age and sex of the participants.

Players make up two teams, usually seven-a-side with up to five substitutes, although five-a-side has been recently introduced by the British Handball Association. The ball is passed among members of the attacking team until an attempt is made to shoot at goal, while the opposition establishes a defense formation around the goal area. The winning team is the one which scores the most goals in the allotted time. Games may be played individually or in the form of tournaments and normally take place on an indoor court, although an outdoor field is acceptable. Rules of the game are controlled by the International Handball Federation, which has 70 affiliated nations. Olympic recognition for handball was not achieved until 1972, when the game was contested by men only, but at the Montreal games in 1976, women's handball was given equal status.

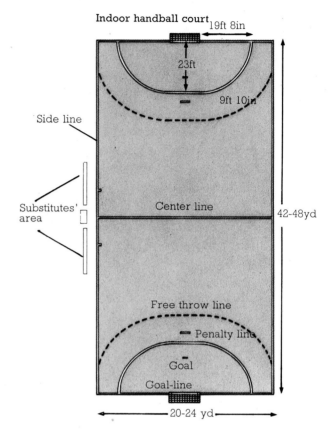

Indoor handball court

19ft 8in

23ft

9ft 10in

Side line

Substitutes' area

Center line

42-48yd

Free throw line

Penalty line

Goal

Goal-line

20-24 yd

BHA British Handball Association; organization responsible for the development and promotion of handball in the United Kingdom.

blocking Defensive move in which the defending player attempts to intercept a shot at any height from an attacker.

chest pass Throw in which the ball is launched with two hands from the chest.

corner throw Awarded to the attacking team when a defending court player (*qv*) causes the ball to cross the goal line to either side of the goal.

court player All members of a team, except the goalkeepers (*qv*), are court players.

court referee Official positioned on the court behind the attacking team in order to watch the ball.

defense formation Method by which a team not in possession of the ball defends its goal. The six court players are positioned in various ways between the free throw line and the goal area line. The simplest is the 6-0 for-

mation, where the court players form a line as close to the goal area line as possible.

disqualification A player is disqualified after serious infringement of the rules or after three suspensions (*qv*) and may not play again in that game.

dive Attacking shot, usually from the side of the goal, in which the player 'dives' towards the goal, both feet off the ground, before shooting.

falling shot Similar to the dive (*qv*) except that one foot remains in contact with the floor. It is mostly used for penalty throws (*qv*).

five-a-side Game developed by the BHA (*qv*) for play where space is not available for a full size seven-a-side court. Each team has ten players, of which two are goalkeepers, with only five players allowed on the court at one time. Rules are identical to seven-a-side (*qv*).

free throw Awarded against the defending team for any one of a number of infringements not

subject to a penalty (*qv*). It is taken from the free throw line and defending players must be at least 9ft 10in from the thrower.

goal Scored when the whole of the ball crosses the goal line. The game is restarted after a goal with a throw off (*qv*) from the halfway line by the team conceding the goal.

goal area Floor area inside and including the goal area line. A court player landing inside this area commits an infringement of the rules if interrupting play or for defensive purposes.

goalkeeper The player responsible for defending his team's goal, for which purpose he may touch the ball with any part of his body, including the feet. He may be substituted by a court player, but may only become a court player himself once he has passed the ball out of the goal area. He may not cross the goal area line while holding the ball.

goal line referee Official positioned near the goalpost. He is responsible for watching players

inside the free throw line and ensuring no infringement of the rules on the goal area line.

goal throw Awarded to the defending goalkeeper if he or an attacking player causes the ball to cross the goal line to either side of the goal. It is taken from inside the goal area.

holding Infringement committed when a player has held the ball for more than three seconds, or when a defending player holds an attacking player with his hands or arms.

IHF International Handball Federation; world governing body of handball.

infringement Any contravention of the official rules of the game, penalized by a penalty throw (*qv*), free throw (*qv*), suspension (*qv*) or disqualification (*qv*). Infringements include holding (*qv*), bouncing the ball with two hands, obstructing a player, contact with the ball below the knee by a court player and taking more than three steps while in possession of the ball.

Below left: Handball may be played indoors or outdoors, the marked out playing area is 20-24yd wide by 42-48yd long. Five-a-side handball uses a smaller playing area of 30-34yd long by 11-21yd wide. This is better suited to schools. At each end of the playing area is a goal area defined by a line 9ft 10in long at a distance of 19ft 8in from the goal and parallel to the goal-line. The ends of this line, the goal area line, are connected with the goal-line by means of quarter circles with a radius of 19ft 8in measured from the back inside corner of the goal posts. The broken free-throw line is similarly marked out 9ft 10in further out from the goal-line.

Right: The diving shot, one of three attacking shots used in handball, allows the attacking player to get in close to the goal before releasing the ball. It is usually made from the side of the goal, with the whole of the body rising above the playing area in this action. Two other shots are the jumping shot and the falling shot, the latter mostly used for penalty shots—the attacker should have one foot in contact with the floor at all times. The jump shot, involving a great leap into the air, is used in front of defenders as it enables the attacker to rise above the level of the defending wall.

Left: The goal has a two-color wooden frame backed by a net and is 9ft 10in wide by 6ft 6in high. In five-a-side handball, the goal is 6ft wide by 3ft 9in high. That part of the goal-line between the posts must have the same width as that of the goal posts 3⅛in, otherwise it is 2in wide as are all the other lines. Each goal is defended by a goalkeeper, who may use any part of his body to save the ball. There are no restrictions on the goalkeeper's action with the ball while in his own goal area, but he is not permitted to carry it out of the goal area nor, having himself left the area, to take it back over the goal-line area. Once the ball is in his possession he throws it out to the court players.

jump shot Attacking shot in which the shooter crosses the goal area line, but does not land inside the goal area, by jumping high in the air before releasing the ball. Also used to dodge a defending player.

long throw Throw made with the hand raised above the head to give extra length.

own goal Goal scored by the attacking team if a defending player causes the ball to enter his team's goal.

penalty throw Awarded when a defending player illegally prevents a likely goal or enters the goal area to defend the goal, or when the goalkeeper takes the ball into his area or is passed it by a defender. A penalty is taken from the penalty line, with all other players remaining behind the free throw line.

referees Two officials, known as the goal line referee (*qv*) and the court referee (*qv*), appointed to supervise a game. In the event of disagreement over an award, the stronger is given (eg a penalty

throw instead of a free throw). The decision of the court referee is final should there be conflict over the team to be penalized. Referees change position half way through a game.

referee's throw Used to restart a game which was halted in error or for any other reason which did not result in an award being made to either side. It is taken by the court referee (*qv*) from the point at which play was interrupted or, if this was inside the free throw line, from the nearest point outside.

secretary Official who keeps a record of the game, including goals, suspensions, etc, and controls the entry of players on to the court.

seven-a-side The usual form of handball in which each team has up to 12 players comprising ten court players (*qv*) and two goalkeepers (*qv*). Only six court players and one goalkeeper may be on the court at one time; the remainder are substitutes (*qv*). The game is played in two equal

halves with a ten-minute interval after which teams change ends. Men play 30 minutes each way, women and youths 25 minutes each way, and younger players 20 minutes each way. Tournament games are of shorter duration (men 15 minutes each way and all others ten minutes each way) and have no interval.

shoulder pass One-handed pass released when the hand is at shoulder height.

substitute Court player or goalkeeper who may replace another at any stage of the game. Substitution is made from the substitute's area (*qv*).

substitute's area Area to one side of the court in which substitutes and suspended players sit. Substitutes may only enter the court from this point.

suspension A referee may suspend a player, usually for two minutes, for repeated or serious infringement of the rules. No substitute is allowed for a suspended player.

throw in Method of restarting a

game when the ball has crossed the touch line. It is awarded to the opposite team to that which last came into contact with the ball, and is taken from the point where the ball crossed the line.

throw off The first pass made by the attacking team from the center of the court to start a game, or to restart after a goal has been scored.

timekeeper Official responsible for timekeeping during a game under the direction of the referees. He also controls the substitutes' area (*qv*). His duties may be combined with those of the secretary (*qv*) up to and including national level.

toss Coin tossed by the two team leaders to determine which team shall start the game. The losing team forms the defence.

underhand throw One-handed pass in which the ball is released from below waist height.

warning A referee may give a player one warning before suspension (*qv*) or disqualification (*qv*) of that player.

53

Netball

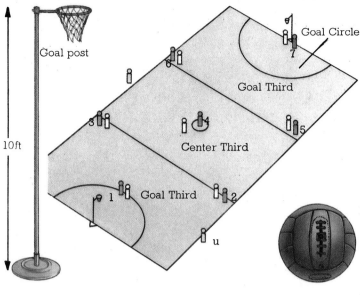

Netball, says the rule book of the All England Netball Association, 'is an International Sport. It is played by two teams of seven players and is based on throwing and catching. Goals are scored from within a defined area by throwing the ball into a ring attached to a 10-foot (3.05m) high post.' There is no mention that it is played almost exclusively by girls and women, although men may play netball. Games, however, must be between members of the same sex.

It originated with the introduction of basketball to England in 1895, but modern netball differs in many ways from its antecedent. Players may not run with or dribble the ball, are restricted to certain playing areas, and must pass the ball within adjacent thirds. Thus it requires teamwork to move the ball into the goal circle — the 'defined area'. Only the goal shooter and the goal attack may shoot at goal. Other players in a side are wing attack, center, wing defense, goal defense and goalkeeper. No player may hold the ball more than three seconds, making quick, accurate passing and sure handling essential skills. Any form of contact or obstruction is penalized, and there are strictly defined rules regarding playing the ball and moving the feet while in possession.

It was with the Ling Association's official rules of 1901 that netball established an identity of its own. Rings with nets replaced baskets as goals, the size of the ball was reduced, and the goal circle put an end to wild, long-distance shooting. Schoolteachers were the game's early disciples, to such effect that today it is played throughout the world. Since 1960 it has been governed by the International Federation of Netball Associations.

Above: The court, with players in position for a centre pass. Only the two centres may stand in the centre third before the whistle is blown.
1 goalkeeper, 2 goal defence, 3 wing defence, 4 centre, 5 wing attack, 6 goal attack, 7 goal shooter; u umpire. Each player is guarded by her partner.

Above: The ball is made of leather, rubber, or a similar material. It must weigh between 14-16oz and have a circumference between 26-27in.

Below: Shooting at goal. The shooter has only 3 seconds in which to shoot from the time of first holding the ball.

advantage Allowing play to continue after an infringement of the rules when penalizing the infringement would put the non-offending team at a disadvantage.

attack An all-embracing name given to the goal shooter, goal attack and wing attack who, together with the center, attack their own goal (*qv*). All are onside in the goal third where they score.

attacker The player in possession.

bibs That part of the official playing uniform on which the initials of the playing position are shown.

blocking Preventing a player who is not in possession of the ball from moving freely.

bouncing Playing the ball onto the ground with the hand. A player not in possession may bounce the ball once and then catch it or play it to another player, but a player already holding the ball may not bounce it and then replay it herself.

center A playing position. The only player allowed in all three thirds, she plays a leading part.

center pass The means of starting play at the beginning of each quarter and after a goal has been scored. It is taken alternately throughout the game by the two centers, first center being one of the options open to the captain winning the toss. The center taking the center pass must stand wholly inside the center circle and pass the ball within three seconds of the whistle. The ball must not go beyond the center third without first being played by another player within that third.

circle The semicircle around each goal post which constitutes the *goal* or *shooting circle*. Only the goalkeeper, goal defense, opposing goal shooter and goal attack are allowed in the circle.

contact Accidental or deliberate personal contact so as to interfere with the play of an opponent is an infringement, regardless of whether or not she holds the ball. Similarly, a player may not use the ball to touch or push an opponent, nor may a player touch or take the ball when it is in an opponent's possession.

defense An all-embracing name given to the goalkeeper, goal defense and wing defense who, together with the center, defend their opponents' goal (*qv*) from opposition attacks. All are onside in the goal third they are defending.

defender The player guarding the person in possession.

double bounce Bouncing the ball twice to gain possession is an infringement.

dragging An infringement of the footwork rule. A player in possession of the ball may not drag or slide her landing or pivot foot along the ground.

dropped ball A player, having held and then dropped the ball, may not replay it.

free Said of a player who is unguarded.

free pass Awarded to the non-offending team for any infringement except personal contact (*qv*) and obstruction of a player.

guarding Each player guards a player of the opposing team by remaining as close to her as possible without infringing the rules of contact and obstruction. Except when trying to intercept a pass or shot, the arms may not be outstretched or held away from the body unless as a natural movement.

half One half of the court from the center circle to the goal line.

hopping An infringement of the footwork rule if the player is in possession of the ball. She may not hop on either foot.

interception Stopping a ball played by an opponent from reaching its intended destination. A player may attempt to intercept provided she is not closer than 3ft to the original position of the landing or pivot foot of the player with the ball. Otherwise it is obstruction.

intimidation Making a player, with or without the ball, afraid to play her normal game. It is an infringement of the obstruction

Left: The nature of the playing uniform is left to each individual team or club to decide, though most choose between dresses or skirts and blouses or shirts. Shorts may be worn. Each player, however, is required to wear 7⅞in high playing initials on her front and back above the waist, and most wear bibs for this purpose. The rules also specify that footwear must be of lightweight material and must not be spiked. Jewellery, except for a taped-over wedding ring, must not be worn and fingernails have to be short.

Right: Obstruction of a player who is not in possession of the ball. The goal defence, standing within 3ft of her opponent, is using her outstretched arms to prevent the other player from moving freely about the court.

Right: A player may defend against an opponent with the ball provided her front foot remains at least 3ft from the opponent's landing, grounded, or pivot foot. The arms may be extended to attempt an interception, provided they are not waved about in intimidatory fashion or brought down onto the ball.

pivot, grounded, or landing foot

Left: The one-handed pass is highly effective for moving the ball quickly around the court, although it requires more practice and control than two-handed passes. Whatever kind of pass is used, however, the ball may not be thrown over a complete third without coming into contact with a player already standing or who lands in that third.

Below: Two examples of offside: stepping into an area other than that allocated to the position, and touching the ground within that area.

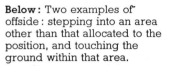

Left: When catching the ball, players must take care not to infringe the footwork rule, especially by dragging or sliding the landing or grounded foot along the ground when trying to recover balance, or by raising and then replacing this foot before passing the ball.

rule.

kicking Deliberate kicking is an infringement, but a ball which is thrown and accidentally hits a player's leg is not considered to be kicked.

landing foot The foot on which a player, having caught the ball in mid-air, lands. If she then lifts it off the ground, she must release the ball before putting it down again.

obstruction Illegally guarding a player with the ball by standing closer than 3ft, the distance being measured on the ground from the original position of the attacker's landing or pivot foot to the defender's nearer foot. A player without the ball is obstructed if an opponent uses her outstretched arm or uses her arms in an unnatural manner to stop her moving freely.

offside Entering any playing area other than those allocated to the playing position.

onside Being in those playing areas allocated to the playing position.

opponent's goal Goal into which the opposition team is shooting.

out of court A player or the ball in contact with the ground, any object, or any person beyond the sidelines or the goal-line.

own goal Goal defended by the opposition.

partner The opponent a player guards.

penalty pass Awarded to the non-offending team for infringements against the contact and obstruction rules. Any onside player may make the pass, but the offender must stand beside and away from the thrower, not moving until the ball is played.

pivot foot The foot on which the player in possession swivels to change direction. If she lifts it, she must release the ball before regrounding it.

play The umpire's command to throw the ball back into play when it is out of court.

playing area One of the five zones of the court: the two goal circles, the remainder of the two goal thirds, and the center third.

quarter One period of playing time in an hour-long game.

rally A tournament, usually held on one day, at which groups of teams compete on a league or knockout basis to produce a winner.

running Running with the ball is an infringement of the footwork rule.

shooter The goal shooter or the goal attack, who are the only two players permitted to shoot at goal.

stepping Lifting and regrounding the landing or pivot foot while still holding the ball. It is an infringement of the footwork rule. However, the player may take any number of steps with the other foot provided the pivot foot remains firmly grounded.

third One of the three equal areas into which the court is divided: the two goal thirds and the center third.

throw in Awarded to the team not responsible for the ball going out of court.

throw up Used to restart play

after an accident or when opposing players simultaneously gain possession, knock the ball out of court, are offside (and one is in possession), or make personal contact. The umpire flicks the ball in the air between the two opposing players, blowing her whistle as she does so.

tip To knock the ball in the air while trying to gain possession.

tossing Throwing the ball in the air and catching it without it first making contact with another player or the goal. It is an infringement.

traveling Making ground illegally while having possession of the ball. The term is also used when a player carries the ball into the goal circle, having caught it before jumping from outside the circle. It is an infringement if the player then tries a shot at goal.

two lines It is an infringement if the ball carries over two transverse lines (ie a complete third) without touching a player.

umpires The two officials who control the game.

Pelota (Jai-Alai)

The generic name for ball and court games developed in the Basque areas of northern Spain and southwestern France, pelota takes a variety of forms. Also known as *pelote Basque* or *pelota Vasca*, it may be a *jeu direct* or *jeu indirect*, played on an open or enclosed court with the players hitting the ball with the bare hand, with a wooden bat or strung racket, or with the curved wicker *cesta* or *chistera*. The *chistera* has given birth to the superbly exciting, fast-moving games such as *cesta punta*, *remonte*, *grand chistera* and *yoko-garbi*, which are played in highly polished three-sided courts known as *jai-alai*.

Each of these follows a similar precept, with the players catching the small, hard ball in the *cesta* and in a continuous motion slinging it against the front wall in the air so that it rebounds into the court where the opposing player or team attempts to return it before it bounces twice. The rally is won when one side fails to return the ball correctly or is responsible for it going beyond the defined playing area.

Today governed by the Federación Internacional de Pelota Vasca (FIPV), which organizes a four-yearly world championship, pelota in one form or another is played in South and Central America, certain parts of the United States and Europe and in north Africa and the Philippines.

One of the main reasons for the game's attraction is that it is an excellent medium for gambling, with special versions such as *quiniela* devised for this purpose. This, in turn, has produced a cadre of professionals whose breathtaking skills make them as much entertainers as sportsmen.

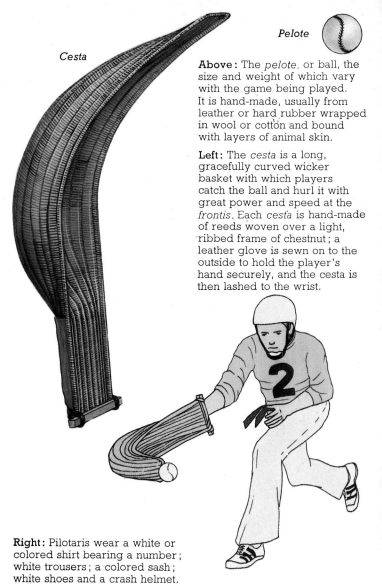

Cesta

Pelote

Above: The *pelote*, or ball, the size and weight of which vary with the game being played. It is hand-made, usually from leather or hard rubber wrapped in wool or cotton and bound with layers of animal skin.

Left: The *cesta* is a long, gracefully curved wicker basket with which players catch the ball and hurl it with great power and speed at the *frontis*. Each *cesta* is hand-made of reeds woven over a light, ribbed frame of chestnut; a leather glove is sewn on to the outside to hold the player's hand securely, and the cesta is then lashed to the wrist.

Right: Pilotaris wear a white or colored shirt bearing a number; white trousers; a colored sash; white shoes and a crash helmet.

arrière The player who takes up a position at the back of the court. In *cesta punta* (*qv*), he is usually the player who decides tactics and calls the plays as he is able to see all the court.

arrimada A backspin shot played close to the side wall with the *cesta* (*qv*) (*cesta punta* and *remonte* [*qv*] only).

atchiki The momentary holding of the ball in the *cesta* before throwing it out again. In some forms of pelota it is a penalty to prolong the *atchiki*.

cancha Any form of court on which pelota is played.

cesta, or chistera The curved basket used for catching and throwing the ball in such games as *cesta punta*, *remonte* and *yoko-garbi* (*qv*). Developed from small wicker fruit baskets around 1860, it has a curved frame of seasoned chestnut and ash and is covered with plaited osier twigs or rattan canes. Size differs according to the type of game and to a player's requirements.

cesta punta The fast-moving *jeu indirect* (*qv*) played with *cestas* in the smooth-surfaced court known as a *jai-alai* (*qv*). It is played as singles, doubles (the most common form) or triples.

cortada A shot played hard and low against the front wall.

cuadros The vertical lines which divide the side wall of a court into numbered areas.

dejada A ball which 'dies' as soon as it rebounds off the front wall; a 'kill'.

fronton General term for the court in which *jeux de place libre* are played.

fronton espagnol A *fronton mur à gauche* (*qv*).

fronton mur à gauche A three-, occasionally two-walled court, either open or covered, in which most *jeux indirects* (*qv*) are played. Literally 'court with a left wall', it is so named because the side wall is on the players' left. The front wall is called the *frontis*, the side wall the *lateral* and the back wall the *rebote*. The right-hand side is open or enclosed with a clear screen so that spectators can view the play.

gant Literally a glove; the name sometimes given to the basket used in *cesta punta* and similar games.

grand chistera A *jeu indirect* played by teams of three in a *place libre* (*qv*). It is similar to *yoko-garbi* (*qv*) except that the ball may be lodged momentarily in the *cesta* to prepare a shot and, as the name suggests, a larger basket is used.

jai-alai The full-sized court with a smooth, highly polished surface for such fast-moving games as *cesta punta* and *remonte*. In the USA, the term *jai-alai* (literally 'merry festival') is used to mean *cesta punta*.

jeux directs One of the two main categories of pelota games. The players face each other, sometimes across a net, and play the ball between themselves as in tennis. Scoring is as in tennis, with a match consisting of a number of games. *See rebot and pasaka.*

jeux indirects The other category of pelota games. The players face a wall against which the ball is hit, either directly or off another wall as in squash. The scoring is by points, either to the side winning a rally or to the serving side, the formula differing with the various games and with local rules.

main nue Literally bare-handed; games played without a bat, racket, or basket.

main nue en fronton mur à gauche A singles or doubles *jeu indirect* played with the bare hand in a small version of the *fronton mur à gauche* (*qv*).

main nue en place libre A singles or doubles *jeu indirect* played with the bare hands in an open, one-walled court, the aim being to hit the ball on the volley or first bounce so that it returns directly to the wall and rebounds within the confines of the court.

main nue en trinquet A singles or doubles *jeu indirect* played with the bare hand in a *trinquet* (*qv*). The aim is to use the hazards to

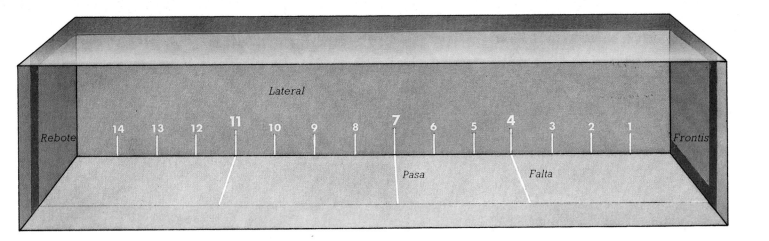

In the court diagram: Lateral, Rebote, Frontis, Pasa, Falta, with numbers 14 13 12 11 10 9 8 7 6 5 4 3 2 1

Above: The three-walled court, known as a *fronton mur à gauche*, in which most *jeux indirects* are played. The red areas are out of bounds. Dimensions vary according to the type of game played and to local practice, but the maximum length is 56m (180ft) with a height of 10-12m (33-40ft). For some forms of pelota such as *cesta punta*, the fronton is divided into numbered areas by *cuadros* with *falta* and *pasa* service fault lines marked at the fourth and seventh *cuadros*. The service line can vary with the form of game being played.

Left: Pilotaris in action during a game of *cesta punta*, a rough, fast game requiring speed, strength, and mental stamina. It may be played as singles, doubles, or triples. The aim is to play the ball, in the air or on the first bounce, and rebound it off the *frontis* so that the opposing players are unable to return it correctly within the strictly defined playing area. Games are played up to 40 points, usually with only the server able to score points, the receiver having first to win the right of service. The service must rebound from the front wall to the service zone between the *falta* and the *pasa*, though it may hit the side wall en route. If the ball lands beyond the *pasa*, a second service is allowed; if it fails to reach the *falta*, the right of service is lost.

prevent the opposing player or side from returning the ball to the front wall correctly.

pala or paleta A form of *pala larga* (qv) played as doubles in a *place libre*.

pala corta A version of *pala* using a shorter bat and played in the smaller *fronton espagnol*. It is played to 35 points, points being scored from every rally.

pala larga A doubles game, played in a *jai-alai* court and similar to *cesta punta* except that a long wooden bat made of beech or ash is used. The server is allowed a third serve in the event of his first two serves passing beyond the *pasa*.

paleta cuir or paleta gomme Forms of pelota played in a *fronton mur à gauche*, *trinquet* or *place libre*.

pasaka A *jeu direct* played as doubles in a *trinquet* (qv). The players hit the ball over the net with bare or gloved hands, the aim being to prevent the opposing pair from returning the ball over the net correctly. The pair

between the net and the front wall are the *refil*, or receiving side; the serving side are the *camp buteur*. They alternate courts after every game. Scoring is as in tennis, with a match consisting of 13 games.

pelote A ball. Its weight, size and composition depend on the type of game for which it is made, the usual composition being of wool, cotton, leather, or hard rubber with an outer covering of skin from a goat, sheep, calf, or dog.

pik A high lobbing shot which lands in the join of the floor and the back wall and then runs along the floor of the court without bouncing.

pilotari A player of pelota.

place libre An outdoor court with only one wall at one end. The playing area may be up to 100m (300ft) long.

quiniela A method of playing *cesta punta* with wagers placed on certain players or teams. Each player or team is allotted a number, numbers 1 and 2 starting on court. When one

side loses a rally it returns to the bench and its place is taken by the number 3 player or side, the game continuing in this manner with the winning side always staying on court. The eventual winner of the game is the player or team to reach a required number of points; the winning bet is that which chooses the first- and second-placed players or sides, either in correct order (*quiniela exacta*) or in any order.

rebot or rebote A five-a-side *jeu direct* played on a 300ft long *place libre* (qv) with *cestas*. The match consists of 13 games, with points scored by making the opposition miss the ball or by preventing them from returning it within the playing area correctly.

remonte A *jeu indirect* played as doubles in a *jai-alai* court. It is as fast as and similar to *cesta punta*, except that the *chistera* is slimmer and less curved, making it possible for players to impart heavy slice to their shots.

sare A *jeu indirect* played as

doubles with a loosely-strung racket in a *trinquet*. Developed in France, where it is also known as *raquette Argentine*, it is similar to most games played in the *trinquet*; the tactics being to use the *tambour*, grille and the *dedans* to prevent the opposing team from playing the ball back on to the front wall.

trinquet A small covered court of rectangular construction with a gallery along three sides and penthouse areas with a sloping roof along the left-hand and back walls. On both are usually found *dedans* nets. At the corner of the front and right walls is a flat, vertical piece of wood called a *tambour*, and near this, on the front wall, is inset a grille which may trap the ball. For *jeux directs*, a net is slung across the center of the court.

yoko-garbi A *jeu indirect* played by teams of three a side using a small *cesta* (*petit chistera*) in a *place libre*. The ball must be played immediately without any hint of *atchiki* (qv).

Squash

Right: A wooden-shafted racket with natural gut stringing and leather grip. In all rackets, the framework of the head is made of wood. The handle shaft may also be made of wood but can be of metal or fiberglass.

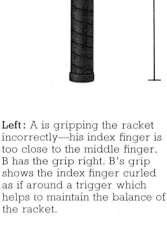

27in

Below: The ball is made of rubber or rubber and butyl and has a matt finish. It weighs 1.05-1.15oz with a diameter of $1\frac{1}{2}$-$1\frac{3}{4}$in.

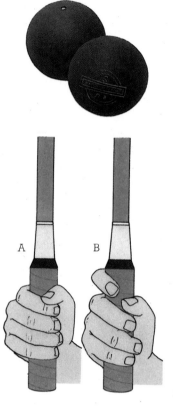

A   B

Squash, also known as squash rackets, developed from the game of rackets and is reputed to have begun at Harrow School, England in the mid-nineteenth century. Harrovians, waiting their turn on the rackets court, evolved a knockabout game which, because it was played in a confined area, required a softer ball than the hard one used for rackets. It was from this ball, which could be 'squashed' in the hand, that the name derived, and soon the game took on its own individual form. Courts were built in country houses, large hotels, and even ocean liners. However, the absence of standardized rules before 1922 led to the Americans and Canadians using a smaller court and a harder ball than those now defined in the rules of the International Squash Rackets Federation. This body, when it came into being in 1967, adopted the English rules which were also used in Australia, New Zealand, Pakistan and South Africa.

The aim of squash, primarily a singles game, is to hit the ball on the volley or on the first bounce so that it rebounds off the front wall, either directly into the court or off another wall, in such a way that the opponent is unable to return it correctly. Each player hits the ball alternately, and it must reach the front wall, directly or off another wall, without first touching the floor or going out of court. It must hit the front wall above the board. Under ISRF rules, only the server may win points, the receiver having to win a rally to gain service. Games are to nine points and matches the best of five games. In North America, points may be scored by the receiver as well as the server, and both singles and doubles games go to 15 points.

Left: A is gripping the racket incorrectly—his index finger is too close to the middle finger. B has the grip right. B's grip shows the index finger curled as if around a trigger which helps to maintain the balance of the racket.

angle A stroke played so that the ball hits a side wall on its way to the front wall.

appeal A player's request to the referee (*qv*) for a let (*qv*), or to question a decision by the marker (*qv*). It is a player's responsibility to make his own appeals.

backhand A stroke played with the racket arm across the central axis of the body and with the reverse side of the racket. Also that side of the court on which a player hits the ball with a backhand stroke.

board The line or strip of wood on the front wall to mark the upper edge of the tin (*qv*). The top of the board is 19in from the floor.

boast An angle stroke played flat on to the side wall so that the ball draws across the face of the front wall, hits it just above the tin, and rebounds short into the front court or off the side wall. It may be a defensive shot made under pressure, or an attacking one to make an opponent move

around the court and lose command of the T-position (*qv*).

court The enclosed four-walled area within which squash is played.

cross-court stroke A drive (*qv*) that makes the ball travel from the striker's side of the court, via the front wall, to the other side.

cut line The line extending across the front wall 6ft above the floor of the court. The ball must be served so that it hits the wall above this line.

drive A firmly hit stroke that travels directly to the front wall and bounces back into the court without being diverted by contact with a side wall.

drop shot A gentle stroke, usually played from in front of the short (*qv*) line to a point on the front wall just above the tin so that the ball merely drops back into the court.

fault A service which hits the wall on or below the cut line, bounces in front of or on the short line, or bounces on the

half-court line or in the server's half-court, If the ball goes out (*qv*) the server loses the service.

foot fault A service fault when the server does not stand with at least one foot in the service box when striking the ball.

forehand A stroke played with the forearm facing the ball. Also that side of the court on which a player hits the ball with a forehand stroke.

game A series of serves and rallies until one player scores 9 points with a 2-points advantage. However, if the score reaches 8-8, the receiving player decides whether to play no set (*qv*) or set 2 (*qv*). In North American singles and in ISRF doubles the game is played to 15 points with no set, set 3 (game to 16) or set 5 (game to 18) called at 13-all.

game ball The point in a game when the server needs only win the next rally to win the game.

half-court line The line which extends from the back wall to the short line, dividing the back

court into two equal halves: right and left half-court.

hammer A powerful shot played with the racket at or above shoulder height. Used as a service or against a volley.

hand A player's right to serve, either because he won the spin to decide first service or because he won the preceding rally. The server is said to be *hand-in*; the receiver is said to be *hand-out*.

ISRF International Squash Rackets Federation; founded in 1967.

kill An attacking stroke hit fast and low to the front wall and just above the board so that the ball dies on bouncing back into the court.

let An undecided stroke which, at the request of either player or the marker, leads to the point being replayed.

lob A stroke played by bringing the racket up underneath the ball so that it travels in a high arc from the front wall to the back of the court.

marker The official who, from the center of the gallery, con-

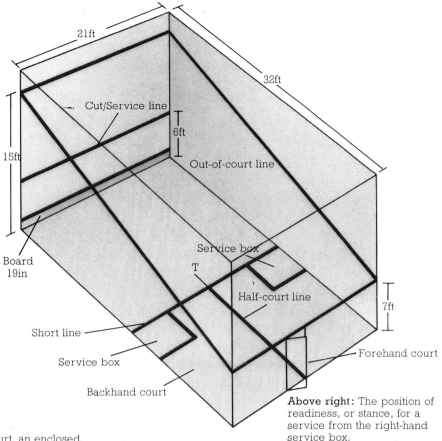

Cut/Service line

6ft

21ft

32ft

15ft

Out-of-court line

Board
19in

Service box

T

Half-court line

7ft

Short line

Service box

Backhand court

Forehand court

Above: The court, an enclosed four-walled area, has smooth walls which are painted white or off-white. The floor is made of hardwood planks laid parallel to the side walls. Standard dimensions for a singles court are as shown. The out-of-court line is 2in wide and painted red. Other court markings may be 2in wide or less and are also painted red.

Above right: The position of readiness, or stance, for a service from the right-hand service box.

Right: Preparation for a backhand drive. The weight is on the back (left) foot at the completion of the backswing but transferred to the front foot as the racket is swept down to meet the ball. Balance and co-ordination of body movements are essentials to fluent stroke play in squash.

trols the game and calls the play and the score. If there is no referee, he assumes the referee's duties as well.

match Normally the best of five games. Apart from an interval of one minute between games, and of two minutes at 2-all, play is continuous.

nick The join between floor and wall, and a stroke played so that the ball leaves the front wall at an angle towards a side wall and lands in the nick. If it lands exactly in the join it is a *dead nick*; if slightly off so that the ball does not die immediately, it is a *half-nick*.

no set One of the options open to the receiver when the score stands at 8-8 (13-13 in doubles). It means that the game ends when one player (or pair) reaches 9 points (15 in doubles).

not up A ball which is hit after the second bounce or fails to hit the front wall above the board, or is incorrectly returned in any other manner except out (*qv*).

out When the ball touches any

of the walls above the red out-of-court line. This is 15ft high on the front wall and 7ft high on the back wall with the side lines extending diagonally from the front wall to the back wall lines. Also when the ball comes into contact with lights or any part of the ceiling. The player hitting the ball out of court loses the rally.

penalty point The rally is awarded by the referee against a player who unnecessarily obstructs his opponent's stroke, or prevents him from attempting a winning stroke.

position of readiness The stance adopted between each stroke.

referee The official to whom all appeals must be directed, including appeals arising from the marker's decisions and calls. He should not interfere with the marker's calling of the game unless on appeal; if he sees that the marker has made an error; or if one player suffers interference from or distraction by his opponent.

reverse angle A stroke in which the ball hits the far side wall before hitting the front wall.

service The first stroke of a rally, played from one service box into the opposite half-court without fault (*qv*) or foot fault (*qv*). In the event of a fault or foot fault, a second service is allowed. The service must be a volley (*qv*). After each point, the server alternates service boxes until losing the service. The new server always has choice of service box for his or her first service of the hand, or at the start of a new game.

service box The 5ft 3in square area at the front edge of the right and left half-courts, two sides of the box being the wall and the short line. The server must have at least one foot in the box in contact with the floor, but not touching the lines at the moment of striking the ball.

set 2 Choosing to play a game to 10 points when the score is 8-all.

short line The line, 18 ft from the front wall, extending trans-

versely across the court.

striker The player whose turn it is to play the ball after it has hit the front wall. He must hit the ball before it bounces twice so that at some time it strikes the front wall between the board and the out-of-court line without touching the floor. Otherwise, he loses the rally.

T The point where the half-court line meets the short line. It is the central point of the court and having command of the T allows a player to move to any part of the court quickly.

telltale Another name for the tin.

tin The strip of resonant material, often metal, fitted all the way along the bottom of the front wall below the board (*qv*). Any ball hitting the tin is not up (*qv*).

volley A stroke played before the ball has bounced on the floor.

warm-up The 5-minute period before the start of a game to allow the players to loosen up—and to try to detect each other's weaknesses.

Table Tennis

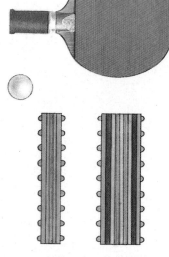

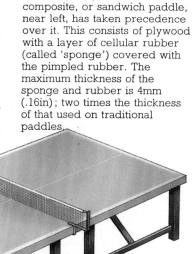

It is not surprising that table tennis rates as one of the world's largest participant sports, given that it is played indoors by both sexes and that equipment — table excepted — is relatively inexpensive. Moreover, in spite of the technology of spins, sponges and pimples. the game remains essentially simple. Play commences with a service, after which each player hits the ball directly over or around the net so that it bounces in the opponent's court. Volleying is not permitted. The rally ends, and the point is won by the opponent, when one player fails to return the ball after the first bounce. The first to score 21 points, or have an advantage of two points should the score reach 20-each, wins. Service alternates after every five points. In doubles, the service is made from the right-hand half-court to the half-court diagonally opposite, after which the four players hit the ball alternately. After five points, the receiver serves to the previous server's partner.

By the early 1900s, the champagne corks and cigar boxes, rubber balls and wood-surface bats of the nineteenth-century had given way to the light celluloid ball and the rubber-pimpled paddles that gave 'ping pong' a new dimension of speed and spin. By 1926, its international popularity was such that the first world championships were staged in London. Lady Swaythling, mother of the Hon Ivor Montagu who organized the tournament and was the ITTF's first president, gave a cup for the men's team competition, and in 1934 Marcel Corbillon obliged the ladies. Europe and the United States held sway until the 1950s, when the Japanese, Chinese and Koreans transformed the game with their supreme speed, skills and innovations with paddle surfaces.

Left: The restrictions on table tennis paddles are few; the size, weight and shape are the prerogative of the player, but the covering on the blade, other than plain wood, must be pimpled rubber and dark in color. The ball is made of celluloid or plastic and can be yellow or white. It must be between 2.4 (.085oz) and 2.5g (.09oz) in weight.

Left: Two types of paddle are now in use. That at the far left is the traditional wood paddle covered in pimpled rubber up to 2mm (.08in) thick. The composite, or sandwich paddle, near left, has taken precedence over it. This consists of plywood with a layer of cellular rubber (called 'sponge') covered with the pimpled rubber. The maximum thickness of the sponge and rubber is 4mm (.16in); two times the thickness of that used on traditional paddles.

Below: A full-sized table is 2.74m long by 1.52m (9 x 5ft) wide. It is constructed of wood, usually painted in dark green matt. It has white side, center and end lines.

backhand Stroke played by a right-handed player on his left-hand side; and vice versa for a left-handed player. If the pen-holder grip (qv) is used, the reverse side is rarely employed to play a backhand stroke.

backspin Spin imparted on the ball by the chop (qv) stroke. The ball rotates backwards in its forward flight over the net, with the result that the forward movement is checked when the ball bounces on the playing surface (qv).

block shot Method of returning the ball by letting it hit the paddle and rebound over the net using its own speed.

center line A white line, $\frac{1}{8}$in wide, running parallel with the side lines. For doubles play.

chop A basically defensive stroke with which a player deliberately imparts backspin on the ball by bringing the paddle downwards, behind and underneath it at the moment of impact. There are several variations, including the low-flight chop

just over the net, and the high-flight chop to the end line. It is also an attacking stroke.

control end The end of the table at which, in training or practice, a partner provides the appropriate balls for the player to practice against. The other end of the table is known as the *worker's end*.

counter-hitting Using topspin (qv) against topspin.

courts The two equal halves of the playing surface as it is divided by the net.

cut To chop (qv).

defensive strokes Those played to slow down the pace of the ball in rallies.

drive An attacking topspin stroke in which the forward speed of the ball and the effect of the topspin are of approximately equal importance. It can be played on either the forehand or the backhand, the paddle finishing the stroke forward and/or upward of the striker.

drop shot Played to deceive an opponent who has been driven

well away from the table. The initial movement is one of driving, but just before making contact the striker arrests his shot to gently lift the ball over the net.

early ball Said of a stroke played as the ball is rising from the bounce.

end line The white line at either end of the playing surface.

expedite system Introduced in its present form in 1963, this rule puts a time limit of 15 minutes on the length of a game (qv). At the end of 15 minutes the umpire calls 'let' and play recommences with service alternating after each point. The server has his service and 12 subsequent strokes with which to win the rally or the point is immediately awarded to the receiver. Once implemented, the expedite system remains in operation for the remainder of the match (qv).

flat drive A hard-hit drive played with little topspin, the power of the shot coming from the forward swing of the shoulder with

the hitting arm. It is best played when the ball is near the net or bouncing high.

foil To take the initiative by preventing an opponent from playing his strongest shots.

forehand Stroke played by a right-handed player on his right-hand side; and vice versa for a left-handed player.

game A series of rallies played until one player or doubles pair scores 21 points; or if the score reaches 20-each, has a two points' advantage.

half-court The right- and left-hand sides of the court for doubles play.

half-volley A push stroke on the ball immediately as it rises from bouncing.

ITTF The International Table Tennis Federation, founded in 1926.

kill To drive the ball fiercely so that an opponent has little chance of returning it.

late Said of a stroke played when the ball has dropped from the apex of its bounce to below the

60

Shake-hands grip

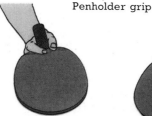

Penholder grip

Above: The shake-hands grip, front and back view.
Above right: The penholder or Asian grip, front and back view.

Right: A player uses a forehand attacking shot from the backhand corner of the table. It might seem more orthodox to reply from this position with a backhand shot, but tactics and imagination play a greater role in table tennis than tradition.
Far right: The follow-through on a backhand topspin, seen head-on.

Below: The forehand chop—contact and follow-through.

Below: The backhand chop—approach and contact.

Above: The service. The ball should be held gently in the steady palm of the free hand. The palm should be open, not cupped, with the fingers together and the thumb out. The hand must be positioned above the table surface. The ball is tossed up vertically, and cannot be struck until after it begins to fall. After contact with the paddle, it must touch the table on the side of the server and pass over or around the net to the receiver's court.

level of the playing surface.
let A rally from which no point is scored. There are six reasons for a let, the main ones being when the ball touches the net or posts in an otherwise fair service, and when it is time to implement the expedite system.
loop drive A variation on the topspin drive, played with an exaggerated action which begins below the level of the playing surface and ends up at or above shoulder height. The effect is to make the ball 'kick' up when it bounces.
match A continuous contest between two players or pairs. It may consist of one game (*qv*), or the best of three or five games.
net The dark green, unsized mesh with a white tape along its upper edge. Hung freely across the middle of the playing surface between two posts, it stands 15.25cm (6in) high along its whole length of 1.83m (6ft).
net cord A shot which hits the top of the net and falls on to the opponent's side of the table

peak timing Hitting the ball at the top of the bounce.
penholder grip Also known as the *Asian grip*. The paddle is held with the thumb and forefinger wrapped around the base of the handle and pressing from the forward surface against the other fingers on the non-striking side. Usually only one surface is used for striking the ball.
playing surface The upper surface of the table, including the top of the extremities. It should be 2.74m by 1.52m (9 x 5ft).
push strokes Forehand or backhand guiding strokes played with no real power but with the bat inclined slightly backwards as it is pushed forwards and downwards. The ball should be steered in a controlled direction.
rally The length of time the ball is in play from when it is served until one player fails to return it correctly.
reverse sandwich A sandwich (*qv*) bat with the pimples facing inwards against the sponge rubber.

sandwich A bat which has a layer of sponge rubber between the wood and the pimpled rubber, the pimples facing outwards.
service The means of starting a rally. The ball is held in the flat and open palm of the non-striking hand above the level of the playing surface, tossed vertically in the air without spin, and struck first time as it descends so that it touches the server's court first, crosses over or around the net without touching it or its supports, and bounces in the receiver's court. The umpire must be able to see the ball throughout the service. The ball must be struck from behind the end line, or a line extending therefrom. An incorrect service results in the loss of a point.
shake-hands grip The paddle handle is held as if the player were shaking hands with it. The front surface is used for forehand strokes, the back surface for backhand strokes. Also known as the *western grip*.

side lines The white lines along the long edges of the playing surface.
sidespin Spin imparted by brushing the paddle across the ball rather than upwards or downwards. The ball spins to the left or right on bouncing according to the sideways movement of the paddle on impact.
soft Said of a light ball; also of pimpled rubber surfaces such as those on sandwich paddles.
swing strokes The topspin and backspin strokes.
tennis style Another type of shake-hands grip.
topspin Spin imparted by brushing the paddle upwards and forwards across the rear of the ball on impact. The effect is to make the ball rotate forwards, dip in flight, and shoot sharply forwards and upwards on bouncing.
volley A ball which has not yet bounced. Hitting a volley (ie volleying) is an infringement of the rules (except in service).
worker's end *See* control end.

61

Tennis

The early ancestor of tennis was 'jeu de paume', a thirteenth-century French game played with a sheepskin ball and bare hands. By the fifteenth century, a racket and net were added refinements, and the English took up the game with enthusiasm. It became 'royal' tennis, and courts at Hampton Court, Windsor and Whitehall testified to its aristocratic popularity. The rules became increasingly complicated and the playing area itself, arraigned with penthouses, grilles and galleries, matched the rules. What survives today as a direct descendant of this exacting pastime is real tennis.

What is more popularly known today as tennis — lawn tennis — evolved three centuries later in Britain. A Major Wingfield applied for a patent on a portable court in 1874. It was hourglass-shaped, with a 7ft high net, and the rules were based on those of badminton. In 1875 slightly different rules were drawn up by the Marylebone Cricket Club and in 1877 the first Lawn Tennis Championships were played at Wimbledon, governed by rules very much like those of today.

Tennis is played by both men and women on courts of a great variety of surfaces. The size of the court also varies depending on whether a singles or doubles game is being played, but the height of the net is constant. Each player has a specialized racket with which a hollow rubber ball is hit. Play begins with a service, each player 'serving' in turn for one game. The opponent returns the ball across the net, so that it falls within the other player's court. The ball is allowed to bounce only once after being struck and a 'rally' is broken when a player allows the ball to bounce twice, causes the ball to hit the net, land outside the court, or misses the ball. In these cases where a rally is broken, the opponent gains a point.

Left: Rackets are assuming more varied designs under the influence of big business interests and popular fascination with the game. Wood is the classic racket frame material, but steel and even plastic are now fashionable. The important points to assess in choosing a racket are balance, sturdy grip and a well-strung head—gut rather than synthetic if possible.

ace A service ball which the receiver cannot play due to its speed or positioning.

advantage The player gaining the first point after deuce (*qv*) is said to have the advantage, and must gain the following point in order to win the game.

advantage server Scoring call indicating that the server has the advantage.

advantage striker Scoring call indicating that the receiver of the service has the advantage.

all Scoring call indicating that the players (or pairs) have an equal number of points (eg 15-all).

All England Lawn Tennis Club Founded in 1874 as an extension of the All England Croquet Club. It is the most prestigious club in the world, composed of a fixed 375 members, with a reputed waiting list of some 40 years. Its grounds are in Wimbledon, where the international 'Lawn Tennis Championships on Grass' take place.

angle To play the ball across the court in a diagonal manner, often away from the opponent.

back court The area of the court between the service line (*qv*) and the baseline (*qv*).

backhand Any stroke played with the back of the hand towards the direction of play. The grip for this stroke involves a quarter turn inward from the forehand grip (*qv*), and the diagonal positioning of the thumb across the back of the handle.

backhand drive A return stroke played after the ball has struck the ground with the racket held in the backhand position.

backhand volley A return stroke played before the ball has struck the ground, with the racket held in the backhand position. The volley is made from the front of the court or net position.

backspin The ball is set in a spinning motion, so that after contact with the ground it is not received by the opponent at the expected speed.

ball boy The person who gathers up the balls during the game and returns them to the players.

ball-in-court A ball falling on a line is regarded as falling in the court bounded by that line. It is only necessary for it to touch the edge of the outside line for the ball to be considered in the court.

ball-in-play The ball is 'in play' from the moment it has been served until a point is decided.

baseline The line indicating the boundary at the end of the court.

baseline player A player who positions himself near the baseline and prefers not to approach the net.

break point The point from which the receiver may win a game. He or she is said to have 'broken' the opponent's service.

cannonball A fast service.

center-line A line positioned centrally on the court and which connects the two service lines.

change-of-ends The players exchange sides on the court at the end of every first, third and alternate games in a set. This system continues in operation throughout the match, with the exception of those sets which end in an even number of games. In this case, the players play the first game of the next set before changing ends.

chop To play the ball with a sharp, chopping action of the racket. This stroke gives the ball a large amount of backspin (*qv*).

continuous play A match cannot be interrupted for players to take advice or refreshment. For some exhausting major matches, however, such as the Wightman Cup, an exceptional 10-minute interval may be agreed by the captains before the match.

court A measured area 27 x 78ft for singles and 36 x 78ft for doubles, in which the game is played. The classic court is smooth rolled grass, but other surfaces include clay, porous cement, wood, carpet and artificial grass.

covered court An indoor court of wood or artificial surfacing.

cross-shot A shot played diag-

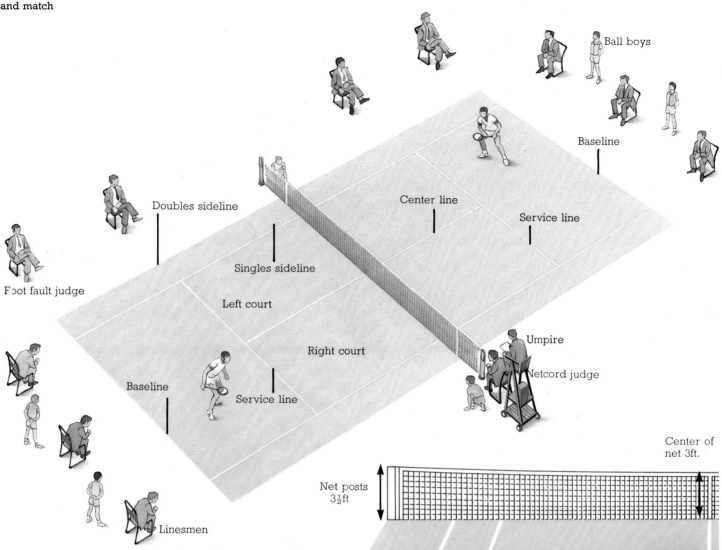

Ball boys

Baseline

Doubles sideline

Center line

Service line

Singles sideline

Left court

Foot fault judge

Right court

Umpire

Baseline

Netcord judge

Service line

Center of
net 3ft.

Net posts
3½ft

Linesmen

onally across the court.

cut A quick stroke, chopping at the ball, causing it to spin. Similar to a slice (*qv*).

Davis Cup Challenge cup presented in 1900 by the American, Dwight Davis, for men's international competition. It consists of four singles and one doubles match.

deep A shot where the ball lands near the baseline.

deuce The score when the players have each gained three points (ie a score of 40-all) in a game, or when the score is even after this.

double bounce Where the ball bounces twice before it is returned. The receiver loses the point.

double fault Two incorrect services. The server loses the point.

draw Method of determining order of play in elimination matches. After the 'seeds' (*qv*) are selected, names are drawn at random and single players or double pairs are pitted against one another in rounds (*qv*).

dress Standard dress for tennis is cool, light and always white, though recent innovations have included some colored trim. Men wear shorts and short-sleeved shirts, women shorts or skirts and blouses or tennis dresses. Tennis shoes are regulation on all courts and consist of canvas uppers with tractioned soles.

drive A stroke played after the ball has bounced once in the receiver's court. It is usually therefore made from the back of the court. *See* forehand drive; backhand drive.

Eastern grip *See* forehand.

fault A contravention of the rules.

Federation Cup Ladies' international team cup, presented by the International Tennis Federation on the occasion of its 50th anniversary in 1963.

fifteen *See* scoring.

final set The deciding set in a match.

first service The first of two services allowed. If this and the second service are faults then

the server loses the point.

first set The opening set in a match.

follow-through The act of completing a stroke after the ball has made contact with the racket. The follow-through is an essential part of the stroke, since the swing governing the completed stroke affects the length, direction and twist of the ball.

foot fault This occurs when the server touches the court or baseline with either foot or is on the wrong side of the baseline center mark at the moment of serving. A *foot fault judge* is an official strategically positioned to decide whether a foot fault has been committed.

forehand Any stroke played with the front of the hand toward the direction of play. It is often called the 'shake-hands' grip because of its similarity to this attitude. Also called the Eastern grip.

forehand drive The most basic stroke in tennis, played after the ball has struck the ground. The

shot is one continuous swing, in which correct form and smoothness of follow-through are essential.

forehand volley A return stroke played before the ball has hit the ground. The force of the shot depends on bodyweight and the locked wrist.

forty *See* scoring.

game Scoring call indicating the end of the game.

game point A point from which the result of a game may be obtained.

Grand Prix The most successful male player and the most successful female player in world-wide major tournaments are presented with these annual awards.

grip (1) The main grips are the forehand (*qv*), the backhand (*qv*) and the advanced or 'chopper' grip. The last is a major modification of the backhand grip. (2) Leather-covered handle of the racket.

ground stroke A stroke played just after the ball hits the ground.

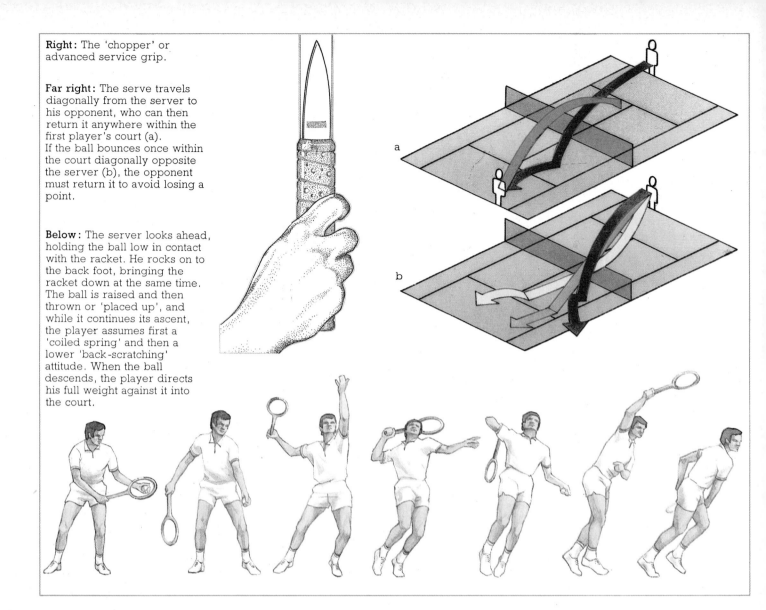

Right: The 'chopper' or advanced service grip.

Far right: The serve travels diagonally from the server to his opponent, who can then return it anywhere within the first player's court (a). If the ball bounces once within the court diagonally opposite the server (b), the opponent must return it to avoid losing a point.

Below: The server looks ahead, holding the ball low in contact with the racket. He rocks on to the back foot, bringing the racket down at the same time. The ball is raised and then thrown or 'placed up', and while it continues its ascent, the player assumes first a 'coiled spring' and then a lower 'back-scratching' attitude. When the ball descends, the player directs his full weight against it into the court.

half volley A stroke which is made just as the ball bounces.

head The strung area of the racket which is used to strike the ball.

ITF International Tennis Federation, the worldwide governing body of the game. It is composed of the national associations of numerous countries. The rules of the game are under the sole authority of this federation.

kill To play a shot with such strength and expertise that it is impossible for the opponent to return it.

let Umpire's call when he judges that a point should be played again. This applies particularly for serving; if the ball hits the net and lands within the service court, let is called and the server may serve that ball again.

linesman Official person who decides whether a ball has landed within the court.

lob To play the ball, in an attacking or defensive manner, so that it curves high into the air.

love No score; zero.

LTA Lawn Tennis Association, the British tennis governing body.

match A complete game of tennis, which consists of the best of five sets for men and the best of three for women.

match point Point on which the result of a match may rest.

mixed doubles A match played for the best of three sets, where the participants consist of one man and one woman on each side.

net (1) Three-foot-high netting fence across the center of the court, dividing the court equally across its width. (2) A ball which hits the net.

net cord Whereby the ball hits the top of the net when it is played.

out Linesman's call if the ball lands outside the boundary lines of the court.

overhead A stroke made with the racket held over the head. *See* smash.

passing shot A shot which passes the player.

poach In a doubles match, to play a shot which one's partner should have played.

post The vertical support for the net situated outside the court.

rally A succession of strokes between the players, on which the result of the point rests.

rankings A list of players drawn up in order of ability.

real tennis Also called royal or court tennis. It has roots as far back as twelfth-century Alexandria, but reached its peak in sixteenth-century France and England. An indoor game, it is played on a four-walled court bordered by grilled penthouses and numerous galleries. The floor is divided by a net into two equal areas, the 'service' and the 'hazard'. A peculiar characteristic of the game is the 'chase', a rally played in the service area when the ball has been allowed to bounce twice or when it lands in a numbered gallery. Points are scored by playing off chases and by hitting the ball directly into the winning gallery.

receiver The player who receives the ball.

referee Official who is the authority of the tournament.

return of service The first shot played by the receiver of the service shot.

reverse shot A shot which deflects to one side on impact.

rough The face of the racket on which the loops of the treble-stringing are evident.

rough or smooth? Question asked when the racket is spun to decide the selection of the ends of court or the service.

round Where several matches in a tournament are played simultaneously to eliminate players.

scoring The system for counting the points to be credited to each player or team as they are scored. The first score gained is called 15, the second 30, the third 40 and the fourth is 'game'. If the score becomes 40-all, deuce (*qv*) is called. It is then necessary for a player to gain two successive points to

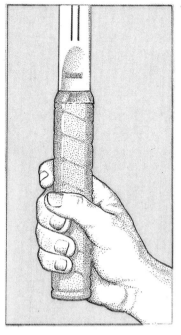

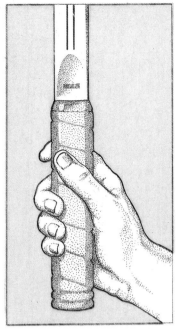

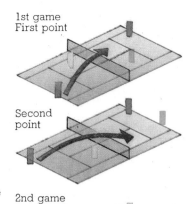

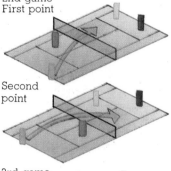

Left: The backhand grip is a quarter of a turn to the left from the forehand position. The V between the thumb and the forefinger is on the corner of the handle. Underneath is shown the backhand drive.

Far left: The forehand grip is much like shaking hands. The back of the hand encircling the handle is directly in line with the flat of the racket. Underneath is shown the forehand drive.

Right: The doubles game is played by members of the same sex or as mixed doubles. One player serves throughout each complete game, beginning from the right-hand court and alternating sides after each point. As in singles, the players change ends after the first game and thereafter when the number of games played in a set is an odd number.

1st game
First point

Second
point

2nd game
First point

Second
point

3rd game
First point

Second
point

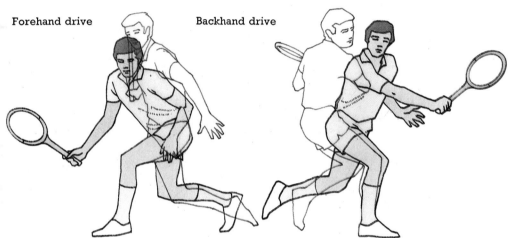

Forehand drive   Backhand drive

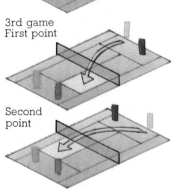

win the game. The player must win six games to win the set and must be leading by at least two games. Otherwise the set continues until this lead is gained or the tie-break (*qv*) comes into operation.

seed To arrange the draw in a tournament so that the best players do not oppose each other until the late stages; a thus selected player.

serve To deliver the ball from the baseline in a diagonal direction across the court into the service court of the opponent to open each point in the game. The server uses a variation of the forehand grip, and strikes the ball which he has tossed up in the air.

server The player who first delivers the ball.

service The act of serving. For each point in the game two serves may be played.

service break A game in which the receiver wins.

service court One of the two oblong areas which are found on both sides of the net and within the boundaries of which the ball must land when served.

service fault Can be a foot fault (*qv*), serving outside the designated area, striking a fixture or net with the ball, running or walking while serving. If the first service is a fault, the server is allowed one more serve; a 'double fault' (*qv*) loses the point.

service line The limiting end boundary of the service courts within which the ball must land when served.

set A finished part of a match, usually where one player or team has reached six games and is in the lead by at least two games. *See* scoring.

set point A point on which the result of the set may rest.

straight sets Match in which the winner has not lost any of the sets played.

singles Games played between two players.

slice Stroke which slices the ball, causing it to spin and curve in flight.

smash A shot played overhead in which the ball is returned very hard.

smooth The face of the racket head on which the loops of the treble-stringing are not evident.

spin the racket To twist the racket in order to select the ends or the choice of service.

stop volley A stroke played softly and close to the net before the ball hits the ground, with the result that the ball falls with little force on the other side of the net.

stroke To hit the ball with the racket. Strokes include forehand and backhand drives and volleys, lobs, smashes, slices and cuts.

team tennis US inter-city league competition for men and women played in eastern and western divisions with a final play-off between winning teams.

tie-break After an agreed score has been reached in a set (6-all or 8-all), a specified number of points are played to determine the winner of the set.

top seed The best player in a tournament who is situated at the top of the draw.

top spin Spin given to the ball by a player hitting it with a rising action and an extended follow-through. It makes the ball dip in flight.

tournament A series of matches.

tramlines The parallel lines down the sides of the court, the outer of which demarcate the boundary for doubles matches and the inner for singles.

treble-stringing The fine binding gut weaved at the top and the bottom of the racket head.

two-handed A grip in which the racket is held with both hands.

umpire Official who is in charge of a match.

volley To play the ball before it hits the ground. See forehand (*qv*) and backhand (*qv*) volley.

warm-up A period prior to a match when players loosen up.

Wightman Cup Ladies team cup presented to the winner of the annual competition between Britain and the US.

Volleyball

An Olympic sport since 1964, volleyball is played by two teams of six players each, although including substitutes a team may consist of as many as 12 players. Both women and men play, but not in mixed teams. The aim of the game, in which the ball may be played with the arms, hands, or any part of the body above the waist, is to ground the ball in the opposition court or to hit it in such a way that the other team is unable to return the ball in accordance with the rules. Once the ball has been served, each team may play it three times before returning it, although no player may hit it twice in succession. The usual tactics are to use two hits to set the ball up at the net for one of the front-line players to spike it into the opposition court. The opposition, meanwhile, attempt to block the spike, two or three players jumping up and reaching over the net to force the ball back into the other court.

In keeping with the intentions of its American founder, W. G. Morgan, volleyball restricts the development of specialist players by demanding the rotation of positions every time a team wins the right to serve. (Only the team serving may score points.) Moreover, there are limitations on the attacking potential of back-line players: if in front of the attack line, they may not hit the ball over the net unless it has dropped below net height. Morgan formulated his game in 1895 for middle-aged businessmen. At first there was not even a net, and not until after World War I was the number of court players reduced from nine to six. World championships have been held since 1949, two years after the formation of the International Volleyball Federation, and, like the Olympic competitions, they have been the preserve of the eastern Europeans and Japanese.

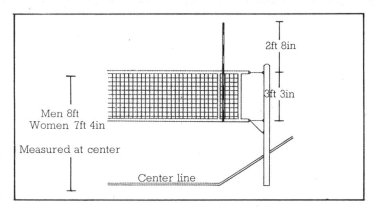

Above: The net is made of 4in square mesh and is 3ft 3in deep by 31ft long. A double thickness of 2in-wide white canvas is stitched across the top through which passes a taut, flexible cable. Vertical white tapes, 2in wide, run down each side of the net. Two aerials projecting 2ft 8in above the top of the net and coinciding with the outer edges of the net are also fastened to the net 29½ft apart. Another cable runs through the lower edge of the net, keeping the net rigid.

Below: The court and players' positions at the time of service. Players (4), (3) and (2) are called front-line players and (5) (6) and (1) back-line players. The rotation order changes each time a team wins the right to serve.

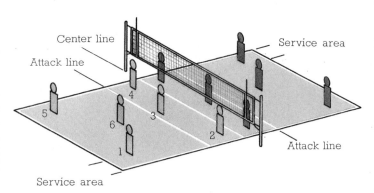

ace A service which the opposition are unable to play.
aerials Sticks or rods of fiberglass or similarly flexible material extending 2ft 8in above the net to indicate out-of-bounds (qv).
back-court spike A spike (qv) by a back-line player. It must be made from behind the attack line.
back-flop set A set (qv) over the setter's head to a spiker (qv) standing behind the setter.
back-line players The three players positioned behind the front-line players (qv) at the time of the service.
block An attempt by front-line players to stop an opposition spike with hands, arms, and/or the upper part of the body. Any player making a block may play the ball a second time, and this counts as the team's first touch.
cover Those players positioned behind a smash or block to play the ball should it rebound.
cross-court shot A shot hit into the diagonally opposite side of

the opposition court.
dead ball When the ball goes out of play following a point or side-out (qv), or when play is temporarily suspended by the referee.
dig A method of playing the ball with one or both arms when it is below shoulder level. The two-arm dig, which is more reliable and accurate than the one-arm dig, is made with the hands clasped and arms extended. The dig is usually used to receive a spike or serve.
dink Another name for a dump (qv).
double hit When one player hits the ball twice in succession in a single attempt to play the ball. Except in the instance of a block (qv), it is a foul.
dump A tactical shot by a player who makes as if to spike but at the last moment lobs the ball over the block.
floater A service that floats or weaves through the air because the server has imparted little or no spin on the ball.

foot fault Occurs when the server, while serving, puts a foot on or over the back line, or when any player puts a foot over the center line into the opposition court.
foul Any infringement of the rules.
front-line players The three players at the front of the court.
held ball A foul when the ball is caught by a player or allowed to rest momentarily on any part of his body before being played.
in the net Said of a player who commits a net fault.
Japanese set A short set (qv) to a spiker who, already in the air, attempts to spike the ball as it is passed up to him.
jump set A set made by a front-line player already in the air, often in an attempt to deceive the opposition that he is making the spike. He then sets the ball to another spiker.
kill A shot which the opposition are unable to return.
match At international and senior national level, the best of five

sets (qv). At lower levels, a game may be the best of three sets. In five-set matches, an interval of two minutes is allowed between the first four sets, with five minutes between the fourth and fifth.
net ball A ball which touches the net or the aerials while in play. Except at the service, it counts as good if it drops into the opposition court.
net fault Occurs when a player touches the net or the aerials while the ball is in play. Unless the ball has pushed the net against the player, it is a foul.
net serve A service which touches the net, the aerial, or its imaginary extensions. It is a foul and results in the loss of service.
out-of-bounds Said of the ball when it touches the ground beyond the boundary lines, the net outside the vertical tapes, or the aerials.
out-of-position A foul if a team is not in its correct order of rotation (qv) at the service. The

Right: A sequence in the underhand method of service. It is the simplest mode of service and is used in the early stages of learning the game. More skilled players use the tennis or hook (hand open or closed) serve. The service is made using any part of the arm or hand. The hand is closed in this service.

Right: The moment of contact with the ball when making a volley. It is the most common way of playing the ball.

Below: Hands clasped for the dig. The dig is used to play fast-moving or dropped balls difficult to volley, or to set up a smash.

Below: Front-line players attempt to block a shot. Blocking is the defensive counter move to the smash.

offending team lose any points scored while their players were out of position.

overlapping A fault occurring at the service when an official is unable to determine a player's correct positioning (qv). Players are judged by any part of their body touching the court.

penetration A tactical move in which a back-line player moves to the net after the service to act as setter, so allowing all three front-line men to play as spikers.

positioning At the moment of service, all players must be in correct positional alignment in relation to the players in front, behind, or alongside, the order having been recorded on the score-sheet at the beginning of the set. Players must adopt the same position for service until rotation (qv).

power serve A service in which the ball is hit with great force, usually with an overhead spike action.

punch serve A serve in which the ball is floated high into the

opposition court with an overhead, open-hand punch (not a closed fist).

receive The tactics the non-serving team adopt to play the service.

rotation The clockwise movement of the players' service positions when their team has won the right to serve.

roundhouse Name given to the style of hitting the ball with the arm fully extended over the head.

scoop To lift the ball in the air with the open hands.

screening Occurs when players on the serving team obscure their opponent's view of the service. It is a foul.

service The method of hitting the ball into play. It is by the right back-line player from the service area behind the baseline on his side of the court. Having released the ball from his other hand, the server may use any part of his hand or arm to hit the ball which, to count as a fair service, must enter the opposi-

tion court without hitting the net, aerials, or a member of the serving team.

set (1) A series of rallies until one team scores 15 points with a margin of at least two points; if the score reaches 14-all, play continues until a two-point margin is achieved. Only the team serving may score points. (2) A high pass to a team-mate near the net to enable him to play a spike (qv).

setter The player who sets up the ball for a spike.

side-out When the serving team forfeit the right to serve by losing a rally. Service goes to the opposition, who must then rotate positions.

smash A spike.

spike A sharply hit shot down into the opposition court. Because of the net's height, the player making the spike is invariably in mid-air. Front-line players may spike from anywhere on the court; back-line players must jump from behind the attack line.

substitute A player who enters the game as replacement for a teammate. Each team is permitted six substitutions a set. Except in the case of injury, a substitute may be replaced only by the player whose place he took, and he may not then return during the same set.

switch A tactical ploy in which front- and back-line players, following the service, move to positions in which their talents are used to best advantage.

tape The 2in-wide removable strip of white material fastened vertically on each side of the net directly above the sidelines to mark the boundary of the court.

toss The toss of a coin is held at the beginning of each set to decide choice of ends or right to serve.

time-out A 30-second rest period. Each team is allowed two time-outs per set, but only when the ball is dead.

volley Using the fingers of both hands to play the ball when it is above shoulder height.

Equestrian Sports

Dressage

From the French *dresser*, meaning to 'teach' or 'school' an animal, dressage is concerned with the development of a horse so that it becomes an enjoyable animal to ride, and to watch being ridden. Dressage, however, is also a sport, both in its own right and as part of eventing, and as such the aim of the dressage tests is to determine how well a horse has learned the lesson of its schooling. It is included in the Olympic Games as an individual (Grand Prix) and team event, and there are world championships for horses at Grand Prix, Reprise Intermédiare (advanced difficulty), and Prix St Georges (medium difficulty) standards. At Grand Prix level, the test is demanding, including pirouettes, changes of direction on two tracks at the canter, canter changes of leg at every stride, and such classical movements as the *piaffe* and the *passage*.

The traditions, theory, and much of the practice of modern dressage stem from the famous European equestrian schools of the seventeenth and eighteenth centuries. Its object, as laid down by the Fédération Equestre Internationale (FEI) is the 'harmonious development of the physique and ability of the horse. . . . it makes the horse calm, supple, and keen, thus achieving perfect understanding with its rider.' Such qualities are revealed by the 'freedom and regularity of the paces; the harmony, lightness, and ease of movements; the lightening of the forehand and the engagement of the hindquarters'. The horse is thus able to give the impression that it is doing on its own what the rider requires. However, dressage does not have to be an end in itself, concerned exclusively with competition. The well-schooled horse, obedient to its rider's commands, is as essential in the hunting field or show jumping ring as it is in the dressage arena.

Above: Perhaps the most difficult times in dressage tests occur when the horse is required to change speed or gait. This must be done smoothly, without fumbling or loss of rhythm. To train a horse to accomplish this feat, the rider must develop his animal's posture, response and reflexes. This is done through suppling exercises, some of the principal forms being renvers, travers, work on circles, serpentines and negotiation of corners. This rider is executing a circle on the left rein; the horse must learn to bend into the movement while keeping its body as straight as possible.

aids Signals used by a rider to convey instructions to the horse.

balance The equal distribution of the weight of horse and rider so that the horse can perform with maximum ease and efficiency.

cadence The measured, rhythmical movements of the horse's stride, revealing precision and elegance.

canter A three-time pace, the three definite steps comprising the one stride. The hooves touch the ground in the following sequence: left hind leg, left diagonal (*qv*), and right foreleg followed by a period of suspension (*qv*). The three recognized canter paces are medium, collected, and extended, with the working canter replacing the collected canter in tests below Grand Prix standard.

capriole An *haute école* movement in which the horse kicks out with its hind legs while jumping with all four legs off the ground.

collected canter A slow, controlled canter in which the stride is more elevated than at the medium canter, the hind legs being placed as far as possible under the horse.

collected trot An energetic controlled trot performed with shortened, elevated steps, the horse showing much forward and upward impulsion (*qv*) and gaiety in its steps, and greater mobility in its stride than at the medium trot.

collected walk A slow walk performed with a shorter and more elevated stride than at the medium (*qv*) walk. The hind feet touch the ground behind the footprints of the forefeet.

collection A controlled combination of elevation and forward movement producing cadence and rhythm in every stride.

contact The manner of holding the rein to allow constant communication from the bit to the rider's hand.

counter-canter A movement on a circle or curve with the horse leading on the leg opposite to the direction of the canter.

courbette An *haute école* movement in which the horse, while its forelegs are off the ground, jumps forward several times on its hind legs.

demi-pirouette A turn of 180° with the forehand (*qv*) of the horse describing a small circle around the hind quarters.

diagonals The fore and hind legs diagonally opposite. The *right diagonal* consists of the left hind and the right fore; the *left diagonal* of the right hind and the left fore.

disunited Said of a canter when the steps change to an incorrect sequence.

extended canter A fast, controlled canter. The steps are longer, but not quicker, than at a medium canter.

extended trot A fast, controlled trot. The steps are longer but not quicker than at medium trot.

extended walk A fast, controlled walk with steps longer, but not quicker, than at a medium walk.

fluid balance The ability to transfer a horse's point of balance forwards or backwards smoothly so that neither horse nor rider makes any jolting movements.

forehand Those parts of the horse in front of the rider.

forward movement The urge of the horse to move forward freely as it develops impulsion from its hind quarters and yet remains under the complete control of the rider.

free walk A walk in which the horse, given freedom of its head and neck, is allowed to move forwards with lively but relaxed strides and with its tail swinging from side to side.

half-halt An exercise to improve a horse's balance and attention before a transition to another pace.

half-pass A movement in which the horse moves forward at an oblique angle on two tracks.

halt The horse standing motionless with its spine straight and its weight evenly distributed over all four legs. Tests (*qv*) begin with a halt and a salute.

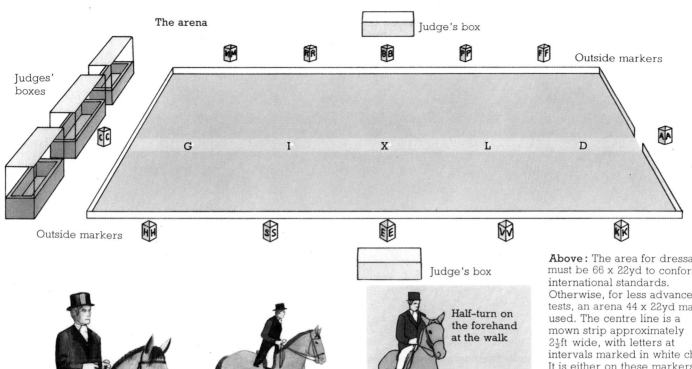

The arena

Judge's box

Judges' boxes

MM RR BB PP FF — Outside markers

CC

G I X L D

AA

Outside markers — HH SS EE VV KK

Judge's box

Above: The rising trot relieves the hind quarters of the horse of some of the rider's weight otherwise present in the sitting trot. It is an exercise used to develop longitudinal suppling.

Left: The halt may appear easy, but it is one of the most difficult movements for the horse and rider to execute correctly.

Half-turn on the forehand at the walk

Half-turn on the haunches to the left

Above: The area for dressage must be 66 x 22yd to conform to international standards. Otherwise, for less advanced tests, an arena 44 x 22yd may be used. The centre line is a mown strip approximately 2½ft wide, with letters at intervals marked in white chalk. It is either on these markers or between combinations of them and outside markers (placed about 6½ft outside the arena at intervals) that the competitor is required to perform his movements.

Left: Change of direction is an integral part of most movements. The horse is capable of turning in different ways: by pivoting on its forelegs, or by turning on both at once. While the last comes naturally to the horse, it is the first two types of turn which are the most attractive and are thus used in dressage.

haute école Literally high school; the style of riding practised at the Spanish Riding School of Vienna.

impulsion The driving action of a horse's hind quarters.

lacking activity Said of a horse showing little impulsion.

lateral work Movements forwards and sideways with the horse at an oblique angle.

levade An *haute école* movement in which the horse holds a raised position on its hind legs.

medium canter A pace between collected and extended canter.

medium trot A pace between collected and extended trot.

medium walk A pace between collected and extended walk.

nappy Term used of a horse that will not go forward in response to aids (*qv*).

passage A slow, very collected trot with plenty of elevation and a definite period of suspension.

piaffe A marking-time on the spot with an elevated trot; resembles a stationary collected trot.

quarters-in Another name for the renvers (*qv*).

rein back A backwards walk with the legs, diagonally paired, raised and set down simultaneously.

renvers A suppling exercise in which the hind quarters remain on the outer track while the horse travels forward at an oblique angle with its forelegs on the inner track and its body 'bent' in the direction of travel. Also known as *tail to the wall*.

rhythm The smooth, regular step of a horse so that it maintains a uniform stride at any pace.

shoulder-in A suppling exercise on two tracks. The horse's inner feet step in front of the outer feet as it travels at an oblique angle with its body bent to the inside; ie away from the direction of travel.

sloppy running Said of a horse which is not properly balanced.

straight A horse is moving straight when the hind legs follow in the same track as the forelegs.

submission The horse's obedience, balance and general de-

meanor throughout a test.

suspension The horse having one pair of diagonals (*qv*) in the air while the diagonal opposites remain on the ground.

test The performance of required movements by horse and rider within the time allowed.

track The line in which a horse moves; eg straight (*qv*) or on two tracks (*qv*). Also the prescribed path to be followed in the execution of a dressage movement. Tracks are designated inner and outer in relation to the centre of the arena.

tracking-up When the hind feet come to the ground at the same spot as the front feet.

transition The change from one recognized pace to another.

travers A suppling exercise on two tracks. The horse moves at an oblique angle with its forelegs on the outer track and the hind legs on the inner track, the outside legs stepping in front of the inside legs. Also known as *head to the wall*.

trot A two-time pace with the legs

moving on alternate diagonals separated by a period of suspension. Steps should be free, lively and equal. The three recognized trotting paces are medium, collected and extended, with the working trot replacing the collected trot in tests below Grand Prix standard.

two tracks An exercise in which the horse moves at an oblique angle with its fore and hind legs on the inner and outer tracks. The forehand is always slightly in advance of the hind quarters.

volte A full turn on the haunches over the smallest circle the horse can manage.

walk A four-time pace in which the four legs follow one another in a regular sequence: left fore, right hind, right fore and left hind. There are four steps to one stride. The four recognized walks are medium, collected, extended and free.

working canter trot A pace between the medium and collected canter trot for a horse not yet properly trained.

Eventing

Best known to the public through its major and international competitive form, the three-day event, eventing developed as a test for officers' chargers and even today some still refer to it as the 'military'. The British call it Combined Training; the French, with their customary accuracy, have named it the *Concours Complet*, the complete test. This aptly describes the nature of the three-phase sport—a comprehensive test of horse and rider in the dressage arena, across terrain and obstacles resembling the hunting field, and in the show jumping arena. Neither the dressage nor the show jumping is of the high standard demanded when these sports are practised in their own right, but each is designed to prove that, in dressage, the horse and rider are trained and able to perform accurately and fluently the basic movements, and, in show jumping, that the horse is still sound, supple and obedient and able to jump a reasonable course after its endeavors in the previous day's speed and endurance phase.

It is this middle phase that is the most demanding—and most thrilling—part of eventing, and it invariably has the most influence on the result. This is determined on a ratio of points from the dressage, speed and endurance, and show jumping, with the winner being the horse with the least penalty points. In a three-day event, which may be for individuals, teams, or both, the speed and endurance consists of four phases: roads and tracks (Phases A and C); the steeplechase (Phase B) over a course similar to a normal steeplechase; and the cross country (Phase D), which in a CCIO may be as long as 12mi. As in the show jumping, an optimum time is set in relation to the distance and speed for each phase, and penalties are incurred for exceeding this time, as well as for faults at obstacles.

Above: In the speed and endurance phase, which includes the cross country, riders wear more casual attire.

Below: In the dressage phase of a three-day event, riders, unless in military dress, wear hunting attire.

cavalletti A series of low rails used in schooling a horse to jump obstacles.

CCI Concours Complet International; a three-day event open to individuals from other nations than that holding the event. The number of individuals allowed to enter is at the discretion of the organizing authority. An unofficial team event is sometimes included. The specifications for a CCI are not as demanding as for a CCIO.

CCIO Concours Complet International Officiel; a major three-day event, such as the Olympic Games or the world or European championships. Countries may enter only one team, plus additional individual competitors.

CCN Concours Complet National; an event in which entry is restricted to nationals of the country holding it.

Chef d'équipe The manager of a national team.

Combined Training The British name for eventing, or horse trials.

deep going Soft, wet ground into which a horse's hooves sink.

deviation A rider's failure to follow the prescribed route. Courses are marked with yellow direction flags or signs, and with red and white flags marking compulsory sections of the course. Riders must keep the red flags to their right and the white flags to their left. To correct any deviation, a rider must return to where he first went wrong.

drop fence An obstacle where the ground on the landing side is lower than on the take-off side.

English-type saddle A shallow-seated spring or tree saddle which must be used in the dressage stage of an international three-day event.

fence An obstacle forming part of the steeplechase, cross-country, and show jumping courses. Failure to jump any obstacle or rejumping an obstacle already taken or not in the correct order results in elimination.

get under Said of a horse that misses its stride and so takes off too close to an obstacle.

good going Ground with sufficient elasticity for a horse to move easily without sinking in or being jarred.

grading The system used in Britain to classify horses according to points won at official horse trials or three-day events. Grade I—41 or more points; Grade II—10-40 inclusive; Grade III—under 10 points.

hard going Bone-dry ground which jars a horse.

Helsinki step-fence A cross-country obstacle comprising two or three steps cut into sloping ground going downhill and reinforced with rails.

horse trials Another name for eventing. Trials are usually over one or two days, when the order of the phases may be varied to suit the organizers' arrangements. It is compulsory to do the dressage phase first and usual to follow with the show jumping, then the cross-country.

in and out A cross-country obstacle comprising two elements, closely related but spaced, so that they cannot be taken in one jump but at the same time do not allow the horse to take more than a few strides between the elements.

island fence A cross-country obstacle isolated from the field boundary.

military Name given to the three-day event by some European countries.

napping A horse's unwillingness to go beyond a certain point. It is penalized by elimination if it resists for more than 60 seconds.

outside assistance Help given to a rider which, in the opinion of the judges, proves advantageous to his or her performance (unless it is to catch a horse, adjust saddlery, or remount following a fall). Such help, even if unsolicited, warrants elimination.

override To exhaust a horse by forcing it beyond its capabilities.

palisade A cross-country obstacle with a top rail across a row of vertical spars.

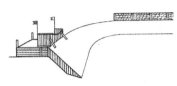

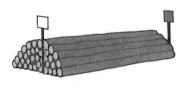

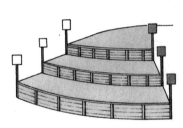

Typical cross country fences

Above and above right: An example of the problems facing horse and rider during the cross country—the phase that is most decisive in determining the overall result of an eventing competition. The obstacle is a facsimile of the Quarry at Badminton, site of the famous three-day event in Gloucestershire, England. Once on the platform, there is little room for the horse to manoeuvre before attacking the fence, and immediately on landing, horse and rider have to adjust to the bank. Some cross country obstacles are constructed so that riders can choose alternative routes— sacrificing time for safety or gambling on saving time by making a more adventurous approach.

Left: A selection of obstacles encountered on the cross country in an eventing competition. Fences should not be so high that it requires acrobatic feats to clear them; rather, they should pose problems to horse and rider by their shape and siting. Where obstacles are lower on the landing side than on the take-off side, the drop must not exceed 6ft from the highest part of the obstacle. Riders must keep the red flag on their right and the white flag on their left.

Below: Final phase of the three-day event is the show jumping. It is not inherently a test of the horse's jumping ability but is designed to prove its obedience, fitness and attitude to fences.

parallel bars A cross-country obstacle, similar to that in show jumping but more solidly constructed. Also known as *double rails*.

peck To stumble on landing.

pedestrian crossing A cross-country obstacle, constructed like parallel bars but with staggered gaps in the rails.

penalties Points lost for errors in any of the three phases of an event. Time penalties are also incurred for failure to finish the course within the optimum time.

penalty zone A rectangular area around each obstacle on the steeplechase and cross-country courses, and in which refusals, falls, voluntary dismounts, and other errors incur from 20 to 60 penalty points or elimination. Extending 11yd in front, 22yd behind, and 11yd to either side of the obstacle's boundary flags, it is marked by sawdust, chalk, pegs or similar means that will not interfere with competitors.

post and rails A cross-country obstacle comprising one or more horizontal bars attached to the top or the sides of vertical posts.

refusal Running out (*see run-off*) or stopping in front of an obstacle to be jumped which is not immediately followed by a standing jump. On the cross-country course, the obstacle must be within the penalty zone for a refusal to incur penalty points. There are no penalty zones in the show jumping phase.

ride A road or lane cut through a wood and used as part of the roads and tracks phase of a three-day event.

roads and tracks Phases A and C of a three-day event, the name being self-explanatory. Riders may choose their own pace and may even walk their horses provided they are mounted when they pass the finishing post.

run-off A deviation from the prescribed route. To continue, the horse has to be brought back to the point of deviation.

run out To miss an obstacle by going to one side or the other.

It counts as a refusal.

spooky Said of a nervous horse. A horse which makes a cautious, erratic jump over an unfamiliar obstacle is said to be *spooking*.

stand back To take off some distance in front of an obstacle.

summer holding Ground conditions where the weather has dried out the surface but left the sub-surface 'sticky', so making galloping tiring.

teams National teams in international events consist of three or four members, with only the best three final scores counting towards a team's total. If fewer than three in a team finish, the team is eliminated; (although in some CCI events for three-man teams the score is taken from the best two riders). Team members' scores are automatically considered for the individual competition as well.

three-day event Staged over three days with one day allocated to each phase. Where there is a large entry, the competition may take four days, with two allocated to the dressage, and one each to the speed and endurance and the show jumping phases.

time limit The period of time within which a rider must finish a course to avoid elimination. It is twice the optimum time for the course.

trakener A cross-country obstacle, built in a ditch and comprising a knife-rest construction with a rail attached to the cross-pieces.

wall A cross-country obstacle, usually of upright construction, made from bricks, concrete blocks, railway ties or stones.

weight cloth A cloth, carried under the saddle, with pockets to hold lead weights. In the speed and endurance and show jumping phases of a three-day event, a weight of 165lb must be carried.

winter holding Ground conditions where the going is wet but at the same time easier to make progress through than ground that is summer holding (*qv*).

Horse Racing

Traditionally the 'sport of kings', horse racing is also the sport of the common man. Today, millions attend race meetings, or follow them via newspapers, radio and television, so supporting a sport that has become an international industry. Owners, trainers and jockeys (or drivers) are able to diversify their interests in several countries, even though most remain within the confines of their branch of horse racing. Basically, there are three main types: flat racing, hurdling and steeplechasing for thoroughbreds, and harness racing for standard-breds. The latter form, in which separate races are held for trotters and pacers pulling a sulky, is most popular in the United States, France, Australia and New Zealand, where it rivals the established thoroughbred racing, and has a more limited following in Europe and Asia. Whatever the racing, however, each follows the same precept: the first horse to cross the finish line wins.

Although the origins of horse racing are lost in time, the racing of thoroughbreds can be dated to England around 1700, when it was discovered that certain mating systems could produce a faster breed of horse. The result is that horses are today bred for short, sprint distances up to five or six furlongs (one furlong = $\frac{1}{8}$ mile or 220yd; or middle-distance races of 1-1½ miles (1.6-2.5km) in which staying ability becomes as important a quality as speed. Handicapping and weight-for-age scales help balance the fields. Races over jumps tend to attract older horses than flat racing. Hurdles are smaller than steeplechase fences (3½ ft to 4½ ft minimum height), while the steeplechase course must include a ditch and a water jump.

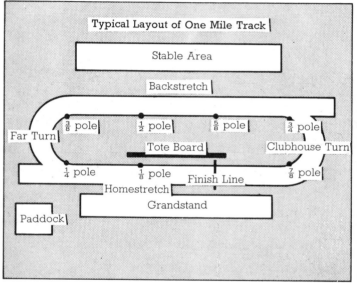

Typical Layout of One Mile Track

Stable Area

Backstretch

Far Turn — $\frac{3}{8}$ pole — $\frac{1}{2}$ pole — $\frac{5}{8}$ pole — $\frac{3}{4}$ pole — Clubhouse Turn

Tote Board

$\frac{1}{4}$ pole — $\frac{1}{8}$ pole — Finish Line — $\frac{7}{8}$ pole

Homestretch

Grandstand

Paddock

---

acceptances Those horses still entered for a race after a specified date.

added money The sum of money added to the prize money made up from entrants' fees.

age In the Northern Hemisphere, a horse's age is calculated from 1 January of the year of foaling; in Southern Hemisphere countries such as Australasia and southern Africa from 1 August; and in South America from the preceding 1 July.

aged A horse which is six or more years old.

apprentice A boy serving an apprenticeship under a trainer for a certain period of time; it must be for a minimum of three years. During this time he learns to ride and look after horses, and if good enough is given rides in races. He can claim weight allowances until his apprenticeship is served or he has ridden a certain number of winners.

auction plate A race for horses bought in public auction. They may be handicapped according to their purchase price.

blinkers Eye-screens attached to the bridle, or a hood, with stiffened shields for the eyes, which fits over a horse's head to limit sideways vision and so keep the horse's mind on its racing.

brood mare A mare used at stud for breeding purposes.

bumpers Amateur riders in flat races.

chalk jockey A little-known or inexperienced jockey; so called because bookmakers chalk his name on a board whereas the names of established jockeys are already painted on boards.

claiming race A race in which a runner may be claimed by a buyer for its entered price.

classics Broadly, the most important races in a country's racing calendar. The classic races vary from country to country, and also within the different forms of racing.

clerk of the course The official responsible for the running of a course and all meetings there.

clerk of the scales The official responsible for the weighing-out and weighing-in of jockeys.

colt A male race horse of four years of age and under.

coupled entry Two or more horses in a race owned and/or trained by the same person. In harness racing, a bet on one horse counts as a bet on all horses coupled as one *entry*.

dam A brood mare who has produced foals.

distance A winning margin of 220yd or more; also, in heat races, the measurement back from the winning post which a horse must have reached when the winner finishes in order to run in the final heat.

field The runners in a race.

filly A female racehorse of four years of age and under.

foal A horse less than one year of age.

futurity A stakes race in which the entries have been nominated before being foaled.

gait The pattern of a horse's stride.

gaiting strap In harness racing, a strap attached to the inside of the sulky (*qv*) shafts to prevent the pacer (*qv*) from moving its hindquarters sideways when running.

gelding A horse that has been castrated and therefore is useless for breeding purposes.

going The ground conditions of a course. It may be described as *hard, firm, good, soft, yielding,* or *heavy,* or degrees in between.

handicap A race in which the weight a horse carries is adjusted to equalize the chances of all the entries. In harness racing, the handicap takes the form of distance allowance.

head pole A small shaft fixed alongside the neck and head of a pacer to keep its head looking straight ahead.

hobbles Leather straps connecting a pacer's fore and hind legs to help it maintain its lateral gait.

horse A male racehorse of five or more years of age.

jumps The obstacles in hurdle and steeplechase races.

Right: Two horses fight it out in a close finish. In the past the judges had the difficult task of sorting out which horse had won in such close finishes. It was not uncommon for doubts to be cast on their verdict, it being suggested that financial inducements had helped them to make up their minds. Nowadays, the judges have a relatively simple task sorting out the winner with the help of the photo-finish camera. Races are also filmed by the camera patrol at crucial points in the race such as the closing stages. The film is used by the stewards to decide objections.

Left: A layout of a typical one-mile race track. The track surface is usually a mixture of clay and sand, but the consistency can vary widely at different locations. The ability of the track surface to handle moisture can make a considerable difference on the betting odds as some horses can handle deep, muddy tracks better than others. Many tracks have a separate turf track on the inside of the dirt track for traces run on grass.

Below: Horses and riders clear a flight of hurdles. Hurdles, which are packed with gorse and are slightly sloped, are so designed to give way on impact when a horse hits them. Hurdling and steeplechasing are known collectively as jump racing in most countries, although Britain still uses the term National Hunt racing – after the National Hunt Committee which governed British jumping until it merged with the Jockey Club in 1969. The name steeple chasing originated in eighteenth century England, where races were held across country to a point marked by a church steeple. Races for steeplechasers and hurdlers must be at least 2 miles (3.22km) long, and national rules stipulate the minimum number of jumps required. For steeplechasing in Britain, there must be a ditch every mile (1.6km) and a water jump.

leathers The straps connecting the stirrups to the saddle. They are set to a length to suit a jockey's riding style.

maiden A horse which has never won a race.

mare A female racehorse of five or more years of age.

match A race between two horses, the terms for the race being arranged by the two owners.

matinee In harness racing, a race for which there is no entry fee.

nursery A handicap race for two-year-olds.

odds The proportion of return offered by the pari-mutuel (*qv*) on a wager.

on the bit Said of a horse which is requiring restraint by its jockey while running easily.

pacer A harness racing horse which moves with a lateral gait, the fore and hind legs on either side swinging in unison.

paddock The collecting area where the horses are assembled prior to going on to the starting area.

Pari-mutuel A betting system used at virtually every track in the U.S. Odds are determined by the total amount bet on any one entry in a race in proportion to the total bet on the entire race. The odds are constantly updated right up to the start of the race.

place The horse finishing second in a race.

plate (1) A race in which the prize money is of a definite value guaranteed by the course. (2) A horse's shoe. A horse with a loose shoe is said to have *spread* or *cast* a plate.

scratch To withdraw a horse from a race.

show The horse finishing third in a race.

silks The blouse (of silk or some suitable material) and peaked cap worn by a jockey and carrying the colors of the owner Harness racing drivers wear jackets.

sire A stallion with progeny.

stallion A male horse at stud for breeding purposes.

starter's orders The field is said

to be under starter's orders from the moment his flag is hoisted. Usually no horse may then be withdrawn from the race.

starting price (SP) The final odds offered by the pari-mutuel system before the start of a race.

stewards The officials who control the running of a race meeting.

sulky The light, two-wheeled cart in which the driver sits in harness racing. It is attached to the horse by two shafts.

sweepstake A race in which all, or a major proportion, of the prize money comprises entry fees, subscriptions, or forfeits from owners, plus any added (*qv*) money.

thoroughbred A racehorse which has its pedigree entered in the General Stud Book.

toteboard The large sign in the infield of the track. It continually flashes the odds on each horse and indicates the winners.

trotted up Said of a horse when it has won with ease.

trotter A harness racing horse

which moves with a high-stepping diagonal gait.

walk-over The result when only one horse is left in a race. The horse has only to be ridden past the judge's box to be declared the winner.

weighing-in The practice of weighing a jockey after a race; usually confined to the riders of the first four horses. If a jockey's post-race weight falls below the weigh-out weight by more than a permitted amount, his horse is disqualified.

weighing-out The practice of weighing every jockey before a race. Weighed with each jockey are his silks, the saddle, breast-plate, martingale, number cloth, blinkers and any lead make-up weight.

weight-for-age Races in which a scale of weight allowances operates according to a horse's age, the distance and the time of year.

win The horse who comes in first.

yearling A horse between one and two years of age.

Polo

A game contested by two teams of four horsemen, polo has its antecedents in the ancient Persian game of *changar*, meaning a mallet. American players still refer to the implement used to hit the ball as a mallet; to the British it is simply a stick, or polo stick. The name polo derives from the Tibetan *pulu* (a ball), reflecting its nineteenth-century discovery in the northern frontier areas of India by British cavalry officers serving under the Raj. They gave polo its modern character and in 1869 took it to Britain; by the early 1880s it was being played in North America, and today there are polo clubs in numerous countries.

The players' aim in polo is to score more goals than the opposition during the number of chukkas played. To achieve this, they display a high degree of teamwork, horsemanship and strokeplay as they move the ball about the field of play or ride-off opponents. There is no offside rule, but right of way must be respected. A unique rule confines all players to using only their right hand for holding the mallet. Play commences with a center-field throw-in, the two teams lining up according to their numbered positions: 1, 2, 3 and 4 (or back). Once the ball is in play, No. 1 becomes the spearhead of the attack; No. 2 is the orchestrator, determining tactics and linking defense and attack. No. 3 and No. 4 play a primarily defensive role, guarding the opposing Nos. 2 and 1 respectively. Nonetheless, because polo is fast and fluid, players must be able to adapt themselves to other roles as the run of play dictates. All players are given a handicap rating within a format initially devised in America in 1891 and adopted internationally in 1910. Polo 'ponies' of any height may be played.

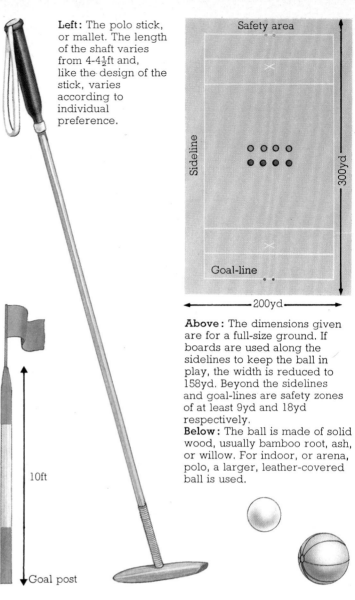

Left: The polo stick, or mallet. The length of the shaft varies from 4-4½ft and, like the design of the stick, varies according to individual preference.

10ft

Goal post

Above: The dimensions given are for a full-size ground. If boards are used along the sidelines to keep the ball in play, the width is reduced to 158yd. Beyond the sidelines and goal-lines are safety zones of at least 9yd and 18yd respectively.
Below: The ball is made of solid wood, usually bamboo root, ash, or willow. For indoor, or arena, polo, a larger, leather-covered ball is used.

Safety area · Sideline · 300yd · Goal-line · 200yd

all risks A captain's command to his team to forsake defensive measures and make an all-out assault to score a goal.
approach shot A long-distance shot intended to stop before the ball reaches the goal so that the striker or a team-mate can attempt a second shot with greater accuracy.
arena polo A three-a-side game played with a soft, leather-covered ball on a ground within an open-air or covered walled area. The playing area is much smaller than that for standard polo. Also known as indoor polo, it is played extensively in Argentina and the United States.
back The No. 4 player.
backhander A stroke which hits the ball in a backwards direction.
boards The barriers which may extend along the sidelines of the playing area to keep the ball in play.
brace The standing-in-the-stirrups position adopted by a player when playing his shot.
change of ends Teams change

ends after every goal (except in the event of a penalty goal) or, if no goals have been scored, at half-time.
chukka The colloquial Indian name for a period of play. The duration of actual playing time is 42 minutes divided into 6 periods of 7 minutes each with specified intervals between each period. Matches played under local rules may not have so many chukkas.
circular wind-up Method sometimes used to play off-side strokes. The mallet is swung through one and a half revolutions on the player's right-hand side before he makes contact with the ball.
crossing Riding across or entering another player's right (*qv*) of way. It is an infringement if there is risk of a collision or danger to any of the players involved.
cut A stroke made at an angle away from the pony's line of advance.
disengage stroke A feint at the ball by a player in an attempt to

draw his opponent into an early hook (*qv*). If successful, he withdraws his mallet and beats off that of his opponent before playing his shot.
drive A forehand or backhand shot made in a line parallel to the pony's line of advance.
forehander A stroke which hits the ball in a forwards direction.
free hit An unimpeded hit at the ball awarded to the non-offending side in the event of an infringement of the rules.
hammer stroke A method of playing an off-side backhander by swinging the mallet all the way through on the right-hand side of the body instead of bringing it from across the body.
handicap The means of rating a player according to his status as a player and his value to a team. Handicaps range from −2 to +10 goals; the higher the handicap the better the player. A *team handicap* is the aggregate of its players' handicaps. The number of goals start awarded to a weaker team is obtained by sub-

tracting its handicap (the smaller total of goals) from the higher one of its opponents. If a full number of chukkas is not being played, the goals start must be reduced in proportion. Under HPA rules, any fractions are reckoned as half goals; under USPA rules, fractions larger than a half count as a goal and those less than a half are not counted.
high goal polo Term used when the team handicap of each team in a tournament is 19 or more.
hit-in The method used by the defending side to restart play when an attacking player hits the ball over the goal-line. It is taken from where the ball crossed the line, but not within 4yd of the goalposts or sidelines.
hooking Using the mallet to beat away or deflect an opponent's mallet, so preventing him from making his stroke.
horse A wooden horse, carrying a saddle and used by learners to practise their strokes.

76

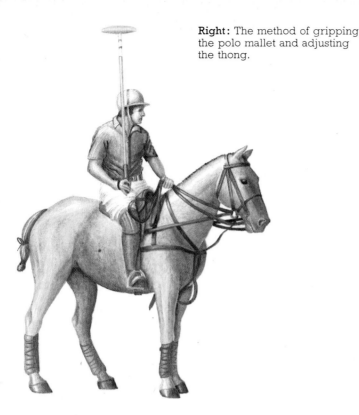

Right: The method of gripping the polo mallet and adjusting the thong.

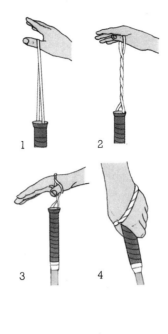

1 2 3 4

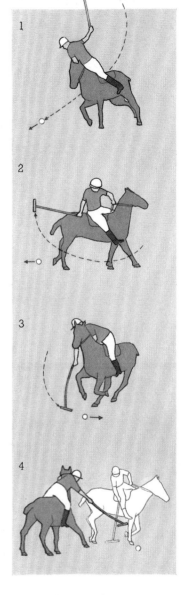

1
2
3
4

Above: Rider and pony in the rest position. Helmets of pith, cork, or a synthetic material of similar hardness and lined with a shock-absorbent substance must be worn and held in position with a chinstrap. Knee pads are not compulsory, but if worn must, like the boots, be free of buckles or studs. Spurs must not be sharp or rowelled.

Provided it is not so badly behaved that it could endanger other horses and players, any type of pony or horse may be played. However, it must be willing to pit its weight against another pony, and must not flinch from the swinging mallet or the ball. Good eyesight is essential, and the rules exclude animals unable to see with both eyes. Boots, fitted like gaiters, or bandages are worn to protect the legs against blows from the ball or mallets.

Right: Playing the ball calls for a high degree of horsemanship, and newcomers to the sport should spend many hours practicing their strokes, first from a wooden horse in a polo pit and then on a quiet pony.
1 The off-side forehander.
2 The off-side backhander.
3 Hitting under the neck from the off-side.
4 Hooking, which is permitted only when an opponent is about to hit the ball and the player hooking is on the same side of his opponent as the ball. Hooking above shoulder height is not allowed.

HPA Hurlingham Polo Association, whose rules of polo, since 1965, have formed the basis of the game in most countries, with the notable exception of the United States.
indoor polo *See* arena polo.
near-side The left-hand side of a pony.
normal grip The grip in which the thumb curls around the handle to rest against the index finger. It is used for off-side forehand shots and near-side backhand shots.
off-side The right-hand side of a pony.
penalty The punishment incurred by a team for an infringement of the rules. It may take the form of a penalty goal, a free (*qv*) hit, a hit-in (*qv*), or the compulsory retirement of a player in the event of injury to a fouled opponent. In addition, a player or a pony may be temporarily or permanently ordered off by an umpire.
penalty goal Awarded by an umpire if, in his opinion, a goal would have been scored but for

a foul by the defending team.
pit, or polo pit The place in which a learner, sitting on a wooden horse, practices hitting the ball.
pony power The allocation of players' ponies so that a team is evenly mounted throughout a match or better mounted in some chukkas than in others.
pull A stroke made at an angle that crosses the pony's line of advance.
referee An off-the-field official appointed to adjudicate in the event of the umpires (*qv*) disagreeing.
reverse grip The grip in which the thumb lies pointing down the handle of the stick. It is used for near-side forehand shots and off-side backhand shots.
ride-off To bump or push against an opponent and his pony to move him from the line of play or stop him from receiving a pass or playing a shot. It must be done while riding in the same direction as the opponent.
right of way A player's entitle-

ment to ride in a forward direction without having to check his pace because of another player. Initial right of way is accorded to any player following or riding to meet the ball on its exact line provided he is taking it on his off-side. If no player is on the exact line, right of way goes to the player following it at the smallest angle.
safety zones Areas set aside beyond the goal-lines and side-lines so that players may cross these boundary lines at speed and at any angle without fear of injury to pony, person, or spectator.
stick The British name for the polo mallet.
stroke The method used to hit the ball. There are four basic strokes: the off-side forehander, off-side backhander, near-side forehander and near-side backhander. Within each of these four categories are the drive, cut and pull. Other strokes include under-the-neck shots, pushes, jabs, disengage (*qv*) strokes and

between-the-legs shots.
throw-in The method of putting the ball into play at the start of a match, after a goal, or when the ball crosses a sideline, lodges in a player's clothing, or becomes damaged. The umpire bowls the ball underhand and hard between the two teams, who line up facing the umpire, each player paired-off opposite his corresponding number.
topping Hitting too high up on the ball as a result of forcing the hand ahead of the stick instead of letting the stick carry the hand along.
umpires The two mounted officials who control the match from the field of play. In most instances, each takes responsibility for one half of the field.
under-the-neck shots Strokes in which the mallet is swung under the pony's neck to hit the ball at right angles to the line of advance.
USPA United States Polo Association.
wooden horse *See* horse.

77

Show Jumping

Show jumping, thanks to television, is today known to millions, and so successfully have the rules been simplified that most understand the formula of competitions. A rider attempts to take his or her horse around the course of jumps without accumulating faults for knocking down an obstacle, or a part of it, stepping in the water, or a refusal to jump. If time is being taken into account—as in a jump-off against the clock—riders try to complete the round as quickly as possible. Scoring of faults depends on the type of competition, of which there are basically three: those testing jumping but also taking into account the time taken; puissance, which tests jumping skill only; and speed competitions, which put the emphasis on speed and agility. The first two, which represent the majority of jumping competitions, are scored according to a rule known as Table A. Other tables are used for speed competitions. Under Table A, four faults are given for every obstacle knocked down or failure to clear the water; eight for a fall by horse or rider. Three faults are given for a first disobedience, six for a second, plus in each instance time penalties if an obstacle is knocked down. For a third refusal a competitor is eliminated. In addition, time faults are given for exceeding the time allowed.

Developed during the nineteenth century by cavalrymen and huntsmen, show jumping today is a major international sport with quadrennial open world championships, inclusion in the Olympic Games, and competitions such as the Nations' Cup. With sponsors generous in their allocation of prize money, there is a succession of indoor and outdoor meetings throughout a long season, and even for the amateur rider, show jumping has become a full-time concern.

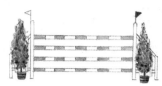
Post and rails

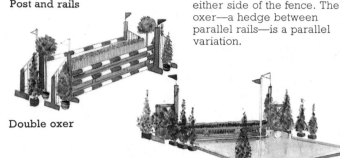
Double oxer

Water jump

Left and below: There are three basic types of fence: vertical, parallel and staircase, as well as permanent hazards such as banks and water jumps. An example of the classic vertical is the post and rails: there are no obstructions on either side of the fence. The oxer—a hedge between parallel rails—is a parallel variation.

A typical course

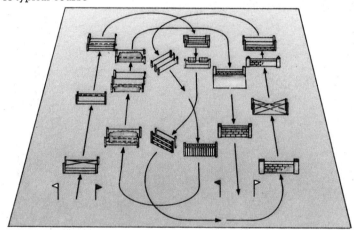

arena The enclosed area within which a show jumping event is contested.

bank A permanent obstacle in an arena but not always included in the course. The horse approaches the top of the bank, sometimes over a jump, and has to get down the face of the bank as best it can.

barème Literally a scale or table; refers to the table of rules used for judging competitions under international rules.

barrage A jump-off (*qv*).

brush and rails An upright obstacle comprising brush surmounted by one or more poles.

clear round A round jumped without incurring any faults.

collecting ring A ring or enclosed area near the main arena and from which riders make their entrance. If there is sufficient space, it may contain practice jumps.

combination jumps Two (double), three (treble), or more obstacles placed within 12m of each other so that the horse is required to

take a definite, and restricted, number of strides between each element. It is considered to be one obstacle and refusal at any element means the whole obstacle must be jumped again.

course The route from start to finish with the obstacles usually being taken in a set order. The maximum length of a course, measured in meters, is the number of obstacles multiplied by 60.

CSI Concours de Saut International; a competition open to foreign riders, run under FEI (*qv*) regulations, provided they have been invited by the host country and have the permission of their own national federation.

CSIO Concours de Saut International Officiel; an official international show, run under the regulations of the FEI, at which a Nations' Cup competition is held. Each country in Europe is limited to one CSIO a year. Other countries are permitted to hold two.

derby A jumping (*qv*) derby.

deviation When a competitor fails to follow the plan of the course, goes the wrong side of a flag, takes an obstacle out of the correct order, misses one, or jumps an obstacle not forming part of the course. If corrected before the next obstacle, the deviation is penalized as a disobedience, but if it is not corrected the rider is eliminated.

disobedience An offense incurring faults for a refusal, running out, or resistance; a rectified deviation; for circling (except after a refusal or running out); or for passing an obstacle and then approaching it sideways, zigzagging, or turning sharply towards it.

fault A penalty point received for knocking down an element of an obstacle or failing to clear the water jump cleanly; for a fall; or for disobedience.

FEI Fédération Equestre Internationale. The international body governing competitive equestrian sport including showjumping.

grand prix The major individual competition at an international show jumped under Table A. In the Olympic Games, it is the competition for the individual medals.

high jump A competition in which there is only one obstacle, which increases in height when it has been successfully cleared. The obstacle should be a spread (*qv*) as opposed to an upright (*qv*).

hog's back A spread obstacle consisting of three parallel poles.

impulsion The horse's power, under the control of the rider, as it approaches and jumps an obstacle.

interrupted time The stopping of the clock during a competitor's round. The reason for interrupted time is when a fence has to be rebuilt after being knocked down by a refusal.

jumping derby A competition over a long course which includes natural obstacles, such as a bank.

jump-off A deciding round held

Left: To the average spectator the water jump is one of the most exciting hazards to watch. In a purely physical sense, it probably demands less of the horse than some other jumps, but its punch lies in its ability to disturb the horse's rhythm after completing a number of high fences. Judging the jump can bring much dissension, and at official and international shows and championships a tape must be placed along the edge of the water to show whether the horse has cleared the jump successfully.

Left: The bank is a spectacular hazard, and one at which balance and judgement are tested to the utmost. The rider and horse must be able to determine the angle at which to distribute their weight, going down at slithering speed.

Below: In competitions judged under Table A, a competitor is penalized four faults regardless of whether the bar is simply dislodged or whether it is fully lowered. Further penalties may be incurred for failure to clear the water jump cleanly, for a disobedience, and for a fall. Under Tables B and C, faults are converted into seconds and the classes judged on a time basis.

Faults

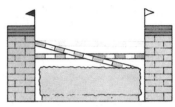

Four faults for dislodging bar

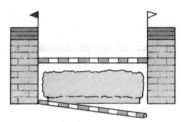

Four faults for bar on ground

after the competition proper to decide the result when two or more riders have tied for first place. Usually, the number of obstacles is reduced, the obstacles raised or widened, and time taken into account.

junior A rider under the age of 18.

Nations' Cup An international team competition held at every CSIO. A minimum of three teams must take part, with at least three riders per team. A team may consist of four riders, in which case only the best three scores in each of the two rounds count towards the team's total. Also known as *Prix des Nations*.

overface To require a horse to jump higher or further than it is capable of achieving.

oxer An obstacle comprising a brush fence or natural hedge with a pole on the take-off side. If there are poles on both sides, it is a *double oxer*. The name derives from the former practice of placing poles alongside hedges to deter oxen.

parallel bars A spread jump made up of poles on separate supports parallel to each other.

placing pole A pole laid on the ground in front of a fence to make sure the horse being schooled meets the fence on the correct stride.

President's Cup The trophy awarded annually to the country with the most points from that year's Nations' Cup competitions. It is effectively the world team championship.

puissance A competition which tests a horse's jumping ability alone over a decreasing number of obstacles, the height of which is increased as the competition progresses. During the jump-offs, the obstacles are reduced to one upright and one spread.

refusal When a horse stops in front of an obstacle and will not jump it. After three refusals it is eliminated.

resistance When a horse fails to move forward. It is eliminated if it resists for more than one minute, fails to pass the starting

line within one minute of the starting signal, or, except in a fall, takes more than one minute to jump an obstacle.

six bar A competition in which six obstacles, all of the same construction and of the same or progressive heights, are placed in a straight line with only two or three strides between them.

speed competitions Competitions in which the result is determined by the time taken to jump the course. Any faults are converted into seconds and added to the time.

spread An obstacle which is made up of elements in different planes so that the horse has to jump both height and width.

staircase A triple bar (*qv*).

Table A Method of determining the result of a round by allocating penalty points for faults on an established scale. Emphasis is on jumping rather than speed. Time may be taken into account only when several horses are tied for first place in certain competitions.

test Name sometimes given to a puissance (*qv*) competition.

time limit Twice the time allowed for a round or competition. Any horse not completing the round within the time limit is eliminated.

top score A competition in which each obstacle is allotted points from 10 to 120 according to difficulty. Riders receive points for each obstacle jumped clear within 60 seconds (45 seconds indoors). Order of jumping is at the rider's discretion.

touch class A class in which faults are incurred for merely touching an obstacle as well as for dislodging part of it.

triple bar A spread obstacle made up of three poles, on separate supports, in ascending order from front to back.

upright An obstacle with the elements placed one above the other in the same vertical plane.

water jump A spread obstacle comprising a ditch of water 4-5m wide. It may be faced with a pole or small brush fence on the take-off side.

Field Sports

American/Canadian Football

Colourful, violent, and demanding a tactical astuteness better suited to warfare, American football was evolved in the early 1880s under the direction of W. C. Camp of Yale University. It is played professionally, and at college and high school levels where cheer leaders, marching bands, half-time shows, and a general orchestration of noise are as important to the spectacle as the game itself. Apart from minor variations, the rules and aims of football, or gridiron as it is commonly known, do not differ greatly from the student game to the professional one. Actual playing time is one hour, divided into four quarters with the teams changing ends after each quarter, and with a halftime break of at least 15 minutes. However, with the time-outs, substitutions, stoppages for injuries and penalties—not to mention breaks for television commercials—a game can easily take up to 2½ hours. Only 11 players per team may take the field, but playing squads, from which coaches draw on new players, even new teams, to meet offensive and defensive situations, number up to 40.

The aim of the game, as in rugby, is to score points by reaching the opponents' goal-line for a touchdown, which allows a try for a conversion. Points are also scored from field goals and safeties. Movement of the ball is essentially by hand, either by running with it or by passing, with the offensive team permitted one forward pass on each play, or down—usually a spectacular, long-range throw by the quarterback to his ends or backs. On each play, the ball carrier is protected from the opposing players by the blocking of his team-mates as he attempts to advance the ball up field. This need to advance the ball is integral to the game, the offensive team having to gain at least 10yd (9.14m) within a series of four downs if they are to retain possession.

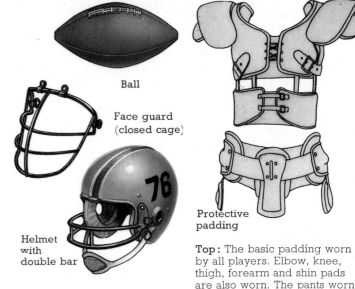

Ball

Face guard (closed cage)

Helmet with double bar

Protective padding

Top: The football has a pointed oval shape. It is about 11in long with a diameter of 7in in the center. Its leather casing covers a rubber bladder inflated to a pressure of 12½-13½lb per sq. in. The ball must weigh 14-15oz one hour before the start of the game.
Above: The helmet is the single most important piece of equipment football players wear.

Most helmets are of the suspension type which never allow the head to come into contact with any solid part of the helmet. They are made to size so that they fit snugly. Every player also wears a face guard—open or closed cage—depending on his position in the field.

Top: The basic padding worn by all players. Elbow, knee, thigh, forearm and shin pads are also worn. The pants worn are specially made of tight-fitting elastic material with pockets on the inside for the knee and thigh pads.

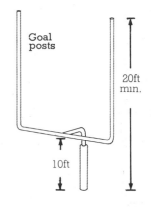

Goal posts

20ft min.

10ft

---

approved ruling An official decision on a play or incident after a discussion of the relevant facts.

backward pass A pass made in a direction backward of the offensive team's advance. If it touches the ground and is recovered by the offensive team, the advance may be continued; if it is recovered by an opponent, the ball is considered to be dead and possession goes to the team making the recovery. Also called a lateral pass.

blitz A defensive play (qv) in which one or more linebackers (qv) or defensive backs rush through the opposition's scrimmage line to get at the quarterback.

block The use of the forearm or body above the knees by an offensive or defensive player to obstruct an opponent without the ball; usually by an offensive player to prevent a defender from getting to the ball carrier.

bowl A football stadium.

broken-field running Carrying the ball against defensive players

without the help of a set-up blocking pattern. The main source of broken-field running is runbacks (qv).

catch To gain possession of a live (qv) ball in flight.

chain gang The official crew stationed on the sideline to measure with the 10-yard chain the distance gained in a series of downs (qv).

clipping Hitting or bringing down an opponent, other than the ball carrier, from behind. Illegal blocking, it carries a penalty (qv) of 15yd (13.7m).

completion Safely catching a team-mate's pass.

conference A group of teams who play against each other as part of a league system. In college football, the conferences tend to be established on a geographical basis.

conversion A successful try for an extra score awarded to a team making a touchdown (qv). In professional football it is worth one point; in college football it is worth one point if a kick over

the opponent's goal, two points if a pass or run into the end (qv) zone. It is taken while the time is stopped. In college football, the play is held on the defensive team's 3yd (2.7m) line; in professional football it is held on the 2yd (1.8m) line. The ball becomes dead as soon as the down ends.

cornerbacks Defensive backs, usually two, who defend against passes and help the linebackers on running plays.

dead ball The ball when it is not live. Among instances of the ball becoming dead are when a player in possession of the ball touches the ground with any part of his body other than his hands or feet, an incomplete forward pass, when the ball goes out of play, or when a fair (qv) catch is made.

defensive backs The backs who are deployed behind the defensive team's linebackers (qv). They are usually the two cornerbacks and two safeties (qv).

defensive team The team which

is not in possession. Defenders try to limit the offensive (qv) team's advance and gain possession of the ball by tackling (qv) the runner, intercepting (qv) a pass, recovering a fumble (qv), or blocking or receiving a punt (qv).

down A unit of play which begins with a snap (qv) from scrimmage and ends when the ball is dead. Within this time the offensive team try to gain yardage by running or passing. They have four downs in which to advance 10yd (9.14m) or they lose possession. A gain of 10yd in four or fewer downs gives the offensive team a new series of downs. The gain is measured by the chain (qv) gang.

encroachment See offside.

end line The boundary line at the end of the field of play on which the goalposts are situated.

end zone The area, 10yd (9.14m) deep, from goal-line to end line.

fair catch The catching of a punt (qv) which has travelled beyond the neutral (qv) zone, by an

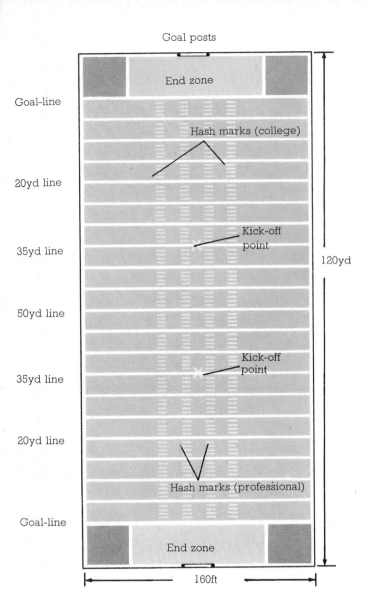

Goal posts

End zone

Goal-line

20yd line

Hash marks (college)

35yd line

Kick-off point

120yd

50yd line

35yd line

Kick-off point

20yd line

Hash marks (professional)

Goal-line

End zone

160ft

A quarterback braces for the handoff

Left: The American football field measures 53⅓yd wide by 120yd long, including two 10yd end zones. Yard lines divide the field at 5yd intervals between the goal lines. Hash marks, in pro football, are placed every yard at 70ft 9in in from each sideline. In college football the hash marks are 53ft 4in in from the sidelines. The Canadian field is

65yd wide by 160yd long, including end zones 25yd deep. Goal posts are situated on the goal line in Canada and at the end line in American football.

opposition player who has clearly signalled his intention to make the catch by raising one hand well above his head. While he is making the catch he may not be tackled or otherwise impeded, and as soon as the catch is made the ball becomes dead. The catcher's team now becomes the offensive (*qv*) team.

field goal A place kick, worth three points, which passes directly between the opposition's goalposts without first touching the ground or a player of the kicker's team. The ball is snapped back to a holder who places it for the kicker. If the kick misses, the ball is returned to the line of scrimmage or to the 20yd (18.3m) line, whichever is further from the goal-line.

first and ten The beginning of a series of downs: first down and 10yd (9.14m) to go. Yardage made on the first down is subtracted to show the yardage still required at the second down; eg 'second and seven' would mean a gain of 7yd (6.4m) is

needed on the next three downs.

flanker back A back who is positioned wide to receive a pass.

forward pass The team in possession is allowed one forward pass in each down; usually by the quarterback with an overhand throwing motion. If the ball hits the ground before being caught, goes out of play, or hits part of a goalpost, it is dead and play resumes at the original line of scrimmage.

free kick A kick-off or any other kick at which players must remain behind established restraining lines until the ball is kicked.

fumble Occurs when the ball carrier loses possession of the ball, either by dropping it or having it fairly knocked from his hands. Unless it is deliberately fumbled forwards (in which event it is an illegal forward pass), either team may recover and advance the ball.

goal-line The transverse line which forms the start of the end zone and on or over which the

ball must be taken for a touchdown (*qv*) to be scored.

goal to go Term used when the yardage to be obtained from a down takes a team to their opponent's goal-line.

gridiron The name given to the field of play as a result of the transverse yardage markings which give it the appearance of a gridiron.

hand-off The action of the ball carrier (usually the quarterback) in handing the ball to a teammate, as opposed to passing it.

huddle The gathering of players on the offensive team prior to the play. While 'huddled' around in a circle, some 9m behind the spot where the ball is lying, they decide on which play to use following the snap. The defensive team may also huddle to prepare their alignment against the offensive team's attack.

illegal motion The illegal forward movement of offensive (*qv*) ends or backs before the snap (*qv*).

illegal procedure The illegal

movement of an offensive lineman after his set and before the ball is snapped from scrimmage. Those players not in the offensive line must be at least 0.9m behind the scrimmage line. The penalty is the loss of 5yd (4.6m).

incomplete forward pass A forward pass which is not held by the receiver and thus results in the loss of the down.

intercept To catch a pass intended for an opponent. Possession then goes to the side making the interception.

lateral pass *See* backward pass.

linebackers Those defensive players positioned a short distance behind the defensive line.

linemen Those players, on both teams, who form up on the scrimmage line. The offensive line usually consists of the center, two guards, two tackles and two ends. The defence may have fewer linemen, usually two tackles and two ends. Linebackers may come up to the line in certain situations.

line of scrimmage *See* scrim-

Below: A place kick being taken. The ball is thrown back by the center between his legs to the holder who places it for the kicker.

Below: The officials' positions at a play's start in a pro game. The referee is in charge and his word is law. The umpire watches for any equipment and line of scrimmage infringements. The linesman has charge of the chain gang. The field judge is responsible for watching kicks and forward passes. The back judge watches pass plays to his side of the field and the number of defensive players on the field at the time of the snap. The line judge has responsibility for timing and scrimmage line plays. The side judge helps the linesman on plays to that side.

Above: The referee is the chief of a team of seven officials responsible for overseeing a game of professional football. The other officials are the umpire, linesman, line back, field judges and side judge. The officials dress in black and white striped shirts and white caps and carry whistles and gold colored flags. Most colleges use five officials; high schools use four.

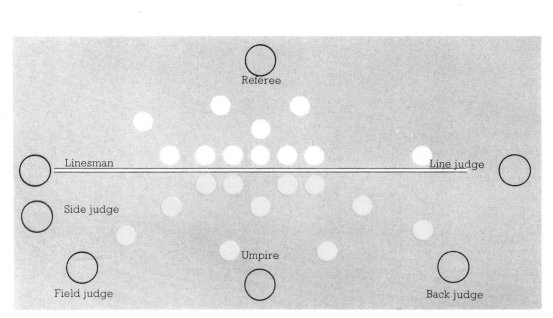

Referee

Linesman — Line judge

Side judge

Umpire

Field judge — Back judge

mage line.

live ball The ball while it is legally in play. When the ball is passed, kicked, or fumbled but has not touched the ground, it is said to be a *live ball in flight*.

loss of a down The offensive team's loss of one of their four downs as a result of a penalty for illegal actions, such as intentionally grounding a forward pass.

major fouls Infringements of the laws involving rough or dangerous play and unsportsmanlike behaviour. Penalties include loss of yardage, and sometimes loss of down, with the ball being moved closer to the offending team's goal-line.

minor fouls Infringements such as offside, illegal procedure and delay of game. Penalties for such offences are a loss of yardage, usually 5yd (4.6m).

NFL National Football League. It consists of two conferences of 13 teams each, the National and the American, each conference being divided into three divisions.

The winners of each division and the runner-up with the best record contest semi-final and final play-offs, the conference winners then meeting in the Super Bowl.

neutral zone The space between the two lines of scrimmage prior to the ball being snapped into play. It is equal to the length of the ball, approximately 11in

offensive team The team in possession of the ball and therefore trying to gain yardage in the direction of their opponent's goal-line.

offside The movement of any player, offensive or defensive, into the neutral zone before the ball is snapped into play. The penalty is the loss of 5yd (4.6m). Also called encroachment.

overtime The sudden-death period of extra time played in the event of a tie. The game is won by the first team to score, but if at the end of 15 minutes there is still no score, the tie stands.

pass A forward throw intended for a team-mate. It ends when the ball is caught, recovered, or considered to be dead (*qv*).

passing play A play (*qv*) in which the quarterback, having received the ball from the scrimmage, drops back to give himself time and balance to make a forward pass to gain yardage. The linemen form a defensive semicircle in front of him to provide protection. The pass must be made from behind the line of scrimmage and, unless the ball is touched by the opposition, may be caught only by the ends or backs.

penalties Major (*qv*) and minor (*qv*) fouls.

platooning The practice of teams who have specialized players for offensive and defensive plays; often even special units who concentrate on select phases such as kick-offs.

play The tactics used by an offensive team in an effort to advance the ball during a down, and by a defensive team to prevent them from making any gain. Plays are decided in the huddle

preceding the snap and are usually called by the quarterback, or sent in by the coach.

punt A kick in which the ball is dropped and kicked before hitting the ground.

quarterback Usually a team's passer of the ball, and often the *alter ego* of the coach; the player who directs the team on offence. At the line of scrimmage he positions himself behind the center to receive the ball.

receiver On an offensive team, the player for whom a pass is intended; on a defensive team, a player who is set to catch the ball from a kick.

recovery Gaining possession of the live ball after it has touched the ground.

runback The advance made by a player after catching an opponent's kick, pass, or fumble.

running play A play in which the quarterback hands the ball off to one of his backs who will try to run around one end of the line or into the line to take advantage of an opening created for him by

84

The snap

Right: A player dives in to tackle another in possession of the ball. Only the ball-carriers may be tackled in this style. There are very strict rules governing the manner in which defense may tackle and offense may block a player. Yet because of the intense rivalry between teams these rules are not always heeded and opponents sometimes are stopped in unnecessarily rough and illegal ways. However, infringements are promptly penalized by having the ball moved closer to the goal-line of the offending team. Players can be disqualified for serious offenses, such as punching and kicking an opponent. It is illegal for a defensive player to tackle or hold an opponent not in possession of the ball.

Left: A quarterback receives the ball from the center The quarterback's hands are placed under the center's crotch with the thumbs together and fingers fanned open to allow him to accept the ball without a fumble. The ball is placed in his hands with the laces of the ball across the fingers of the throwing hand. This allows him to throw or hand the ball off without rotating it in his own hands, which might lead to a fumble. The quarterback is the general of the offensive team, responsible for initiating each play. It is his skill, or lack of it, which determines the outcome of the play. The one forward pass allowed during each play is usually thrown by the quarterback who can make accurate passes of up to 60m.

---

the blocking linemen.

rushing Gaining yardage by running with the ball.

safety (1) A method of scoring in which two points are awarded to the opposition when an offensive team cause the ball to become dead in their own end zone or to go out of bounds from the end zone. Play is restarted by a free kick from their own 20yd (18.3m) line by the team giving up the safety. (2) Name given to the players stationed at the back of a defensive line-up. They are usually positioned further behind the line than the others to provide pass protection or catch the ball if the other team kick.

scrimmage line The imaginary lines, parallel to the goal-lines and passing transversely through the ends of the ball as it lies with its ends pointing up and down the length of the field. Each team, therefore, has its own scrimmage line behind which it must remain until the ball is in play. The area between the two scrimmage lines is the neutral (qv) zone. The number of players on the line depends on a team's tactics, except that the offensive team must have at least seven players on the line.

snap The action of a player in the offensive line, usually the center, in handing or passing the ball back to the quarterback. The movement of taking the ball off the ground and passing it through the legs must be quick and continuous, and the player making it must not move his feet or lift his hand until the ball is snapped.

spotter A coach who is positioned high up in the stadium so that he gets an overall view of the game and sees developments perhaps not immediately obvious from ground level. He is in radio contact with the head coach on the bench.

stiff-arm A method used by the ball carrier to fend off a tackler with his hand. The hand must remain open, not be clenched into a fist.

substitutes Players who come on for tactical reasons or to replace an injured team-mate. Substitution is virtually unlimited (each team may have up to 40 players in uniform) but is allowed only when the ball is dead.

Super Bowl The annual play-off game between the winners of the two NFL conferences to decide the League champions for that season.

T-formation One of the basic offensive formations with the quarterback behind the center and the other three backs behind in a row parallel to the line of scrimmage.

tackle (1) Using the hands or arms to grapple with the ball carrier or to throw him to the ground so that the ball becomes dead. (2) One of the line positions. On offence, the two tackles operate on the left and right of the line between the ends and guards. On defence, they form the line with the ends and sometimes with the linebackers. They are usually the biggest men on the team.

time-out A charged rest period given at the request of a team's captain. Each team is allowed three time-outs of $1\frac{1}{2}$ minutes each per half for tactical discussions, etc, and three minutes for repairs to equipment.

touchback Occurs when the ball, in the defending team's end zone as a result of action by the offensive team, becomes dead in the possession of a defensive player as the result of a kick, pass or fumble by the offensive team; or when a kick carries over the end line. Possession then goes to the defensive team at the 20yd (18.3m) line.

touchdown A score of six points when an offensive player carries the ball into his opponent's end zone, or catches or recovers it on or behind their goal-line.

try An attempt for a conversion (qv).

zone of intense resistance The area near a team's goal-line when their opponents are in possession and are therefore in a likely position to score.

Australian Football

A spectacular, physically demanding game, Australian football—formerly known as Australian Rules—is played by two teams of 18 players on the largest field of any football code. The laws—those there are—have been devised for the safety of the players rather than for such technical niceties as offsides, and this refreshing attitude has produced a game in which stoppages are minimal. Play commences each 25-minute quarter, and after goals, with the field umpire bouncing the ball high in the center circle for the followers to contest and palm-out to team-mates. The aim is to score points, either from goals or behinds, and to achieve this the ball is moved quickly about the field by kicking, punching, or running with it until a player is in a position to try to kick at goal. If run with, the ball must be bounced or touched to the ground every 10m.Throwing the ball, as opposed to punching or palming, is not permitted; nor is direct kicking over the boundary lines. Infringements are penalized by free kicks, which are also awarded for marks. The high-flying marks are a speciality of Australian football, as is the long accurate kicking to team-mates.

Australian football attracts a devoted and aggressively partisan following in its country of origin. Beyond Australia it is virtually unknown. The NFL claim support in all states, and in Papua-New Guinea, but it is only in Victoria (its true home), Western Australia, South Australia and Tasmania that the game really flourishes. Nonetheless, few sports can better the crowds of more than 100,000 that pack the Melbourne Cricket Ground for the annual Premiership grand final. Players in the top leagues receive payments, plus special 'retirement bonuses', but only a few are fully professional.

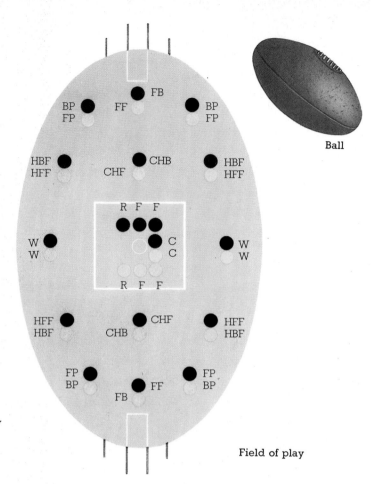

Ball

Field of play

Above: The field of play showing players' positions at the start of play and after a goal. The yellow team is attacking the goal at the top of the diagram. Positions are as follows: FB full-back, FF full-forward, BP back pocket, FP forward pocket, HBF half-back flanker, HFF half-forward flanker, CHB center half-back, CHF center half-forward, W wing, C center, F follower, R rover. Play commences with a field umpire bouncing the ball in the center circle.

all-clear The field (qv) umpires' signal to the goal (qv) umpire that there were no breaches of the laws either before a kick at goal was made or before the goal umpire has signalled. The goal umpires then signal whether a goal (qv) or behind (qv) was scored.

attack All-embracing term for the six forwards (qv).

back pockets The two defensive players flanking the full-back to guard the opposition forwards.

backs The six players who defend their team's goal against the opposition forwards. They consist of three half-backs and three full-backs, two of the latter being designated back pockets.

behind One point scored when the kicked ball touches a goalpost or passes between the goalposts after first touching any player, is kicked or knocked between the goalposts by a defender, or passes directly over a goalpost, or between a goalpost and a behind post. The point is signalled by the goal

umpires waving one flag. Play restarts with a kick by a defender from the goal (qv) square.

behind posts The two shorter posts flanking the goalposts. Each behind post is positioned 6.4m from its corresponding goalpost.

boundary umpires The two umpires responsible for signalling when the ball crosses the boundaries. In addition, they return it to play by standing with their back to the field and throwing it over their head towards the center of the field. Should the ball be kicked out in the air, however, a penalty is awarded to the non-offending team.

centers The three central players whose role is to link defense with attack. The center players near the boundary line are known as wings or *wingmen*.

checking The action of a player who protects a team-mate with the ball from being tackled, either by blocking, pushing, or shouldering the opponent. Such action is legal within 4.5m of the

ball-carrier; otherwise it is penalized. Also known as shepherding.

crumbs gatherer A player who specializes in winning the ball when it comes clear from a pack of players.

defense All-embracing term for the six backs (qv).

field umpires The two officials responsible for controlling the game. They alone rule on infringements, award penalties, and add time-on (qv). They start play at the beginning of each quarter and after a goal by bouncing the ball high in the air in the center circle. Also known as *central umpires*.

flanker Name given to the half-forwards and half-backs positioned near the boundary line.

flying Making a spectacular leap for a mark (qv).

followers The two players on each team whose essential role is to win the ball at set pieces—the center bounces and the boundary throw-ins—and deflect it to the waiting rover (qv). Other-

wise, theirs is a free-ranging brief. Also known as *ruckmen*, followers are among the tallest and strongest players in the team, possessing an ability to leap to prodigious heights, withstand the buffetings from mid-air contact with opposing ruckmen, and at the same time to catch or palm-out (qv) the ball.

forwards The six players who attack the opposition's goal. They consist of three half-forwards and three forwards, the principal forward being the *full-forward* and the other two being the *forward pockets*.

free kick A kick awarded to a player following a mark (qv) or a penalty infringement. It is taken without interference by the opposition, who must remain at least 10m from the kicker. Following a mark, one member of the opposition may stand on the free-kick spot, also known as the *mark*. Any movement over the spot is further penalized by a gain of 15m to the kicker.

goal Six points scored when the

Below: Players flying high in an attempt to claim a mark or to palm out the ball to a waiting team-mate. The mark, or marking—catching the ball above the head or clasping it to the chest—is the most spectacular aspect of Australian football, especially when the giant ruckmen are involved and the marks are of the high-flying variety colloquially known as screamers. It is not uncommon to see players leap 1.5m off the ground to make a mark and so win the right to a free kick.

Left: Dimensions of the oval field of play vary within the minimum-maximum specifications of the NFL: length 135-185m, width 110-155m. The center square is 45 x 45m and the center circle 3m in diameter. The rectangular goal squares extend 9m from the goalposts.

Above: One of the special features of Australian football is the accurate long-range kicking, either at goal or as a way of passing the ball to a team-mate. Kicks are either punts, as in the illustration, or drop kicks.

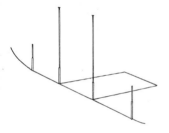

Left: The scoring area, which is marked at each end of the oval. The two central posts, often as high as 15m, are the goalposts; the shorter, flanking posts are the behind posts. The distance between each post is 6.4m.

ball is kicked between the goalposts by an attacking player and has not touched another player en route. The goal umpires signal the goal by waving both their flags. Play restarts with a center bounce.

goal square The 9m-long rectangle extending into the field of play in front of the goalposts. Also known as the *kick-off square*.

goal umpires The two officials, one stationed at either set of posts, who signal whether a goal (*qv*) or a behind (*qv*) has been scored. The umpire at the non-scoring end acknowledges the score by waving his flag or flags at the same time. Both goal umpires, easily recognizable in their white hats and coats, keep an official scorecard.

goalposts The two tall posts, set 6.4m apart, at either end of the oval playing area.

guernsey The player's jersey.

handball The unique Australian football method of hand-passing by holding the ball in the palm of one hand and punching it with the fist of the other. Throwing or handing the ball to another player infringes the hand-passing laws.

high marking *See* mark.

hit-out The action of players, usually the followers (*qv*), in leaping up for the ball and deflecting it to the rover (*qv*) or some other team-mate.

holding the man Law which gives the player with the ball the right to kick or handball it while he is being held by an opponent.

interchange The two players per team who may be used as replacements at any time during a game.

key positions The central positions along the 'spine' of the field between the goalposts. They are usually occupied by tall players.

lead-out The action of a player who makes a sudden move away from his guard to make himself available to receive the ball.

major Colloquialism for a goal.

mark The action of a player catching the ball cleanly on his chest or above his head after it has been kicked. For a free kick to be awarded for taking the mark, the ball must have travelled at least 10m.

NFL National Football League, the governing body of Australian football.

palm-out Deflecting the ball, while in mid-air, to a team-mate. Also known as a *tap-down*.

penalty A free kick awarded to the opposing team in the event of an infringement of the laws.

poster When the ball hits a goalpost. A behind is scored.

Premiership The title contested in a four-match elimination series at the end of the VFL (*qv*) season between the four leading teams in the league.

rover The player who works in concert with the two followers, collecting the ball from their palm-outs and initiating fresh attacks.

ruck Name given to the two followers and the rover, whose free-ranging role takes them all over the field to contest possession of the ball.

screamer Colloquialism for a spectacular mark.

shark To wait around a pack of players jumping for the ball in order to gain possession should it bounce loose.

shepherding *See* checking.

shirt-front Colloquialism for a vigorous shoulder charge on an opponent's chest or running with full force directly into him.

spearhead A full-forward; also the team's leading goal-kicker for a season.

stab pass A fast, low-trajectory drop-kick to a team-mate.

tackle The means of stopping a player with the ball. Tackles must be made below the ball-carrier's shoulders and above his knees.

time-on The time added on at the end of each quarter to compensate for any time lost from stoppages in play. It is signalled to the timekeepers by the field umpires.

VFL Victoria Football League.

wings The center players positioned near the boundary line.

Baseball

Baseball was developed in the United States even though its origins date back to 17th century England. Regarded as America's national game, baseball is not, however, restricted to the United States alone. It is a major spectator sport in Japan, while it has strong support in Latin America, some European countries, and, to a lesser degree, in Australia. Softball, which was derived from baseball, is even more widely played. The basis for the game's rules were drawn up in 1845 by Alexander J. Cartwright, whose New York Knickerbockers played in the first game under his rules in 1846, going down 23-1 to the New York Baseball Club in a four-innings game. At that time, the first team to 21 won. Although baseball was at this time an amateur pastime, it did not take promoters long to see its viability as a commercial venture, and in 1871 the National Association of Professional Baseball Players was established as the first professional league, becoming in 1875 the present National League. Today's other major league, the American League, was formed from the Western League in 1900. Teams within these two leagues are enfranchised to cities across the United States and play in Eastern and Western divisions throughout the season. The respective divisional leaders then play off for their league's pennant, and the two champions compete in the World Series, an annual battle watched by the entire nation.

The game itself is played over nine innings by two teams of nine players each. One bats while the other fields. The aim is to score runs by having a batter complete a circuit of the four bases around the diamond, either on one hit or by advancing from base to base during plays. The teams alternate every time three of the team at bat have been put out.

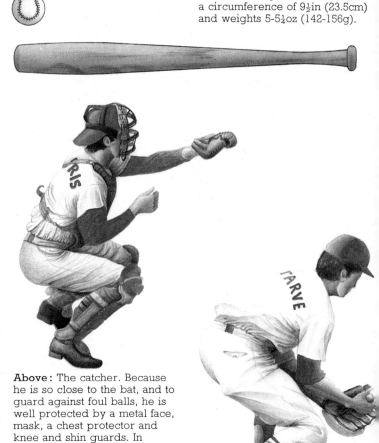

The baseball bat, which is made of hardwood, must be no longer than 42in (1.07m) with a maximum diameter of 2¾in (7cm) at its thickest part. The ball has a circumference of 9½in (23.5cm) and weights 5-5¼oz (142-156g).

Above: The catcher. Because he is so close to the bat, and to guard against foul balls, he is well protected by a metal face, mask, a chest protector and knee and shin guards. In addition, because the ball is pitched at high speed, he wears a larger mitt than the other fielders (right). The players wear shoes fitted with steel cleats.

balk An illegal move by the pitcher. When there are one or more runners on base, it entitles the base runners to move up one base.

ball A pitch which does not pass through the strike zone (qv) and is not struck at by the batter.

base The small area of canvas or rubber set at each of the four corners of the diamond. First, second and third bases are marked by small canvas bags fastened to the ground, while fourth base is the home plate (qv). The base runner must touch every base without being put out in order to score a run, and only one runner may occupy a base at any one time.

base on balls The free walk to first base given to a batter who has received four balls (qv). If there is a base runner (qv) on first base, he moves to second, second moves to third and third to home. However, a base runner already on base is not entitled to advance to the next base if the preceding base is not occupied.

base runner A player of the team at bat who is on or running towards any base.

bases loaded Base runners on all three bases. When there is a force play (qv), all three must run.

batter The player at bat. As soon as he hits the ball to fair territory he becomes a base runner.

battery Term used to denote the combination of pitcher and catcher.

batting average The average number of hits (qv) by a batter in relation to his times at bat. The average is always given to three decimal places. For example, a batter hitting once every four times at bat would have a batting average of .250.

beanball An illegal pitch aimed at, or hitting, the batter's head.

bench Where team officials, players and substitutes sit when they are not taking an active part in a game. It is also known as the *dugout*.

bullpen The special enclosure for the relief pitchers, who warm up there.

bunt A tapped hit, the batter letting the ball come on to the bat instead of swinging at it and following through after contact. The ball stops short within the infield. A bunt rolling over either foul line always counts as a strike. If an attempted bunt on the third strike goes foul, the batter is out, the pitcher being credited with a strike out.

catcher The member of the fielding team who crouches directly behind the batter to catch the pitched ball.

coach Two members of the coaching staff who each stand in designated boxes next to first and third bases. They relay signs (qv) from the manager to the batter and base runners and assist the runners in running the bases.

curve A pitch which, from a right-handed pitcher, swerves in the air downwards and away from the swing of a right-handed batter. The left-handed pitcher's curve swerves away

from the left-handed batter.

designated hitter In the American League only, he is a player named by the manager before the game to bat and run bases in place of the pitcher. The pitcher stays in the game and the designated hitter does not field.

diamond The main part of the infield, so-called because the square area bounded by the four bases, when looked at from behind the home plate, resembles a diamond.

double A hit which enables the batter to reach second base.

double header Two games, played by the same teams on the same day, for which the spectators pay the one admission price.

double play The putting out of two base runners on one play. It is achieved by swift interplay by the basemen, the one obtaining the first put-out throwing the ball immediately to a base to which another runner is advancing in time to put him out also, making two outs.

double steal A stolen base (qv)

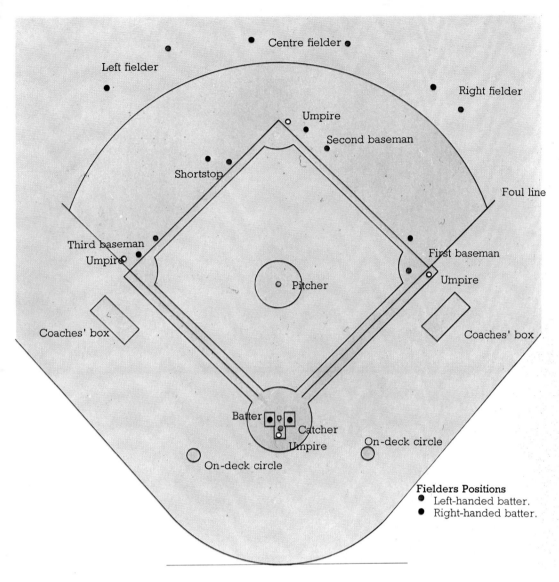

Left fielder

Centre fielder

Right fielder

Umpire

Second baseman

Shortstop

Foul line

Third baseman

Umpire

First baseman

Umpire

Pitcher

Coaches' box

Coaches' box

Batter

Catcher

Umpire

On-deck circle

On-deck circle

On-deck circle

Fielders Positions
● Left-handed batter.
● Right-handed batter.

The game of baseball is played on a field which is divided into an outfield and an infield. The main part of the infield is the 90ft (27.4m) square area known as the diamond. At the right-angles of the diamond, and so 90ft (27.4m) apart, are the four bases through which the base runners travel in an anticlockwise direction. First, second and third bases consist of canvas bags measuring 1ft 3in × 1ft 3in (38 × 38cm) and fastened to metal pegs in the ground; home base, or plate, is a five-sided piece of whitened rubber 1ft 5in (43cm) wide where it faces the raised pitcher's mound. Set in the centre of the mound, and 60½ft (18.45m) from the rear of the home plate, is the pitcher's rubber 2ft (61cm) wide by 6in (15.5cm) long. When at bat, the batter stands in the 6 × 4ft (1.83 × 1.22m) box beside the home plate; the side he uses depends on whether he is a left- or right-hander. When next up to bat, he waits in the '-on-deck circle'.

by each of two base runners at the same time.

duster A fast inside pitch, close to the batter, used to intimidate batters who are crowding the plate. It is differentiated from a bean ball (qv), which is an illegal pitch.

error A mistake by a fielder on a play that should have put out one of the batting team

fair ball Hit that goes into fair territory, the area between foul lines.

fast ball A ball delivered with a backspin, which causes it to break upwards or hop during its flight to the batter. It is held in the fingertips and released with the thumb beneath the ball and the two first fingers pointing over the top towards the batter.

fielder's choice The decision of a fielder to throw to a base, other than first, to put out a preceding base runner rather than the batter.

fly ball A hit that goes in the air. If the ball is caught, regardless of whether the ball was fair or foul, the batter is out, and the

base runners, unless tagging up (qv), may not advance.

force play When the base runner on a base is forced to run because the batter has become a base runner and is advancing to first base forcing base runners on bases ahead of him to move to the next base. The fielder puts the runner out by stepping on the base with the ball in his hand. He does not have to tag the runner.

foul ball A hit which goes behind the foul lines. A batter's first two fouls, but no subsequent ones except for an attempted bunt (qv), count as strikes, and any caught foul is an out. Base runners may not advance on a foul ball unless it is a foul fly ball that is caught.

foul lines The lines extending at right-angles from the home plate through first and third bases to the edge of the playing area.

ground ball A batted ball which skips along the ground.

hit Any hit from which the batter

advances at least as far as first base. It is also called a base hit.

hit and run Runner on base starts for the next base on the pitch with the batter having to swing to protect him.

hit by pitched ball A batter not swinging at a ball is allowed to reach first base if the pitched ball hits him.

home plate The five-sided piece of whitened rubber set in the ground that constitutes home base. The apex of the plate fits into the right-angle of the right-field foul line and the left-field foul line.

home run A complete circuit of the bases by the batter off one hit.

infield fly A ball struck in the air within the infield. If the fly is in fair territory, and if there are fewer than two batters out and runners on at least first and second bases, the umpire rules the batter out automatically if he considers the catch will be taken by an infielder. This is to prevent the fielder dropping the catch

intentionally to set up a double play (qv).

infielders The four fielders who guard the infield area around and in the diamond. They are the three basemen and the short-stop.

inning The turn of both teams at bat. One team's turn at bat is a half-inning. There are nine innings in a game, with extra innings played if the score is tied after nine innings. The team batting second does not have to bat its ninth half-inning if it is already in the lead. The first half-inning is accorded to the visiting team.

intentional pass Allowing a base on balls for tactical reasons, usually to prevent a strong hitter getting base runners on second or third bases home, or to put more than one runner on base to promote a possible double play, or force out. However, the pitcher would not usually walk the batter if first base was already occupied. The side at bat might counteract

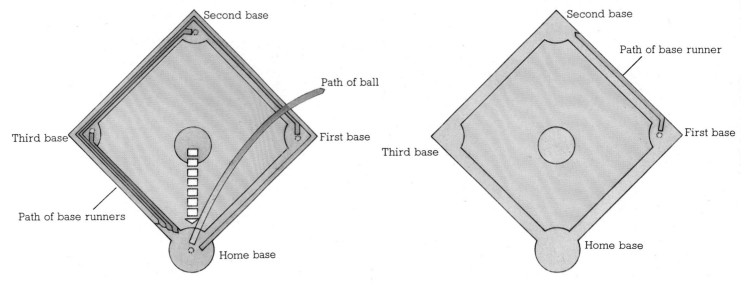

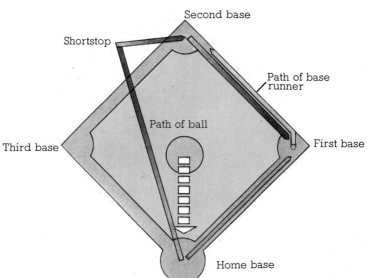

Above: A grand-slam homer, with the three base runners and the batter making home base off the batter's home run hit. A situation in which all three bases are occupied by runners is known as bases loaded.

Above: A stolen base, or steal. The base runner advances from first to second base as the pitcher delivers the ball. He runs the risk of being put out if the pitcher sees him and throws the ball to second base, or if the catcher gets the ball to second base before he arrives.

Left: A double play. Batter hits ground ball to shortstop, shortstop flips ball to second baseman who steps on bag forcing runner from first. He then throws to first to get the batter.

this by introducing a pinch hitter (*qv*).

interference An umpire's ruling that the catcher has interfered with the batter's swing. The batter is allowed to proceed to first base. Or, a batter or base runner interfering with a defensive player who is making a play on another base runner. He is called out by the umpire.

knuckle ball A ball held with the knuckles of the first two or three fingers pressed behind it by the thumb, and delivered in much the same motion as a fast ball (*qv*). The knuckle ball is highly unpredictable and is used by only a few pitchers who specialize with it.

line-up The order in which a team bats throughout the game, also known as the *batting order*.

mitt The glove worn on the non-throwing hand by the fielders.

no hitter A game in which a team fails to make a safe hit. Credit is given to the pitcher who is said to have pitched a no hitter.

obstruction An illegal act by a

fielder who, while not trying to field the ball or not having hold of it, gets in the way of a base runner.

outfielders The three fielders who patrol the wide area of the outfield beyond the base lines. They are called right-fielder, center-fielder and left-fielder, the direction being relative to the right or left hand of the catcher as he faces the pitcher.

passed ball A pitch that the catcher fails to take cleanly and so allows a base runner the chance to move to another base.

pennant The American League and the National League championships. Since 1969 the two leagues have each been split into Eastern and Western divisions and the winners of each division play off for their league pennant.

perfect game A game in which no batter on one team reaches first base by any means.

pinch hitter A substitute batter brought into the line-up in place of a weak hitter when the team

is in need of a hit. The player he replaces is officially out of the game.

pinch runner A substitute base runner brought on to replace a slow-running batter when he reaches base.

pitch The delivery of a ball from the pitcher to the batter.

pitcher The member of the fielding side who delivers the ball to the batter.

pitchout A deliberate ball called for by the catcher when he suspects a base runner will attempt to steal. The pitch is usually thrown wide of the plate to make it easier for the catcher to catch it and throw to the base to get the runner.

play Any action between pitches is known as play generally resulting from an action of the offensive team trying to get on base and score runs while the defensive team tries to get them out.

put-out The act of dismissing a batter or base runner.

relief pitcher A substitute pitcher

brought into the game for tactical reasons, usually because the pitcher is allowing too many hits.

rubber The pitcher's plate set on the pitcher's mound.

run Scored by a member of the batting team who progresses through first, second and third bases to the home plate without being put out.

rundown When a base runner is caught between bases by the infielders.

runs batted in (rbi) The runs credited to a batter in the statistical analysis of his game, seasonal, or career performance. They include his own runs, and also runs scored by any base runner off his hits, bases on balls, or if he is hit by the pitcher and allowed his base.

sacrifice A tactical play by the batting team with men on bases and no more than one man out. The batter hits a long fly into the outfield, or a sacrifice bunt into the infield, knowing he will probably be out, but that these

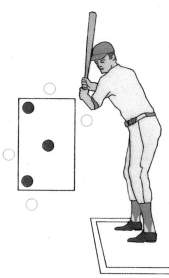

Left: From an initial stance (1), the pitcher goes through a series of movements prior to throwing the ball, the actual delivery action being unique to each pitcher. He may go into his pitch from the hands-above-head position (2) followed by the actual delivery (3). He has at his disposal a variety of techniques to make the ball rise, dip, or swing in flight as it reaches the home plate at tremendous speed. When releasing the ball, he must keep one foot in contact with the rubber, and he must always face the batter when pitching. Should he want to interrupt his delivery to put out a runner stealing a base, he must step in the direction of that base before throwing the ball.

Path of batter's swing

Left: The strike zone. The width of the imaginary box is that of the home plate, while the height is taken as the line from the batter's shoulders to his knees when he is adopting his normal stance. Balls passing inside this area are called 'strike whether or not the batter swings at them; those passing outside are called 'ball'.

moves may allow the base runners to advance.

safe A base runner's arrival at a base without being put out. The ruling is made by the base umpire.

screwball A reverse curve that curves to the right when thrown by a right-handed pitcher and to the left when thrown by a left-hander.

shortstop The infielder positioned between second and third bases.

shut out A game in which a team fails to score.

sign (1) Signal from catcher to pitcher indicating what kind of pitch he wants thrown. (2) Signals relayed from manager to coaches then to batter and base runners directing their actions on the next play.

single A hit which enables the batter to reach first base.

slide The action of a base runner to reach the base and avoid being tagged (*qv*) by a fielder. He may slide feet first to make contact with the bag or dive headlong

and try to grab the canvas with his hand.

slider A curve thrown with the speed of a fastball that breaks late and horizontally on the batter.

southpaw A left-handed pitcher.

spitball An illegal pitch in which saliva or grease is applied to the ball making it move in an erratic manner.

squeeze play An attempt to bring a base runner home from third with a bunt.

stolen base A base runner's advance to another base without the batter making a hit.

stretch One of the two positions used by a pitcher to deliver the ball to the batter. It is often used when there are opposing players on the bases, since he can easily pivot and throw the ball to a baseman, should a player attempt a stolen (*qv*) base. The pitcher must set himself, or stop his motion, before throwing to the plate or to a baseman.

strike A pitch called against the batter. Three strikes and he is

out. The umpire calls 'strike' on a legitimate pitch if the batter swings at the ball and misses it; if it passes through the strike zone; if a hit is a foul, unless the batter has already fouled twice; and if a bunt rolls over either foul line.

strike zone The area the width of home plate between the line of the batter's armpits and his knees when he is adopting a normal stance.

substitute A player brought on to replace a member of the original line-up. Any member of either team may be replaced, but he then cannot return to the game.

switch hitter A batter who can hit the ball right- or left-handed.

tag The fielder's action to put out a base runner. With the ball in his gloved hand, he will put out the runner by touching him before he arrives at the base or by touching the runner while he is between bases.

tagging up A base runner's remaining on his base until a fly ball is caught. He may then

try to advance to next base.

triple A hit which enables the batter to reach third base.

triple play The putting out of three base runners on the one play.

umpire(s) The official(s) controlling the game. The chief umpire stands behind the catcher and calls each pitch 'strike' or 'ball' accordingly.

walk Sometimes used for a base on balls. A pitcher who allows a batter a base on balls is said 'to walk' the batter.

wild pitch A pitch which bounces in front of the catcher or passes so wide of or high over the home plate that he cannot reach it.

windup One of the two pitching positions. Once the pitcher starts his windup he must deliver the ball to the batter in one continuous motion.

World Series The world championship of baseball, contested on a best-of-seven-games basis between the American League and National League pennant winners.

Bowls

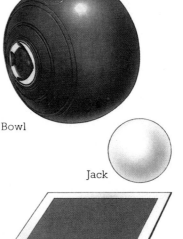

Bowl

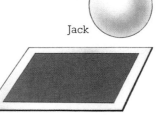

Jack

Mat

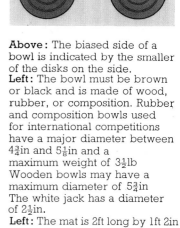

Above: The biased side of a bowl is indicated by the smaller of the disks on the side.
Left: The bowl must be brown or black and is made of wood, rubber, or composition. Rubber and composition bowls used for international competitions have a major diameter between $4\frac{3}{4}$in and $5\frac{1}{8}$in and a maximum weight of $3\frac{1}{2}$lb Wooden bowls may have a maximum diameter of $5\frac{3}{4}$in The white jack has a diameter of $2\frac{1}{2}$in.
Left: The mat is 2ft long by 1ft 2in wide with a 2in white border

It is not surprising that W. G. Grace, legendary figure of English cricket, was keenly interested in bowls; in 1903 he was elected first president of the English Bowling Association. The game demands all those qualities which Grace possessed in abundance: judgement of pace and length, competitiveness, and a modicum of gamesmanship. The aim of the player (in singles) — team in pairs, triples and fours — is to deliver his or her bowls with sufficient draw so that he or she groups as many as possible around the small white jack resting at least 75½ft from the mat. One point is received for each bowl closer to the jack than any of the opponent's bowls. Because of this, resting out an opponent's bowls or trailing the jack is very much part of the game's tactics. In all but singles, tactics are decided by the skip, who advises the other players on the type of bowl to be delivered. In singles, the first player to score 21 points wins; in pairs and fours they play 21 ends and in triples 18 ends, victory going to the team with the most points.

Called lawn bowls to distinguish it from crown green bowls, bowls is controlled for international competition by the International Bowling Board (IBB). It is played extensively by men and women of all ages in the British Isles, Australasia, South Africa, the United States and Hong Kong, while its popularity extends to most countries where Britain has had influence. An indoor form, played on carpets, was propounded by the ubiquitous Dr Grace in the early 1900s and today is widely practiced. Crown green bowls is similar in its aims, differing mainly in that the green is higher in the center than at its boundaries, and that the jack may be bowled in any direction by the player winning the end.

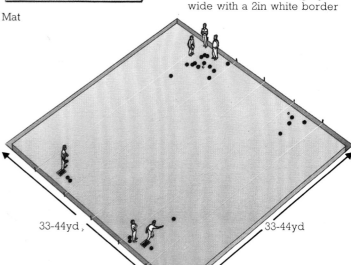

33-44yd   33-44yd

The green

backhand The left-hand side of the mat for a right-handed bowler as he bowls at the jack; the right-hand side for a left-handed bowler.
bias The reason why the bowl runs on a curved, rather than straight, line. It is caused by the built-in imbalance in the spheroid bowl, and is indicated by the disc on the biased side being smaller than that on the side opposite.
block A bowl in the draw (*qv*) or near the center line (*qv*) which prevents an opponent from drawing the jack (*qv*) or firing (*qv*) at it or any bowls in the head.
burned Said of the jack or any bowl that is moved or displaced from the rink, except by a bowl in play.
center-line An imaginary line running the length of the rink between the rink numbers. Sometimes it is partly indicated at either end.
chalk To mark a toucher (*qv*).
cot Colloquialism for the jack.

counter A bowl that has been conceded as a shot (*qv*).
covered Said of the jack when a bowl is in front of it.
dead bowl A bowl that is out of play. Also an illegally delivered bowl.
dead end An end considered not to have been played, and so replayed in its entirety. The usual reason for a dead end is the jack's being driven outside the rink's bounds.
draw The line a bowl should take, allowing for the effect of the bias, when approaching the jack.
drawing the jack Delivering the bowl with sufficient speed and draw that it comes to rest touching or close to the jack.
drive To deliver a bowl forcefully in order to break up the head, so opening the way to the jack for subsequent deliveries, or to force the jack into the ditch.
end The delivery of all bowls from all players to one end of the rink. When the scores have been taken, the next end is bowled in

the opposite direction.
eyes The disks on the bowls which indicate the biased and non-biased sides.
firing shot A drive (*qv*).
follow-on A bowl delivered with sufficient strength to remove any bowls covering the jack and then go on to the jack.
forcing shot A delivery halfway in strength between a running wood (*qv*) and a drive.
forehand The right-hand side of the mat for a right-handed bowler as he bowls at the jack; the left-hand side for a left-handed bowler.
fours A match played between two teams of four players, each delivering two bowls. The leads (*qv*) play their two bowls alternately, followed by the seconds, thirds and skips (*qv*).
green The area on which a number of games are played concurrently. It is divided into a number of rinks (*qv*), six where possible, by linen thread boundary markers. The speed of the green is gauged by the time it

takes a bowl to run from the point of delivery until it comes to rest 30yds (27m) from the front edge of the mat.
hatful The maximum score in one end: four in singles, eight in pairs and fours, nine in triples.
head The jack and all live bowls (*qv*) in play at any given time in an end.
heavy A bowl delivered with so much strength and pace that it overruns its objective.
jack The small white ball delivered at the beginning of each end for the players to bowl to.
jack-high A bowl level with the jack.
kill an end To drive the jack out of the rink, so bringing about a dead end (*qv*).
kissing A bowl just touching the jack.
kitty Colloquialism for the jack.
land The amount of green it takes for a bowl to come to rest in the required position, taking into account the curve of the bias.
lead The first player in a pairs, triples, or fours. The lead of the

The basic grip.

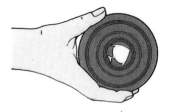

The claw grip.

The cradle grip.

Upright stance

Crouch stance

The delivery

Below: Delivery must be made with one foot on or over the mat.

Right: Examples of tactical moves. In each instance it is black's turn; the red bowl indicates black's move.
1 Black, having the shot, decides to rest out one of yellow's bowls behind the jack in case yellow tries to trail the jack on to it.
2 Black trails the jack away from its original position.
3 In (a), black, trying to anticipate what yellow's next move will be, foresees a possibility for yellow to bring another bowl on to the jack. In (b,) he draws his own bowl in to the jack, so shutting out yellow's chances of getting close without disturbing the head.
4 Black's firing shot rests out yellow's bowl from its advantageous position.

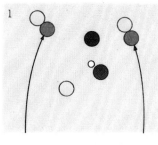

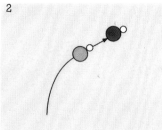

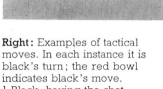

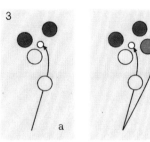

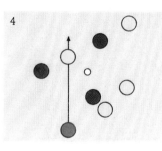

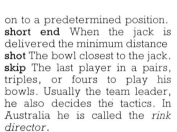

side winning the previous end is responsible for laying the mat and rolling out the jack. As he and his opposite lead play their bowls alternately before the others, he should set the draw (*qv*).

live bowl A bowl which forms part of the head (*qv*) within the rink, or one in the ditch which has been chalked (*qv*).

long end Playing to a jack that is more than 33yd from the mat.

mat The rectangular piece of rubber or canvas from which each bowler delivers his bowls, having one foot on or over it as he does so. It must be placed on the center line (*qv*) and once positioned must not be moved during the end.

measure The device used to determine the distance from bowls to the jack. In instances when the difference is minimal, a micrometer is used.

merry A bowl which is running too fast.

minimum jack Playing to a jack (*qv*) which has been delivered the minimum distance.

narrow A bowl which is not given enough land (*qv*) to compensate for its bias and so runs away from the jack.

opening the head Clearing a path to the jack by scattering those bowls in front of it.

pairs A match played between teams of two players; the lead and the skip. Each player has four bowls, although in some countries both the number of bowls and the order of play varies.

pot A group of bowls, belonging to one player or team, lying behind the jack so that it may be trailed to them.

rest out To push an opponent's bowl from an advantageous position.

rink The playing area defined by the boundary markers which subdivide the green.

rinks Sometimes used to mean fours.

running wood A bowl delivered with enough strength to rest out (*qv*) a certain bowl and then run

on to a predetermined position.

short end When the jack is delivered the minimum distance.

shot The bowl closest to the jack.

skip The last player in a pairs, triples, or fours to play his bowls. Usually the team leader, he also decides the tactics. In Australia he is called the *rink director*.

spring the jack To draw a bowl on to a bowl resting against the back of the jack so that the jack moves forward slightly.

take-out A bowl which removes an opponent's shot (*qv*).

taking the green Using the maximum width of the rink for the bias to take full effect.

tilting Delivering the bowl so that the bias rotates over and over instead of being at the side of the bowl. It is done in an attempt to make the bowl travel in a straight line.

toucher A bowl which hits the jack and is chalked as such before the next bowl is delivered. If it runs on, or is later hit, into the ditch it remains in play

and could still win the head.

trailing A bowl moving the jack from an opposition bowl and staying with the jack as it runs.

triples A match played between teams of three players, each playing three bowls.

tucked in Said of the jack when it is hidden from the view of the bowler by other bowls in the head.

weight The amount of force needed to deliver the bowl a normal length in relation to the speed of the green.

well-paired Two bowls of one player or team close together in the head.

wicking Deflecting a bowl off another so that it changes direction.

woods Another name for bowls. They were originally made of wood (lignum vitae), but can also be composition or hardened rubber.

yard-on shot A delivery which moves an opposition bowl from the jack or trails the jack away from it.

Cricket

Cricket's origins owe as much to speculation as to fact. However, its development from rustic pastime to professional sport is unquestionably English, and it is in the countries of the former British Empire — Australia, New Zealand, South Africa, the West Indies, Pakistan, India, and, of course, England — that the game is strongest.

Although there are references to an early form of cricket in 1300, it was in the eighteenth century that the game made its strongest advance with the first county match — London *v* Kent — in 1719, the drawing up of the laws of cricket in 1744, the addition of a third stump to the wicket, and in 1787 the emergence of the MCC. With the nineteenth century came widespread popularity throughout England, the beginning of a county championship, tours abroad, and in 1877 the first Test match, at Melbourne between Australia and England. There developed a first-class game, shared by players (professionals) and gentlemen (amateurs), a distinction abolished in 1963. The first half of the twentieth century saw cricket follow the pattern established at the end of the previous century, but a drop in support for English county matches brought about a financial crisis which in turn led to the introduction of competitions limited to one innings and with limited overs. These, with their formula to produce a winner at the end of the day, appealed to a greater mass of spectators, and put new life into county cricket.

Despite the subtleties of its laws, cricket is intrinsically simple. One team bats to score as many runs as possible while the fielding team attempts to dismiss ten of the eleven batsmen. This achieved, or the batting team declaring, the teams change roles. A match may consist of one or two innings per team.

The equipment required for cricket includes a bat, ball, stumps, a box or abdomen protector, batting gloves, wicketkeeping gloves and pads. Two types of batting gloves are shown. Batsmen choose a bat to suit their physique and their style of play. The maximum length of the bat is 3ft 2in; the maximum width is $4\frac{1}{4}$in.

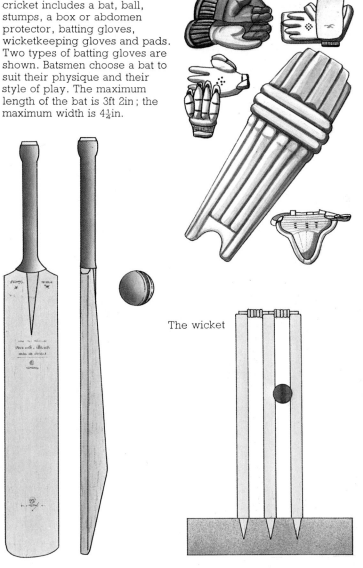

The wicket

---

appeal A question asked of one umpire in the words 'How's that?' by any member of the fielding side when he considers a batsman to be out. An appeal must be made before an umpire can order a batsman out.

Ashes A traditional symbolic trophy, dating from an obituary in the *Sporting Times* in 1882, contested by Australia and England in every Test match series.

body-line A bowling theory in which a fast bowler (*qv*) delivers the ball in an intimidatory fashion on line (*qv*) with the batsman's leg stump (*qv*), and consequently his body.

bouncer A delivery (*qv*), often short-pitched, which rises sharply towards the upper part of the batsman's body or head.

boundary The perimeter surrounding the field of play. *See also* four.

bowler A member of the fielding side who delivers the ball from the stumps at one end of the pitch (*qv*) to a batsman guarding the stumps at the other end. He

may bowl underhand or overhand, provided the umpire knows his intentions, but must not throw (*qv*) or otherwise contravene the no ball (*qv*) law. No bowler may bowl consecutive overs (*qv*). He is credited with dismissing any batsman bowled, lbw, caught out or stumped off (*qv*) his bowling.

bowling crease The line extending either side of the stumps.

box Colloquial name given to the abdomen protector.

bump ball A ball hit so hard into the ground that, on rising into the hands of a fieldsman, it appears to be a catch.

bye An extra (*qv*) scored when the batsmen run when the ball, not having been called no ball or wide (*qv*), has passed the striker without touching him or his bat.

chinaman A left-handed bowler's off-break (*qv*) (to a right-handed batsman).

chucker Name given to a bowler who deliberately throws (*qv*).

covers The sector of the field at

right angles to and 45 degrees in front of the striking batsman's off side (*qv*).

cut An off side stroke played with the bat more horizontal than perpendicular in the sector between cover point (square cut) and third man (late cut).

dead The ball is considered dead if, in the opinion of the umpire, it is settled in the hands of the bowler or wicketkeeper, has crossed the boundary, has lodged in the dress of either batsman or umpire; or if a batsman is out, or if the umpire has called over or stopped play.

declare To conclude the batting side's innings (*qv*) before all ten wickets have fallen. The declaration is made by the captain of the batting side because his batsmen have made sufficient runs, or for tactical reasons.

delivery A ball bowled by the bowler.

draw The result of a match which is not completed within the allowed playing time.

duck A batsman's dismissal without scoring.

extras Runs credited to the batting side but not to the batsman. Byes (*qv*), leg byes (*qv*), no balls (*qv*) and wides (*qv*) are extras, and must be signaled as such by the umpire.

fielder A member of the non-batting side placed in a certain position to catch batsmen out, stop runs, or run out (*qv*) batsmen. One of the fielding side is the wicketkeeper, and any member of the fielding side may bowl except a substitute.

first-class Status given to a match of three or more days' duration between teams adjudged first-class under ICC laws.

flight Variation in the ball's trajectory through the air. Used mostly by slow bowlers in an attempt to make the batsman misjudge where the ball will pitch.

follow on A team is said to follow on when its second innings directly follows its first innings. The captain of the fielding side

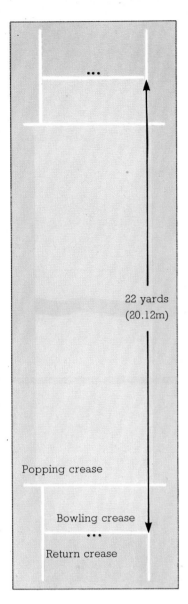

22 yards
(20.12m)

Popping crease

Bowling crease

Return crease

Left: The pitch, which should be set as centrally as possible on the field of play.

Below: The field of play, showing a range of fielding positions that could be deployed against a right-handed batsman (yellow figure). The red figures represent a field setting that might be used when a medium-paced seamer is bowling.
1 Bowler; 2 Wicketkeeper; 3 First slip; 4 Second slip; 5 Third slip; 6 Third man; 7 Gully; 8 Point; 9 Silly mid-off;

10 Cover; 11 Extra cover; 12 Deep extra cover; 13 Mid-off; 14 Long off; 15 Long on; 16 Mid-on; 17 Deep mid-wicket; 18 Mid-wicket; 19 Mid-on; 20 Forward short leg; 21 Short leg; 22 Square leg; 23 Deep square leg; 24 Backward short leg; 25 Leg slip; 26 Fine leg; 27 Deep fine leg; 28 Long leg.

---

may enforce the follow on if the opposing side is a certain number of runs behind his team's first innings' total.

four, or *boundary* Four runs are scored automatically when the ball, having first touched the ground, crosses the boundary.

googly An off-break (*qv*) (to a right-handed batsman) bowled with a leg-break (*qv*) action to deceive the batsman.

half-volley A delivery which pitches (*qv*) just in front of the batsman within the straight flow of the bat. A batsman may turn a good-length ball into a half-volley by moving his feet to the pitch of the ball.

handled ball Unless given permission to do so by the fielding side, a batsman is out if he touches the ball with his hands while it is 'in play' (*qv*).

hat-trick A bowler's taking three wickets with consecutive balls.

hit the ball twice Unless doing so to defend his wicket, a batsman is out if, having hit the ball once, he deliberately hits it again.

ICC International Cricket Conference, the body with international responsibility for cricket. England, Australia, West Indies, India, Pakistan and New Zealand have full membership, while other cricket-playing countries are associates.

in play The ball is in play from the time the bowler commences his run-up until the umpire considers it dead (*qv*). A batsman can be dismissed or runs scored as long as the ball is in play.

in-swinger A delivery which curves in the air into a batsman from his off side (*qv*).

innings One man's or one team's turn at batting. A team continues batting until ten of its eleven batsmen are out, the captain declares, or, in the case of a limited-overs match (*qv*), the allotted number of overs has been bowled. All first-class matches are of two innings per side, whereas a limited-overs match is of one innings per side. A team is said to have won by an

innings if it dismisses its opponents twice while having to bat only once itself.

leg before wicket (lbw) A means of dismissal. The striker, hit on any part of his body or clothing while in a straight line between the wickets, is out if the umpire considers that the ball would otherwise have hit the wicket. He is not out if the ball hits his bat or hand first.

leg-break A delivery which, on pitching, spins into a right-handed batsman from his leg side (*qv*).

leg bye An extra scored when the batsmen run after the ball has struck some part of the striker, except bat or hand, while he was playing a stroke. If no stroke is played, the batsmen cannot run.

leg glance A stroke played by turning the face of the bat to the leg as it makes contact with the ball, so directing the ball down the leg side.

leg side The side of the field of play behind the batsman as he takes up a sideways stance

to the bowler.

length The pitch of the ball after being bowled.

limited-overs match A game, usually played within a day, in which each team's innings is restricted to a certain number of overs.

line The direction, related to the wickets, in which a delivery is bowled.

long-hop A very short-pitched, bad length delivery that allows the batsman plenty of time to get into position before playing his stroke.

maiden over An over from which no runs are scored off the bat.

matting wicket A pitch (*qv*) of cork or synthetic mat over a concrete or packed earth strip.

MCC The Marylebone Cricket Club. Until 1969 the governing body of cricket, it retains responsibility for the laws of cricket. Its headquarters are at Lord's, London.

no ball An illegal delivery, called as such by the umpire if the bowler throws (*qv*) or, at the

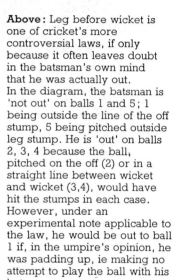

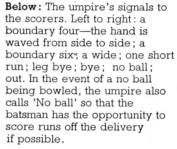

Above: The action a bowler uses to deliver the ball depends to a large extent on the way he feels is most natural, although a coach should try to remedy any faults affecting his performance. One of the basic principles of bowling, fast or slow is, co-ordination of run-up, or approach, delivery, and follow-through. It is important for the bowler to be sideways on in his delivery stride, looking over the top of his forward shoulder at the batsman. Cricket, whether for batsmen or bowlers, is essentially a side-on game, and the bowler who is 'open-chested' in the delivery stride handicaps himself by limiting the body swing he puts into the delivery as he brings his arm over and then across his body in the follow-through.

Below: The umpire's signals to the scorers. Left to right: a boundary four—the hand is waved from side to side; a boundary six; a wide; one short run; leg bye; bye; no ball; out. In the event of a no ball being bowled, the umpire also calls 'No ball' so that the batsman has the opportunity to score runs off the delivery if possible.

Above: Leg before wicket is one of cricket's more controversial laws, if only because it often leaves doubt in the batsman's own mind that he was actually out. In the diagram, the batsman is 'not out' on balls 1 and 5; 1 being outside the line of the off stump, 5 being pitched outside leg stump. He is 'out' on balls 2, 3, 4 because the ball, pitched on the off (2) or in a straight line between wicket and wicket (3,4), would have hit the stumps in each case. However, under an experimental note applicable to the law, he would be out to ball 1 if, in the umpire's opinion, he was padding up, ie making no attempt to play the ball with his bat.

moment of releasing the ball, does not have part of his front foot behind the popping crease (qv) or both feet within (not touching) the return crease (qv). The striker cannot be bowled, caught out or stumped off a no ball but, if he hits it, he may run and those runs are credited to his score. He may, however, be run out (qv). If the batsmen do not run, one extra is scored. The bowler delivers an additional ball for every no ball bowled during an over.

off-break A delivery which, on pitching, spins into the batsman from his off side.

off side The side of the field in front of the batsman as he takes up his sideways stance to the bowler.

out of his ground Said of a batsman who, while the ball is in play, has no part of his held bat or person grounded behind the line of the popping crease.

out-swinger A delivery which curves away in the air from the batsman towards the off side.

over Six or, as in Australia, eight consecutive deliveries by one bowler from one end of the pitch. The umpire signifies the end of the over by calling 'over' when he feels the ball is no longer in play.

over the wicket A method of delivery in which the bowler delivers the ball from the hand nearer the stumps.

overthrow A throw from a fielder which carries past either wicket and allows the batsmen to take another run or runs.

pitch The prepared strip between the two wickets. In addition, the ball is said to 'pitch' when it hits the ground after being bowled.

played on A means of dismissal in which the ball goes off the bat on to the stumps and dislodges a bail. It is recorded as bowled.

popping crease The line 4ft in front of and parallel to the stumps and extending a minimum of 6ft to either side.

retire To conclude a batsman's innings voluntarily.

retire hurt To conclude or interrupt a batsman's innings because of injury or illness. The batsman may resume his innings, with the permission of the opposing captain, on the fall of a wicket.

return crease The line running at right-angles from the popping crease and extending beyond the bowling crease.

round the wicket A method of delivery in which the bowler delivers the ball from the hand further from the stumps.

run Scored when both batsmen cross and safely make their ground behind the popping crease at the opposite end from which they started. If a batsman is dismissed while running, that run does not count.

run out A means of dismissal in which a fielder breaks the wicket with the ball or with the hand holding the ball while the batsman is out of his ground. If both batsmen are out of their ground at the time, the one nearer the broken wicket is out. If the batsmen have already crossed, that run does not count.

runner A player or a substitute who runs between the wickets for a batsman who is incapacitated. He must wear pads and gloves and carry a bat.

scorers Record runs scored and deliveries bowled in official score-books, entering the runs against the name of the batsman scoring them or against the appropriate extras.

seamer Name given to a bowler who attempts to make the ball move off the seam of the ball on pitching.

short run When a batsman, while running, fails to ground his bat over the popping crease prior to setting off on another run. It does not count as a run.

six Six runs are scored without the batsmen having to run them when the ball crosses the boundary on the fly.

spin To impart rotational movement in the ball by turning the wrist or flicking the fingers at the moment of delivery so that the ball moves into or away from the

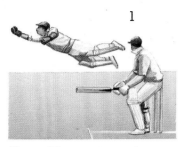
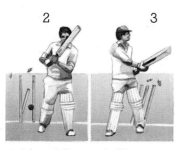

Above: Five ways to end an innings. The batsman can also be dismissed leg before wicket (see opposite). 1 Caught out; in this instance 'caught behind', or by the wicketkeeper. 2 Bowled. 3 Hit wicket. The batsman is out if, when playing at the ball or in setting out on a run immediately after playing at the ball, he breaks the wicket with his bat or person, including his clothing. 4 Stumped. The batsman, having played at the ball and missed, is still out of his ground when the wicketkeeper breaks the wicket. 5 Run out. The batsman, while attempting a run, has failed to regain his ground before a member of the fielding side breaks the wicket, either ball in hand, or by throwing from a distance.

Below: A selection of batting strokes. Left to right: the forward defensive; the sweep (by a left-handed batsman); the hook; the pull; the off-drive.

batsman on pitching.
square leg A fielding position on the leg side, approximately midway between the boundary and stumps in a direct line with the popping crease.
straight bat When the bat is perpendicular in its swing prior to and at the moment of impact with the ball.
striker The batsman facing the bowling. The batsman at the other end is the *non-striker*.
stroke The technique of hitting the ball. Strokes can be defensive or attacking and played off the front or back foot.
stumped A means of dismissal in which the wicketkeeper, without assistance from another fielder, breaks the wicket with the ball, or with the hand holding the ball, while the striker is out of his ground. If he is attempting a run, any dismissal is a run out.
stumps The three cylindrical pieces of wood which, when surmounted by two bails, comprise the wicket. They are known as the off stump, middle stump

and leg stump.
substitute A replacement fielder, usually the twelfth man (*qv*). The opposing captain may object to a substitute fielding in a position at which he is a specialist.
sundries Term used by Australians for extras.
swing The movement of the ball in the air, either into or away from the batsman.
take first innings To bat first in a match.
TCCB Test and County Cricket Board, responsible for Test matches and county cricket in England.
Test match An international match between any two of the six full members of the ICC. Test matches are normally of five days' duration, but may be of four or six days.
throw An illegal delivery and thus a no ball. A bowler is deemed to throw if, at the moment of releasing the ball, he straightens his arm from a bent-elbow position.
tie The result of a match in which

the final scores are level after the team batting last has been dismissed.
toss The tossing of a coin between the two captains. The captain winning the toss may have the option of putting his team in to bat or field first. His decision is of much tactical importance and has to be taken with regard to the playing conditions, strength of both sides, and the duration of the game.
turn Movement of the ball off the pitch on pitching.
twelfth man A team's reserve player. He may field as substitute or act as runner, but he may not bat or bowl. The twelfth man may be changed during a match.
umpires The two officials responsible for controlling the match within the laws of cricket. While one umpire stands behind the stumps at the bowler's end, the other takes up his position at square leg. At the end of the over, they alternate positions. On appeal, they judge wheth-

er a batsman is out, either individually or in consultation, and signal to the scorers any extras, short runs, or boundaries.
wicket The set of three stumps surmounted by two bails at either end of the pitch. For the wicket to be broken, at least one of the two bails must be dislodged. The term wicket is also used to describe the pitch.
wicketkeeper The fielder, protected by pads and gloves, who stands behind the wicket to stop the ball when it passes the batsman.
wickets fallen Term used to denote the number of batsmen dismissed. Only ten wickets can fall in an innings.
wide An extra scored when the umpire considers that a delivery was too high over or too wide of the stumps for the batsman to reach from his normal batting stance. The bowler delivers an additional ball.
yorker A ball bowled without bouncing that passes under the bat as a stroke is being played.

Croquet

Croquet, as it is played today in Britain, Australia, New Zealand and South Africa, owes its development to Victorian England, but its origins are more obscure. A version of the game, known as *Pell-Mell* or *Pale-maille*, was played in London's Pall Mall in the sixteenth century, while *le jeu de mail,* in which a mallet was used to hit a ball through hoops, was a favorite pastime of the French king, Louis XIV. The first championships were held at Evesham, England, in 1867, and in 1870 a set of rules was formulated and the championships moved to the All-England club at Wimbledon. The Hale setting of six hoops and two end pegs was introduced in 1871 and lasted until 1922, when the present-day Willis setting was adopted. Roque, a similar game to croquet but using a different layout, is played in the United States.

The game is played with four balls, one player (or side in doubles) using the blue and black ones, the other the red and yellow. The aim is to run the hoops twice in the correct order and then peg out, the first to peg out both balls winning. The number of strokes taken is irrelevant, and the score is shown as the difference between a maximum total (26) and the hoops scored by the loser. Each loop and the peg is worth one point. Once each player has put his balls in play from one or the other balk line, they take alternate turns, hitting whichever of their own balls they wish. They may extend their turn by making a roquet (two extra turns, the first of which is the croquet stroke), or running a hoop (one extra).

The game, however, demands great skill — considering that the hoops are a mere ⅛in larger than the balls. It involves a wide range of strokes and tactics, calling for concentration and an ability to plan far in advance.

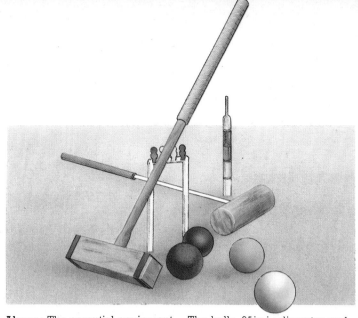

Above : The essential equipment for croquet. The length and weight of mallet used, and whether it is square- or round-headed, depends on the player. The mallet head must be made of wood.

The balls, 3⅝in in diameter and weighing 15¾-16¼oz are made of compressed cork covered with composition or plastic. The iron hoops are 3¾in wide between the uprights and stand 1ft out of the ground. The wooden peg, excluding the detachable piece at the top for the clips, stands 1½ft out of the ground.

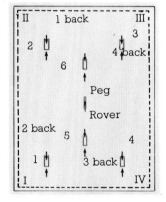

Left : The layout of the court, which measures 35 x 28yd. The longer sides are designated West and East, the shorter sides South and North. The dotted lines represent the balks : south balk from corner I, north balk from corner III. The corner hoops are set 21ft in from the lines, with the penultimate and rover 21ft from the central peg.

angle of divergence The angle at which the balls travel after a croquet (*qv*) stroke.

approach The striker's positioning of his ball to run a hoop (*qv*).

backward ball The ball which has not run as many hoops as a player's or side's other ball.

balk Half of the end yard-lines from corner I to the center and from corner III to the center. The balls may be played into the court from either balk line.

bisque An extra stroke (*qv*) in a handicap game. It may be taken anytime during the game. The number of bisques awarded a player is determined by the difference between his and his opponent's handicap.

break A turn (*qv*) in which two or more hoops are run.

cannon A stroke in which the striker's ball hits two or three other balls. It occurs mostly when the ball to be croqueted is against or close to a third ball so that the striker makes a croquet and then roquets (*qv*) the third ball in the same stroke.

clip The colored marker attached to a hoop to indicate which ball is to run that hoop next. The clips correspond in color with the balls.

continuation stroke The stroke which follows the croquet stroke. The striker may use it to run a hoop or make a roquet.

corner To play a ball into one of the corners as a defensive move.

croquet The first of two extra strokes played by the striker after making a roquet. The striker's ball is placed in contact with the roqueted ball and struck so that they both move. The player is said to *take croquet.*

cut-rush A rush (*qv*) in which the roqueted ball is sent off at an angle to the direction of the stroke.

double tap A foul stroke in which the ball is heard to be struck more than once.

drive A croquet stroke played with the mallet head parallel to the lawn and with a normal follow-through. The term is also

used to denote a rush.

forward ball The ball which has run more hoops than a player's or side's other ball.

four-ball break A break involving all four balls.

free shot A stroke that can be attempted without any danger of giving away some advantage.

full-roll A croquet stroke in which the croqueted ball travels about the same distance as the striker's ball.

half-bisque An extra turn in which no hoop may be scored. A half-bisque is included in handicaps up to 7½.

half-roll A croquet stroke in which the croqueted ball travels two or three times as far as the striker's ball.

hammer shot A stroke in which the mallet is brought down on the ball. It is used mostly when the striker's ball is so close to another ball or a hoop that the striker cannot swing his mallet freely at it.

in hand Used to describe the ball which has made a roquet.

lay a break To position the balls in such a way that a break can be made in the same turn or in the next turn.

lay up To arrange the balls at the end of a turn.

leave The position of the balls at the end of a turn.

lift Moving a ball from where it was lying, perhaps in the instance of a wire (*qv*), and playing it from balk.

make a hoop To score a hoop in its correct order. The ball must enter through the playing side (*qv*) and pass completely through the uprights. It entitles the striker to another stroke.

middle ball Also known as the pivot (*qv*).

ordinary stroke A stroke with which a player can either run a hoop or roquet another ball.

outplayer The non-striking player or side.

pass-roll A croquet stroke in which the striker's ball travels further than the croqueted ball.

peel For the striker to send any other ball apart from the one he

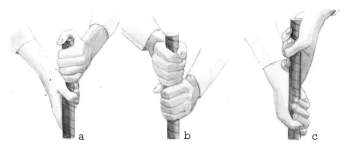

a   b   c

a   b

Left: The side style (a) and the center style (b). The side style, in which the mallet is swung outside the feet, may be played with either foot forward, balance while swinging the mallet being one of the important deciding factors. In the center style, the left foot should be placed ahead of the right so that the right arm has more room to swing.

Left: The grip used is as individual to a player as his or her style. The standard or reverse palm grip (a) can be used for either the center or the side style, with the hands moving as much as 11¾in apart up and down the shaft. The Solomon grip (b) and Irish grip (c), in which the hands may also be interlocked, are used for the center style.

Right: Two examples of the rush, a roquet stroke that sends the roqueted ball to a predetermined position. In the top illustration, the striker's yellow ball hits red at an angle to rush it in the direction of the arrow. The lighter colors denote the original positions of the balls. In the center illustration, yellow rushes the red ball in a straight line.

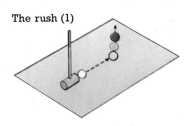

The rush (1)

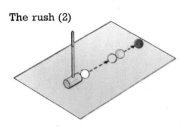

The rush (2)

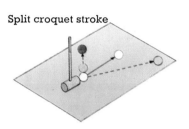

Split croquet stroke

The grip and the stance for the pass-roll. To play a more conventional roll or a half-roll, the striker has his hands higher up the shaft.

The hammer stroke is used where a hoop or another ball prevent a free swing. The player is aiming to hit the ball between his legs.

A jump stroke is played by hitting down on the ball. The mallet is swung through the legs with the head at an angle.

Above: A split croquet stroke. The lighter colors denote the position of the red and yellow balls before being hit. White is an imaginary ball which the striker has in his mind's eye as the line of aim for his swing. Its position is determined by fixing a point midway between the positions to which he wants to send red and yellow.

is playing through its next hoop in order.

peg out To hit the peg and thus remove that ball from the game.

penultimate The name given to the next to the last hoop.

pick up a break To arrange the balls for a break and then make the break during that same turn.

pilot The ball off which the striker makes a hoop in a four-ball break. Having made the hoop, he roquets and croquets the pilot so that it becomes the pioneer for his hoop after his next hoop.

pioneer The ball the striker has positioned at the hoop after his next hoop in order to make his four-ball break. When he arrives at the second hoop, the pioneer becomes his pilot.

pivot The ball the striker has positioned between his next two hoops in a four-ball break.

playing side The side of the hoop through which a ball must pass in order to run that hoop correctly.

pull The tendency of the cro-

queted ball in a split shot (qv) to come round towards the angle of the striker's ball.

roll A croquet stroke in which both balls travel some distance.

roquet The striker's ball hitting another ball, provided the striker has not already roqueted that ball since last running a hoop. A roquet entitles the striker to a croquet stroke and a continuation stroke.

rover The last hoop. The term is also used to denote a ball that has run the last hoop.

run a hoop To make a hoop (qv).

rush A roquet stroke that sends the roqueted ball to a predetermined place.

scatter To separate balls lying close together.

single peel A break in which another ball is peeled through the rover hoop and pegged out to finish the game.

split shot A croquet stroke in which the two balls travel at different angles. If the stroke is, say, a roll (qv) or stop-shot (qv), it is known as a split

half-roll or split stop-shot.

stop-shot A croquet stroke in which the croqueted ball travels the greatest possible distance in relation to the striker's ball.

striker The player whose turn it is to hit the ball.

stroke Can be one of several things: a single hit; the mallet's hitting a ball and so moving it, however accidentally; failing to make contact with the ball following a swing. It also counts as a stroke if a player signifies that he does not wish to take his turn.

take-off A croquet stroke played so that the balls part almost at right-angles. A *fine take-off* is one in which the croqueted ball hardly moves, while a *thick take-off* is one in which the roquet ball travels a short distance but the striker's ball goes further.

three-ball break A break involving only three balls.

tice A ball, usually played from balk, which is hit a certain distance to entice the outplayer to

aim at it and, so the striker hopes, miss.

triple peel A break in which the striker, while running hoops for his own ball, peels another through the last three hoops and pegs it out.

turn One stroke or a series of strokes from one player. The turn ends when he fails to roquet or run a hoop, if he plays a foul stroke or the wrong ball, or, while taking croquet, either his own ball (without having first made a roquet or running a hoop) or the croqueted ball goes off the lawn.

two-ball break A break involving only two balls.

uprights The sides of the hoops.

wired Term used to describe a ball which cannot be hit by the striker's ball because a hoop or the peg is in the way. It also applies if a hoop or peg interferes with the swing of the mallet when the striker is trying to roquet another ball. The ball is said to be *wired* from the striker's ball.

Golf

Poor Robert Robertson; convicted and fined in 1604 for 'profaning the Lord's Sabbath, by absenting [himself along with others] from hearing of the Word, and playing at the Gowf on the North Inch, Perth, in time of preaching'. In more modern times it has been known for services to be shortened to allow golfers in the congregation to be on the first tee in time to commence their games. Such has become the hold of golf: a game so simple in concept and yet so frustrating in execution. It consists of hitting a small ball with a club from the teeing ground to the green, where it is putted into a small round hole. The whole operation should be performed with the least number of strokes. Unhappily, courses are designed to make this more difficult than it need be, once the actual technique of hitting the ball has been mastered. Rough terrain beside the fairways, trees, water hazards and bunkers: all are much beloved by course architects as they do their best to recreate the hazards that confronted sixteenth- and seventeenth-century Scots as they sent balls flying over heather and sand on improvised seaside courses.

In golf, each player has theoretically an equal chance of victory, thanks to the system of handicapping which operates wherever the game is played. Indeed, for many players the aim is not just to beat an opponent but to reduce that handicap, so proving tangibly that their game has improved. There are two principal forms of competitive play—stroke play and match play—and games may be between individuals or pairs, the latter either as fourballs or foursomes. In the United States stroke play predominates at club level, elsewhere, while match play is the more commonly used form, stroke play is reserved for tournaments.

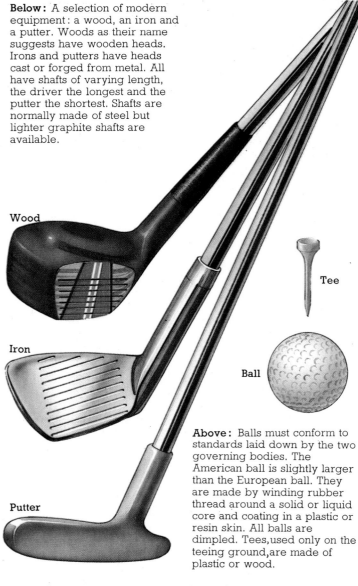

Below: A selection of modern equipment: a wood, an iron and a putter. Woods as their name suggests have wooden heads. Irons and putters have heads cast or forged from metal. All have shafts of varying length, the driver the longest and the putter the shortest. Shafts are normally made of steel but lighter graphite shafts are available.

Wood

Iron

Putter

Tee

Ball

Above: Balls must conform to standards laid down by the two governing bodies. The American ball is slightly larger than the European ball. They are made by winding rubber thread around a solid or liquid core and coating in a plastic or resin skin. All balls are dimpled. Tees, used only on the teeing ground, are made of plastic or wood.

---

address To adopt a stance prior to commencing the swing (*qv*).

air shot A swing of the club which fails to make contact with the ball. Nonetheless it counts as one stroke (*qv*).

albatross A score which is three strokes under par (*qv*) for the hole (*qv*).

apron The area surrounding the green (*qv*), but is not mown as closely as the green itself.

backspin Spin imparted on the ball so that it pulls up quickly on pitching or, if the conditions are suitable, rolls backwards.

balloon To hit the ball almost vertically so that there is negligible forward movement.

bare lie When the ball comes to rest on a hard patch of ground with no grass.

birdie A score which is one stroke under par for the hole.

bisque A stroke conceded as a handicap. It may be taken at any time of the match, provided it is claimed before the player begins play on the hole.

block shot A shot that goes to the right (or left if played by a left-hander); caused by an open club face.

bogey A score which is one stroke over par for the hole.

borrow The amount a putt will move from a straight line when putted on a slanting green.

brassie The name given to the No. 2 wood (*qv*).

bunker A deliberate hazard built into a course to emulate those sandy depressions, caused by wind erosion, which are a feature of Scottish links.

caddie The person who carries or handles a player's clubs and generally advises him on the distance of holes and the best way to play them.

card The official scorecard for the course, showing the distance, par and stroke index of each hole as well as leaving a place for the player's score at each hole.

carry The distance the ball travels from the point where it was struck to where it first bounces on landing.

casual water A temporary accumulation of water, usually the result of heavy rainfall and not a planned feature of the course.

chip A low approach to the flagstick (*qv*) from a lie (*qv*) close to the green. It is not recommended if a hazard is in the way.

choke down To play a shot with less than the full power normally associated with the club because a full shot would be too strong and the next club up would not be strong enough. It is played with the hands lower down the shaft and the stance narrower than normal.

club The implement for striking the ball. Basically there are four categories: woods, irons, wedges and putters. The number of clubs a player may carry is limited to 14.

course The laid-out area on which golf is played. A full course has 18 holes, but where there is insufficient land a course may have only 9 holes.

cut-up A high shot played with spin.

divot A strip of turf lifted out of the ground while playing an iron shot. Golfing etiquette demands that a player replaces and treads down any divots for which he is responsible.

dog-leg Name given to a hole which changes its direction to the left or right between the teeing (*qv*) ground and the green.

dormie Term used in match (*qv*) play for the state of the match when a player is as many holes up as there are holes still to play. His opponent, therefore, must win all the remaining holes to draw level.

draw A shot which intentionally makes the ball in flight curve slightly to a right-handed player's left; or a left-handed player's right.

drive To hit the ball from the tee, using either the woods or irons. It is the essential golf shot.

driver The name given to the No. 1 wood.

driving range A practice facility of US origins. It usually consists

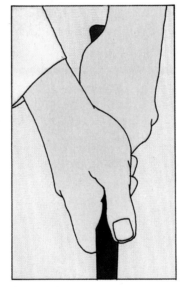

Above: Swings differ because of differences in both physique and technique, but the key to a good swing is the golfer's ability to repeat it constantly. The swing begins from the address position. The arms, shoulders and hands swing the club back in an arc to a position that allows the golfer to swing down powerfully and smoothly at the ball. The head remains still throughout the movement. The legs drive the shot forward and the body and arms follow through towards the target. The purpose of the swing is to allow the clubhead to hit the ball squarely and solidly on impact.

Left: The correct address is essential for a proper backswing. It allows the arms to swing freely through the ball.

Left: Correct positioning of the hands on the club is most important. The hands are united by overlapping or interlocking the little finger on the right hand with the index finger on the left (right-handed player). Two knuckles will be visible on the left hand and the palm of the right hand should face the target. The Vs formed between both thumbs and index finger should point over the right shoulder.

of a row of bays from which golfers hit a succession of balls into an open space.

drop A player's right, under the rules of the game, to put down a new ball for a ball lost in a hazard or remove the ball from an unplayable lie and put it down where it can be played. Depending on the circumstances the drop may be allowed free of penalty, or it may incur one penalty stroke. It is made by the player dropping the ball over his shoulder while facing the hole.

duck-hook A hook (*qv*) which veers sharply to the left (right for a left-handed player) and hardly leaves the ground.

eagle A score which is two strokes under par for the hole.

explosion shot The shot used to play out of a bunker; so called because the clubhead sends up an 'explosion' of sand with the ball.

fade A shot played intentionally to make the ball in flight curve slightly to the right-handed

player's right; or the left-handed player's left.

fairway The stretch of specially prepared turf between the teeing ground and the green.

flagstick The shaft which is placed in the center of the hole, a flag flying from the top end to indicate the position of the hole. The player may ask for it to be removed before he plays a shot. If, from a shot off the green, the ball comes to rest against the flagstick and falls into the hole when the stick is removed, the player holes (*qv*) out. If a putt on the green hits the flagstick, a penalty is incurred.

flier Term for a ball which is hit when there is grass between the surface of the clubhead and the ball. The ball flies further than intended.

forward press A slight forward movement of the hands before commencing the swing.

fourball A match in which four players compete, each playing his own ball. If playing as

partners, they take the better score at each hole as their score.

foursome A match in which four players compete in pairs, playing with one ball per pair. The players in each partnership play alternate shots and alternate the drive from the tee at each new hole.

green The specially prepared putting surface into which a hole of 4¼in diameter is sunk. The hole is marked by a flagstick.

gross score The total number of strokes taken, including penalties, to complete a round before the handicap allowance is deducted.

handicapping The system of awarding players bonus strokes so that they can meet other golfers on equal terms. Many countries establish handicaps on a rating known as the Standard Scratch Score, which is based on the aggregate length of the course. For stroke play, a player's handicap, which is adjusted according to each course, is subtracted from the

actual number of strokes taken to play a round of 18 holes to determine his or her score. Handicap allowances for other forms of golf matches are computed on a system devised for the type of match. The highest handicap for men is 24 strokes; for women 36 strokes.

hole The playing area from the teeing ground to the green. Also the specially cut hole in the green into which each player must hit his ball to hole out.

hole out To hit the ball into the hole and so conclude playing that hole.

honor The right to play first off the tee. It is accorded to the player or partnership who won the previous hole.

hook A shot which makes a more pronounced curve to the left (or right for a left-handed player) than a draw (*qv*), and is usually unintentional.

irons Name given to clubs which have a metal head. They are numbered 1 to 9, plus the wedges, their striking length

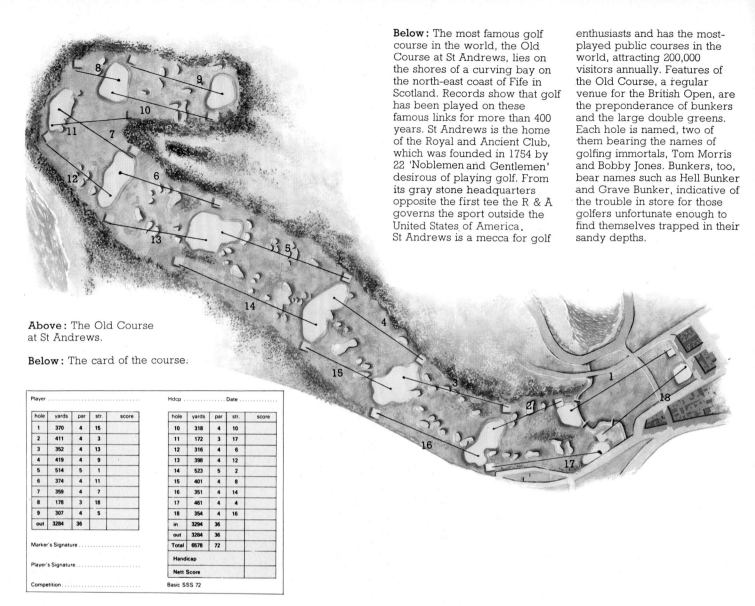

Below: The most famous golf course in the world, the Old Course at St Andrews, lies on the shores of a curving bay on the north-east coast of Fife in Scotland. Records show that golf has been played on these famous links for more than 400 years. St Andrews is the home of the Royal and Ancient Club, which was founded in 1754 by 22 'Noblemen and Gentlemen' desirous of playing golf. From its gray stone headquarters opposite the first tee the R & A governs the sport outside the United States of America.

St Andrews is a mecca for golf enthusiasts and has the most-played public courses in the world, attracting 200,000 visitors annually. Features of the Old Course, a regular venue for the British Open, are the preponderance of bunkers and the large double greens. Each hole is named, two of them bearing the names of golfing immortals, Tom Morris and Bobby Jones. Bunkers, too, bear names such as Hell Bunker and Grave Bunker, indicative of the trouble in store for those golfers unfortunate enough to find themselves trapped in their sandy depths.

Above: The Old Course at St Andrews.

Below: The card of the course.

hole	yards	par	str.	score	hole	yards	par	str.	score
1	370	4	15		10	318	4	10	
2	411	4	3		11	172	3	17	
3	352	4	13		12	316	4	6	
4	419	4	9		13	398	4	12	
5	514	5	1		14	523	5	2	
6	374	4	11		15	401	4	8	
7	359	4	7		16	351	4	14	
8	178	3	18		17	461	4	4	
9	307	4	5		18	354	4	16	
out	3284	36			in	3294	36		
					out	3284	36		
					Total	6578	72		

Player ....

Hdcp .... Date ....

Marker's Signature ....

Player's Signature ....

Competition ....

Handicap

Nett Score

Basic SSS 72

diminishing the higher the number.

length The distance a player is able to hit the ball with a certain club.

lie The place where a ball comes to rest in play; and from where the next stroke has to be played unless a penalty stroke is incurred.

links A seaside golf course.

loft The angle of the face of the clubs. The higher the degree of angle, the less distance the ball travels but the greater the loop of its trajectory.

mashie The name given to the club that is now the No. 5 iron.

mashie-niblick The name given to the club that is now the No. 7 iron.

match play A match in which the result is decided on the number of holes won, as distinct from the number of strokes taken. The match is won when one player is more holes ahead of his opponent than there are holes to play.

medal play A match or competition in which the result is decided on the total number of strokes taken by each player. The winner is the player with the lowest net score. Also known as stroke play.

niblick The name given to the club that is now a No. 8 or No. 9 iron. The term is loosely used for any iron with a widish angle of loft for approach shots.

nineteenth hole The clubhouse; more specifically, the bar therein.

out of bounds Beyond the confines of the course as defined by the club committee.

par The number of strokes required by a scratch player at each hole when playing in average conditions.

Par measurements are as follows. Holes to 250yd (228m) are rated par 3; from 251 to 475yd inclusive (229-434m), par 4; 476yd (435m) and over, par 5.

piccolo Said of a grip when the first three fingers of the top hand let go of the shaft.

pin Flagstick.

pitch To make a lofted approach, usually with a high-number iron or a wedge.

pitch and run A lofted approach pitched short and allowed to run on to the flagstick.

pitch and stop A lofted approach played with backspin so that the ball will not run on after landing.

press To make too great an effort to hit the ball hard, the result being that it is mishit.

provisional ball That used by a player when it is thought his original ball might be lost (except if in a water hazard) or out of bounds. He must choose to play the provisional ball before searching for the original one, as the purpose of the provisional ball is to save time. If, on reaching the area where the ball was thought lost, it is found in play, the provisional ball must be abandoned and the original ball played; if it is found out of bounds, the provisional ball is played and the stroke and distance rule (*qv*) applied.

pull A shot which, although hit in a straight line, goes to the left (right for a left-hander) of the intended direction.

punch shot A shot which keeps the ball on a low trajectory, perhaps to avoid branches or to prevent losing forward momentum when driving into a strong wind.

push A shot which, although hit in a straight line, goes to the right (left for a left-hander) of the intended direction.

putt The shot with which the ball is hit across the green towards, and hopefully into, the hole. It is played from a sideways-on stance with a *putter*, a special metal club. Before making the putt the player may clean his ball and clear away any loose obstructions between it and the hole, but he must not use the putter to smooth down the green.

quitting Pulling up on the downswing of a shot with the result that the clubhead has lost some of its momentum by the time it hits the ball.

rough The parts of the course, to

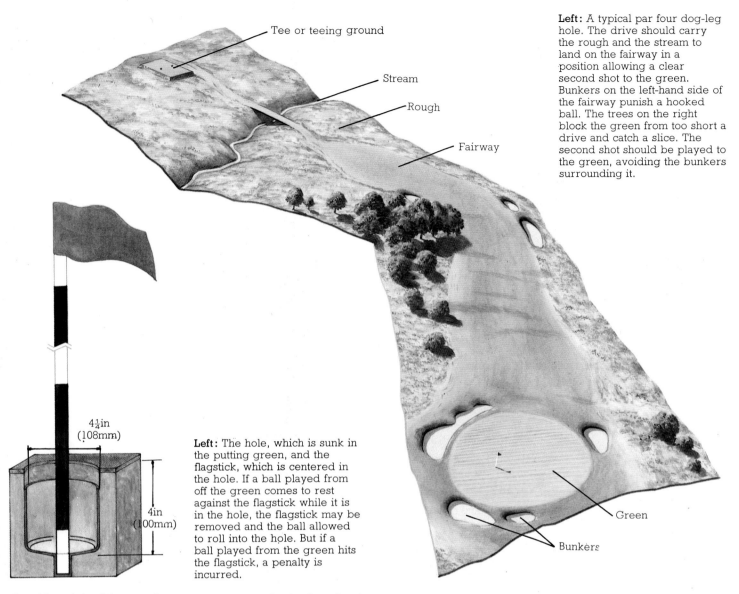

Tee or teeing ground

Stream

Rough

Fairway

Green

Bunkers

4¼in (108mm)

4in (100mm)

Left: A typical par four dog-leg hole. The drive should carry the rough and the stream to land on the fairway in a position allowing a clear second shot to the green. Bunkers on the left-hand side of the fairway punish a hooked ball. The trees on the right block the green from too short a drive and catch a slice. The second shot should be played to the green, avoiding the bunkers surrounding it.

Left: The hole, which is sunk in the putting green, and the flagstick, which is centered in the hole. If a ball played from off the green comes to rest against the flagstick while it is in the hole, the flagstick may be removed and the ball allowed to roll into the hole. But if a ball played from the green hits the flagstick, a penalty is incurred.

the sides of the fairway, where the grass has not been cut smoothly and so constitutes a hazard.

round Playing one circuit of an 18-hole course. If the course has fewer than 18 holes, some of the holes are played twice.

rub of the green An occurrence of good or bad fortune which is not specifically covered by the rules. A most common example is when the ball is stopped or deflected by an outside agency (not the player or his caddie).

sand iron/wedge A wedge (*qv*) specifically for bunker play and pitching.

score The number of strokes, including any penalties, it takes a player to complete a round, less his handicap. For example, a player on a 10 handicap who goes round the course in 84 strokes would have a score of 74.

scratch A handicap of zero. Those playing off scratch in a match neither give nor receive bonus strokes in medal play.

shaft The metal tube from head to grip. Length of shaft varies with the physical requirements of each player and also with the individual clubs, the basic criterion being that clubs which hit over a greater distance have longer shafts.

shank A mishit which sends the ball flying off at 45-90 degrees to the right (left for a left-hander) of the intended line of direction. It results from hitting the ball between the heel of the club and the bottom of the socket.

slice A shot which makes a more pronounced curve to the right (left for a left-hander) than a fade (*qv*) and is usually unintentional.

spoon The name given to the No. 3 wood.

stableford A type of match in which the object is to acquire points in relation to the strokes taken at each hole. For example, 1 point is scored for one stroke over par, 2 for par, 3 for a birdie, etc.

stroke An attempt to hit the ball

with a club. Every attempt counts towards a player's score irrespective of whether or not the ball is hit.

stroke and distance The rule which allows a player whose ball is out of bounds, lost, or unplayable to play another ball from where the original shot was played. He incurs a penalty stroke.

stroke play Medal (*qv*) play.

stymie The situation on the green when one player's ball blocks an opponent's ball's path to the hole. It is no longer possible, but prior to 1951, when the stymie was abolished to allow every player an open path to the hole, the laying of stymies was a deliberate tactic.

sudden death The method of deciding a tie in stroke, match or medal play. Those involved in the tie play an extra hole (or holes), the first to win the hole taking the match.

swing The method of returning the clubhead to the ball so that, at the moment of impact, it is in

exactly the same position as it was at the address (*qv*). There are two distinct elements: the backswing, which takes the club back over the shoulders into the preparatory position, and the downswing, which brings the clubhead back to the ball and into the follow-through.

tee, or tee peg The small, brightly colored plastic or wooden support on which the ball is placed to be driven from the teeing ground.

teeing ground The flat, usually built-up, area from which the first stroke of a hole is played. Also known as the *tee*.

topping Hitting the ball above its center. Also known as *thinning*.

underclubbing Using a shorter iron than necessary for the shot.

wedge A broad-soled iron with maximum loft for playing out of bunkers and for hitting short, lofted shots to the green.

woods Name given to clubs which have a wooden head. Of many kinds, they are used for the longer shots.

103

Hockey

Hockey is played by men and women using a curved stick to hit a small, hard ball over a smooth field, usually grass covered. It is a major international sport which can trace its ancestry to pre-Christian times. To distinguish it from ice and roller hockey, it is sometimes referred to as field hockey. Men, and in some instances women, play under the auspices of the FIH; women of the IFWHA. Basically they play the same 11-a-side game with the aim of scoring goals, worth a point each, by hitting the ball between the goalposts and under the crossbar of the opposing team's goal. Play commences with a bully, after which the players control, dribble, pass, or hit the ball with the face of their sticks in order to get it into the opposing team's shooting circle: to score, a player must shoot from within the shooting circle. Use of the hand is allowed to stop the ball dead. Otherwise only the goalkeeper may stop the ball with his or her body or kick it, and then only within his or her shooting circle.

As in soccer, playing formations have become more fluid with the evolution of new tactics, although hockey has always placed an emphasis on the coordination and interdependance of attack and defense. Even with the basic pyramid formation, it is as much for convenience as strategy that players are designated backs, wing-halves, center-half, center-forward, inside-forwards and wing- or outside-forwards. In women's hockey, the inside-forwards are called right and left inner. The men's game has been an Olympic sport—with a few interruptions—since 1908. Women's hockey is to be played in the Olympic Games for the first time in 1980.

Left: Hockey is a fast-moving game played on a rectangular grass field 100 x 60yd. The two teams each have a goalkeeper, two fullbacks, three halfbacks and five forwards, although modern playing formations are more flexable. Play always begins on the center line.

Indian stick

English stick

STRIKE

Ball

Left: The English stick, which is still favored by many women players, and the Indian stick, which is now used by most men. Length and weight of a stick are individual to each player. The portion of every stick below the top of the splice must be wood, while the grip can be of tape, leather, rubber or towel. The classic ball is white leather, but plastic and composition balls are gaining acceptance.

assault wave In men's hockey those players whose role at a corner (*qv*) is to get near the goal to collect rebounds off the goalkeeper or defenders, or to deflect into goal a shot going wide. It comprises the corner hitter and at least two other players.

bully The method of starting play at the beginning of each half, after a goal has been scored, after an injury, and after simultaneous fouls have been committed. A bully may also be played if the ball lodges in the goalkeeper's pads, or in a player's or the umpire's clothing, or in some cases after an accident. One player from each team stands over the ball, facing a sideline with his/her own goal on the right-hand side. With the stick, each then taps the ground behind the ball and the opponent's stick above the ball, repeating this twice more before making an attempt to gain possession of the ball. If a bully is held inside the shooting (*qv*)

circle, it must be at least 5yd. from the goal-line.

circle The shooting (*qv*) circle.

corner The means of restarting play when a defender unintentionally puts the ball over his/her goal-line (except in the event of a goal) from within the '25' (*qv*). It is taken by an attacking player on either the goal-line or sideline from a point up to 5yd from the corner flag on the side of the goal on which the ball went out of play. Apart from this, the provisions of a penalty (*qv*) corner apply: up to six defenders may stand behind the goal-line; the others in the defending team are restricted to beyond the center line until the corner is taken. Attackers must remain outside the circle until the corner is taken.

dribbling Keeping the ball under close control with the stick while running.

face The flat side of a stick's head. It is the only side which may be used for striking the ball.

FIH Fédération Internationale de

Hockey, the world governing body for men's hockey. It also has affiliated women's associations.

flick A stroke used to lift the ball off the ground. It is similar to a push (*qv*), but with a flick of the wrist at the moment of contact.

free hit A hit awarded to the non-offending side in the event of an infringement. Except for certain offenses within the shooting circle, it is taken where the offense occurred. The free hit is also used to restart play when the attacking side puts the ball over the goal-line or a defender unintentionally hits it over the goal-line from outside the '25' (*qv*) In men's hockey the free hit is taken on any spot within 16yd of the goal-line in a line with where the ball crossed it. In women's hockey a free hit awarded against an attacker in the circle may be taken from any spot within the circle.

hit Means by which the ball is propelled by striking it with the face (*qv*) of the stick.

hit-out In men's hockey, the stroke which puts the ball into play from a corner or penalty corner.

hitter-in The player who makes the hit-out (*qv*).

IFWHA International Federation of Women's Hockey Associations, the world controlling body for women's hockey.

IHRB International Hockey Rules Board (men's hockey).

indoor hockey A form of hockey for teams of up to six players and six substitutes. Rules have been established by the FIH, two main differences from field hockey being that the ball must be pushed (*qv*), not hit, and may be lifted above the surface only when a player is shooting at goal within the opponents' circle.

inner Name given to the inside-forwards in IFWHA hockey.

jab A stroke used to prevent an opponent from playing the ball. It is made by pushing the stick out quickly so that the face jabs under the ball, making it jump off the ground over the oppon-

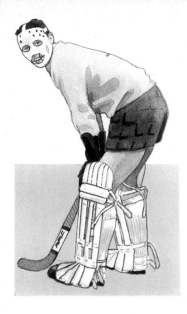

Left: The hockey goalkeeper must be well protected to guard against hard deliveries. Gloves, leg pads and face masks have become standard equipment.

Right: The scoop is the most common stroke used to lift the ball and send it a distance over the field. It should be used only when players are sure of clearing opposition players. The player holds the stick with the face open and uses a forward and upward heave to propel the ball.

The hit

The scoop

Right: The bully, which is used to start play and restart play after a goal. In such instances it is held on the center line. It is also used to restart play in the event of injury or a simultaneous foul. The two players concerned in the bully face each other and the ball is placed between the blades of the opposing sticks. The two players then execute a formula, tapping three times on the ground and striking their opponent's stick three times alternately. The ball may then be played by either player, who will try to pass it to a team-mate.

Above: The hit is the elementary stroke in hockey. It is made up of the backswing and the forward swing, the strike and the follow-through. The player shown here is at the top of his backswing. Unlike the golf stroke the backswing is short. There is no reason to bend the left arm and the stick should not rise above shoulder level. On the downswing the player will shift his weight on to the left foot. Undercutting the ball to produce possibly dangerous lift is forbidden.

ent's stick to deny him control.

links Name given to those players deployed behind the forwards and ahead of the halfbacks in a 4 - 2 - 4 - goalkeeper formation. Their role is to support the forwards in attack and to guard the opposing inside-forwards in defense.

long corner Name sometimes used for a corner (*qv*).

mixed hockey Games played between teams with equal numbers of men and women on each side. IHRB rules apply.

offside An infringement when an attacking player inside his opponents' half has fewer than two opponents between himself and the opponents' goal-line at the moment the ball is played forward to him by a team-mate, and is in a position to gain an advantage or affect an opponent's play.

penalty corner The means of restarting play when a defender intentionally puts the ball over his/her goal-line (except in the event of a goal). It is also awarded against the defending team for a deliberate offense within their '25'. The penalty corner is taken in a similar manner to a corner (*qv*) except that the corner hit is from a point on the goal-line 10yd or more from the goalpost.

penalty stroke A free push, flick, or scoop at goal awarded to the attacking team for certain offenses committed by the defending team in the shooting circle. These offenses are; an intentional foul in the circle to prevent a goal being scored; an unintentional foul in the circle that would probably prevent a goal; positioning infringements at a penalty corner. It is taken from a penalty spot 23ft in front of the goal, with all other players but the penalty-taker and the goalkeeper standing beyond the 25yd line.

pitch The playing field.

push A stroke which begins with the stick already in contact with the ball and sends it along the ground.

push-in The method used to restart play when the ball crosses the sidelines. All players other than the one taking the push-in, who may not play the ball more than once, must stand at least 5yd from the ball.

pyramid The playing system in which players are deployed in a five forwards, three halfbacks, two backs, and goalkeeper formation.

reverse stick Turning the stick over so that the toe points downwards. It enables players to play the ball with the face when the stick is on the left side of the body.

scoop A stroke used to lift the ball into the air over the heads of opposing players. It begins with the stick several inches behind the ball; on contact the ball is propelled upwards as the stick is lifted in the follow-through.

shooting circle The area surrounding each goal. It consists of a straight line, 4yd long and 16yd out from the goalmouth, with a quarter-circle linking each end to the goal-line.

short corner Name sometimes used for a penalty (*qv*) corner.

sticks Raising the stick above shoulder height when playing or attempting to play the ball. It is an offense.

stop The act of bringing a rolling ball under control by 'trapping' it with the stick.

sweeper Name given to a defender deployed behind the other defenders (excluding the goalkeeper) in some playing formations. Rather than being responsible for guarding a certain player or zone, he has freedom to position himself where he feels the greatest danger to his goal lies.

tackle Use of the stick to rob an opponent of the ball or force him to pass or lose possession. It is not permitted to hit, hold, or otherwise interfere with an opponent's stick.

'25' The area between the goal-line and the transverse line 25yd from the goal-line.

WIHRB Women's International Hockey Rules Board.

Lacrosse

A game in which the aim is to throw a ball from a crosse into the opposing team's goal, lacrosse is played by men and women, though not together and to different rules. An obvious difference is in the number of players to a team: 10, plus up to 9 substitutes in the men's game; 12 plus 1 substitute in the women's. The field dimensions and layout also differ—the women have no marked boundaries—and the men play four 15-minute quarters, the women two 25-minute halves. But a more significant difference is that men's lacrosse permits bodily contact, in the form of shoulder-to-shoulder charging when competing for a ground ball, and blocking. It also has an offside law, which the free-flowing women's game does not. Nor, for that matter, do women, apart from the goalkeepers, find any need for the protective equipment—helmet, visor, elbow pads, and heavy gloves-required by the robust nature of the men's game. Both games feature crosse and body checking to stop an opponent's progress, and both demand a high degree of fitness in addition to the skills of running with, passing, and catching the ball. Handling is not allowed, except by the goalkeepers, who may deflect a shot within the goal crease but may not catch it.

Played principally in the United States, Canada, Australia and Britain, lacrosse originated in North America from the Indians' lengthy, religious-orientated game *baggataway*. French missionaries and settlers named it lacrosse because the racket resembled a bishop's crozier (*crosse* in French) with a net looped over the end.

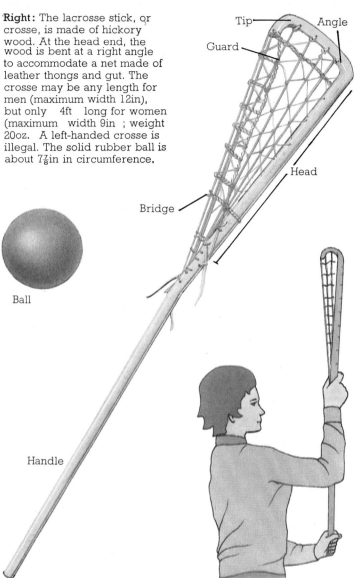

Right: The lacrosse stick, or crosse, is made of hickory wood. At the head end, the wood is bent at a right angle to accommodate a net made of leather thongs and gut. The crosse may be any length for men (maximum width 12in), but only 4ft long for women (maximum width 9in ; weight 20oz. A left-handed crosse is illegal. The solid rubber ball is about $7\frac{7}{8}$in in circumference.

Tip Angle Guard Head Bridge Ball Handle

---

angle The part of the crosse (*qv*) where the top curves at a right angle to the rest of the stick.

assists Passes from which goals are scored. Players are credited with assists by the scorer.

attack Name given to the three men whose prime objective is to score goals. In women's lacrosse, the attack players are first, second and third home, and right and left wing attack.

block In men's lacrosse, the action of an attacking player who stands in the path of a defending player to prevent him from moving to guard another attacker. In women's lacrosse it is the action by a defender of stopping or deflecting a pass with her stick.

body checking In men's lacrosse impeding the forward progress of an opponent in possession by standing with the crosse, held flat, in the path of that player and the goal. In women's lacrosse body checking must not involve contact.

box lacrosse A form of lacrosse played in Canada.

checking, or crosse checking Using the crosse to strike an opponent's crosse in order to rob him or her of the ball, or to prevent him or her from catching the ball or shooting.

cover point The central or pivotal defense in women's lacrosse.

cradling The rhythmical swinging movement of the crosse made by a running player so that the ball remains in the crosse.

crease The circular goal area. A player is not allowed into the opposition crease, but may enter his or her own crease to retrieve the ball or pass through it to retrieve a wide ball. No player may carry the ball into the crease or retain possession of it for more than four seconds while in the crease (but *see* goalkeeper).

crosse The lacrosse racket; also known as the stick. It is so designed that the ball moves freely in the net at all times.

cutting Escaping from a guarding opponent and running into space to receive a pass.

defense Name given to the three men who guard the attacks (*qv*) and with the goalkeeper, defend the goal. At the face-off they stand behind the defense restraining line. In women's lacrosse, the defense players are point, cover point, third man and right and left wing defenses.

draw Used in women's lacrosse to put the ball in play at the start of each half and after goals. The two center players face each other with one foot toeing the center line, their crosses at about hip height : wood to wood, angle to collar, back to back. When the umpire, having placed the ball between the crosses, says 'Ready, draw,' the centers pull their crosses up and away so that the ball goes into the air. Other players must be at least 32ft 10in from the draw. It is also used to restart play after some stoppages.

expulsion foul A deliberate foul on another player or an official which may warrant a player's suspension from the men's game.

face The open side of the crosse, and the only side in which the ball is carried.

face-off Used in men's lacrosse to put the ball into play at the start of each quarter and after goals. The two centers crouch facing each other with their crosses back to back $\frac{3}{4}$-$1\frac{1}{4}$in apart, the wooden frames parallel to and touching the ground. The ball is placed between the crosses, and at the referee's whistle the centers try to win possession. Until one does so, only the midfield players may move beyond their restraining lines. The face-off is also used to restart play following some stoppages, in the event of which no other players may be within 15ft of the face-off.

feeder The player who makes an assist (*qv*) or the pass from which a shot at goal is made.

first home One of the attacking positions in women's lacrosse. She plays mostly in the area

106

Left: The draw. The ball is placed between the two crosses which are held back to back. At the start of play the crosses are pulled up sharply by both players to set the ball in motion.

Below: Three lacrosse techniques. In the crosse checking illustration, the player on the right is about to bring her crosse down on her opponent's crosse in an attempt to dislodge the ball. There must be no bodily contact. Cutting is a movement to escape from an opponent's marking.
The overhand shot is made with the bottom hand providing the power while the top hand directs the ball.

Crosse checking

Cutting

Overhand shot

Above: The goalkeeper wears leg pads and a body pad which extends to protect the thighs. In addition a face mask may be worn. Shoes have studded rubber soles.

Left: The grip. One hand is positioned at the top with the knuckles facing outwards; the other grips the bottom of the handle at waist level.

closest to the crease.

forcing A tactical move with a defense carrying the ball upfield in an attempt to draw an opposing defender out of position, so creating space for an attack.

free play In men's lacrosse, the method of restarting play when the ball, or a player carrying it, crosses a boundary line. Except when the ball is out of play after a shot at goal, the free play is awarded against the team last touching the ball. Players must be at least 15ft from the player taking it.

free position The penalty awarded to the non-offending team in the event of a foul. No player may be within $5\frac{1}{8}$yd ($4\frac{1}{4}$yd for women) of the player taking the free position, while the offending player is positioned in line with or behind the taker according to the nature of the offense.

goalkeeper The player who defends the goal. He or she is the only player allowed to handle the ball, but only within the crease. Having done so, the

goalkeeper in the men's game must immediately put the ball in the crosse and proceed with the game. The woman goalkeeper has ten seconds in which to do so.

midfield The center and left and right wing midfield players in men's lacrosse.

neutral throw *See* throw.

offside In men's lacrosse, a team infringes the offside rule if it has fewer than four players in its own (defending) half or fewer than three players in the opposition half. There is no offside in women's lacrosse.

penalty box An area beyond the playing field in which men players must remain while under suspension.

personal fouls Infringements against an opponent's person or crosse. In women's lacrosse, any form of body contact is a foul. In men's lacrosse, foul play is penalized by time suspensions; in women's lacrosse by free (*qv*) positions.

point The last defender before

the goalkeeper, in women's lacrosse.

ragging Term used in the men's game to describe the deliberate slowing-down of play.

riding out The action of attacking men players who, on losing possession, man-to-man guards the defending players to prevent the ball being cleared.

second home One of the attacking positions in women's lacrosse.

slow whistle Used in men's lacrosse when the referee, having allowed play to continue to the advantage of a fouled player or his team, later whistles up the player who committed the foul.

stand A rule in women's lacrosse preventing any movement of players after the whistle has been blown. The rule also applies in British men's lacrosse as *dead ball*.

stick Another name for the crosse (*qv*).

tackle To body check or crosse check an opponent with the ball

so that he or she loses possession or is forced to pass.

technical fouls Territorial infringements in men's lacrosse, such as offside and entering the crease, or offenses not involving contact.

third home One of the attacking positions in women's lacrosse.

third man One of the defensive positions in women's lacrosse. She guards third home

throw Used in women's lacrosse to restart play when neither side is fully responsible for the stoppage. It is contested by two players who stand side by side, 3ft 3in apart. The umpire, her back to the rest of the game and $5\frac{1}{2}$-11yd from the two players, releases the ball with a short, high throw for them to catch to restart play.

time-out In men's lacrosse, a period of time allowed during a game for tactical discussions or to allow officials to caution players.

time-out penalty The temporary suspension of a male player for committing a foul.

Rugby

A sport which evolved in the English universities and public schools of the 1800s, rugby football today has two separate codes: rugby union, a strictly amateur sport played by 15-man teams, and rugby league, in which players may be amateur or professional and teams have only 13 men. However, both are games in which an oval ball is handled, run with, and kicked with the object of scoring tries, which entitle the scoring team to a conversion attempt. Points may also be scored from penalty tries, penalty kicks and drop kicks. The ball must not be passed or knocked forward; nor may players gain advantage from an offside position.

The differences, apart from the number of players, arise in the way the ball is brought back into play following breakdowns. Rugby league employs the scrum and the play-the-ball; rugby union employs the scrum, lineout, ruck and maul. Kicking for territorial gain is more prevalent in rugby union, but kicking into touch on the full is limited to defenders behind their 25yd line. In league, kicking into touch on the full is prohibited except, as in union, for penalty kicks.

Prior to 1895 there was only one handling code, owing its origins to Rugby School in England and its rules to the Rugby Football Union. It was in England that the split occurred. The cause for the dissent was the amateur RFU's refusal to allow 'broken-time' payments to compensate players who lost money taking time off from mining and factory shifts to play rugby. The result was that 21 clubs in the north of England broke away to form the Northern RF Union which, in 1922, changed its name to the Rugby Football League. Rugby is a popular sport in Australia, New Zealand, South Africa, France, Britain and Ireland.

Left: The oval-shaped rugby ball is made of leather or other approved material and weighs 13½-15oz. The league ball is slightly narrower than the union ball, with a length of 11-11¼in and long and short circumferences of 30-31in and 24-25½in.

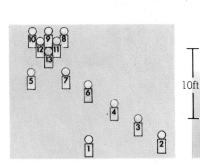

Above: The layout of players at the scrum. The positions are: 10 & 8 Front-row prop forwards; 9 Hooker; 12 & 11 Second-row forwards; 13 Loose-forward; 7 Scrum-half; 5 Left wing-threequarter; 6 Fly-half; 4 Center-threequarter; 3 Center-threequarter; 2 Right wing-threequarter; 1 Fullback.

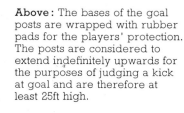

Above: The bases of the goal posts are wrapped with rubber pads for the players' protection. The posts are considered to extend indefinitely upwards for the purposes of judging a kick at goal and are therefore at least 25ft high.

Where a term is exclusive to one code, it is followed by (r.l.) if rugby league and (r.u.) if rugby union. These abbreviations also apply in the explanations.

accidental offside When a player in an offside position cannot avoid making contact with the ball or player carrying it.

advantage law Allows the referee to use his discretion whether or not to stop play for an infringement when such action would be disadvantageous to the non-offending team.

All Blacks (r.u.) Name given to New Zealand's national and touring teams.

amateur A player who plays rugby simply for the enjoyment of the game and does not receive any financial reward for doing so.

ankle tap A method of bringing down a ball carrier running at speed by touching his ankle with a hand, so unbalancing him.

backs Those players who take up positions behind the scrum. They consist of the halfbacks,

threequarters and fullback.

blind side The side of the field opposite that on which the backs line out from a scrum (qv), line-out (qv), ruck (qv), maul (qv), or play-the-ball (qv). At the latter, it is usually the side of the field closer to the touchline (qv).

box The open space behind a scrum, or lineout, between the scrum-half and fullback.

center-threequarters The two backs who take up a position between the fly-half (qv) and the left or right wing-threequarter. The two centers are called either inside or outside, or left or right according to the practice of the country. In New Zealand, only the outside center is a threequarter, the inside center being called a second five-eighth (qv).

Chanticleers (r.l.) Name given to France's national and touring teams.

charge-down Blocking an opponent's kick with the hands, arms, or body. If the ball ricochets on to the ground, it is not consider-

ed to be a knock-on (qv).

conversion A successful place kick at goal following a try (qv). The kick must be made from a place in line with where the try was scored. It is worth two points.

differential penalty (r.l.) A penalty kick which does not entitle a direct kick at goal.

dribbling Controlled kicking of the ball along the ground.

drop kick Kicking the ball on the half-volley after it has been dropped from the hands.

drop out Means of restarting play with a drop kick: (r.u.) Following an unconverted try, touch in goal, and a touch-down (qv) if the defending team has not carried the ball into their in-goal (qv) area. (r.l.) Following a defender's touch-down and touch in goal, or if he is tackled or kicks the ball directly into touch while in his in-goal area.

dropped goal A goal (qv) scored with a drop kick from open play (as opposed to a penalty or free (qv) kick). In r.u.

it is worth three points; in one point.

dummy To make as if to pass the ball while intending to retain possession of it.

fair catch (r.u.) Made by a player who, standing stationary with both feet on the ground, catches the ball on the full from an opposition kick, knock-on, or throw forward, and at the same time shouts 'Mark!' He is awarded a free kick.

field goal A dropped goal.

five-eighth Name given to inside backs in Australia and New Zealand, the fly-half and inside center are called first and second five-eighth respectively; in Australian r.l., the fly-half is called the five-eighth.

flankers (r.u.) The two loose forwards who pack down on either side of the scrum and stand at the tail of the lineout. Also known as wing-forwards and breakaways.

fly-half The back who acts as a pivot between the scrum-half and the rest of the backline.

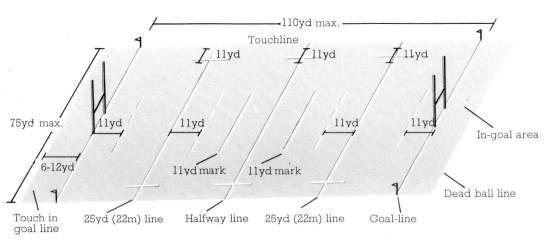

Left: The rugby league pitch differs in its markings from the union pitch but the playing area has the same overall dimensions. Flag posts are placed at the corners of the goal and touch lines and at least 4ft high with rounded tops. The touch lines do not form part of the playing area.

Below: An attacker about to score a try despite the attempted tackle of a defending player. A try is scored when an attacker grounds the ball in the opposition's in-goal area, which includes the goal-line.

Below: Playing-the-ball, the procedure used by a tackled player who retains possession to bring the ball back into play. The common practice is to heel the ball back to a teammate, known as the acting half-back, who stands directly behind the player playing-the-ball.

forward pass A pass or throw that is made in a forward direction towards the opposition goal-line. In r.u. it is officially a *throw forward*.

forwards Those players who pack down in the scrum and, in r.u., contest the lineout to win the ball. There are eight r.u. forwards (3 front row, 4 second row, and number 8) and 6 r.l. forwards (3 front row, 2 second row and loose-forward).

free kick (r.u.) A kick awarded to the player who makes a fair (*qv*) catch. It may be a place kick, punt, or drop kick and must be taken by the catcher himself on or behind the mark of the catch.

front row The two prop forwards and the hooker who comprise the front row of the scrum.

fullback The back who adopts a solitary position behind the backline as the last line of defense. He also attacks by running and linking up with teammates or by creating an overlap.

garryowen (r.u.) An up and under (*qv*), so called after the Irish club of the same name.

goal A place kick or drop kick which carries over the crossbar between the line of the goal posts. In r.u., a try plus the conversion (six points) is called a goal.

halfbacks The scrum-half and fly-half. In Australia and New Zealand, the scrum-half is called a halfback.

hand-off A method of fending off a would-be tackler by pushing him away with an open hand.

heel Using the foot to rake the ball backwards out of the scrum or ruck.

hooker The front-row forward who strikes with his leg and foot to hook the ball out of the scrum to his scrum-half.

in-goal area The area between the goal-line and the dead-ball line.

international (r.u.) A match between national teams of the eight International Board countries, and the British Isles. The Inter-national Board countries are England, Ireland, Scotland, Wales, Australia, New Zealand, South Africa and France.
(r.l.) A match between two countries which is not given test (*qv*) status; eg England v Wales. International Board countries are Britain, Australia, New Zealand, France, and Papua-New Guinea.

Kangaroos (r.l.) Name given to Australia's national and touring teams.

Kiwis (r.l.) Name given to New Zealand's national and touring teams.

knock-on When the ball bounces forwards off the hand or arm of a player attempting to catch it or pick it up.

lineout (r.u.) The means of re-starting play when the ball goes into touch. The forwards on each side form a line at right-angles to and 5½yd in from the touchline and the ball is thrown straight between the two lines.

Lions Name given to the British Isles r.u. touring team and the Great Britain r.l. touring team.

lock (r.l.) Australian name for the loose-forward (*qv*).

locks (r.u.) The two players who pack down behind the front row and bind the scrum together.

loose-forward (r.l.) The forward who packs down at the base of the scrum.

loose forwards (r.u.) The two flankers and the number 8 (*qv*); fast-moving players whose role is to spoil the opposition attacks, back up their own attacks, cover, defend, and to win or kill the ball whenever it is loose. Sometimes called the back row from the time when the scrum packed in a 3-2-3 formation.

loose head The prop forward who packs down on the side his scrum-half puts the ball into the scrum.

mark (r.u.) A fair catch; so called because the player making the catch must shout 'Mark!' as he takes the ball.

maul (r.u.) A scrimmage of players from both teams around the player holding the ball. If the ball is dropped on the ground

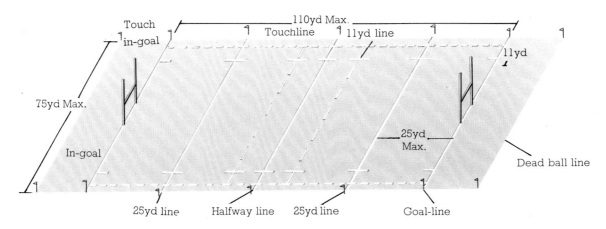

Touch
in-goal
110yd Max.
Touchline
11yd line
11yd
75yd Max.
In-goal
25yd
Max.
Dead ball line
25yd line
Halfway line
25yd line
Goal-line

Above: Rugby union is played on a grass, sand, or clay pitch measuring a maximum of 110yd long by 76yd wide and marked out as shown. The touchlines do not form part of the playing area, and so the ball is out of play whenever it, or a player touching it, lands on or goes beyond the touchline. At each end of the playing area, centrally placed along the goal-line, are the goal posts. They are positioned 6yd apart and joined by a crossbar at a height of 3yd.

Right: The 3-4-1 formation which is favoured by almost all teams today for the scrum. Customary positions in Britain are: 1 Prop forward (loose head); 2 Hooker; 3 Prop forward (tight head); 4 & 5 Lock forwards; 6 & 7 Flank forwards; 8 No. 8 forward; 9 Scrum-half; 10 Fly-half; 11 Left wing-threequarter; 12 Center-threequarter; 13 Center-threequarter; 14 Right wing-threequarter; 15 Fullback. 1-8 are known as forwards, 9-15 as backs.

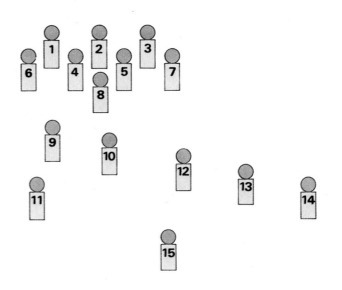

the maul becomes a ruck (*qv*).

number 8 (r.u.) The loose forward who packs down at the base of the scrum. So called because he wears the number 8 jersey.

obstruction An infringement when a player impedes the progress of an opponent who does not have the ball.

offside A player is offside when he is in front of the ball. He must attempt to retire behind the ball or take no part in the play until put onside. He is put onside by a team-mate who, having kicked the ball ahead of him, runs past him; or by an opponent who passes or kicks the ball, or in r.l. runs 5yd with it. There are also offside laws for a scrum, lineout and play-the-ball.

overlap When the team in possession has more players in their attack than there are defenders to mark them.

pack To go down in a scrum. Also used collectively for a team's forwards.

penalty goal A goal scored from a penalty kick. In r.u. it is worth three points, in r.l. two points.

penalty kick A free kick awarded to the non-offending team in the event of serious infringements. It may be taken as a punt, tap kick, or drop kick or place kick at goal. Not all penalty kicks are at goal (*see* differential penalty). In r.l. the kick may be taken as a punt into touch followed by a tap kick 11yd infield from where it went out.

penalty try A try awarded when the referee considers an obstructed player would have scored a try had he not been impeded. The conversion attempt is taken from directly in front of the posts.

place kick A kick taken with the ball resting on the ground. The ball may be held in position provided part of it is in contact with the ground.

play-the-ball (r.l.) The method of bringing the ball back into play after a tackle. The tackled player stands up, facing forward, and an opponent stands in front of him. An acting halfback stands behind each player while the rest of the players retire at least 5yd behind the ball. As soon as the tackled player puts the ball on the ground it may be kicked or heeled in any direction by either player, although in practice the ball carrier rolls it behind him with his foot or, if he is loosely marked, kicks it ahead and chases after it. In Britain and Australia a team may play-the-ball for five successive tackles; on the sixth a scrum is held.

professional (r.l.) A player who receives a match fee plus bonuses for playing rugby. However, the game must not be his only source of income.

prop forwards The two front-row forwards who support the hooker.

punt To kick the ball before it touches the ground.

replacement (r.u.) A player who comes on in place of a team-mate considered medically unfit to continue. In an international match each team is allowed up to two replacements.

round-the-corner A style of place kicking with the kicker taking a curved, rather than straight, run-up to the ball.

ruck (r.u.) A scrimmage of players from both teams around the ball when it is on the ground.

scrum (r.l.) A set method of restarting play following an infringement or when the ball goes into touch. It must take place at least 11yd from the touchline and be no closer than 5yd to the goal-line. The forwards pack down in a 3-2-1 formation. (r.u.) A set method of restarting play following an infringement. Although the minimum number required for a scrum is three per team, normally all eight players are involved, packing down in a 3-4-1 formation with the front row interlocking with their opposite numbers. The forwards should not attempt to gain any advantage by shoving until the ball has been put into the tunnel between the two packs.

Right: A typically orthodox rugby tackle. The player in possession is brought down by a combination of the unbalancing forward momentum of the tackler diving headlong into him from behind and from being firmly grasped round the thighs and legs. A common alternative is the smother tackle in which the man in possession is held round the arms to prevent him from passing the ball during the tackle.

Below: The lineout is formed by the forwards of both teams to receive the throw-in after the ball has gone into touch. It must be formed at least 5m infield from the touchline.

Left: A successful kick at goal from a place kick, the most used method of kicking penalty goals or conversions. In rugby union the drop kick may be used for penalties and conversions, but in rugby league, conversion attempts must be a place kick. Since the 1960s, the style of place kicking has changed, with many modern kickers favoring the round-the-corner approach to the traditional straight approach. Kickers also have their own theories on the way they place the ball on the ground; either upright or at an angle.

scrum-half The link player between the forwards and the backs. He is often the team's tactician and must be able to judge when to pass to his backs, to run and link with his forwards, or to kick for territorial gain.

second-phase (r.u.) The practice of deliberately creating a ruck or maul after a set piece. The aim is to commit the opposition loose forwards to the breakdown and then get the ball back quickly in an attempt to take advantage of any openings in the defense.

second row (r.u.) The two locks and the two flankers.

second-row forwards (r.l.) The two forwards who pack down behind the front row and bind the scrum together.

set pieces (r.u.) The scrum and lineout. (r.l.) Planned moves when restarting the game.

sevens A fast form of rugby with only seven players to each team. Team formations are four backs and three forwards, or five backs and two forwards.

Springboks Name given to South Africa's national and touring teams.

stand-off half Another name for the fly-half.

substitute (r.l.) A player who replaces an injured player or is brought on for tactical reasons. Two substitutes are permitted. Any substituted player may in turn be a substitute, but once only.

tackle A method of stopping the progress of an opponent holding the ball. The player may be dropped to the ground or held (provided the tackle is not made with a stiff arm or is not to the head), and is considered tackled when unable to play the ball or, while in his hands, it touches the ground. In r.u. the tackled player must release the ball immediately; in r.l. he must immediately signify his wish to play-the-ball.

tap kick A nominal kick with the player tapping the ball with his foot and then running with, passing, or kicking it.

test A r.l. international involving a touring team; also used in Australia, New Zealand and South Africa for a r.u. international.

threequarters The two centers and the two wings.

tight head The prop forward who packs down on the side the opposition scrum-half puts the ball into the scrum.

touch-down The grounding of the ball by a defending player in his own in-goal area. A touch-down is not a try, although it is incorrectly used as a synonym for one.

touch in goal When the ball goes out of play behind the goal-line.

touchline The sideline. The ball is said to be *in touch* when it or any player in contact with it touches or crosses the touchline. In r.l. play restarts with a scrum; in r.u. with a lineout.

Tricolours (r.u.) Name given to France's national and touring teams.

triple crown (r.u.) A mythical prize contested annually by England, Ireland, Scotland and Wales. To win it, one country has to defeat the other three in the course of the season.

try Awarded to a player for grounding the ball in the opposition's in-goal area. It then entitles his team to a conversion attempt. In r.u., it is worth four points; in r.l., three points.

up and under A high, lofted kick which gives the kicker's forwards time to position themselves under the ball before it comes down, so putting the defenders under extreme pressure.

Wallabies (r.u.) Name given to Australia's national and touring teams.

wing-threequarters The two backs on the right and left extremities of the field. Traditionally they are the fastest players on the field, adept at using their speed to finish off try-scoring moves. They also play a defensive role in covering the fullback.

111

Soccer

The most universal of sports, association football, or soccer, may well have its origins in ancient civilizations. But its development and organization are modern, stemming from mid-nineteenth century England where, from being a glorified street brawl, it became first the preserve of the private schools and universities and then the recreation of all classes. The British propagated the game abroad, and by the early 1900s there were national associations in Europe and South America. Today, some 146 nations are affiliated to FIFA and may contest soccer's four-yearly world championship, the World Cup.

Although it hardly accounts for the passions soccer arouses, one reason for its worldwide appeal is its intrinsic simplicity: two teams of 11 players attempting to score goals by forcing the round ball into their opponents' goal during two 45-minute halves. To do so they may use any part of the body except hands and arms, handling the ball being restricted to the goalkeepers, and then only in their own penalty areas. Skills revolve around the ability to kick, head and control the ball and to rob an opponent by tackling. However, all deliberate bodily contact, apart from a fair charge, is against the laws. Foul and dangerous play, hand-ball and ungentlemanly conduct are penalized by direct or indirect free kicks, in addition to which the referee may caution and even send off any players guilty of serious or persistent infringements. Tactics have evolved as international competition has provided stimulus and an interchange of ideas. The old 2-3-5 formation of goalkeeper, two fullbacks, three halfbacks and five forwards has given way to a more fluid pattern in which players are labeled defenders, midfield players and strikers.

Left: The round ball is made of leather or some other approved material and has a circumference of 27-28in. It must weigh 14-16oz and be inflated to a pressure of 14lb per sq in at the start of a game. During a game the ball can be changed only with the referee's consent.

Above: The goal is defined by two goalposts placed centrally, 8yd apart, along the goal-line. A crossbar spans both posts and is 8ft above the playing surface. The bar and posts may be made of wood or metal and their width and depth should not exceed $4\frac{3}{4}$in; they are painted white. A net is usually used with the goal and in certain competitions is compulsory.

Left: The light-style football boot favoured by modern players. The plastic studs on the sole of the boot can be changed to suit different ground conditions.

8ft 8yd

---

advantage The referee's decision to allow play to continue after an infringement when a stoppage would be disadvantageous to the non-offending team.

back four The two fullbacks and two center-backs who form the line of defense in front of the goal.

banana kick A kick that makes the ball swerve, or bend (*qv*), in flight.

bend To make the ball swerve in flight by kicking it with the inside or outside of the foot.

blind side The side of a player, or the referee, where it is difficult for him to see the ball.

booking A caution (*qv*); so called because the referee enters the name of the offending player in his note-pad.

by-line The goal-line.

catenaccio A tactical formation, first used by the Swiss and perfected by the Italians. Essentially defensive, it positions a sweeper (*qv*) behind four backs, three midfield men and two strikers.

caution A formal warning by the referee to a player guilty of persistent infringement of the laws, ungentlemanly conduct, dissent, or leaving or rejoining the game without his permission. A player who continues to infringe the laws after receiving a caution may be sent off.

center To pass the ball towards the goalmouth from a point near the touchline.

center-back One of the two players deployed in the centre of the defense between the fullbacks.

center-forward The spearhead of a team's attack. He must be able to score goals and set them up for team mates by winning and laying-off the ball despite tight marking. Also called a *striker* or *target man*.

chip A short, lobbed kick over the head of a defender or defenders.

corner kick The method of restarting play when the ball, having last touched a player of the defending team, goes out of

play behind their goal-line. The kick is taken by one of the attacking team from the corner quarter-circle where the relevant goal-line and touchline meet, and is a goal (*qv*) if it goes directly into the goal. The defending players must retire at least 10yd from the ball.

cross A center (*qv*).

dangerous play Attempting to play the ball in a fair manner but in such a way that could cause injury. Frequent types of dangerous play are raising the kicking foot too high above the waist or dropping the head very low to head the ball.

direct free kick A free kick from which a goal may be scored directly, ie without the ball having to touch any other player.

dive To fall to the ground spectacularly in an attempt to convince the referee a foul has been committed. Occurs most often in or around the penalty area.

dribbling Close control of the

ball at the feet while running.

dropped ball The method of restarting play after the referee has stopped the game for reasons other than an infringement. The referee drops the ball between two opposing players who may not attempt to play it until it touches the ground.

dummy Feinting as if to perform some particular action and then doing something different in order to outwit an opponent.

fair charge A charge made shoulder to shoulder on an opponent when the ball is within playing distance, or from behind if an opponent is intentionally obstructing (*qv*).

far post The goalpost or side of the goal farther away from the player with the ball.

FIFA Fédération Internationale de Football Association, the controlling body of world soccer. It was formed in 1904.

foul An infringement involving physical contact, other than a fair charge, on an opponent.

four-four-two (4-4-2) A tactical

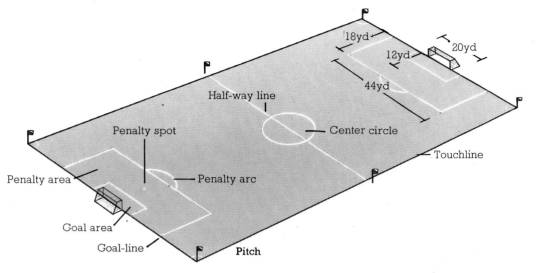

18yd
12yd
20yd
44yd
Half-way line
Penalty spot
Center circle
Touchline
Penalty area
Penalty arc
Goal area
Goal-line
Pitch

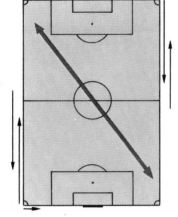

formation, basically defensive, with four defenders, four midfield men and two strikers.

four-three-three (4-3-3) A tactical formation employing four defenders, three midfield men and three strikers.

four-two-four (4-2-4) A tactical formation, more attacking than defensive, employing four defenders, two midfield men and four strikers.

free kick Awarded to the non-offending team after an infringement. It may be direct or indirect.

fullback One of the two defensive players deployed on either the left or right of the defense. He may also play an attacking role by overlapping up his side of the field to support the player with the ball.

goal The two goalposts and the crossbar; also the point scored when the whole of the ball passes over the goal-line into the goal, provided this is not the result of an infringement by the attacking team.

goal area The smaller of the two rectangular areas in front of the goal.

goal average A method of deciding the superior team in a league when two or more finish with equal points. The average is obtained by dividing the number of goals scored by the number of goals conceded, the team with the higher average being the superior team. This method has been largely superseded by goal difference.

goal difference A method of deciding the superior team in a league when two or more finish with equal points. The difference is obtained by subtracting the number of goals conceded from the number of goals scored, the team with the higher difference being the superior team.

goalkeeper The player who guards the goal. He may handle the ball anywhere inside his own penalty area.

goal kick The method of restarting play when the ball, having last touched a player of the

attacking team, goes out of play behind the goal-line. The kick may be taken from any point inside the goal area on the relevant side and must travel outside the penalty area before it is in play.

halfbacks Originally those players deployed in the middle of the field between the fullbacks and the forwards, but both the term and position have little relevance to modern formations.

hand-ball An infringement which occurs when any player, except the goalkeeper within his own penalty area, plays the ball intentionally with his hand or arm.

head To strike the ball with the head. The result of such action is called a *header*.

hospital pass A pass to a teammate who is so closely marked by the opposition that he has little chance of keeping possession without a struggle.

indirect free kick A free kick from which it is not possible to score without the ball first touching another player. It is

awarded against a player for dangerous play; shoulder-charging an opponent when the ball is not within playing distance; intentional obstruction; unlawfully charging the goalkeeper; and against the goalkeeper for taking more than four steps with the ball or for wasting time.

inside The goal side of a player moving forward.

inside-forward Originally the player who supported the center-forward and wingers and carried the ball from defense to attack.

jockeying The action of a defender who positions himself between an opponent with the ball and the goal to make it difficult for him to play the ball towards the goal.

kick off The method of starting play at the beginning of each half and of restarting after a goal. The ball is placed on the mark in the center of the field and must be kicked forward the distance of its own circumference before

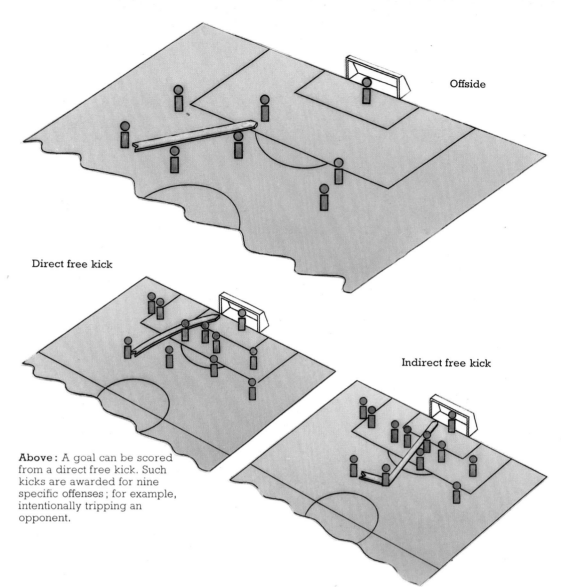

Offside

Direct free kick

Indirect free kick

Above: A player intentionally handles the ball. A direct free kick is awarded against the offending team.

Above left: The attacking player to whom the ball is played is offside. A player who, in the opinion of the referee, is not interfering with play or an opponent, or who is not seeking to gain advantage by so positioning himself, is not penalized. An infringement of the offside law results in an indirect free kick being awarded to the defending team.

Left: An indirect free kick from which a goal can be scored only after the ball has been touched or played by a second player.

Above: A goal can be scored from a direct free kick. Such kicks are awarded for nine specific offenses; for example, intentionally tripping an opponent.

being played by a player other than the kicker.

lay off (the ball) To pass the ball to a teammate.

linesmen The two officials, one on each touchline, who assist the referee by indicating when and where the ball goes out of play and which team has the right to return it into play. They may also indicate when any infringement occurs, but the referee is not obliged to act on their signals.

linkman A midfield player.

man-to-man marking A defensive strategy with certain players responsible for marking specified opponents.

marking Covering a player so that he is unable to make constructive use of the ball should he receive it.

midfield player The player who links the defense with the attack.

near post The goalpost or side of the goal nearer the player with the ball.

nutmeg To kick the ball through a marking player's legs.

obstruction An infringement

when a player, not attempting to play the ball himself, positions himself between an opponent and the ball to stop that opponent playing the ball. The player being obstructed is allowed to shoulder-charge the obstructing player from behind.

offside A player is offside if he is in front of the ball and there are fewer than two defenders between him and the goal-line when the ball is played to him; also if, while in an offside position, he interferes with play in such a way that his team gains some advantage. He cannot be offside on a goal kick, corner kick, or dropped ball; in his own half; if the ball was last touched or played by an opponent; or if, while in an offside position, the ball is not played towards him and he is not interfering with play or trying to gain any advantage. One of the most controversial laws of soccer.

outside The touchline side of a player moving forward.

outside right/left The right/left

winger. *See* winger.

over-the-top Going over the top of the ball in a tackle and kicking the opponent instead.

overlapping Running up the touchline outside the player with the ball to provide support should he need someone to pass to.

park Scottish term for the field of play.

pass To kick the ball to another player, preferably a teammate.

penalty area The larger of the two rectangular areas in front of the goal.

penalty kick A direct (*qv*) free kick to the attacking team in their opponents' penalty area. The kick is taken from the penalty spot 12yd out from the center of the goal, with all other players but the goalkeeper and the penalty taker outside the penalty area and at least 10yd from the ball.

professional foul *See* tactical foul.

red card The card shown to a player by the referee to indicate

he is being sent (*qv*) off.

referee The official who controls the game, keeping the time and enforcing the laws.

reverse pass A pass made in one direction while the player making it moves in another direction.

running off the ball The activity of players who move into a good position to receive the ball from a teammate or to divert the attention of defenders from the movements of teammates.

screening The action of a player who, while in possession of the ball, uses his body to shield the ball from an opponent.

sending-off The referee's action in dismissing a player from the game for violent conduct, serious foul play, foul or abusive language, or continued infringement of the laws after a caution.

set piece A corner, throw in, free kick, or goal kick from which pre-planned moves can be put into practice.

shoot To kick at goal.

shoulder charge A fair (*qv*) charge.

Above: The player has gone into the tackle and played the ball cleanly. The opponent, coming in late to get possession, falls over his outstretched leg. This is not a foul.

Above: In his attempt to kick the ball, the player is putting his opponent in danger of injury. An indirect free kick is therefore awarded against the offending side for dangerous play.

Above: An unfair charge. The charge is directed at the opponent's body instead of his shoulder. A direct free kick is awarded against the offender.

Above: A player moving across the path of his opponent to prevent him from reaching the ball. This is obstruction, and an indirect free kick is given.

Left: The ball may be played with any part of the body, excluding the hands or arms. Thus a player may use his thighs (1), feet (2), chest (3) or head (4) to pass, stop or control the ball. There are two situations in which this does not apply. First at throw-ins, when the player is required to use both hands to throw the ball back into play. Second: inside the penalty area, where the goalkeeper may use his hands or arms. Outside the area he is subject to the normal restrictions.

square ball A pass across the field rather than in a forward direction.

stopper Name given to the center-half in the W-formation (*qv*); if used of modern players it refers to one of the center-backs.

striker The player whose prime role is to score goals. He operates mainly in the opposition's half of the field.

substitute A player who replaces a teammate because of injury or for tactical reasons. Substitutes must be named before the start of the game and throughout it are subject to the referee's authority. A player who is substituted cannot return to the game.

sweeper The player deployed behind the back four in a *catenaccio* (*qv*) formation, or in front if he is adopting a more attacking role. He has no special marking responsibilities but 'sweeps up' any loose balls or players who get away from their marking defenders.

tackle Using the foot or feet to take the ball away from an opponent's control. The intention of the tackler must be to play the ball, not the man, or he commits a foul if contact is made.

tactical foul A foul or hand-ball committed by a defending player to rob the attacking side of an obvious advantage, the subsequent stoppage and free kick giving the defense time to regroup. The offense may warrant a caution for ungentlemanly conduct. Also called a *professional foul*.

target man The striker who receives clearances from the defense or provides a target for the midfield players' passes.

third-back game A tactical formation resulting from the change of the offside law in 1925. The center-half was moved back from a midfield position between the halfbacks to play as a stopper between the fullbacks, so forming a defensive line of three backs.

through ball A pass through or over a defense which is intended for a teammate to run on to.

throw in The method of restarting play after the ball has crossed the touchline. It is taken by a player of the team opposing that of the player off whom the ball went out of play. He may not play it again until it has touched or been played by another player, nor can he score directly from the throw in.

trap To control the ball with the foot, chest, stomach, or thigh.

ungentlemanly conduct Any action that is considered against the spirit of the laws. It is punishable by an indirect free kick (unless accompanied by a more serious offense) and a caution.

volley To kick the ball before it has bounced, although the term is often used for any kick made while the ball is off the ground.

W-formation The tactical formation of the forwards in the third-back game, so called because the disposition of the forwards resembled a W with the two inside-forwards deployed behind and between the center-forward and the two wingers. More accurately, it was a W-M formation because the defense, with the two wing-halves deployed ahead of the fullbacks and stopper, resembled an M.

wall The line-up of defensive players between the ball and the goal at a free kick.

wall pass A pass quickly laid off by the receiver for the original passer to run on to. So called because the original passer is using his teammate as a 'wall' to rebound the ball from in order to beat a defender.

winger The forward player whose attacking role is to take the ball down the touchline and as close as possible to the goal-line before crossing into the goalmouth.

yellow card The card shown to a player by the referee to indicate he is receiving a caution.

zonal defense A defensive strategy with each player responsible for covering any attacking players who move into a specified area, or zone, of the field.

Gymnasium Sports

Gymnasium Sports

Gymnastics

Beam

Gymnastics, which played such a major role in the lives of the Ancient Greeks and Romans, lapsed into obscurity until revived at the end of the eighteenth century in Germany. Since then, interest and enthusiasm have spread worldwide. Men's gymnastics has been an Olympic sport since 1896 and women's events were introduced in 1928. At international level, the eastern European countries and Japan have dominated the sport in recent years.

Gymnastics falls into three general categories: free exercises (without apparatus), exercises with light apparatus, and those performed on fixed apparatus such as the parallel bars and the vaulting horse. At international level, gymnastics is contested separately by both sexes. Men compete on the floor, pommel horse, rings, vaulting horse, parallel bars and horizontal bar. Women's exercises, with a greater emphasis being placed on style and fluency of movement rather than strength, are performed on the vaulting horse, asymmetric bars, beam and floor. Women's floor exercises are performed to music. At the Olympic Games and world championships, which are held every four years, there are three fields of competition: team, individual events and the individual combined event. A team consists of six gymnasts who perform a compulsory and optional exercise on each apparatus. For the individual combined event, the best 36 competitors are selected from the teams to perform an optional exercise on each apparatus; and for the individual titles, the best six competitors on each piece of apparatus compete once more on that piece of apparatus alone. The compulsory exercises comprise set combinations of movements and are changed every four years.

Above: The beam, 5m long and 10cm wide. The maximum height is 1.20m, but this should be adjustable. Exercises on the beam are designed to test a gymnast's balance while performing along the length of the apparatus.

Below: The asymmetric or high and low bars consist of two wooden bars aligned with each other along their lengths but of varying heights. The top bar should be 2.3m high, and the bottom 1.5m. The distance between the bars, which are on the same plane, is adjustable.

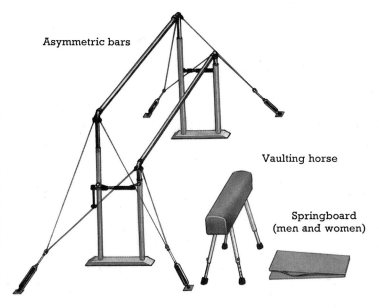

Asymmetric bars

Vaulting horse

Springboard (men and women)

aerial A movement (*qv*) which is performed in the air without the hands or feet touching the apparatus; eg an aerial cartwheel.

arab spring Alternative name for a round-off (*qv*).

arabesque A scale (*qv*) in which both arms are stretched out and the free leg is extended above horizontal.

asymmetric bars Apparatus used by women as one of their four exercises. The gymnast moves between the high and low bars using swinging and circling movements.

attention Upright body position with arms by the sides assumed before and after performance.

back lever Element on the rings in which the body hangs horizontally from straight arms, the stomach facing the floor.

balance An essential element of any gymnastic routine. Loss of balance is a fault and would be penalized in competition.

beam Apparatus used by women as one of their four exercises. It is mounted on adjustable sup-ports.

bent-body position Position in which the body is bent forward from the waist with the legs straight or bent.

body Leather covered part of a horse or buck.

boundary line Line marking the outer limit of the floor (*qv*). A competitor who steps on or over the boundary line is penalized by a deduction of points.

bridge Another name for the crab (*qv*) position.

buck A short side horse (*qv*).

cabriole Leap on the beam or floor in which take-off is from one leg, and both legs are brought together in the air before landing separately.

callisthenics Exercises designed to promote strength and grace in the gymnast.

cartwheel A sideways rotation of the body through 360° with the weight being taken alternately on the hands and then back to the feet. Legs kept straight and wide apart through-out.

cast A transitional movement on the asymmetric or parallel bars in which the body is swung from a support position (*qv*) to a clear (*qv*) support position.

cat leap A leap with flexing of the legs in front of the body.

chalk Magnesium carbonate compound used by gymnasts to keep their hands dry.

clear A position with a hand support with neither the body nor legs touching the floor or apparatus.

clubs Hand apparatus used in gymnastique moderne (*qv*) routines.

coach Person responsible for the training and welfare of an individual or team of gymnasts.

code of points The list which provides the degree of difficulty of the moves in the exercises and details the deduction of points for poor performance etc.

connecting move Position or movement performed between two elements in order to effect a smooth transition.

crab Position in which both

hands and feet are on the floor with the tips of the fingers pointing towards the feet; the body is arched with the stomach facing upwards.

croup Right end (*qv*) of a pommel or side horse, or the landing zone (*qv*) nearer to take-off point on a long horse (*qv*).

crucifix Position on the rings in which the body hangs straight down from outstretched arms in the form of a cross.

Diamidov A forward swinging full turn (*qv*) around one arm to a handstand on the parallel bars.

dismount Any method of leaving a piece of apparatus at the end of a performance or exercise.

dive handspring Another name for a flyspring (*qv*).

double back somersault A back somersault (*qv*) with a rotation through 720°.

double leg circle A movement on the pommel horse in which both legs pass right round the body (*qv*) of the horse under the left and right hands in succession.

elbow lever Lever (*qv*) in which

Men's equipment

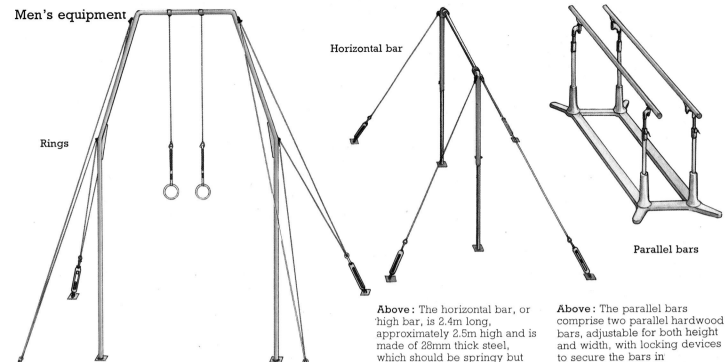

Rings

Horizontal bar

Parallel bars

Above: The rings are suspended from a metal frame, stabilized by guy cables or from the rafters of the gym. They hang approximately 2.5m from the floor and are attached to the suspending cables either by leather or webbing straps. The gymnast begins his routine by leaping up to take a grip of the rings.

Right: The vaulting horse comprises a heavily padded leather-covered body, mounted on adjustable legs. It stands at 1.2m high for women's exercises and at 1.34m high for men's. For competition, it is divided into croup, saddle and neck by lines defining the area of the saddle.

Above: The horizontal bar, or high bar, is 2.4m long, approximately 2.5m high and is made of 28mm thick steel, which should be springy but resilient. The bar may be on an independent base, stabilized with guy cables or mounted on a wall, although the latter presents certain difficulties for the performer.

Above: The parallel bars comprise two parallel hardwood bars, adjustable for both height and width, with locking devices to secure the bars in place at the required point. The bars are strong but flexible, and the base is heavy enough to ensure stability.

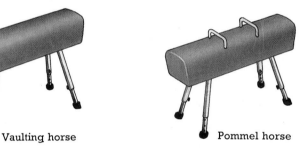

Vaulting horse

Pommel horse

the arms are bent at the elbows. Both a single elbow lever and a double elbow lever may be performed.

element A movement, position or balance performed by a gymnast.

Endo A Stalder (*qv*) performed in undergrasp (*qv*).

ends Parts of the pommel horse to either side of the saddle (*qv*).

face vault A vault in which the front of the body passes over the apparatus.

fall Should a gymnast fall from a piece of apparatus, he or she has a set time allowed in which to remount and continue; 10 seconds on the beam, 30 seconds on the asymmetric bars, etc.

FIG (Fédération Internationale de Gymnastique) Organization governing the world regulations of gymnastics, including the specifications for equipment.

first flight The second part of a vault from the take-off from the springboard to arrival on the horse.

flank vault A vault in which the

side of the body passes over the apparatus.

flic-flac Backward flyspring (*qv*).

float A movement in which the body swings under a bar, straightening as it goes.

floating support A support (*qv*) position in which no part of the body other than the hands comes into contact with the bar.

floor Padded area 12m² on which floor exercises are performed.

floor exercise Any exercise performed on the floor (*qv*). In competition, men perform for 50-70 seconds without music, and women 60-90 seconds to the accompaniment of one musical instrument. A floor exercise routine should make use of the entire area available, and should include leaps, spins, balances and tumbling techniques. The emphasis is on skill, grace and harmony for all competitors; in addition, men should display evidence of power and strength. Judges award marks according to the difficulties of the performance.

flyspring Handspring in which take-off is from both feet. Also called a *dive handspring*.

forward seat rise Technique in which a sitting position is attained on the bar from an inverted pike hang position (*qv*).

free A position or movement achieved without hand support.

front lever Ring exercise similar to the back lever (*qv*), but with the body facing upwards. It is harder to control than the back lever.

front support Position in which the gymnast is supported on his arms with his front facing the apparatus. *See* support.

giant Hecht A Hecht vault (*qv*) performed from the neck (*qv*) of the long horse.

giant stoop vault A stoop vault (*qv*) in which the push-off (*qv*) is from the neck (*qv*).

giant swing A swing around the horizontal bar with the body straight.

gymnasium Hall designed for the practice of gymnastics, and equipped with the appropriate

apparatus.

gymnastique moderne *See* modern rhythmic gymnastics.

handguard *See* palm strap.

handspring A forward or backwards turn through 360° starting from an upright position and springing from the hands back to the feet.

handstand Element in which the body, held in a straight line, is supported on the hands.

hang A position in which the body is suspended from straight arms, feet pointed towards the floor.

hang swing Any swing performed from a hang (*qv*) position.

hang turn Movement from a hang position to a straight arm support position on the rings by bringing the legs up over the head. Also called a *turn somersault*.

headspring A spring or upstart performed through a headstand (*qv*) position to bring the gymnast full circle back into a standing position.

headstand Element similar to the

Women's exercises

Backward walkover

Left: Individual floor exercises were introduced at the Olympic Games of 1952. The gymnast has the opportunity to show great creativity in the way she fits the sequence of movements to the musical accompaniment. Leaps, jumps, somersaults and dance movements can be combined into a highly artistic performance.

Above: The backward walkover to splits. From the starting position (1), the body is bent backwards and the arms lowered to the floor (2) to take the weight of the body. The legs are then swung into the splits position (3) before being lowered to the floor (4) and the splits position (5).

Right and far right: Exercises on asymmetrical bars consist mainly of swinging and circling movements. The changes from one bar to the other must be performed in continuous motion, without stopping. The gymnast needs to have great strength and suppleness in order to complete each exercise with continuity and accuracy. Dismounts can be accomplished in various ways. Each technique requires a high degree of balance to be performed without fault.

handstand, but with the weight on the head and hands. The hands also provide balance.

Hecht dismount A dismount from the asymmetric bars following a backward circle. As the body completes the circle the hands are released and, pushing from the thighs, goes over the bar with the body straight in a 'Hecht' position.

Hecht vault Vault performed from the croup (qv) of the long horse in which the body is horizontal, legs together, during flight, and the gymnast lands with his back to the horse.

high kick Limbering up exercise in which first one leg and then the other is kicked up in front as high as possible, keeping both legs straight.

hip circle Circle performed on a bar through 360° with the hips in contact with the bar throughout. It may be performed backwards and forwards.

horizontal bar Movements performed on the horizontal bar should demonstrate a continuous

swing motion—any form of hesitation is penalized. A routine, which usually lasts around 30 seconds, comprises some 12-15 movements.

in Movement whereby one or both legs is moved under one hand from a front support (qv) to a rear support (qv) position on the pommel horse.

inverted hang Reverse of the hang position (qv) on the rings in which the head is towards the floor and the feet point in the air.

inverted pike Hang (qv) position with the body piked (qv) and legs up over the head.

jeté A leap from one foot to the other.

judges Four judges and a referee are appointed for each event at international competitions. In addition, line judges and timekeepers are also nominated to check that competitors keep within the regulations.

kick uprise Technique by which a gymnast alters from an inverted hang (qv) position to a straight arm support (qv) position by

swinging the legs out and, at the same time, pulling himself up on his arms.

landing zone Term sometimes used for the croup (qv) and the neck (qv), the 60cm long areas at either end of the long horse (qv).

leotard Close-fitting all-in-one stretch costume worn by female gymnasts and also by men under trousers or shorts.

lever Position in which the body is held perfectly horizontal, supported on straight arms. May be performed on the floor, beam or rings.

long horse Alternative name for a vaulting horse without pommels. Men's vaults are performed from end to end. For women, the horse is turned sideways.

L-support Support (qv) position in which the body is upright and the legs stretched out at right-angles.

lunge Step on the floor or beam in which the leading leg is bent, the other trailing behind, and the

arms are stretched out, one forwards and one backwards.

marking Gymnastic events are marked by four judges (qv) on a points system from 0-10. Strict rules govern the deduction of points according to the degree of seriousness of a fault. The highest and lowest marks awarded are disregarded, and an average then taken of the middle two.

mat Portable floor covering of a non-slip, resilient material used for floor exercises and as a safety aid in the gymnasium.

mixed grasp Bar grip in which one hand is in the undergrasp (qv) and the other in the overgrasp (qv) position.

modern rhythmic gymnastics Branch of gymnastics for women in which the emphasis is on grace and fluency of movement. Exercises are performed on the floor with the aid of various hand apparatus, including the ribbon, ball and rope.

Moore A movement on the pommel horse in which the body

Free forward roll

Handspring vault

Left: A handstand on the beam with the legs in the stag position. Balance is the essential ingredient of beam exercises. The hands are used to grip the top and sides of the beam; the thumbs are placed on top while the fingers grip the sides. Although the beam was originally intended to be an apparatus on which women demonstrated mastery of balance, its leading exponents have incorporated many of the spectacular skills associated with floor exercises.

Below: The free forward roll. Starting with a crouching position with raised arms (1), the body is bent forward (2, 3, 4) until the head and shoulders rest on the beam (5). The feet are then released and swung over the head. Other beam routines include steps, jumps, spins, twists, sitting and prone elements, and held balances.

Right: The handspring vault. The gymnast leaves the springboard (1) with great speed to accomplish the first flight (2). Her hands momentarily come into contact with the horse (3) in order to push herself into the second flight (4) and the landing (5). In men's competition, the gymnast vaults over the horse lengthways, first going over the croup and then the neck. Both men's and women's vaults are assessed on the smoothness of the flight and landing and on the difficulty of the movement.

circles around one arm and over the horse.

movement An element (*qv*) in which swing or forward or backward movement is involved.

muscleuphandstand Method of attaining a handstand by use of strength alone rather than with the aid of swinging, etc.

neck Left end (*qv*) of the pommel or side horse, or the landing zone (*qv*) farther from take-off point on a long horse.

neckspring Maneuver in which the gymnast places his weight on his neck and follows through with a spring to a standing position.

out Opposite movement to an in (*qv*) in which the gymnast passes from a rear support (*qv*) to a front support (*qv*) position.

overbar somersault Forward or backward somersault performed in the air after swinging off from a support position on the parallel bars.

overgrasp Grip on a bar in which the palms of the hands face forwards.

palm strap Leather device designed to protect the hands from friction. Also called a handguard.

parallel bar grips In addition to the overgrasp (*qv*), undergrasp (*qv*) and mixed grasp (*qv*), the hands may grip the parallel bars either with palms facing outwards or inwards.

peach basket Another name for an underbar somersault (*qv*).

pike Position in which the body is bent forward from the hips with the legs straight.

planche Support position in which the body is horizontal and facing downwards, and is supported on straight arms above the apparatus.

pommel horse Apparatus used by men as one of their six exercises. It is similar to the vaulting horse but with handles, or pommels, 40-45cm apart in the center of the upper surface. The gymnast grasps the pommels and performs a routine of continuous swinging movements.

preflight First part of a vault, from the beginning of the run

to the take-off from the springboard.

push-off Point in a vault at which a gymnast pushes himself off from the horse with his hands.

rear support Support (*qv*) position on the pommel horse performed with the back to the apparatus.

resin Substance used to improve the traction of the soles of shoes, and to render the surface of the beams less slippery.

ribbon Hand apparatus used in modern rhythmic gymnastics.

ring exercises These should combine swinging and balancing movements and display the strength of the gymnast. Two handstands (*qv*) should be included in a performance, both of which should be held for two seconds. The gymnast is expected to perform without swinging the rings at any time.

rings Apparatus used by men. The two rings (inside diam. 18cm) are suspended from wire cables 50cm apart, the rings being attached to the cables by

looped straps. The height of the rings above floor level is a maximum of 2.50m.

roll A 360° turn on the floor or beam, either from a squat or a standing position. It may be performed forwards or backwards.

round-off A move designed to change forward movement to backward movement.

run-in Short run taken before a jump to gain momentum.

saddle Section of the pommel horse between the pommels, and the marked center section (40cm long) of the vaulting horse between the croup (*qv*) and the neck (*qv*).

safety belt Protective device worn around the hips when learning or practicing a difficult exercise. A cord attached to each side is held by a spotter (*qv*).

scale Element in which the gymnast balances on one leg (or knee) and holds the other leg in one of a number of positions. In a Y-scale, for example, the second leg is held up to the side so that

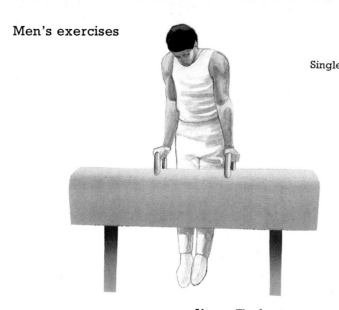

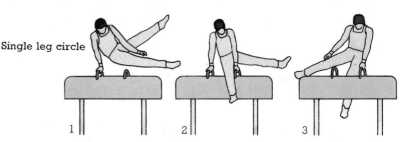

Single leg circle

Above: The front support position on the pommel horse, in which the front of the gymnast's body rests against the horse. In the rear support position, the back of the body rests against the horse. In the third support position, the straddle, one leg is behind the horse and the other is in front.

Left: Ring exercises probably demand the most strength from a gymnast. At the same time great balance and control are needed, for the rings should remain static between each movement.

Above: The single leg circle. The legs are raised to the left in a swinging motion. The left hand is released to bring the right leg over the horse (1) and then replaced while the legs are in the straddle position (2). The body is then tilted to the left and the right leg swung over while the right hand is released (3) to complete the movement.

Below: A sequence of movements showing the back uprise to an L-support. The body starts in a swing (1). On the backswing (2) the body is lifted to a horizontal position with the arms straight and vertical. From this position, the legs are swung forward, with the arms in the support position (3), and are then raised to the L position (4).

Back uprise to an L-support

the body forms a 'Y'.

scissors *See* shears.

second flight Second part of a vault, from push-off (*qv*) to landing.

shears An open-legged vertical swinging movement on the pommel horse in which each leg swings alternately to the back and front of the apparatus. Also known as scissors.

shoulderstand Similar to a headstand (*qv*), but with the weight resting on the shoulders.

side horse Another name for the pommel horse, or the vaulting horse used by women on which vaults are performed from one side to the other.

side splits Method of doing the splits (*qv*) whereby the legs are out to the side with the body facing forwards.

side travel Double leg circles on the pommel horse while moving from one part of the horse to another.

sole circle Full circle executed, forwards or backward, on the asymmetric or horizontal bar

with the arms straight, the body piked (*qv*) at the hips, and the soles of the feet on the bar. The legs may be together or in the straddle (*qv*) position.

somersault Turn performed in mid-air through 360°, beginning and ending in a standing position. It may be executed forwards, backwards or sideways, with the body tucked, bent or stretched out. Also known as a *salto*.

splits Element in which the body faces forwards with the legs outstretched and completely in contact with the floor, one forwards the other at 180°.

spotter Partner or helper when performing an exercise. Spotters are allowed in official competitions, but may not speak to competitors or help them in any way.

squat vault Elementary vault in which the legs are tucked up over the apparatus.

stag handstand Lunge (*qv*) handstand.

Stalder A movement performed

on the horizontal bar from an overgrasp (*qv*) giant swing (*qv*) with the legs straddled (*qv*) and the body piked (*qv*). The swing is from handstand to handstand.

stockli A rear travel (*qv*) out (*qv*) followed by an immediate rear travel in (*qv*) on the pommel horse.

stoop vault Vault performed on the long horse in which the gymnast springs from the croup (*qv*) with legs straight and body bent forward, then stretches out completely before landing with his back to the horse. This was the compulsory vault at the 1976 Olympic Games.

straddle Position in which the legs are wide apart, as in a straddle vault.

straddled L-support Support (*qv*) position in which the body is parallel to the apparatus and the legs straddled.

straight somersault Somersault (*qv*) performed with the body stretched out, rather than in the tuck (*qv*) position.

Streuli A backward roll (*qv*) into

a handstand (*qv*) on the parallel bars.

stutz A forward or backward swing with a half turn on the parallel bars.

support Any position in which the bodyweight is supported on the arms.

support seat Position in which the body is in a seated position in one of a number of angles and is supported on the arms.

swan dive Graceful stunt in which the gymnast leaps from a standing position, body stretched out, and dives into another position, eg a roll, handstand, etc.

swing uprise A movement in which the gymnast swings forwards or backwards and upwards from a hang (*qv*) or upper arm support (*qv*) on the rings, horizontal bar, or parallel bars.

Swiss handstand Handstand (*qv*) in which the legs are at right-angles to the body and in the straddle (*qv*) position.

tinsica A walkover (*qv*) performed sideways in a cartwheel motion with one foot and the

Left: Performances on the parallel bars are judged for strength, skill and aesthetic qualities, skill being considered more important than strength. The program must include one movement in which both hands are off the bar simultaneously.

Swing and support

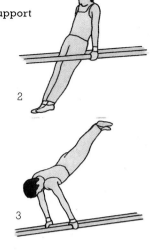

Above: The swing and support. The swing is made with straight arms and legs (2). At the end of each swing (1, 3) the body is above the bars.

Right: Exercises on the horizontal bar consist of continuous swings, any hesitation of flow being penalized.

Pull over

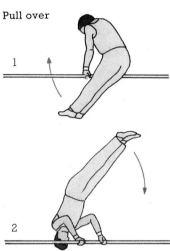

Left: The pull over on the horizontal bar. The body is drawn up towards the bar in a pike position and the legs pulled forward and upwards (1). From this position the legs are brought round the bar (2) to finish the movement.

---

corresponding hand in advance of the other.

trampoline Apparatus consisting of a rectangular metal frame on supports at about table height across which is stretched a sheet of canvas or nylon webbing approximately 3.6 x 2.4m. Exercises are based on a simple bouncing technique, from which a wide variety of stunts may be performed. It may be used as a training aid, but is not included in any of the general gymnastic categories.

travel To move between the saddle (*qv*) and the end (*qv*) of a pommel horse or vice versa.

tromlet Side travel (*qv*) movement completed by a double leg circle (*qv*).

Tsukara vault A vault with either a $\frac{1}{4}$ or $\frac{1}{2}$ turn on to the horse followed by one and a half somersaults off.

tuck Crouched position with the knees against the chest and toes pointed. The basic position for a somersault (*qv*).

tumbling Exercises comprising

turns or rolls (*qv*) are categorized as tumbling stunts.

turn A revolution around the long axis.

twist A rotation around an imaginary axis running the length of the body, using the head and arms for the turn.

underbar somersault A movement on the parallel bars from a support (*qv*) position whereby the gymnast swings backwards to a hang (*qv*) position and executes a backward somersault from under the bars to support. Also called a peach basket.

undergrasp Grip on a bar with the palms of the hands facing backwards.

underswing dismount Dismount in which the bar is released at the peak of a forward swing.

upper arm support Support position in which the arms are held along the top of the parallel bars.

upstart Technique whereby a gymnast raises the body from a hang (*qv*) position to a support (*qv*) position.

valdez A backward tinsica (*qv*)

starting from a sitting position. The character of the movement stems from the initial swing upwards.

vaulting In competition, each woman member of a team performs two compulsory and optional vaulting exercises. Points are awarded for the better of the two in each category. A competitor's hands must touch the horse when vaulting—on the long horse, the hands may not fall outside the landing zone (*qv*). A maximum run-up of 20m is permitted before a vault. Men perform one vault.

vaulting box Layered wooden box, the top of which is padded and covered with leather, similar to the body of a horse.

vaulting horse Apparatus used by men and women in the vaulting competition. The gymnast may twist (*qv*) or turn (*qv*) before landing upright. Women vault the horse sideways; men lengthways.

V-support seat A position in which the body forms a 'V' with

the legs pointed upwards.

walkover A movement executed on the floor or beam in which a turn through 360° is effected by bringing first the hands and then one leg after the other over to return to the standing position. It may be performed either forwards or backwards.

wall bars Basic gymnastic apparatus in the form of a series of wide wooden ladders joined together and attached to a wall.

warm-up Short period prior to a performance for carrying out simple exercises to loosen the muscles, and thus prevent strain.

wheel A 360° turn in either direction on the rings or the horizontal bar. On the rings, it commences and finishes with a handstand (*qv*), and on the horizontal bar in the hang position (*qv*). The latter is also known as the giant swing.

whip back Flic-flac (*qv*) without hand support.

Yamashita vault Handspring (*qv*) vault in which the body pikes in the second flight (*qv*).

Weightlifting

Weightlifting is much more than an attempt to lift the heaviest weight by sheer muscle power. The precise techniques and the mental training required make it anything but a simple sport. Speed and skill are essential attributes, while a sharp intelligence is needed to take full advantage of the tactical developments that add to the fascination of a competition.

In international competitions under the auspices of the IWF, lifters in the ten bodyweight categories have three attempts at each of the recognized two-handed lifts: the snatch and the clean and jerk. A third lift, the clean and press, was withdrawn in 1972 because of difficulties in judging. Order of lifting is decided by drawing lots, and each lifter may decide the weight he wishes to attempt. However, he may not then request a lighter weight. If the weight of the barbell is increased, the second weight must be at least 5kg greater and the third at least 2.5kg greater than the second. The lifter may attempt a heavier weight despite a failure, but failure at all three attempts on either lift means elimination from the competition.

At the end of the two lifts, the heaviest weights in each are added together and placings are determined on the totals. In the event of a tie for first place, the lifter with the lighter bodyweight at the weigh-in is the winner, or, if bodyweights were equal, the lifters involved are re-weighed and the lighter is declared the winner. Should there still be no difference, first place is shared. Amateur and for men only, weightlifting is on the program of major sports festivals such as the Olympic Games and has its own world championships.

Power lifting is also a popular sport and weightlifting routines are practiced by many athletes as an aid to improved performance.

The disks, loaded on the barbell with the heaviest on the inside and the lightest on the outside, are locked in position by collars. Weights are increased in multiples of 2.5kg. The collars and the bar, which is a maximum length of 1.31m between the inside collars, weigh 25kg.

Below: The two-hands snatch position achieved by the split technique. From this position the lifter must recover to an erect standing position still holding the bar overhead with his arms locked.

barbell The apparatus that is lifted with two hands. It consists of a steel rod with evenly distributed metal disc or rubber weights attached to either end by collars (*qv*). In order to facilitate turning the bar during a lift, each end of the bar has a revolving sleeve.

bench press One of the lifts in the power set (*qv*). The lifter, lying on his back on a bench, raises the barbell from his chest by an even, upward extension of the arms.

bodyweight The weight at which a lifter weighs in before a competition. Under IWF rules there are ten bodyweight categories: 52kg; 56kg; 60kg; 67.5kg; 75kg; 82.5kg; 90kg; 100kg; 110kg; over 110kg.

clean The continuous movement of the barbell from the platform to the shoulders without any 'violent' contact with the body, although a light brushing of the thighs is permitted. At the completion of the movement, the lifter must stand erect with his legs on a line parallel with the bar.

clean and jerk The second of the two competition lifts under IWF championship rules and the one in which the heaviest lifts are achieved. The barbell is lifted to the shoulders in a clean (*qv*) movement, using either the split (*qv*) or squat (*qv*) technique, and then, to complete the lift, is jerked in an explosive manner above the head. Because he uses his legs to provide impulsion during the jerk, the lifter must bring them back into a line parallel with the bar before standing motionless with arms and legs braced. The referee (*qv*) signals when he may lower (not drop) the barbell.

clean and press Until 1972 one of the recognized competition lifts. It was withdrawn because referees had difficulty controlling the dubious or borderline techniques being used. After the clean movement, the bar is lifted evenly above the head until the arms are fully extended. During this movement, there should be no movement of the feet, bending of the legs, or any exaggerated leaning back of the body.

collar The locking device used to keep the weighted disks on the end of the bar.

dead lift One of the lifts in the power set (*qv*). Gripping the bar with both hands, the lifter raises it by straightening his thighs and back until he is standing erect with the bar touching his thighs.

deep knees bend Another name for the squat (*qv*) in the power set.

dumb bell The apparatus that is lifted with one hand. It consists of a short steel rod with disk weights attached to either end by collars. So called because the weight was originally a piece of lead shaped like a bell (and was therefore a silent, or dumb, bell), it is used in weight training and in some countries in competition, although these lifts are not IWF-approved events.

IWF (International Weightlifting Federation) It was founded in 1920 at the request of the International Olympic Committee to provide the sport with an official set of rules.

jerk An explosive movement in which the bar is lifted from the shoulders to an arms-extended position above the head. It is often used to denote the clean and jerk (*qv*).

lift A weightlifting event, such as the clean and jerk or snatch. It is also used to denote a successful attempt to lift the barbell.

lifter A weightlifting competitor.

lights See signals.

locked arms The full extension of the arms with the barbell above the head.

no lift An attempt which fails to meet with the approval of the referees because of an infringement of the rules for the particular lift.

platform The wooden area of 172sq ft on which all competition lifts must be made. It must be so built that the planks run crosswise, or parallel to the line of the

124

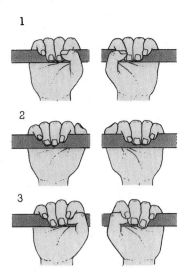

1

Left: Three main ways of gripping the bar.
1 The normal grip.
2 The thumbless grip.
3 The hook grip.

Right: The two-hand snatch position achieved by the squat technique. Although at one time considered more difficult technically, the squat offers a greater weight potential and in modern lifting has largely superseded the split technique.

Below: The two-hand clean and jerk. From the initial position (1), the lifter must get the bar to his shoulders in a single, clean movement, first heaving it above his thighs (2) and then using a split or squat technique (3). From here he adopts an erect standing position prior to the jerk—the movement to extend the bar overhead. To accomplish the jerk, most lifters favor a split technique (4) with the body below the bar in a supporting position. The lifter then recovers to an erect and motionless position (5) with his feet in a line parallel to the bar.

barbell. A lifter has three minutes in which to come to the platform to make his lift or he misses that attempt. If, during an attempt at a lift, he touches the floor beyond the platform or leaves it he is disqualified.

power set Three lifts which depend more on sheer strength than skill and speed. They are the bench press (*qv*), the dead lift (*qv*) and the squat (*qv*). Though not included in the Olympic Games, the power set has world championships and is contested at national and international meetings.

press An even extension of the arms. It is often used to denote the clean and press (*qv*).

referees The officials who determine whether or not the lifts conform to the IWF rules. There are three referees for each weight category, and each judges the lift independently, signaling his verdict on the light signals (*qv*). One of the three acts as chief referee, and it is he who gives the signal to lifters to

lower the bar at the completion of the lift. He sits directly in front of and at least 20ft from the lifter, while the others take up a position to either side so that they study the lift from different angles. If one referee differs in his opinion of the lift, the decision of the other two applies. There may not be any appeal against the referees' decisions.

signals At major events, the referees signify their opinion of a lift by means of light signals: white for a fair lift and red for a no lift. Each referee has his own panel on the signals indicator in relation to his position around the platform. However, the indicator does not light up until all three referees have operated their switches. On the board, the white lights form the top row and the red lights the bottom.

snatch The first of the two competition lifts under IWF championship rules. The barbell is lifted from the platform to the locked arms overhead position in one explosive movement that

takes less than two seconds to perform. The lifter must then establish an erect standing position with legs and arms braced. During the first 'snatch' movement he may use either the squat (*qv*) or split (*qv*) techniques, but apart from a brushing of the thighs the bar must not come into contact with the body. The referee signals when the barbell may be lowered.

split Technique used by lifters to assist in a lift. As he lifts the barbell, the lifter performs the splits by simultaneously moving one leg forward and the other backward while at the same time thrusting the barbell to shoulder height or to the overhead locked arms position.

squat (1) Technique used by lifters to assist in a lift. As he lifts the barbell past his waist, the lifter bends his knees and drops into a squatting position, simultaneously bringing the barbell to his shoulders or thrusting it overhead with an extension of the arms. It is now more commonly

monly practiced than the split (*qv*).

squat (2) One of the lifts in the power set (*qv*). It is also called the deep knees bend. Taking the barbell from between two upright stands, the lifter rests it across the back of his neck and shoulders and adopts a squatting position with his thighs parallel to the floor. He then has to rise to his original standing position without moving his feet.

weigh-in The proceedings at which the bodyweight of the lifters is established. For championships and international competitions, lifters are weighed in the nude two hours before the start of their category. If anyone is too heavy, he has one hour from the start of the weigh-in to reduce to the correct bodyweight limit. If still too heavy he may compete in the next category provided he has met the qualifying weight and his presence in that category comes within the rules for the competition.

Target Sports

Archery

Given man's ingenuity for ensuring his own survival, it is not surprising that the bow was one of his earliest weapons. Even in its simplest form it is an effective means of attack and defence. Not that all early bows were crude constructions. In Asia and southeastern Europe nearly 4,000 year ago, the first composite bows were made from horn, sinew and wood coated with lacquers. Today, the composite bow is a masterpiece of technology, and arrows are made of aluminium and fiberglass tubing more often than of wood. Only the longbow retains its heritage, scarcely altered from the days of Crécy and Agincourt.

Archery, however, is no longer concerned with war. It is a rapidly growing international sport with around 50 countries affiliated to FITA and IFAA. In 1972 target archery returned to the Olympic Games, and there are biennial world championships and international tournaments. Britain's Grand National Archery Society celebrated its centenary in 1961, and the US National Archery Association celebrates its 100 years in 1979.

Of the two main types of archery, target and field, target archery is the most popular in Europe. Archers shoot a round in groups of two to six to a target, the number of arrows loosed varying from six to twelve dozen, at distances varying from 40-100yds (36-91m), according to the particular round. A round consists of a series of ends in which the archers, shooting in rotation, loose two sets of three arrows each before taking their scores and retrieving their arrows. In field archery the targets are laid out on a course in rural surroundings. Groups of three to six archers loose four arrows at each target, scoring them before proceeding to the next target. Shots may be uphill or downhill and are at distances from 10-80yds (9-73m). A round comprises 28 targets.

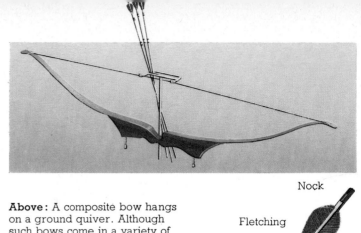

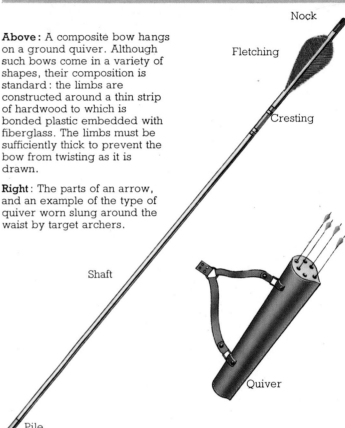

Above: A composite bow hangs on a ground quiver. Although such bows come in a variety of shapes, their composition is standard: the limbs are constructed around a thin strip of hardwood to which is bonded plastic embedded with fiberglass. The limbs must be sufficiently thick to prevent the bow from twisting as it is drawn.

Right: The parts of an arrow, and an example of the type of quiver worn slung around the waist by target archers.

Nock

Fletching

Cresting

Shaft

Pile

Quiver

---

arrow rest The feather or plastic fitting above the arrow shelf (*qv*).

arrow shelf A protrusion or cutaway above the grip on a composite bow.

bare-bow A class of shooting in which sighting devices are not permitted. Sometimes called *instinctive* shooting.

belly The inner side of the bow. The outer side is called the *back*.

boss The circular target of coiled straw rope over which the colored target face is stretched.

bowsight An instrument above the arrow rest which enables the archer to aim directly at the target. It is adjustable for sightings at any distance.

brace To string the bow.

bracer An arm-guard worn on the inside of the forearm, preventing clothing, or the arm itself, from deflecting the bowstring.

butts The field in which shooting takes place (or in field archery the bales against which the target face is placed).

cast The ability of a bow to shoot an arrow swiftly and cleanly. It can also denote the distance it will shoot.

clout shooting A form of archery in which the target is marked out on the ground by a cloth or flag.

cock feather The feather set at right-angles to the nock (*qv*). It may be a different color from the other two feathers.

composite bow A bow made of different materials, such as wood, fiberglass and plastic—as opposed to a self-bow (*qv*).

compound bow A bow whose holding weight at full draw is less than the 'peak' weight with which the arrow is projected.

cresting The distinctive colored pattern below the fletching (*qv*) to aid identification of arrows.

draw weight or bow weight. The effort, expressed in pounds, required to draw an arrow to a specified amount. Bows are graded according to draw weight.

end A specified number of arrows, usually six, shot by

archers before the score is taken and the arrows retrieved. A round is broken up into ends.

face See target face; field face.

fast An order to archers to stop shooting immediately. It is an abbreviated form of 'stand fast'.

field face The paper target affixed to the butts in field archery rounds. The faces are either concentric circles, or pictures of animals with scoring areas superimposed on them. Generally there are three scoring zones, scoring five, four, or three points.

FITA Fédération Internationale de Tir à l'Arc, the world governing body of target archery.

fletching The three or occasionally four vanes (*qv*) set at equal distances around the nock end of the arrow to keep it on a straight and steady flight.

flight shooting A form of archery in which the aim is to shoot the arrow as far as it can go. There are three classes: target bows, the specially designed flight bows, and freestyle.

freestyle A class of shooting in which sighting devices are permitted. The most usual style for target and field archery.

gold The inner circle, colored yellow, of the target. It is not called a 'bull' or 'bull's eye'. In field archery the inner circle is called a *spot*.

handle See riser.

IFAA International Field Archery Association, the world governing body of field archery.

junior An archer under 18 years of age.

kisser A small guidemark on the bowstring which comes into contact with the archer's lips when the arrow is fully drawn, to help the archer know his draw and alignment are consistent.

lady paramount A traditional office dating from medieval times when a lady of importance was patron of a tournament. Today she is the person who hands out the prizes.

let down To disengage slowly from the full draw position without releasing the arrow.

FITA target: the outermost zone scores 1 point. Scoring progresses by 1 point with each zone, so that the center zone scores 10 points.

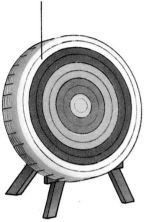

9 7 5 3 1

Above: The small leather 'tab' which fits over the drawing fingers to protect them against the bowstring and also to help obtain a smooth release.

Left: An archer with a longbow, the most popular of self-bows. On the inside of his forearm, the archer is wearing a bracer as protection against the bowstring.

Above: An international 10-zone target face used under FITA rules, and the standard 5-zone target face. The scoring value of each zone or band is indicated. For rounds under FITA rules there are two sizes of target face; the 31½in and 48in, the latter being used for distances of 66yd and over. On the 48in 10-zone targets, the yellow or gold-colored area is 9⅝in wide, while the other colors are 4¾in wide. On the 31½in target face, the gold-colored area is 6¼in and the other colors 3⅛in wide.

33yd
55yd
77yd
99yd

33yd
55yd
66yd
77yd

Men's round

Ladies' round

Right: An archery range for rounds shot under FITA rules. Once they have shot the required number of ends at one distance, the archers move forwards to the next line.

limb The upper or lower part of the bow, thick enough to prevent the bow twisting as it is drawn.

longbow A self-bow (*qv*) traditionally made of yew.

loose To release the arrow and the bowstring when full drawn.

nock The notch at either end of the bow and at the end of an arrow into which the bowstring is inserted. To put the bowstring into that notch on the arrow.

nocking point The correct point on the bowstring where the arrow should be engaged.

petticoat The part of the target face not covered by the colored scoring rings.

pile The point of the arrow.

pin hole The exact center of the target.

popinjay shooting practiced mainly in Europe, this form of archery uses blunt arrows to dislodge wooded 'birds' from their 'roost' on top of a 85ft mast. The 'birds', called cocks, hens and chicks, each have a point value.

quiver A receptacle in which

arrows are kept ready for use.

release aid A mechanical device which releases the bowstring from the fully drawn position, without the archer having to relax his fingers.

riser or *handle*. The center part of the bow between the limbs.

round The shooting of a specified number of arrows at set distances. Rounds vary according to the proficiency, sex and age of the archer. The rounds in target archery include: the Albion, the American, the Bristol (juniors), the FITA (shot under international rules), the Hereford, the Long National, the Long Western, the Metric (juniors), the National, the New National, the Portsmouth, the St George, the St Nicholas, the Short Metric, the Stafford, the Western and the York, which is the longest round of all being 144 arrows at distances up to 100yds (91m). The Portsmouth and the Stafford are indoor rounds, and the Portsmouth is the shortest round being 60 arrows at 20yds (18m).

The rounds in field archery include: the Field, the Hunters, the International, the Big Game and the Foresters. The last two rounds are sometimes shot 'unmarked', which means that the archers are not given information as to the distances at which the targets are placed.

self-bow A bow made from one piece of the same material.

serving Additional thread wound around the center of the bowstring to prevent fraying.

shaft The body of the arrow between the pile (*qv*) and the nock (*qv*). It can also mean the whole arrow.

sighters Six arrows shot at the start of a target archery round by each archer. They are not part of the round and do not count towards the score.

spine The thickness of the arrow, or in tubular arrows the relation of the wall thickness to overall diameter. It determines the weight and flexibility of the arrow and its suitability for use with a particular bow.

spot *See* gold.

stabilizer Additional weights attached to the bow, to add physical weight and thus stability, or strategically placed to 'balance' the bow.

tab A small piece of leather which fits over the drawing fingers to protect them against the string and obtain a smooth release.

target face The canvas, or similar fabric, which is stretched over the boss (*qv*). It has five colored scoring rings painted white, black, blue, red and yellow (or gold). On the standard target face each color is worth 1, 3, 5, 7 and 9, respectively. The international target face consists of ten zones, each of the five colors being halved and having a value of 1 to 10 from the outer to the inner ring. There are two sizes of 10-zone face, 31½in and 48in.

tassel A cloth, usually in club colors, for cleaning muddy arrows.

vane The feather or thin plastic used to make the fletching.

Rifle Shooting

An Olympic sport since the first modern Games in 1896, and with world championships since 1897, target rifle shooting is today practiced under UIT rules at a 10-zone target over 11yd for air rifles, 55yd for small-bore rifles, and 328yd for full-bore rifles. Shooting is three-positional, except in the case of air rifles and the small-bore English match. Away from international competition, however, the sport is enjoyed under the rules of individual national governing bodies, whose classes frequently derive from historical motives for the growth of rifle shooting. For example, in Britain, which had lagged behind Europe in the adoption of the rifled gun, full-bore shooting developed under the auspices of the British NRA, formed in 1860 to fulfill a semi-military function: '. . . the encouragement of Volunteer Rifle Corps and the promotion of rifle shooting. . . .', and in small bore under the auspices of the NSRA. Britain's empire followed the example of the motherland, and the close ties between the shooters of the British Commonwealth are epitomized by the attendance at the annual Imperial Prize Meeting at Bisley in Surrey.

Rifle shooting is practiced extensively in the United States, the Soviet Union and Scandinavia. Its appeal in middle Europe, though no less fervent, is perhaps not quite as widespread. It was to the United States that many central European gunsmiths emigrated in the eighteenth century, taking with them a knowledge of weaponry and marksmanship accrued by their forefathers since the fifteenth century. Essential to that knowledge was the value of rifling—the grooves cut into the bore of the barrel to make a bullet spin in flight. A discovery of the mid-sixteenth century, it gave the handgun an accuracy to equal that of the bow as a target weapon.

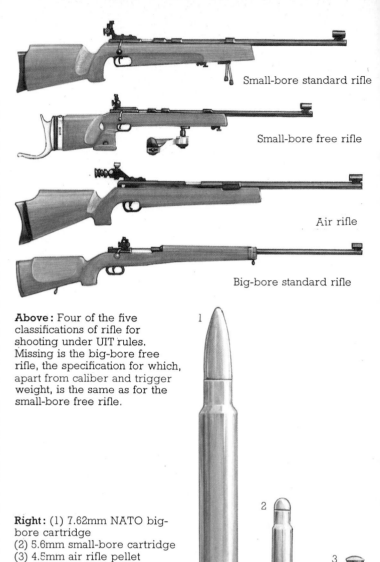

Small-bore standard rifle

Small-bore free rifle

Air rifle

Big-bore standard rifle

Above: Four of the five classifications of rifle for shooting under UIT rules. Missing is the big-bore free rifle, the specification for which, apart from caliber and trigger weight, is the same as for the small-bore free rifle.

Right: (1) 7.62mm NATO big-bore cartridge
(2) 5.6mm small-bore cartridge
(3) 4.5mm air rifle pellet

action The firing mechanism on a breech-loading, bolt-action rifle.
aiming off Making allowance for the effect of the wind on the bullet when taking aim.
air rifle A class of shooting for compressed air or CO_2 gas rifles with a caliber of 4.5mm. Shooting under UIT rules is from the standing position at 11yd; the course of fire is 40 shots in 90 minutes.
back, or back position A shooting position in British and Commonwealth match rifle shooting. The shooter lies on his back with his feet pointing towards the target, one knee bent and the rifle fore-end resting on the other knee. The head may be supported by the non-firing hand or by a sling.
backers Plain white cards placed at a certain distance behind each shooter's target, to trace the origin of shots, to determine when two shots are fired through the same hole, and to help the shooter spot his shots.
backsight A device, mounted

behind the breech, comprising an eyepiece with a small circular hole, or aperture, for aiming. It may be moved vertically or horizontally.
bedding Internal adjustments to a rifle to control barrel vibration. Also known as *stocking-up*.
big-bore See full-bore.
bull The center mark of the target. On the UIT decimal (10 points) target its value is 10; on targets for British and Commonwealth shooting its value is 5.
canting Allowing the rifle to turn sideways when aiming, with the result that the sights are not perfectly upright when the shot is fired.
compensation The effect of barrel vibration in a vertical plane.
course of fire The number of shots to be fired in a competition and the time in which they must be fired.
drag The slowing-down effect that air turbulence, caused by a bullet's flight, has on the bullet.
dummy frame Used in British and

Commonwealth full-bore shooting for marking. When the target frame is lowered after each shot, it is replaced by a frame with a colored panel. The position of this panel indicates the value of the shot.
English match A UIT competition for small-bore free rifle shooting from the prone (qv) position at 55yd. The course of fire is 60 shots plus 10 or 15 sighters in two hours. The term is also used for any shooting in the prone position.
foresight A device mounted on the fore-end of the barrel to aid aiming.
free rifle A class of shooting under UIT rules for modified full-bore and small-bore rifles. Aids to holding are permitted, as is the use of aperture sights fore and aft. Telescopic and optical sights are forbidden.
full-bore Shooting with rifles with a maximum caliber of 8mm. Under UIT rules it is for standard and free rifles from three positions at 328yd. Course

of fire for free rifles is 120 shots plus 30 sighters in 5 hours 15 minutes; for standard rifles it is 60 shots plus 18 sighters in 2 hours 30 minutes. Under British and Commonwealth rules, full-bore shooting is for rifles suitable for firing 7.62mm NATO or .303in (7.69mm) Mark 7 bullets and is divided into target (qv) rifle, service (qv) rifle, and match (qv) rifle classes.
handstop A metal device screwed to the underside of the fore-end of the stock to provide support for the non-firing hand. It is permitted on target and free rifles but not on service and standard rifles.
hangfire An abnormally lengthy time between the firing-pin striking a bullet's percussion cap and the propellant charge igniting.
jump The upwards or downwards movement of the barrel resulting from recoil when the rifle is fired.
kneeling A shooting position in which, under UIT rules, the

The tunnel foresight

Twin-zero backsight for lateral and vertical adjustment.

The three shooting positions for competitions under UIT rules.
Far left: Kneeling. The toe of the right foot, the right knee, and the left foot must make contact with the ground, although the shooter may use a cushion to support his right instep. A sling may be used as a holding aid.
Above left: Standing. The shooter may rest his left arm on his chest or hip, but use of a sling as a holding aid for the rifle is prohibited. A glove may be worn on the left hand to improve the support as well as for comfort.

Left: Prone, The rifle is supported only by the shooter's hands, one shoulder or armpit, and a sling, which is looped around the left arm. The rifle may be rested against the shooter's cheek.

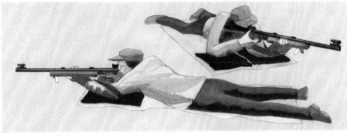

Above: An UIT 55yd target, with scoring zones from 1 to 10. The number of targets and the size vary with the distance being shot.
Right: Three basic support holds when shooting with the standard rifle in a standing position. The nearer the hand is to the trigger guard, the greater the height of the rifle.

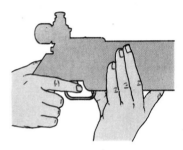
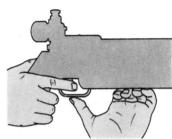
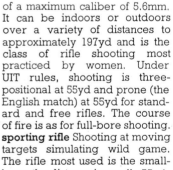

shooter must touch the ground with only three points of contact: the toe of the right foot, the right knee and the left foot (reverse for left-shoulder shooting).
magpie The scoring ring of white with a value of 3 on a British NRA target.
match rifle A class of shooting in British and Commonwealth competitions for any rifle of 7.62mm caliber. Magnifying or telescopic sights may be used Shooting is usually from the back position over ranges in excess of 875yd. Course of fire may be a series of 7, 10, 15, or 20 shots at 45 seconds per shot.
NRA National Rifle Association.
possible The maximum score a shooter can obtain.
NSRA National Small-bore Rifle Association, formed in 1901.
prone A shooting position in which the shooter lies face down towards the target, the upper part of the body supported on the elbows. The arms from hand to elbow must be clear of the

ground and all other objects. The rifle is supported only by the shooter's hands, a shoulder or armpit, and a sling.
receiver The main body of a rifle into which the barrel is screwed or breeched.
service rifle A class of shooting in British and Commonwealth competitions for self-loading 7.62mm-caliber rifles without unauthorized alterations or additions. Both sights must be as issued, though the blade of the foresight may be undercut. The use of slings is not permitted except for deliberate' shooting. The number of shots and the range distances are as for target rifle.
shoulder-to-shoulder Shooters taking up positions at stations (qv) in a horizontal line.
sighters Practice shots to check the accuracy of zeroing.
sitting A shooting position in which the shooter sits on his buttocks. His back must not be supported.
small-bore Shooting with rifles

of a maximum caliber of 5.6mm. It can be indoors or outdoors over a variety of distances to approximately 197yd and is the class of rifle shooting most practiced by women. Under UIT rules, shooting is three-positional at 55yd and prone (the English match) at 55yd for standard and free rifles. The course of fire is as for full-bore shooting.
sporting rifle Shooting at moving targets simulating wild game. The rifle most used is the small-bore; the distance is usually 55yd.
squadding The allocation of stations and a time of shooting to competitors.
standard A full- or small-bore rifle conforming to the UIT standard rifle specifications. Aperture sights and bedding are permitted but, except for a sling, not the use of holding aids.
standing A shooting position in which the shooter stands erect on both feet without any artificial support for himself or the rifle.
station The section of a firing

range allocated to a shooter.
stock The woodwork on a rifle.
stop-butt A mound rising behind the targets.
target rifle A class of shooting in British and Commonwealth competitions for bolt-action 7.62mm or .303in-caliber rifles of conventional design. Backsights may be fitted for horizontal as well as vertical adjustment and tubular foresights added. Handstops are permitted, as are slings. Shooting is from the prone position at 200-1,000yd (183-914m) and comprises series of 7, 10, or 15 shots plus two sighters.
three-positions Shooting at the prone, standing and kneeling positions in one competition with the points from each making the final score.
UIT Union International de Tir, the world governing body of target shooting, founded in 1907.
zeroing The process of ensuring that the line of sight to the target is in correct relationship to the line of the bullet's projection.

131

Water Sports

Canoeing

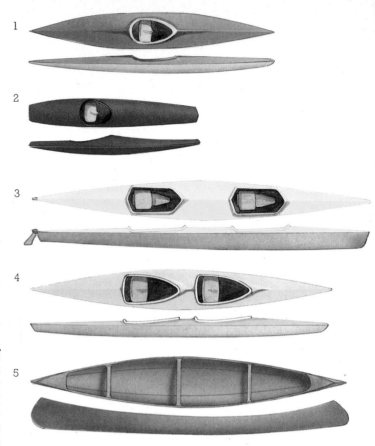

Both as a leisure activity and a competitive sport for men and women, canoeing has enjoyed worldwide growth in the twentieth century. For many, it provides an invigorating and sometimes exciting means of touring, for a carefully packed canoe is able to carry all the holiday camper requires. On a competitive basis, its appeal has been recognized with the inclusion of men's Canadian and kayak sprint events in the Olympic Games since 1936; women's since 1948. Slalom was included at the 1972 Olympics, but apart from then the adherents of slalom and wild-water, or down-river, racing have had to make do with separate biennial world championships. The sprinters also have annual championships, while canoe sailers, racing the single-hulled 10-square-metre craft, have world championships every four years.

Although the word canoe is used generically to cover both Canadians and kayaks, more precisely it referred originally to the Canadian which, before the influence of modern design and materials, was an open craft, pointed at both ends and paddled in a kneeling or half-kneeling position with a single-bladed paddle. Today's sleek racing craft bear little resemblance to their progenitor, and to the uninitiated there appears little difference between the slalom and wild-water Canadians and kayaks. The rules for these events, however, specify that the highest point of the Canadians' cross-sections must not be higher than a line between the highest points of stem and stern. Sprints are restricted to flat water and defined distances, and long-distance racing is appropriate to most waters. But for slalom and wild-water events, waters are needed that test the canoeists' control. Slalom courses should have a current flow of around 2yd/second over 875yd, while wild-water courses must be at least 1⁴/₅mi long.

Above: Various types of canoes. 1 Slalom kayak; 2 Surf kayak; 3 Marathon racing double kayak; 4 Touring double kayak; 5 Touring Canadian canoe. (1) and (2) show two of the three basic kayak designs, the modified Sweden form and the Sweden form, respectively. The third design is the Fish form.

Right: Forward paddling is the basic kayak paddling stroke. The canoeist grips the paddle as shown and begins the stroke as far in front of him and as close to the canoe as possible, finishing it when his hand is in line with or slightly astern of his hip. A straight course is maintained by making strokes on alternate sides of the kayak.

aft The area of a canoe between amidships and the stern (qv).

amidships The center of a canoe, being an equal distance from stern and stem (qv).

back-paddling Reverse paddling to stop or to travel backwards.

bilge The hull section of the canoe below the waterline.

blade The broad end of the paddle used for propulsion.

bottom board A removable board, inside the hull, which takes the canoeist's weight.

bow The forward part of the canoe.

bowman The paddler sitting nearest the bow.

bow rudder Paddling stroke used to turn the bow towards the side on which the bowman is paddling.

brace A recovery (qv) stroke with which the paddler, by leaning on the paddle, prevents the canoe from capsizing.

breakout A stroke forcing a canoe out of the mainstream.

buoyancy Aids placed at the bow and stem to prevent the

canoe from sinking.

C Initial used to denote a competition Canadian canoe. A figure following the initial denotes the number of crew.

Canadian A type of canoe, rudderless, in which the paddler, squatting, uses a single-blade paddle. Sprint canoes are open; slalom and wild-water canoes are decked.

chute A narrow, clear channel through rapids.

coaming The raised board or edge around the cockpit to stop water washing into the hull. Also known as the *washboard*.

cockpit The space in the hull of a decked canoe in which the paddler sits.

deck The top covering of a closed canoe.

deep-water rescue Method of using another canoe or canoes to help a capsized canoeist right his canoe and re-enter it.

down-river racing *See* wild-water racing.

draw stroke Paddle stroke used to pull the canoe sideways.

drip rings Plastic or rubber rings fitted around the neck of a double-blade paddle to prevent water running off the upraised blade, down the loom (qv), and up the paddler's arms.

eddy Where part of a current runs against the normal flow because of an obstruction, or the contour of the waterbank or bed.

Eskimo kayak A decked canoe with a small cockpit and upswept stem.

Eskimo roll A full 360° turn through the water.

ferry glide Using the current to cross a river at right-angles to its direction by setting the canoe at a diagonal to its flow.

fish form A hull shape in which the maximum beam is forward of amidships.

freeboard The area from the waterline to the gunwale when the canoe is loaded.

free gate A slalom gate which may be taken in any direction. It is marked with black and white rings.

gate The slalom obstacle, comprising two hanging poles through which the canoe must pass cleanly in order not to suffer penalties. The port side pole is red and white, the starboard side green and white.

gunwale, or gunnel The upper edges of the hull.

haystack A standing wave topped with white water, usually caused by fast water encountering slower water or some submerged obstacle.

j-stroke Used when single-blade paddling to steer the canoe. The steering action comes at the end of each stroke.

K Initial used to denote a competition kayak. A figure following the initial denotes the number of crew.

kayak A rigid, decked canoe after the style of the Eskimo kayak. The paddler uses a double-blade paddle and is enclosed in a cockpit. It may have a rudder for steering, but not for slalom and wild-water racing.

keelson An internal part of the

Kayak canoe and paddle

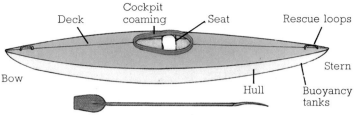

Deck · Cockpit coaming · Seat · Rescue loops · Stern · Hull · Buoyancy tanks · Bow

Canadian canoe and paddle

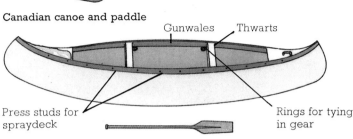

Gunwales · Thwarts · Press studs for spraydeck · Rings for tying in gear

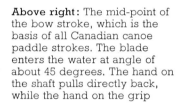

Above right: The mid-point of the bow stroke, which is the basis of all Canadian canoe paddle strokes. The blade enters the water at angle of about 45 degrees. The hand on the shaft pulls directly back, while the hand on the grip pushes forward from the shoulder until the midpoint is reached. Straight travel is maintained by pushing outwards at the end of the stroke, most canoeists preferring not to alternate as with the kayak.

Left and below: The sequence in the put-across roll, one of the three main Eskimo rolls. Rolling enables the paddler to right his canoe, in the event of a capsize, without having to leave it.

canoe running lengthwise along the keel.

leeboards Boards set down in the water at the sides of a sailing canoe to stop it drifting sideways.

line-down Leading the canoe by a painter (qv) through obstacle-strewn water.

long-distance racing Competitive canoeing over courses of varying length and conditions. Races may take place on rivers, lakes, or open water.

loom The shaft of the paddle as far as the blade.

marathon See long-distance racing.

modified Sweden form A hull shape in which the maximum beam is amidships. Also known as *symmetrical form.*

open water The sea or an estuary.

painter A rope attached to the bow or stern.

pawlata A method of righting a kayak by the Eskimo roll, where the paddler leans forward throughout the action.

pry-over A stroke used to move a Canadian canoe sideways, by prying the paddle away from the side of the boat.

recovery The stroke used in the Eskimo roll to bring the canoe upright. Also the period from the completion of one single-blade paddling stroke to the beginning of the next.

rib A part of the frame which runs at right-angles from the keel up to the gunwale.

riffle A small, shallow rapid.

run-off Extra water in a river as a result of heavy rain or thawed snow.

screw A method of performing an Eskimo roll with the hands remaining in the normal paddling position.

sculling An action of the paddle blade by which a canoe can be moved sideways, or by which a canoeist can support himself in a near-capsize position.

slalom A fast water competition event in which K1s, C1s and C2s negotiate a course of gates, plus some natural obstacles over two timed runs.

spooned blade A blade scooped like a spoon to obtain a better pull through the water.

spray cover A form of apron fitted over the coaming (qv) and wrapped around the canoeist's waist to prevent water from entering the hull.

sprint A competition event for kayak and Canadian canoes over flat water courses as still and free of wind as possible. Under international rules, races are for K1, K2, K4, C1, C2 and C7 over 500m, 1000m and 10,000m.

stem The pillar at the front edge of the hull.

stern The rear of the canoe. The sternpost fulfills the same function as the stem.

steyr A method of righting a kayak by the Eskimo roll, where the paddler leans backwards throughout the action.

stopper A wave sufficiently large to cause a capsize. It is usually found in rapids or below a dam where water rolls back on itself and so is flowing both up and down stream. Also known as a *hydraulic jump.*

Swedish form A hull shape in which the maximum beam is aft of amidships. Also known as *Sweden form.*

sweep A stroke used to turn the canoe to starboard or port.

Telemark A stroke made by holding the paddle out to one side and leaning inwards on it to effect a sharp turn.

tiller bar Foot control for a rudder.

trim The level at which a canoe rides in the water.

white water Turbulent water found where fast water flows over rocks or obstacles. Correctly known as *wild water.*

wild water racing A competition event for K1s, C1s and C2s over stretches of fast-moving water with natural and man-made obstacles. Races consist of one timed run.

yaw To go off course by swinging from side to side.

yoke Crosspiece on a rudder to which control lines are attached.

Diving

Diving, at its most elementary, is entering the water, irrespective of the method used. Originally, in competition, that method was the so-called plain one: a development of the English header and known as the Swedish swallow. The body was kept straight with the arms extended sideways at shoulder level until being brought above the head prior to entry. Events consisted of a series of similar dives from platforms of varying heights. Gradually, under the influence of Swedish divers, 'fancy' movements were introduced into the period of flight, and today diving, with its male and female practitioners performing breathtaking twists and somersaults in piked and tucked positions, appears to have more in common with gymnastics than with its aquatic counterpart, swimming. It does, however, share the same governing body—the Fédération Internationale de Natation Amateur (FINA).

Diving, like gymnastics, requires its champions to possess physical qualities of balance, co-ordination, agility and strength in addition to such mental qualities as application. A further essential quality may well be courage, for there are few sports, if any, which require their participants to launch themselves at a barrier, albeit water, which they strike at more than 25 mph.

In competition, diving takes two principal forms, highboard and springboard. Dives are classified in the international diving tables according to type and body position. There are six types—forward, backward, reverse, inward, twist and armstand—and four body positions—free, piked, straight and tucked. Divers are required to perform a specified number of dives, each of which has a degree of difficulty, and the classification of dive must be listed in the divers' entries. Men's diving has been an Olympic sport since 1908; women's since 1912.

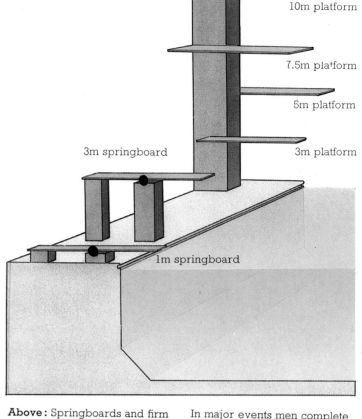

Above: Springboards and firm boards used in diving. Highboard diving is done from the 5, 7.5 and 10m boards. Springboard diving offers the most exciting spectacle as well as aesthetic satisfaction to the diver. The time gained in rising to the peak of the dive from the board allows divers to make more complicated movements.

In major events men complete 11 and women 10 dives from the 3m springboard. Five of these dives, in both cases, are compulsory. In highboard diving men make six required dives with a combined degree of difficulty not greater than 11.2 and four voluntary dives without limit. Women make four required dives and four voluntary dives

armstand Starting position in which the diver adopts a handstand stance at the end of the board. Performed only from the highboard.

back dive Dive in which the diver commences facing backwards and enters the water backwards.

break-out Moment in flight when the diver changes position from tuck (*qv*) or pike (*qv*) to the straight (*qv*) entry position.

degree of difficulty, or tariff The established figure by which the judges' marks are multiplied to give the total score for a particular dive. There are 195 possible springboard dives and 166 highboard dives listed in the international diving tables, and each is given a degree of difficulty. The 3m springboard tariffs range from 1.2 for the inward dive with tuck (ie with no somersaults or twists) to 3.0 for the forward dive with 3½ somersaults piked and the reverse 2½ somersaults piked; the 10m highboard tariffs range from 1.1 for the inward

dive with tuck to 2.9, carried by four dives. Judges do not take the degree of difficulty into account when marking.

entries In competitions, each diver must hand his/her list of dives to the secretary. He/she is then bound to perform those dives listed or be penalized.

entry Making contact with the water after the flight (*qv*) stage of a dive. In competitive diving, the entry into the water must be made vertically, with the body straight and the toes pointed. In head-first entries the hands must be extended above the head, and are usually grasped together to strengthen the diver's position and reduce splash. In feet-first entries the hands must be clasped to the sides of the body. Because the whole body is often rotating on entry, various saving (*qv*) techniques are used to maintain or effect the desired vertical position.

failed dive A dive which the referee is certain was not that announced by the diver in his/

her entries (*qv*).

flight The part of the dive from take-off to entry, during which time the diver is in the air.

forward dive Dive in which the diver commences the dive facing forward and enters forwards. May be standing or running (*qv*).

highboard diving Diving from a rigid platform which, for the purposes of competition, is sited at 5m, 7.5m and 10m. The board must be covered with a non-slip surface, while the depth of water at entry (10m) must be 4.5m. Highboard competition for men consists of four voluntary dives, the total degree of difficulty for which must not exceed 7.5, and six voluntary dives without limit; a total of ten dives. Women's competition comprises four voluntary dives as above and four voluntary dives without limit; a total of eight dives. Also known as *platform* or *tower* diving.

hurdle A jump upwards from one foot executed before the final two-footed take-off in running dives.

inward dive The diver commences the dive facing backwards and appears to dive inwards.

Isander Former name for the reverse (*qv*) dive; named after its Swedish originator.

judges The panel of officials who award marks on the merits of the dives performed. In major games there must be seven judges, in international and big domestic meets seven. After each dive, at a signal from the referee, they show their marks which are based on the four sections of the dive: stance, take-off, flight and entry. Each dive is marked out of 10 on the following scale: completely failed 0; unsatisfactory ½-2; deficient 2½-4½; satisfactory 5-6; good 6½-8; very good 8½-10. Marks are deducted as follows: incorrect starting position 1-3 (for taking less than four steps in a running dive, the referee deducts 2 points from the mark of each judge); not showing a steady armstand position 1-3 (the referee deducts 2 points

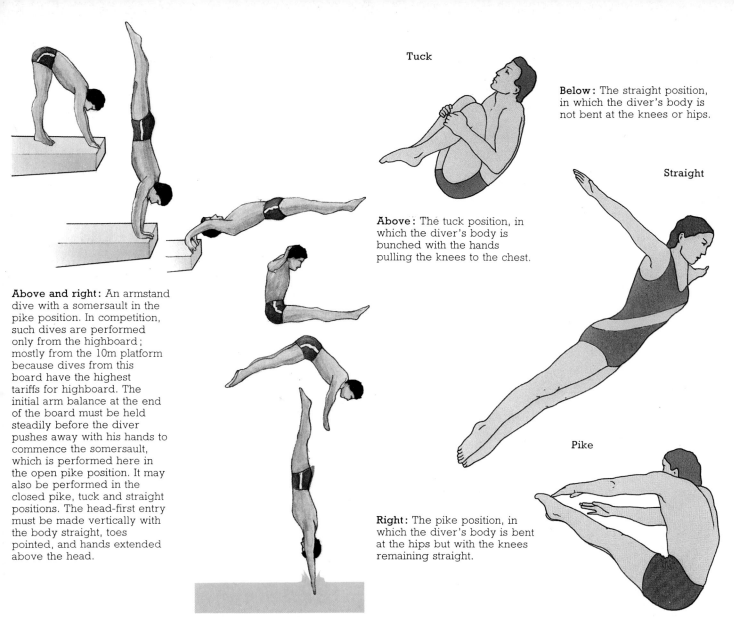

Tuck

Below: The straight position, in which the diver's body is not bent at the knees or hips.

Straight

Above: The tuck position, in which the diver's body is bunched with the hands pulling the knees to the chest.

Above and right: An armstand dive with a somersault in the pike position. In competition, such dives are performed only from the highboard; mostly from the 10m platform because dives from this board have the highest tariffs for highboard. The initial arm balance at the end of the board must be held steadily before the diver pushes away with his hands to commence the somersault, which is performed here in the open pike position. It may also be performed in the closed pike, tuck and straight positions. The head-first entry must be made vertically with the body straight, toes pointed, and hands extended above the head.

Pike

Right: The pike position, in which the diver's body is bent at the hips but with the knees remaining straight.

from each judge's mark if the diver takes two attempts at the armstand; this also applies to other dives started twice); arms not in correct position on entry 1-3. In feet-first dives, if the arms are held above the head on entry the dive is marked out of 4½ points. (*See* scoring).

Mollberg Former name for the reverse somersault dive; named after its Swedish originator.

pike The body position adopted in somersaults in which the diver's body is bent at the hips with the knees straight. In slow-rotating somersaults the 'open pike' position, with the arms extended sideways and the hips bent at roughly 90°, is sometimes adopted. If fast somersaults are required, the 'closed pike' position, in which the arms pull the knees close to the shoulders, is used.

reverse dive Dive in which the diver commences the dive facing forward and, by pulling the feet forwards and upwards, enters the water in a backward position.

running Dives in which the diver approaches the end of the board at a slow run or walk of at least four steps before take-off. The approach must be continuous and only one jump is allowed. From the springboard the take-off must be from two feet; from the highboard it may be from one or both feet.

saving Underwater movements performed by divers to enable them to attain or maintain the desired entry (*qv*) position.

scoring The method of calculating a diver's score from the marks awarded by the judges. For example, the marks for a dive in a world championship event might be as follows: seven judges' marks—6½, 6½, 7, 7, 7, 7½, 8. The highest and lowest marks (6½ and 8) are discarded and the remaining marks multiplied by a tariff of, say, 1.5, to give a total of 42.5. This figure is then adjusted to average the marks of three judges (ie x 3/5), producing a final score of 31.5 for the dive.

secretary The official who records the marks and computes the score for each dive and diver. Also known as the *recorder*.

somersault A movement in which the body rotates fore and aft around the center of gravity. In diving, somersaults may be performed in one of three positions: straight, piked, or tucked.

springboard diving Diving from a flexed and springy platform. Competitive springboards are sited at 1m and 3m, and are normally made of fiberglass-coated laminated wood or steel with a movable fulcrum which allows the diver to adjust the amount of 'whip' in the board. Springboard competition for men consists of the following dives: five required dives (forward, backward, reverse and inward dives, and forward dive with ½ twist), and six voluntary dives chosen from the five groups; a total of 11 dives. Women's competition comprises the five

required dives as above, plus five voluntary dives; a total of ten. Dives may be performed from 1m or 3m boards, but as 3m dives carry higher tariffs (*qv*) that board is used to the almost complete exclusion of the other. Separate 1m competitions are organized at domestic level and occasionally internationally.

starting position *See* armstand, back, forward, inward and reverse dives.

straight The body position during a dive in which the diver's body and legs are kept in a straight line,

swallow dive Forward dive in which the arms are held out sideways until just before entry.

tariff *See* degree of difficulty.

tuck The body position adopted in somersaults in which the whole body is bunched up as compactly as possible, bent at the hips and knees. The hands pull the knees, which should be kept together, to the chest.

twist A sideways rotation around the body's longitudinal axis.

Rowing

Principally an amateur pursuit, rowing developed as a sport in eighteenth-century England as a result of races staged between professional watermen. It was in 1715 that Thomas Doggett initiated the famous Doggett's Coat and Badge sculling race for watermen just out of their apprenticeship. Some 60 years later, rowing regattas were a popular feature on the Thames, and by the turn of the century clubs were being formed and rowing adopted at some public schools. In 1829 Oxford and Cambridge universities met at Henley in the first Boat Race, which was to prompt local businessmen to initiate their own Henley Regatta in 1839. Elsewhere rowing was developing in similar fashion: the Harvard-Yale Boat Race was inaugurated in 1852 and clubs were formed in Australia and Europe as well as in the United States. It was the Americans who, in 1856, introduced keelless boats and, a year later, sliding seats. Outriggers were an English innovation of the previous decade, as was the Carvel-hulled smooth-skinned boat.

The sport has two forms, rowing and sculling, though for convenience both come under the generic title of rowing. The main distinction is that the rower has one oar whereas the sculler has two sculls. Rowing events are for coxed and coxless pairs, coxed and coxless fours, and eights which, by necessity, are coxed. Sculling events are the single, double and quadruple sculls. In Olympic, world championship and other international regattas, events are contested in lanes over standard FISA distances of 2000m for men, 1500m for junior men (under 18) and 1000m for women. Heats are usually held, with a repêchage system operating, to produce the required finalists. Other forms of rowing that have achieved popularity are Head of the River races, bumps and coastal rowing.

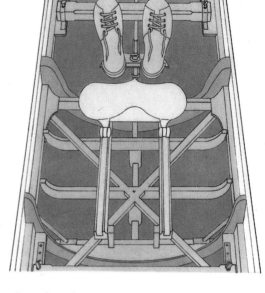

Above: A section of a shell showing the stretcher, to which the oarsman's clogs, or traps, are attached; the sliding seat at the frontstops; and the runners on which the slide travels.

A four with conventional rigging. In the 1950s, to compensate for the snaking effect of the conventional rig, the Italians devised a rig with two center oars on one side, stroke and bow on the other.

backstops The furthest point of travel of the slide (*qv*) in the direction of the bows.

best boat A light racing boat with a smooth skin; usually of carvel construction.

blade The wide end of the oar that is put into the water to provide impulsion.

Boat Race The annual race on London's Thames between the eights of Cambridge and Oxford universities.

bow The oarsman rowing nearest the bow, or front, of the boat.

bowside The starboard side of the boat on which the bow usually rows; those rowers whose oars are on that side.

bumps, or bumping races A traditional form of racing at Cambridge and Oxford universities; also practiced in other parts of England, especially where waters are not wide enough for side-by-side racing. The crews start in line ahead formation and attempt to touch (bump) the boat in front so that they can move up a place in the line on the following day's racing. Any crew that is bumped must stop rowing.

button An adjustable collar fitted to the shaft of the oar to prevent it from slipping through the rowlock (*qv*).

canvas A margin of victory by the length of the bow or stern section of a boat; so called because these sections are covered with thin linen (or, nowadays, dacron).

catch a crab To feather (*qv*) the blades before the finish of the stroke. As a result, the water catches the oar and the momentum of the boat upsets the oarsman.

clinker A method of hull construction with overlapping planks laid fore and aft.

cox, or coxswain The person who steers a boat that is not steered by the oarsmen themselves. He also calls the rate (*qv*) of striking.

double A boat for two scullers (*qv*).

eight The fastest and longest boat with eight oarsmen and a cox. It is 52-59ft long, 24in across at the beam and only some 13in deep. Its weight is approximately a sixth of the total weight of its crew.

élite class The top category in rowing; reserved for oarsmen who have won six races as seniors.

feather To turn the blade flat and parallel to the water between strokes to lessen wind resistance and to avoid hitting the water on the recovery.

fin A small metal protrusion under the hull of a racing shell to aid stability and steering. It is set near the stern.

FISA Fédération Internationale des Sociétés d'Aviron; the governing body of rowing, founded in 1892.

fours An event for four-oared boats, either coxed or coxless.

frontstops The slide's furthest point of travel in the direction of the stern.

gate The device on the rowlock (*qv*) which is unscrewed and lifted so that the oar may be inserted or removed.

Head of the River A form of rowing race in which the boats set off at regular intervals and are individually timed, the fastest crew winning the event. As there are no stations (*qv*), the overtaking crew has right of way. The term is also used for the crew which finishes first at the end of bumping races.

inboard That part of the oar from the handle to the button.

Macon blade See spade blade.

novice An oarsman who has never won an open event at a regatta.

oarsman Strictly, a person who rows with one oar, although the term is often used to mean anyone who rows or sculls.

outboard That part of the oar from the button to the tip of the blade.

paddling The pressure applied by the rower or sculler in combination with the rate of striking is classified as *full pressure*, *half pressure* or *light paddling*.

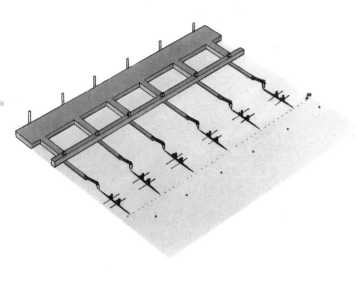

Left: The start of a sculling doubles, with the boats held steady from the quays. Where such facilities are not available, moored stake-boats are used for keeping the boats in alignment.

Below: An oarsman's stroke, from bringing the slide up to the frontstops with the blade feathered (1). At the frontstops he squares the blade (2) then immerses it into the water (3), and as he commences to pull the oar his body swings back on the slide, making his legs (the journey on the slide) last as long as the stroke (4 and 5). At the completion of the stroke (6), the blade is feathered and the oarsman moves his oar, body, and slide into position for the next stroke.

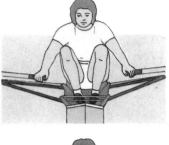

1

2

3

4

5

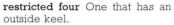

6

Above: Three stages of the sculler's stroke: (top) body in position to immerse the blades in the water; (center) pulling the blades through the water and swinging back on the slide; (bottom) the completion of the stroke. Because the handles overlap in the middle of the stroke, the sculler has to scull with one hand higher than, or ahead of, the other.

pairs An event for two-oared boats either coxed or coxless.

petite finale The race for seventh to twelfth places at an international regatta or FISA championship

pinch the boat To begin the stroke at such an acute angle to the boat that the pressure is applied inwards rather than forwards.

puddle The swirl of water left by the blade after a stroke.

quadruple scull A sculling boat, either coxed or coxless, crewed by four scullers.

rake The angle of inclination on the stretcher (*qv*).

rate of striking The number of strokes rowed per minute.

recovery The period from the end of one stroke to the beginning of the next.

repêchage A system whereby the losing crews in the heats of an event are given a second chance of going through to the finals. The aim of the repêchage heats is to ensure that the best crews contest the final.

restricted four One that has an outside keel.

rigger The outrigger which protrudes from the side of the boat and supports the rowlock.

rigging The way the riggers and stretchers are set to obtain optimum efficiency from the crew.

rower Term in modern usage to replace oarsman (*qv*).

rowlock The support for the oar. Modern rowlocks swivel on a vertical pin attached to the end of the rigger. Also called a *swivel*.

rudder A wooden or metal flap with which the boat is steered.

sculler A person who rows with two sculls, one in each hand. Sculls are shorter and lighter than a normal oar and have a smaller blade area.

shell A racing boat with a smooth external surface and without an outside keel, although it does have a fin.

skiff A heavy, clinker-built boat which is propelled by sculling.

sky To raise the blade too high

above the water before beginning a stroke.

slice To place the blade too deeply in the water during the stroke.

slide The seat on which the oarsman or sculler sits. So called because it slides along on runners to allow the oarsman to achieve a much larger stroke.

spade blade The shorter, wider blade which pioneered the move towards more efficient blade shapes and was the forerunner of the *Macon* blade now used almost universally.

squared The position of the blade as it moves through the water. From the feathered position the oar is turned so that the blade is just past a right-angle to the water.

stakeboat A moored boat or pontoon from which the stern of a boat is held before the start of a race.

station The lane or section of a course allocated to a boat.

stays The metal tubes which together form the rigger.

stretcher The part of the boat on which the oarsman rests his feet, and against which he pushes during a stroke. His rowing clogs, or flexible shoes, are attached to it.

stroke The oarsman sitting in the stern seat. He is responsible for setting the rate of striking and the rhythm for the crew to follow. A stroke is also the cycle of the oar from entry into the water through to recovery (*qv*).

strokeside The port side of the boat on which the stroke's oar is usually placed; those oarsmen who row on that side.

swivel A rowlock that pivots from a vertical pin attached to the outer end of the rigger.

tub A wide, heavy boat equipped with riggers and sliding seats for teaching rowing to beginners.

washing-down The positioning of a boat in front of another, thus causing the opposing crew to row in its wake or puddles.

wash out To partially remove the blade from the water before the finish of the stroke.

Sailing

At one time the prerogative of the wealthy classes, sailing is today very much everyone's sport and pastime, attracting participants from all walks of life. Not all may be able to afford the challenge and excitement of a transatlantic or Round the World race in a sleek offshore racer, but the advent of the many dinghy classes in the years following World War II has given millions of people the opportunity to 'mess around in boats'. If sailing competitively, all yachtsmen must comply with the rules of the IYRU which cover all aspects of pre-race organization, starting signals and procedures, right of way when racing, and the infringement of rules.

The term yacht applies to a craft with living accommodation for its crew, but it is also used collectively to embrace the many day-sailing classes of dinghies, keel boats and multi-hulls. Depending on the number of masts and the disposition of their sails, yachts may be sloops, cutters, ketches, yawls or schooners. This diversification of rigs has evolved as a method of harnessing the power of the wind by using sails which can be easily handled by the crew. When set, the sails assume an airfoil section and act as deflector plates, with the result that the movement of the wind over these surfaces, combined with the yacht's natural resistance to sideways motion, produces forward movement. The sole limitation to progress is the yacht's inability to sail closer than 45° to the wind. To overcome this, in order to attain a windward objective, it has to zigzag towards its goal close-hauled on alternate tacks and is said to be beating. When its course is at 90° to the wind, the yacht is on a reach, and when sailing away from the wind it is running.

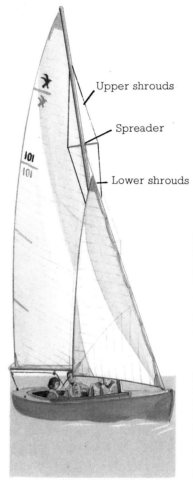

Knockabout day-sailer

Upper shrouds

Spreader

Lower shrouds

Cat-rigged one-man dinghy

Left: A family day-sailer, which is Bermudian rigged to carry a mainsail and a single triangular foresail, or jib. As its name suggests, the spreader (also known as a crosstree) helps spread the angle of the shrouds which carry through it to the masthead.

aback Said of the sail when the wind is on the wrong side (ie what was formerly the lee side).
abaft Behind; nearer the stern than another part or person; eg abaft the mast.
abeam On the beam (*qv*); at right angles to the boat's center line.
Admiral's Cup An international competition for teams of three Class 1 offshore (*qv*) racing yachts per country. It is held every two years to coincide with Cowes Week on the Isle of Wight and is determined on results in four races: the Channel Race, Britannia Cup, New York YC Cup and Fastnet Race.
America's Cup An international challenge trophy named after the schooner *America* which won it for the United States in a race against 15 British boats around the Isle of Wight in 1851. Since then the New York YC has resisted all challenges to win the trophy. Racing today is between two 12 meter (*qv*) yachts off Newport, Rhode Island, with the

challenge decided on the best of seven races.
apparent wind The wind that is felt by a moving boat; a combination of the true wind and the boat's speed.
back To trim the sails to windward to slow down the boat or turn away from the wind.
backing Said of the wind when it changes in a counterclockwise direction.
backstay The rigging (*qv*) that stretches from the top of the mast to the stern to prevent the mast from moving forward.
balanced lug A rig in which the boom and gaff are on the leeward side of the mast. The lugsail (*qv*) is lowered when tacking.
ballast Weight added to a yacht to improve its stability and provide counter-leverage against the effect of the wind on the sails. Most yachts, apart from dinghies and catamarans, have built-in ballast in the form of a keel, while internal ballast may also be used for trimming.
bar An underwater ridge or

sandbank across the mouth of a river, so making the water very shallow there. It is formed by the action of the tide or current.
batten A thin strip of wood or plastic in the leech (*qv*) to control the tautness of the sail.
batten down To make secure hatches, portholes, and anything likely to fly about in disturbed conditions.
beam The widest part of a craft, or the measurement thereof. Also a transverse wooden or metal fixture supporting the deck.
beam reach Sailing with the wind at right-angles to the line of the yacht from bow to stern.
bear away To alter course away from on the wind until the yacht is dead before the wind. Also known as *falling off the wind*.
bear down on To steer towards a certain object or area.
beat (1) To sail to windward on alternate tacks. (2) The upwind leg of a race.
belay To secure a line around a cleat with figure-of-eight turns.

bending sails Securing sails to their spars.
Bermudian or Bermudan A rig that sets a high triangular mainsail with the luff (*qv*) parallel to the mast and the foot (*qv*) attached to the main boom. Perhaps the most common rig, it is suitable for all craft from dinghies to offshore racers and cruisers.
bilge The curve of the hull from topsides to the bottom of the boat. Also refers to the lowest part inside the hull.
bilge keel A fin or keel attached to the bilges to provide stability.
blue peter The preparatory flag, blue with a white rectangle in the center, hoisted five minutes before the start of a race.
bolt rope A line which is sewn along the edge of a sail to strengthen it.
boom The spar attached at right angles to the mast to hold the foot of the sail along its length.
bow The forward end of a craft.
bowsprit The spar projecting forward of the bows for the

Left: A cat-rigged dinghy. The cat is sometimes called the Una rig. The unstayed cantilever mast was a revolutionary feature of the Finn class, which first appeared in 1949 and has been the Olympic one-man class since the 1952 Games in Finland.

Dragon class

Below: A cutter-rigged cruiser, the cutter having two or more foresails. The mainsail may be either a Bermudian (as illustrated) or gaff sail. Ease of handling, as well as its versatility, is one of the reasons for the popularity of the Bermudian rig over the gaff rig, although its mainsail can be difficult to lower when sailing off the wind. When it first appeared, in the years preceding World War I, this rig was known as the Marconi rig on account of its tall mast

and elaborate stays and shrouds resembling the then-new radio masts. Depending on the disposition of her sails and spars, a yacht is a sloop, cutter, yawl, ketch, or schooner. Whatever its rig, though, a cruiser should have a considerably less complicated sail plan than that employed on a racing yacht, the principal reason being that the cruiser may often have a smaller (and perhaps less experienced) crew than her racing sister.

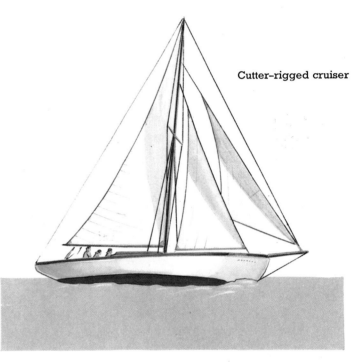

Cutter-rigged cruiser

Above: The Dragon class, a three-man racing keel boat which carries a genoa and spinnaker in addition to a mainsail. Its low freeboard is characteristic of those classes designed for inshore racing. The Dragon, originally designed to be a fast two-man cruiser which could also be raced, was an Olympic boat from 1948 to 1972, when it lost its status. One reason was the high cost of carvel-planked building, a method in which the planks are butted edge to edge and caulked. In 1976, the six Olympic classes were the Finn (1-man dinghy), Flying Dutchman (2-man dinghy with trapeze), 470 (2-man dinghy with trapeze), Soling (3-man keel boat), Tempest (2-man keel boat with trapeze), and Tornado (2-man catamaran).

purpose of setting an extra or bigger foresail.
bring up To stop or come to anchor.
bumkin A short spar which extends aft over the stern to support the backstay or the mizzen sheet lower block.
burgee The small triangular or swallow-tail flag flown from the mast to indicate the yachtsman's club. When racing, it is common to fly a rectangular racing flag.
cat rig Rig which sets only one sail—the mainsail. It is used on one-man racing dinghies such as the Finn class.
catamaran A twin-hulled yacht with the hulls held parallel to each other by a bridge deck.
center-board A hinged or sliding keel. It is a flat plate of wood or metal raised and lowered through a slot on the centreline of the hull to enable the yacht to steer a course close to the wind.
chinese jibe An uncontrolled jibe (qv) in which only the lower half of the sail swings over to catch the wind on its

opposite side, the top half of the sail remaining on its original side. The shape of the sail in such a jibe is described as an 'hour glass'.
cleat A T-shaped fitting to which a line can be secured.
clew The lower aft corner of a sail where the leech (qv) joins the foot.
close-hauled Sailing as close to the wind as possible. Also known as on the wind.
committee boat A craft which is manned by the race officers and so positioned that they are able to control the races. It must be rigged to fly the necessary class and warning flags. It may be anchored to form one end of the starting line.
cutter rig A rig in which there are two or possibly more foresails as well as the mainsail.
dagger-board A vertical plate used in small dinghies instead of a center-board. It is not hinged to pivot as a center-board does, but has to be pulled up or pushed down by hand.

dinghy An open, unballasted sailing craft ranging in length from 8-20ft approximately. Lateral resistance is obtained by means of a center-board (qv) or dagger-board with the crew providing moving ballast against the wind's force on the sails.
dipping lug A rig in which the lugsail, when the boat is tacking, is released at the tack which is taken behind the mast. The gaff is 'dipped' to the new leeward side. The halyard is slackened off to facilitate dipping and set up on the windward side.
displacement The weight of a vessel, which is equivalent to the amount of water it displaces.
draft or draught The measurement of the hull from the water-line to the lowest part of the keel or center-board. It determines the amount of water needed to sail the boat.
draw Said of the sails when filled by the wind; also used in reference to a boat's draft. It is said to draw so much water.
drop keel Another name for a

center-board or center-plate.
ease sheets To let out the sheets (qv) to trim the sails; also to alter course away from the wind.
eye of the wind The direction from which the wind blows.
fall The part of a halyard on which a crew member pulls.
fathom A nautical measure of depth equivalent to 6ft. The term is also used as a measurement for lengths of line.
feather the rig Letting the sheets off to leeward as much as needed to partially stall the sails. It is performed to slow down the boat while at the same time keeping it under control.
flake To stow a line in a serpentine fashion so that it can be run out easily.
foot The lower edge of the sail.
foresail Any sail set forward of the main mast.
forestay The rigging fastened from the front of the mast to the bow.
free Said of the wind when it is blowing from the beam or abaft.
freeboard Term describing the

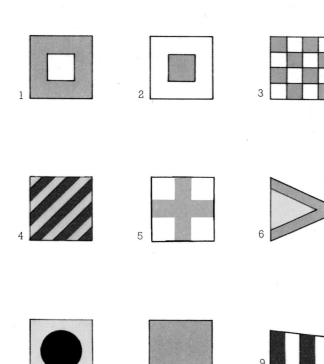

Below: The Olympic course is three-sided and marked out by three buoys laid out shortly before the start of the race. The reaching mark, Buoy 2, is laid to make an angle of 60 or 90 degrees with Buoys 1 and 3. The angle chosen depends on the classes sailed. Buoy 2 may be laid to the right. The course is sailed in three rounds which can be divided into six legs. The first leg is a beat from start to Buoy 1. Two reaches from Buoy 1 to Buoy 3 form the second and third legs. The fourth and fifth legs consist of a beat from Buoy 3 to Buoy 1 and a run from Buoy 1 to Buoy 3. The last leg is the beat from Buoy 3 to finish. The beat is usually 1.5 nautical miles.

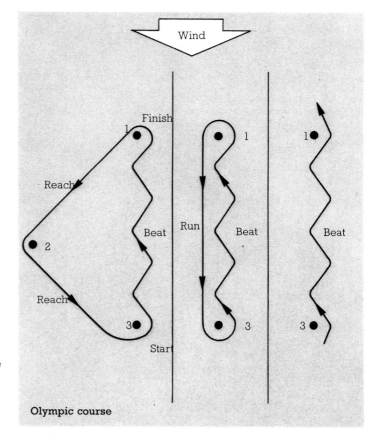

Olympic course

Above: International flags and pennants used for signalling in races. 1 Flag 'P', the 'Blue Peter' is hoisted on the starting boat 5 minutes before the start of the race; 2 Flag 'S' indicates that the course has been shortened; 3 Flag 'N' signals all races are abandoned; 4 Flag 'Y'—sailors should put hull above the waterline. on their life jackets; 5 Flag 'X' recalls boats crossing the starting line too early; 6 'First Substitute' pennant recalls the whole class; 7 Flag 'I'—1 minute rule in force; 8 'Finishing Signal'—hoisted on the finishing boat; 9 'Code and Answering' pennant—all races not started are postponed. time.

gaff The spar at the top of a four-cornered sail. A craft using this gaff sail is said to be gaff rigged, as opposed to Bermudian rigged.

genoa A large jib (qv) which extends aft of the mast to overlap the mainsail.

go about To sail from one tack to the other so that the bows pass through the eye of the wind and the wind blows on the opposite side of the sails.

gooseneck The fitting which joins the boom, or any other spar, to the mast.

Gunter rig A rig that sets a triangular mainsail with the upper part of the luff (qv) attached to a vertical yard (qv).

guy A wire or rope attached to a spar to hold it in position.

halyard A line or wire used for hoisting and lowering sails, flags or spars.

handicap The time allowance given to yachts according to their rating (qv) when they are not racing level. The smaller the rating, the larger the handicap

hank A clip which holds the luff of a foresail to a stay (qv).

hard-chine construction A method of boat-building which uses flat sheets of plywood, steel, or aluminium in angled rather than complete curved sections. A hard-chine boat has a definite angle instead of a curve in the bilge.

harden in To haul in sheets.

head The top corner of a triangular sail, or the top side of a gaff sail.

headsail A sail set forward of the mast.

head up To alter course towards the wind.

heave to To bring a yacht almost to a standstill by keeping the bow head on to the wind or sea. It is achieved by slackening off the mainsail in its sailing setting, backing the headsail into the wind and, if necessary, setting the tiller to the leeward side of the yacht.

helm A device attached to the rudder to steer the yacht. It is either a tiller or wheel.

helm down To move the tiller in a leeward direction so that the bow turns to windward. The opposite maneuver is known as *helm up.*

helmsman The member of the crew who operates the helm. On a one-man dinghy the helmsman is also responsible for adjusting the mainsheet.

in irons Said of a yacht when she is stopped head to wind and is unable to be steered.

international classes Classes of yacht sailed in many countries and thus suitable for international competition. Yachts are determined to be international by the IYRU.

IOR The International Offshore Rule, the formula introduced in 1970 to level the handicap of offshore racers throughout the world. It has been, and is, subject to frequent revision. Ratings are expressed in meters or feet, the measurement being the computation of a formula which takes into account the yacht's length, beam, depth, girth, sail area, freeboard, and other factors. The rating is not the actual length of the yacht.

IYRU The International Yacht Racing Union, the governing body of yachting throughout the world. It was formed in 1906.

jib The leading headsail

jibe To alter course away from the wind when running (qv) so that the stern passes through the eye of the wind which then blows on the opposite side of the sails. If jibing is badly performed in heavy weather, it can lead to capsizing or dismasting.

jury rig A temporary rigging made after the standard rig has broken; any makeshift form of propulsion.

kedge To move a boat by pulling on the anchor rope, hauling up the anchor, re-anchoring, and then repeating the process. A kedge is a light anchor for kedging and to supplement the main anchor.

keel boat A yacht with ballast provided by a keel fitted to the

1

Below: Two of the numerous knots which every sailor must be well versed in tying. 1 Figure-of-eight knot used to prevent a line from unreeving through an eye or block. 2 Clove hitch, which can be made more secure by finishing off with two half hitches. A knot must be very firm, becoming more secure as the strain on it increases, yet must undo easily, even when wet.

Figure-of-eight

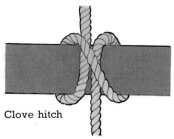

Clove hitch

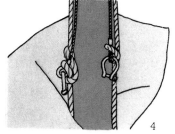

2

3

4

Left: One useful way of tidying up the halyards. First an eye is made (1), through which a loop is pushed (2). Through this loop is pushed part of the halyard holding the shackle and this is then pulled tightly downwards (3). The shackles can be stopped from banging about by hanging them down far enough to be covered by the boom cover(4).

Below: Some of the sails used on keel boats. Sails were originally made from pure cotton but are now made of man-made fibres such as dacron. These sails are less prone to tear and are water repellant, enabling them to be stored wet in the sail bag without losing shape. There are two main types of sail, square and loose-footed.

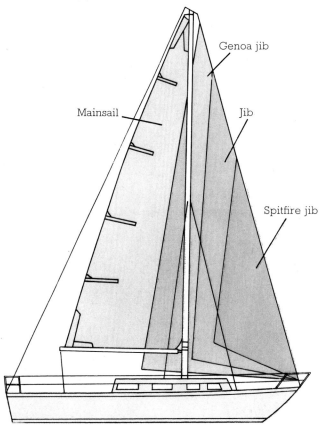

Genoa jib

Mainsail

Jib

Spitfire jib

---

bottom of the hull.

keel boat classes Day-racing yachts with fixed keels. They come in a number of classes, among them Dragon, Soling, Star, and the meter classes, and are controlled in their design by a formula incorporating LOA, draft, sail area and other factors in a mathematical equation.

ketch A sailing vessel which, in addition to the mainsail and headsails, has a mizzen (*qv*) stepped forward of the rudder.

kicking strap A wire or rope from the foot of the mast to a point on the boom to prevent the boom from lifting when the sheets (*qv*) are eased.

knot A nautical mile (1.85km) per hour.

lee bowing Sailing across a tidal stream with the current flowing against the lee bow.

lee helm Said of a yacht which has a tendency to turn its bow away from the wind. It has to be checked by holding the tiller to leeward, so bringing the head

round more to windward.

lee shore The shore on to which the wind is blowing.

leech The aft edge of a sail.

leeward The side of the yacht opposite that on which the wind blows.

leeway The sideways movement of a boat to leeward when sailing. It is caused by the force of the wind and counteracted by lateral resistance from keel, center-board, dagger-board, or the crew providing moving ballast.

leg A stretch of water between two racing marks.

LOA Length overall; the extreme measurement of the hull from stem to stern.

luff The leading edge of a sail.

luffing To head up in order to slow a boat down or to take pressure out of the sails to enable the crew to haul in sheets.

lug rig A rig to set a lugsail. The upper leading edge of the sail is bent on to a spar.

lugsail A four-sided sail, a large part of which extends forwards of the mast.

mainsail The principal sail attached to the main mast.

mare's tails White, feathered clouds which indicate an imminent increase in the force of the wind.

mark Buoys, moored boats, posts, etc, deployed on a racing course to mark the route. They must be rounded on the specified side.

mast A vertical spar on which the sails are set and on which other spars may be attached according to the nature of the rig.

meter boats Keel boats designed to a specific mathematical formula with the rating expressed in meters; eg 5.5 meter and 12 meter yachts. Taken into account are the length, girth, measured sail area and freeboard.

miss stays Said of a boat when the helmsman fails to bring it about on to a new tack and it reverts to the original one.

mizzen A mast smaller than and set aft of the main mast.

multihull Yacht with more than one hull, eg catamaran, trimaran.

national classes Types of yachts individual to one country only and recognized by the national racing association of that country.

nautical mile One-sixtieth of a degree (1 minute) measured along the equator; approx. 1.85km or 6076ft.

neaped Said of a boat which goes aground during spring tides and does not receive enough water from the next tide to float her off.

neaps Those tides with the smallest range of rise and fall.

obstruction to sea room Any object, including other craft under way, that forces a yacht to alter its course in order to avoid it.

off the wind Said of a yacht when it is not close-hauled.

offshore racing Racing practiced by sea-going yachts which are equipped with accommodation, navigational equipment and other elements considered compulsory under IYRU rules. Yachts are divided into offshore classes according to their IOR rating. Also known as ocean racing.

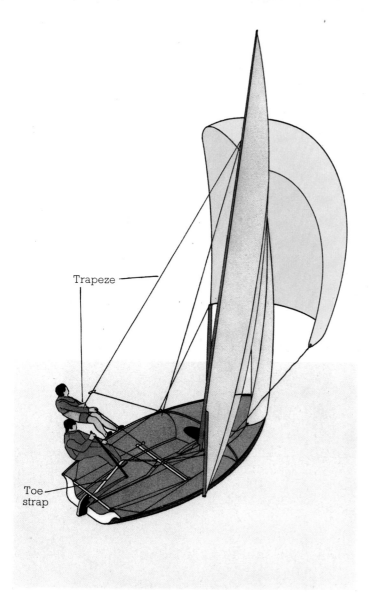

Trapeze

Toe strap

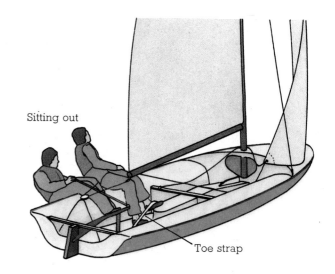

Sitting out

Toe strap

Left: The helmsman uses the toe strap, a length of webbing running along the length of the cockpit, to lean out to windward while his crew stands out from the hull on the trapeze, a device which enables planing boats to be sailed as upright as possible. It consists of a steel wire fastened to the shroud fitting on the mast with a hooking system at its end to which the crew clips his trapeze belt. The trapeze wire is kept under tension by a rubber shock cord. One advantage of such an arrangement is that the boat can carry much more sail than would otherwise be possible, and can thus achieve higher speeds.

Below: It is essential, in particular when the wind is strong, that sailing boats—especially dinghies—are sailed as upright as possible. Sailing trim (the attitude of the boat when moving) can be achieved by the crew positioning themselves correctly in the boat or by sitting out. By sitting out the crew are able to use their bodyweight to counteract the heeling force of the wind, thus keeping the dinghy upright. In stronger winds the crew should sit out further. In light breezes it is better to have the boat heeling slightly to the lee side, which can be done by removing weight from the stern.

There are four categories: 1 for long-distance races well offshore for extended periods; 2 for long-distance races along or near a shoreline; 3 for races on relatively well-protected open water; 4 for short races in protected waters.

on the wind Said of a yacht when it is close-hauled.

one-design Any class of yacht in which all the craft are built and rigged to the same measurements and specifications. Emphasis is therefore on sailing and tuning skills rather than individual design.

overlap When the bow of one yacht moves ahead of the stern of another.

overtaking A yacht is said to be overtaking when she establishes an overlap from clear astern and is within two lengths of the side of the other boat.

pay off To turn the bow away from the wind so that the sails will fill.

peak The upper, aft, corner of a four-sided sail.

pinching Sailing too close to the wind with the result that the sails are unable to draw efficiently.

planing Skimming over the surface of the water rather than through it. Applicable only to light boats; not keel boats.

points The points of the compass, of which there are 32. Each point is $11\frac{1}{4}$ degrees. Thus 45 degrees is referred to as four points.

pooped Said of a boat running before a stormy sea when a wave breaks over its stern.

port The left-hand side of a boat, the point of direction taken while facing the bow.

port tack Sailing with the wind coming from the port side.

pram A dinghy with a transom (qv) at both ends.

proper course Any course taken by a yacht after the starting signal to reach the next mark or the finishing line as quickly as possible. It is not necessarily a straight line but takes into account the wind and tidal streams.

pursuit race A method of handicap racing which eliminates the need to calculate the places of finishers once they have crossed the line. Yachts are started according to their rating, and the first to finish correctly is the winner.

race An area off a headland or between islands where there is a strong, rapid tide which, in bad weather, gives rise to very broken seas.

race level To race against yachts of the same one-design class, thus eliminating the need for handicaps.

racing A yacht is said to be racing from the moment the blue peter (qv) preparatory signal is flown until she has crossed the finishing line or retired.

rake The angle of a boat's mast off its vertical line.

rating The formula to which the design of a yacht must conform in order to fit within an established class.

reaching The course of sailing with the wind blowing from the beam. Because the sail reaches its maximum efficiency as an airfoil and the resistance of the hull is reduced, this is the fastest point of sailing.

reefing Reducing the sail area by rolling the sail around the main boom or by tying down slabs of sail to the boom. It is done when the force of the wind suddenly increases or threatens to do so.

restricted class A one-design boat for which the regulations are not quite as strict, allowing certain leeway with regard to building materials, the size of cockpit and the stay system for the mast. The Flying Dutchman is a restricted class.

rig (1) To set up the rigging. (2) The arrangement of the sails, masts and spars on a sailing boat. It is by its rig that a boat's type is defined.

rigging A boat's standing and running lines.

roach The curved edge to the leech (qv).

rudder The board or plate which

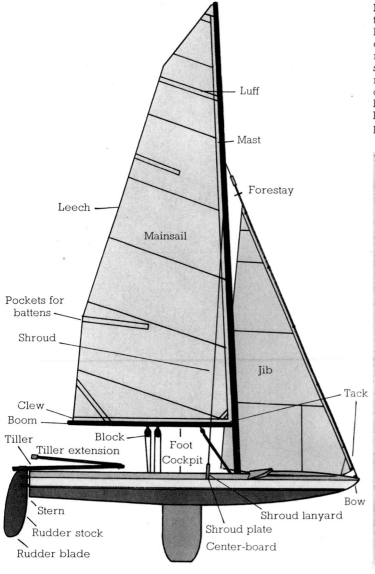

Luff

Mast

Forestay

Leech

Mainsail

Pockets for battens

Shroud

Jib

Clew

Boom

Tiller

Block

Tiller extension

Foot
Cockpit

Tack

Stern

Rudder stock

Rudder blade

Shroud lanyard

Shroud plate

Center-board

Bow

Left: Some basic dinghy terminology. It is usual for the boat to fly a burgee at the top of the mast or, when racing, a racing pennant. In modern small boats the center-board is retractable. The simplest center-board is the dagger-board which is raised or lowered by hand and can be pulled right out.

Below: Sailing expressions related to the position of the boat and the direction of the wind. If the boat alters course in the direction of the arrow to port, it is said to be luffing; if to starboard it is bearing away.

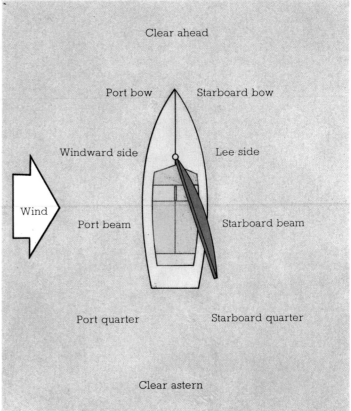

Clear ahead

Port bow

Starboard bow

Windward side

Lee side

Wind

Port beam

Starboard beam

Port quarter

Starboard quarter

Clear astern

is fitted at the aft end of the boat to steer it. It is connected to the helm.

running Sailing downwind, ie with the wind dead aft.

running rigging The halyards (*qv*) and the sheets (*qv*).

sheets The lines used to trim the sails.

shrouds The rigging wires that run from the mast to the side of the boat.

sloop A boat rigged to set one foresail in addition to the main-sail.

spar A solid or hollow piece of wood or metal alloy on which a sail is set. It may be a boom, a gaff, or a mast.

spinnaker A three-sided sail cut very full and set forward of the mast to increase speed when broad reaching or running.

spring tides Those tides with the greatest range of rise and fall. They occur at new and full moons and alternate with neap (*qv*) tides.

spritsail A four-sided sail, almost rectangular, which is spread by a

spar set diagonally from the foot of the mast to the peak (*qv*).

standing lug A rig in which the lower forward corner of the lugsail is made fast at the foot of the mast and the top corner is laced to a yard (*qv*) which is hoisted by a single halyard. A standing lug remains in position.

standing rigging The stays (*qv*) and the shrouds (*qv*) which support the mast in place.

starboard The right-hand side of a boat, the point of direction taken while facing the bow.

starboard tack Sailing with the wind coming from the starboard side.

stays The wires which run from the top of the mast to the fore and aft of the yacht to brace the mast.

step The fixture into which the bottom of the mast is made secure.

tabernacle A box projecting above the deck and in to which the mast is stepped and secured by two pins. One pin is removed so that the mast can be lowered on to the deck.

tack The bottom forward corner of a sail where the luff and foot meet.

tacking Altering course from a starboard or port tack to the opposite tack with the bow passing through the eye of the wind.

tier A strip of canvas used to tie the mainsail to the boom when lowered.

tiller The lever fitted to the head of the rudder and held by the helmsman.

topsides The side of the hull above the waterline.

transom The flat board forming the stern of a yacht.

trapeze A wire and harness worn by one of the crew to enable him to balance outside the boat and keep it upright in heavy winds. The harness is clipped to the wire which is attached high up the mast.

trimaran A multi-hulled craft with a main central hull flanked by two smaller hulls that act as outriggers.

trimming Adjusting the sails with the sheets so that they are

filled with more or less wind as required.

twelve meter The keel boat which, since 1956, has been the class that contests the America's Cup.

unbend To remove a sail from its spar.

veering Said of the wind when it moves in a clockwise direction.

wear To alter course from one tack to the other while stern on to the wind.

weather helm Said of a boat which has a tendency to turn its bow into the wind.

windward The side of the boat on to which the wind blows.

yard A spar, slung from a mast, on which a sail is hung. Also the gaff of a lugsail.

yaw To swing about off course as a result of bad steering or wrongly trimmed sails.

yawl A sailing vessel which, in addition to the mainsail and fore-sails, has a mizzen stepped at or aft of the rudder post. Its mizzen sets a smaller sail than that on the ketch rig.

Water Skiing

A sport in which a person uses skis and propulsion from a motor boat to plane on the water, water skiing has enjoyed an increasing popularity since the end of World War II. Its origins, however, go back to the early twentieth century. But it was not until 1924, when the American Fred Waller patented his design for water skis, that the embryo sport developed its own identity. Large crowds watched the first competition at Long Island in 1935, and four years later the American Water Ski Association was founded. Elsewhere the sport was making similar progress, especially in the western Mediterranean, and in 1946 the World Water Ski Union was formed to control the sport internationally. Britain did not take to the sport until the end of the decade, but today the British federation is second only to the American body. World championships, first contested in 1949, are held every two years.

Championships feature trick skiing, slalom and jumping, plus an overall category for the best all-round performer. In tricks, the skier has a limited time within which to perform a series of freestyle movements for which points ranging from 20 to 450 are awarded according to their difficulty. Mono-ski tricks have a higher point value. In Slalom — a timed run through two lines of buoys — half a point is awarded for every buoy successfully rounded and also for returning to within the boat's wake before the next buoy. Upon completion of the course the boat speed is raised by $1\frac{7}{8}$ mph up to a set maximum of 36 mph for men, 34 mph for women. If the course is still successfully negotiated at these speeds, then the rope is shortened by predetermined amounts, until the skier falls or misses a buoy. In jumping each skier receives three attempts over the ramp and the longest jump scores.

Jump ski   Slalom ski

Figure or trick ski

Above: Three types of grip: 1 The slalom grip, sometimes called the 'baseball' grip, used for slalom and jumping. 2 The toe hold for tricks. 3 The standard two-handed grip for general-purpose and trick skiing.

Above left: The tow handle for trick skiing features a specially adapted toe-strap between the bridle.

The competitive skier has a different type of ski for each event. Jump skis, which have wooden or alloy fins, are longer, wider and more robust than general-purpose skis. Slalom skis have a tapered tail to assist speed of turning, and a deeper fin to prevent sideslipping in tight turns. Trick skis, or 'bananas', are much shorter and have no directional fins.

---

bad gate Getting off to a bad start to the slalom course by taking the wrong line through the gate (*qv*).

banking A way of going through the air after jumping. The body is more horizontal than upright and the skis go out to the left-hand side, although still pointing in the correct direction.

barefoot Planing on the water without skis. An American innovation, and equally popular in Australia, barefoot skiing is mainly concerned with tricks, but slalom and jumping are also practiced

beachie A barefoot start from the beach.

binding The toe and/or heel piece usually of rubber, designed to hold the foot in place on the ski. The heel binding is on a movable metal runner, whereas the toe binding is mounted on a fixed metal shoe.

cut (1) To shorten the tow rope during slalom. After the first run through the course at maximum speed, the tow rope is reduced from 59ft 10in to $52\frac{1}{2}$ft and subsequently to 46ft 9in, 42ft 8in, 39ft 4in and 36ft 11in. The reductions, which are made from the boat, are called first cut, second cut, etc.
(2) A maneuver in jumping with which the skier increases his speed above that of the boat on his approach to the ramp. Having crossed the wake and swung out as far to the opposite side of the jump as possible, he pulls himself sharply back across the wake to make his diagonal attack on the ramp. It is sometimes called a *double cut*.

deepie A barefoot start in deep water.

deepwater start Method of starting in which the skier crouches in the water with the skis pointing out of the water and in line with the boat. As the boat accelerates, the skis rise to the surface.

dock start A method of starting in which the skier sits on a dock or pontoon with the front of the skis pointing out of the water. As the boat accelerates, he is launched on to the surface.

early buoy To take a good line around the first slalom buoys and so make a good start to the pass.

figure skiing Another name for trick skiing.

flying beachie A spectacular barefoot start off dry land. The skier runs to the water's edge, launches himself in the air, and lands on his back in the water, where he does a deepie (*qv*).

gassing Giving the boat more power to compensate for the sudden drag of the skier pulling on the tow-rope to make his cut (*qv*) prior to approaching the jumping ramp.

gate Twin marker buoys 8ft 2in apart at either end of the slalom course and through which the boat and the skier must pass. The skier has to take the gate at an angle in order to get round the first buoy of his pass.

helicopter A 360° turn, either off the ramp or off the wake.

hooking The action of a slalom skier whose ski, as he rounds the buoy, turns too far in so that he appears to be going back on himself instead of taking a line for the next buoy.

hot-dogging Performing spectacular tricks such as somersaults and helicopters (*qv*).

jumping One of the three main competition events in which a skier jumps from a ramp back on to the water. The ramp is set at 5ft 11in for men and 4ft 11in for women. Although the speed of the boat is approximately 35mph the skier approaches the ramp at around 50mph.

line-off An American term for shortening the tow-rope during the slalom.

mono-skiing Skiing on one ski.

observer The person in the boat who faces the skier, interprets his signals to the driver and generally has regard for his safety.

parakiting, or parasailing A branch of the sport in which a parachutist is kept aloft by being towed by a boat. As his 'chute is

154

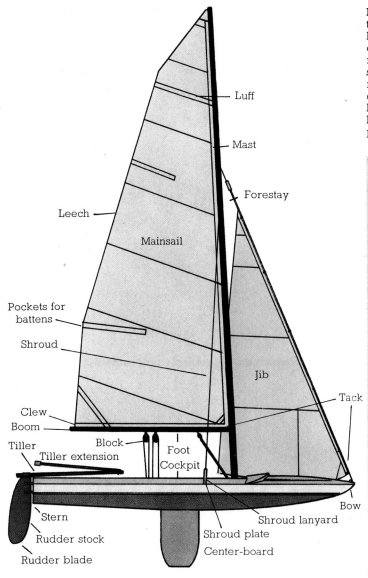

Luff

Mast

Forestay

Leech

Mainsail

Pockets for battens

Shroud

Jib

Clew

Boom

Tack

Tiller

Block

Tiller extension

Foot

Cockpit

Stern

Rudder stock

Shroud lanyard

Shroud plate

Center-board

Rudder blade

Bow

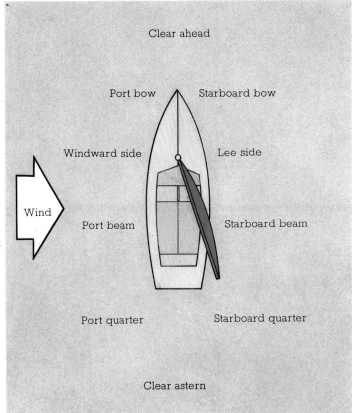

Left: Some basic dinghy terminology. It is usual for the boat to fly a burgee at the top of the mast or, when racing, a racing pennant. In modern small boats the center-board is retractable. The simplest center-board is the dagger-board which is raised or lowered by hand and can be pulled right out.

Below: Sailing expressions related to the position of the boat and the direction of the wind. If the boat alters course in the direction of the arrow to port, it is said to be luffing; if to starboard it is bearing away.

Clear ahead

Port bow

Starboard bow

Windward side

Lee side

Wind

Port beam

Starboard beam

Port quarter

Starboard quarter

Clear astern

is fitted at the aft end of the boat to steer it. It is connected to the helm.

running Sailing downwind, ie with the wind dead aft.

running rigging The halyards (*qv*) and the sheets (*qv*).

sheets The lines used to trim the sails.

shrouds The rigging wires that run from the mast to the side of the boat.

sloop A boat rigged to set one foresail in addition to the mainsail.

spar A solid or hollow piece of wood or metal alloy on which a sail is set. It may be a boom, a gaff, or a mast.

spinnaker A three-sided sail cut very full and set forward of the mast to increase speed when broad reaching or running.

spring tides Those tides with the greatest range of rise and fall. They occur at new and full moons and alternate with neap (*qv*) tides.

spritsail A four-sided sail, almost rectangular, which is spread by a

spar set diagonally from the foot of the mast to the peak (*qv*).

standing lug A rig in which the lower forward corner of the lugsail is made fast at the foot of the mast and the top corner is laced to a yard (*qv*) which is hoisted by a single halyard. A standing lug remains in position.

standing rigging The stays (*qv*) and the shrouds (*qv*) which support the mast in place.

starboard The right-hand side of a boat, the point of direction taken while facing the bow.

starboard tack Sailing with the wind coming from the starboard side.

stays The wires which run from the top of the mast to the fore and aft of the yacht to brace the mast.

step The fixture into which the bottom of the mast is made secure.

tabernacle A box projecting above the deck and in to which the mast is stepped and secured by two pins. One pin is removed so that the mast can be lowered on to the deck.

tack The bottom forward corner of a sail where the luff and foot meet.

tacking Altering course from a starboard or port tack to the opposite tack with the bow passing through the eye of the wind.

tier A strip of canvas used to tie the mainsail to the boom when lowered.

tiller The lever fitted to the head of the rudder and held by the helmsman.

topsides The side of the hull above the waterline.

transom The flat board forming the stern of a yacht.

trapeze A wire and harness worn by one of the crew to enable him to balance outside the boat and keep it upright in heavy winds. The harness is clipped to the wire which is attached high up the mast.

trimaran A multi-hulled craft with a main central hull flanked by two smaller hulls that act as outriggers.

trimming Adjusting the sails with the sheets so that they are

filled with more or less wind as required.

twelve meter The keel boat which, since 1956, has been the class that contests the America's Cup.

unbend To remove a sail from its spar.

veering Said of the wind when it moves in a clockwise direction.

wear To alter course from one tack to the other while stern on to the wind.

weather helm Said of a boat which has a tendency to turn its bow into the wind.

windward The side of the boat on to which the wind blows.

yard A spar, slung from a mast, on which a sail is hung. Also the gaff of a lugsail.

yaw To swing about off course as a result of bad steering or wrongly trimmed sails.

yawl A sailing vessel which, in addition to the mainsail and fore-sails, has a mizzen stepped at or aft of the rudder post. Its mizzen sets a smaller sail than that on the ketch rig.

Surfing

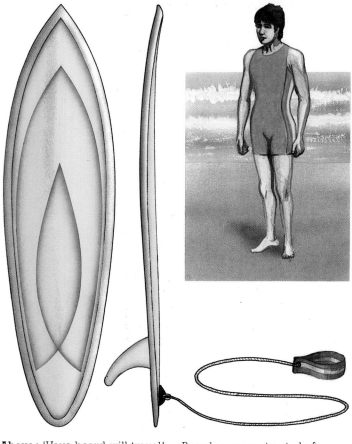

Few sporting activities have captured the imagination as vividly as surfing. The thought of planing over water at express speed, propelled only by the force of the onrushing wave, is exciting enough: actually performing the sport, the wave driving the body and board down and across its face as it breaks in a cascade of spray behind the surfer, remains one of the most exhilarating experiences known. It is a challenge: man's skills against the sea's moods.

Of the various ways of surfing, that most associated with the sport is riding the Malibu-type boards in a standing position. However, there are equally fervent adherents of body, mat, canoe and belly board surfing, and each initially has the same problem: to find the right wave and join it. The best waves are generally found on long, gently sloping beaches that face an open sea. They are formed by the action of winds on the surface; their shape determined by the distance traveled and the contours and depth of the ocean floor as they approach land. It is when the sea bed becomes too shallow, or some obstacle such as a reef is met, that the forward movement of the wave under the surface is arrested and the top of the wave builds up before breaking.

The surfer awaits his wave outside the point where it breaks. When it is almost on him, he paddles or kicks furiously to stay ahead of it as its momentum carries him forwards and upwards until he begins the slide down the face. He is surfing. How long he does so depends on his ability to keep ahead of the breaking section of the wave, while the distance of the ride will be increased by his ability to slide diagonally across the face, rather than in a straight line towards the shore.

Above: 'Have board will travel' was the slogan of the 1960s' surfers and it still stands. The only extra luggage a surfer needs are his swim suit (or wet suit in colder weather) and some board wax. Today's boards are shorter and lighter than earlier versions, but what they have lost in size they have gained in maneuverability.

Boards are constructed of fiberglass and vary in length according to the size of the surf the rider frequents. The 'skeg' at the back acts as a rudder and enables the surfer to steer the board. The surfboard should be equipped with an ankle 'surf leash' so that if the rider is swept off, the board is easily recovered.

back off To change one's mind just prior to take off. A back off is a wave that has already been broken and reformed, the white water having backed-off.

backhand turn A natural (*qv*) rider's turn to the left; a goofy-footer's (*qv*) turn to the right. It is more difficult than a forehand (*qv*) turn.

beach-break Waves that break close in to the shore on a sand bottom.

beach bunny A girl who hangs about where surfers gather, and, if nothing else, brightens up the scenery.

belly board A short rigid surfboard made of marine-ply or fiberglass. It is ridden mostly in a prone position.

blown out Said of the conditions when the wind is so strong that the waves are choppy and not forming a surf suitable for riding.

body surfing Catching waves and surfing without a board by keeping the body outstretched with the arms in front of the head.

bombora A term for a wave which is formed further out to sea than the normal line-up (*qv*).

boomer A large, heavy-breaking wave—and usually unrideable.

bottom turn A turn made at the bottom of the wall (*qv*) of a wave.

bumps Colloquialism for the callous skin on the instep or knees as a result of surfing.

catch a wave To ride a breaking wave.

close-out Said of a place where the waves break all the way along their crest at one time, making the surf unrideable.

corner To travel sideways across a wave.

crack a wave Australian colloquialism for catch a wave.

crest The highest point of a wave before it breaks.

crouch A surfer's leaning forward, squatting position on the board.

curl The curve that forms as the top of the wave breaks and makes a space between the main section of the wave and the spilling crest.

custom board A board specially made to a rider's specifications.

cut-back A maneuver in which the rider surfs diagonally across and up the wall of the wave, then turns back to continue his ride.

cut-out A maneuver in which the rider surfs diagonally across and up the wall of the wave, going out through the back of it to end his ride.

deck The top surface of a board.

ding Damage to the surfboard.

drop in To take off on a wave and slide down its face. Also used to describe the action of a surfer who interferes with another surfer by taking off on a wave he is already riding.

dumper A tall wave that crashes down suddenly in an arc.

face The front of a wave before it breaks.

fins Fitted to a surfboard for stability.

flippers Another name for swim fins.

forehand turn A natural rider's turn to the right; a goofy-footer's turn to the left.

fremlin A female gremmie (*qv*).

glassy The smooth condition of a wave when there is no disturbance to the water from wind.

goofy-foot(er) A surfer who rides with his right foot forward.

green An unbroken wave before there is any white water.

gremmie, or gremlin An inexperienced surfer.

hanging five Placing the toes of the leading foot over the nose of the surfboard while riding a wave.

hanging ten Placing both feet at the front of the board and hanging all ten toes over the nose.

head dip Dipping the head into the wave or white water while riding the board crouching.

heavies Big waves.

highway surfie Someone who has a board on top of his car but rarely actually surfs.

hollow A wave which curls right over instead of forming a tube.

hot-dogging Performing tricks on the board, usually near the

Below: Back view of a long-line drive sliding on the shoulder of a wave. The edge or rail of the board is lifted toward the surfer as he begins to turn the board to the right. Surfers pride themselves on their individual style and no two show quite the same form when hitting a wave. Usually, however, the left foot is placed forward, slightly left of centre toward the bow of the board. The right foot is about 30cm behind it, toward the opposite side of the board. The weight is then shifted back and forth between the two feet, depending on the direction the surfer wishes to go.

1

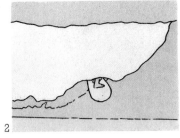

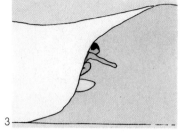

Above and right: Surfers usually prefer hollow waves or 'tubes'. In this type of wave the breaking surf resembles a kind of churning cylinder, slowly turning over from one end to the other. The expert surfer can ride just in front of the wave (1), duck as it begins to break over him (2 and 3), and quickly shoot out into the clear at an angle (4 and 5), playing chase with the breaker.

3

4

5

shore or in the white water.

humpers Medium-to-large unbroken waves.

inside Used to describe the position of a surfer riding on the shore side of a breaking wave.

kick-out A maneuver in which the surfer steps off the back of the board into the wave, often in an effort not to lose his board in a wipe-out (*qv*).

kook A novice surfer; one who generally gets in the way in the surf.

line-up The point where the waves break most consistently and where the surfers gather to take off.

locked in Said of a surfer who prefers to ride inside the curl.

Malibu The long board on which the surfer rides standing up.

mat An inflatable rubber mattress often used by children for catching waves.

natural A surfer who rides with his left foot forward on the board.

outside The position of a surfer riding on the seaward side of the breaking wave. It can also mean the seaward side of a breaking wave.

out-the-back An Australian term for a surfer who is outside the breaking wave.

over the falls Being caught and carried over in the crest of a wave.

pearling When the nose of the board dips into the water and the surfer is thrown off.

peeler A fast wave that curls perfectly without breaking ahead of itself.

pintail A board whose tail tapers to a point.

pull-out Similar to a cut-out (*qv*) or kick-out (*qv*); often performed in white water to end the ride.

quasimodo A hunchback style of riding.

rails The rounded edges of the board.

reverse kick-out A finishing maneuver similar to a normal kickout except that the rider performs a further turn through 180 degrees so that he is facing out to sea with the board in front.

rip The current that runs from the shore out to sea as the water that has come in with the breaking waves escapes.

rogue A wave that appears unexpectedly and does not follow the pattern of previous waves.

section A part of the breaking wave.

set A group of waves rolling in one after the other.

shooting the curl Riding the wave at the point where it loops over to form a curve or tube (*qv*).

shoulder The section of the wave that tapers away in front of the curl or the white water.

skeg The fin of a surfboard.

slide To ride the face of a wave in a line more or less parallel to the shore.

slot The perfect place in the wave.

soup The white water or foam of a broken wave.

spinner A 360-degree turn.

stall A slowing up of the board.

surf's up Colloquialism describing good conditions for surfing.

swell The water in front of the wave on which a surfer usually takes off.

swim fins Artificial rubber limbs worn on the feet by body and belly board surfers to aid their movement through the water.

switchfoot A surfer who can ride with either his left foot or right foot forward.

tandem surfing Two people riding and performing acrobatic maneuvers on an extra-large surfboard.

trim To speed or slow up the board by walking or leaning forwards or backwards on the board.

tube The hollow, semi-cylinder section of a wave.

turn To change a board's direction on a wave.

walk the nose To move foot over foot towards the nose of the board.

wall The face of a wave before it breaks.

white water The foam that results from a breaking wave.

wipe-out The end of a ride occurring when the surfer loses control and is engulfed by the breaking wave he is riding.

Swimming

Swimming is a pleasurable activity or serious athletic pursuit practiced worldwide by people of all ages. The pinnacle of achievement in swimming, is represented by an Olympic or world championship final. But just as significant, perhaps more so, are the thousands of small meets held every week and the laps swum by recreational swimmers. At its most rudimentary, swimming requires no equipment at all. But to produce a world-class performance the champion is provided with near-laboratory conditions. The Olympic pool, eight lanes wide and 50m long, is designed with perfect conditions in mind—water heated to an exact temperature, anti-turbulence lane dividers, wave-inhibiting gutters. Performances are timed to one-thousandth of a second by electronic equipment.

Swimming has taken over a century to reach its present development. In the early days harbors and docks were the scene of many races. Slowly man-made pools appeared, and swimming was popular enough in 1896 to be one of the original Olympic sports. Since 1908, when the first truly international Olympic Games were held, the sport has been dominated by the USA, though from time to time this supremacy has been challenged, though never for long, by successively, Japan, Hungary, Australia, and East Germany.

World records are recognized for the following events for men and women: 100, 200, 400, 800 and 1500m freestyle; 100 and 200m breaststroke, butterfly, and backstroke; 200 and 400m individual medley; 4 × 100 and 4 × 200m (men only) freestyle relay; 4 × 100m medley relay.

Above: The wind-up start. 1 On the command 'Take your marks!' the swimmer steps forward to the front of the block and assumes the starting position. 2 On the signal to start (a shot, klaxon, whistle, or a command 'go'), the arms are swung upward, outward, and forward, the forward swing co-ordinating with the leg drive (3). 3 The legs drive the body forward toward the water. 4 The hands touch the water first, followed by the rest of the body in an almost horizontal position. Where starting blocks have a 'lip', some swimmers use a variation known as the grab start to make a faster start.

age group swimming A method and philosophy of swimming organization and development in which swimmers compete in age bands against other swimmers of their own age. The age groups used for both sexes in the United States and Canada, and subsequently recognized for some international purposes by the FINA (*qv*) are: 10 years and under; 11-12 years; 13-14 years; 15-17 years (ages on 1 January).

alternate strokes Shorthand term for back and front crawl strokes.

American crawl Name given to the now-conventional front crawl stroke in which a complete arm cycle is accompanied by six flutter leg kicks.

Australian crawl Type of front crawl stroke common among Australian swimmers, especially in the 1900s and 1910s. The timing was one leg kick to one arm stroke, in contrast to the Trudgen and later American crawl strokes.

backstroke A style of swimming in which, for competition purposes, the swimmer must remain on the back throughout the race, except for a moment during the turn. It is the only racing stroke in which competitors are in the water at the start. In the early years of the twentieth century swimmers used a form of inverted breaststroke (*qv*), but gradually this was superseded by the back crawl stroke, in which the arms pulled alternately windmill-fashion while the legs performed a balancing and (to some extent) propulsive flutter kick. The refined modern racing stroke, which is the third fastest of the four racing styles, dates from as recently as the mid-1950s.

breaststroke The oldest stroke used in competition and probably the most natural. At all times the arms and legs remain under the water. The arms pull back simultaneously with a circular motion and are pushed forward together from under the chest; the legs are drawn up together, with the feet turned outwards, and kick outwards and backwards. Propulsion comes from the pull of the arms and the backward sweep of the feet and shins. At the turns and finish the hands must touch simultaneously and on the same level under or over the water; at the start and turn only one complete stroke is allowed under water. Breathing takes place as the hands pull backwards. It is the slowest of the four racing styles.

butterfly A stroke which developed from breaststroke, and similarly requires simultaneous movements of arms and legs. The arms pull back and recover above the water to the starting position, the breath being taken late in the pull or early in the recovery (*qv*). The leg kick is a simultaneous vertical dolphin (*qv*) movement, the most common and natural timing being two kicks to one arm cycle. As in breaststroke, the touch at turns and finish must be made with both hands together. Recognized as a stroke separate from breaststroke in 1957, it is the second fastest of the four racing styles.

consolation final A race swum by the fastest competitors not qualifying for the final of an event to determine places 9 to 16 (in an eight-lane pool).

cross-over kick A kick in which one leg kicks across the other. A natural balancing movement, it is common in front crawl, rare in back crawl.

dolphin kick A flexible vertical leg kick in which both legs and lower trunk undulate through the water with an action resembling that of a dolphin.

endurance training A term commonly applied to long steady-state swims done during the pre-season phase of a swimmer's training.

false start A competitor or competitors starting before the signal. Two false starts are allowed, but the perpetrator of a third, whether previously guilty or not, is automatically disqualified.

Below: The Olympic swimming pool is 50m long. It is divided into eight lanes, numbered one to eight from right to left. Each swimmer is given a lane, and must remain there for the race. In all events except for backstroke, the competitors start by diving in from starting blocks. The starter may call two false starts, but then has to warn the swimmers that if there is a third false start, a swimmer who breaks before the signal will be disqualified. For backstroke races, swimmers line up in the water, facing the edge of the pool. They push away from the wall at the starting signal, when their feet must be beneath the water, not on the rail.

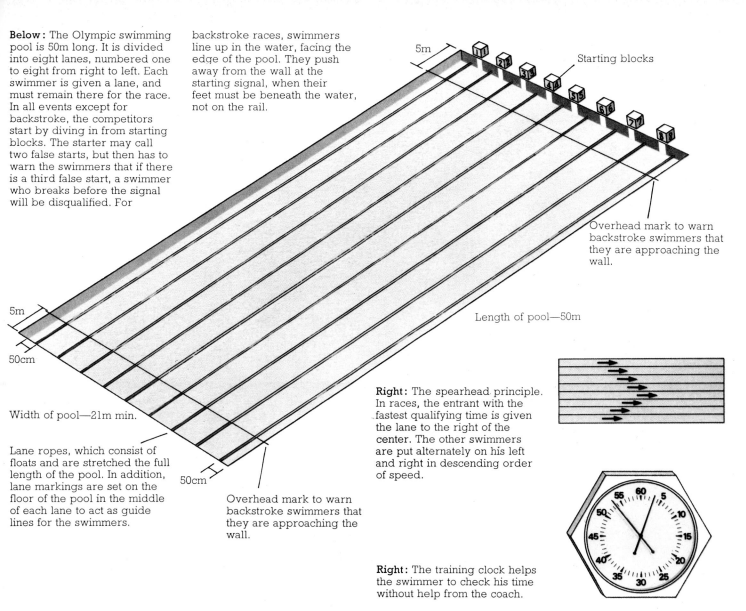

5m

Starting blocks

Overhead mark to warn backstroke swimmers that they are approaching the wall.

Length of pool—50m

5m

50cm

Width of pool—21m min.

Lane ropes, which consist of floats and are stretched the full length of the pool. In addition, lane markings are set on the floor of the pool in the middle of each lane to act as guide lines for the swimmers.

50cm

Overhead mark to warn backstroke swimmers that they are approaching the wall.

Right: The spearhead principle. In races, the entrant with the fastest qualifying time is given the lane to the right of the center. The other swimmers are put alternately on his left and right in descending order of speed.

Right: The training clock helps the swimmer to check his time without help from the coach.

---

fast pool A pool in which fast times may be expected. This is the result of a pool design which discourages the build-up of waves—by employing deep water, effective lane lines, wave-inhibiting gutters, etc—and of atmosphere (both physical and psychological).

FINA Fédération Internationale de Natation Amateur. Founded at the London Olympic Games of 1908, it is the world governing body for swimming, diving, water polo, and synchronized swimming.

final The race to determine the top placings in an event. The fastest swimmers in the heats qualify for the final, being assigned lanes according to the spearhead (*qv*) principle.

flags A line of flags is strung across the pool to warn backstroke swimmers of the imminence of the turn. It is recommended the flags be 5m from the end.

flutter kick A vertical leg kick in which the legs move alternately.

flyer Term used when the outgoing swimmer on a relay (*qv*) team leaves the starting block before the incoming swimmer touches (*qv*). It results in disqualification of the team.

freestyle Literally any stroke, but though any stroke may be used in a freestyle race, the almost universal choice is the *front crawl*, which is the fastest of the four racing styles. It is performed in the prone position, with the arms pulling alternately downwards and backwards under the body and recovering above water while the legs perform a balancing flutter kick. The breath is taken to the side every two or more strokes. Only in a freestyle race may a swimmer stand: but he may not walk.

grab start A method of starting in which the swimmer takes a hold of the 'lip' found on some starting blocks, pulling on them to cause overbalance and so make a faster start.

heats Preliminary rounds of an event. Swimmers are distributed in heats in three ways: at random; by seeding, whereby the fastest swimmers are distributed throughout the heats systematically; by grading, in which the swimmers are arranged in time order, slowest first, so that the fastest swimmers all go in the final heat. Progression from heats to semi-finals and finals is dependent upon times alone.

hypoxic training A training technique in which swimmers cover short distances without breathing to improve their tolerance to oxygen debt. Used only by the most experienced and expert coaches.

interval training Swimming a series of repeats, usually slower than race speed, with a controlled rest between efforts. Examples are 30 × 50m with a 10-second rest (slow interval training); 30 × 50m with a 40-second rest (fast interval training).

judges There are three varieties of judge in swimming events. Style judges ensure that swimmers in the style events conform to the rules. Turning judges rule on the legality of swimmers' turns. Placing judges adjudicate on the order of finishing and act as turning judges at the finishing end.

junior A competitor who is under 17 years of age during the year of competition.

keyhole pull Name given to shape of the butterfly pull when seen from below: the hands enter in front of the shoulders, pull outwards and downwards and then together until they almost touch under the stomach, finally pushing backwards and slightly outwards.

kick That part of a stroke performed by the legs and feet.

kicking Training drill in which only the legs are used.

lanes The individual swimming areas into which a racing pool is divided by lane markers. These range from simple ropes with occasional cork floats to sophisticated constructions designed to eradicate waves. Lanes are numbered from the right, facing the

Right: In the breaststroke the limbs remain submerged throughout. The body is streamlined and the swimmer pulls both arms down, sideways and back, breathing in as his arms recover. He now draws up his feet to his seat, turns them outwards, and drives back and slightly out. Finally the arms are extended again, and the feet sweep back together. For the breastroke turn (far right), the swimmer touches the wall with both hands simultaneously, tucking his body, flexing his elbows and pushing to one side with his arms. The body swivels, one hand sculling to keep it near the wall. The feet push strongly against the wall.

Breaststroke

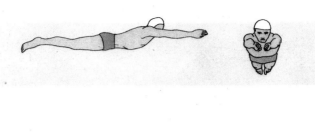

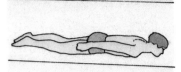

Butterfly

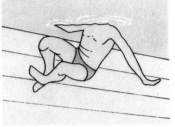

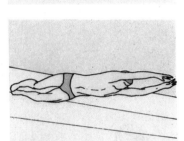

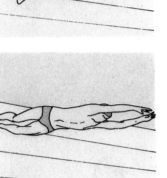

Far left: The dolphin-butterfly is the newest of the recognized strokes. The legs kick together and provide considerable propulsion. The arms enter the water a shoulders-width apart, pulling down and back. The legs beat up and begin their down-beat as the hands pass the shoulder-line. The swimmer breathes in as his arms finish pulling. The arms now leave the water, palms up, to swing past the shoulder-line ready to start the stroke cycle again. The butterfly turn (left) is almost the same as the breast-stroke turn. The swimmer must touch with both hands at the same time and on the same level. He pulls his feet under his body, pushing off against the wall.

course, and FINA recommends they should be 2.5m wide.

leg The distance swum by one member of a relay team.

life-saving An activity in which the main objects are the practicing of techniques of rescue and the resuscitation of water-users who have gotten into difficulties.

long course A 50m pool: sometimes 50m pools are referred to as Olympic pools.

long-distance swimming A term which embraces all kinds of open water (lake, river, sea) swimming, whether competitive races or solo efforts. Purists would restrict the term to swims of 6mi, or even 10mi or more. The classic test is the English channel (22mi).

masters competitions A new development in swimming which enables older swimmers who may be past their prime to swim against one another in age bands. These commonly start at 25 years and ascend in five or ten-year groups.

medley A race involving all four

styles of swimming. In the individual medley (IM), swimmers swim equal legs of butterfly, backstroke, breaststroke and freestyle (a stroke other than the preceding three and invariably front crawl). In a medley relay, the order of strokes is backstroke, breaststroke, butterfly and freestyle.

meet Any competitive swimming meeting, but usually used of an occasion in which swimmers from more than one organization are taking part, eg open meet, invitation meet.

negative split Swimming the second half of a race faster than the first.

Olympic pool *See* long course.

plunging Diving for distance. A once popular contest, in which competitors would dive in and rely on the dive alone for their impulsion, it is rarely seen now.

pull That part of a stroke performed by the arms.

pulling Training drill in which only the arms are used.

recovery The movement of a

limb back to the start of the propulsive movement, as in the over-the-water recovery of the arms in backstroke, butterfly and front crawl and the underwater recovery in breaststroke.

referee The official in overall charge of a meet.

relays Events in which teams of swimmers swim in sequence. Freestyle (*qv*) and medley (*qv*) relays are an integral part of swimming at all levels. A relay team usually consists of four swimmers, but occasionally larger numbers are used. Disqualification of the team results if a swimmer's feet leave the block before the incoming swimmer has touched.

repetition training A refinement of interval (*qv*) training. The swimmer has more rest, but swims close to race speed over short distances (eg a 200m swimmer might swim 6 × 100m with a 6 minute rest, the speed being faster than his best 200m pace).

S-pull Name given to the backstroke pull used by top swimmers

since the mid-1950s. Seen from the side, the hand tends to follow the path of an elongated S; from the entry in front of the shoulder, the hand appears to move back and down, being deepest level with the shoulder, then up close to the surface level with the hips, then down at the back of the pull.

semi-final Second round of eliminators between heats (*qv*) and final (*qv*). In some major competitions semi-finals are held for the 100m events, 16 qualifying from the heats to the semis, and 8 of those 16 for the final.

short course In theory any pool less than 50m long, although a strong body of opinion holds that the term should be applied only to 25m pools.

sidestroke A stroke which developed from breaststroke and, in the days before the Trudgen (*qv*), was the fastest style. By swimming on the side the swimmer was better streamlined; if recovering one arm above water he further reduced friction.

slow pool A pool which, because

Right: The front crawl is the fastest stroke, since the body is being propelled continuously. It makes very effective use of the strong muscles of the chest and shoulders. The swimmer keeps the body streamlined, and his arms pull alternately under the water, recovering over the surface. The legs kick alternately, balancing and helping propel the body. The swimmer turns his head to the side in order to breathe. The front crawl 'tumble' turn (far right) is usually used in competition. It consists of a forward somersault clear of the pool's edge, when the swimmer's speed is enough to carry him to the wall ready to push off again.

Front crawl

Right: For the backstroke the body is horizontal, with the hips just below the water-line. The head rests in the water with the ears just submerged. Since the face is above water, breathing is nearly normal. There are normally six leg beats per completed arm action. The legs move in a similar way to that in front crawl, except that they bend at the knees for added depth on the downward beat, followed by a whip-like action, starting from the hips, on the upward beat. The pulling arm bends to 90° as it passes the shoulders, straightens, and begins to recover as the other arm enters the water. In the backstroke flip turn (far right), the swimmer flips his legs over the surface while turning.

Backstroke

of its poor construction, does not help swimmers produce fast times.

spearhead principle The arrangement of swimmers in finals, and sometimes heats, according to their heat or submitted times. In an eight-lane pool the fastest qualifier swims in lane 4, the second fastest in lane 5, the third in lane 3, and so on until the slowest is in lane 8. This arrangement places the fastest swimmers together and also helps the judges.

splits Intermediate times taken during a race. Pace judgement is vital in swimming and it is important for swimmers to know their split times.

sprint training Towards the end of preparation the swimmer will swim a few all-out efforts, often deliberately running into oxygen debt.

start The beginning of the race. In backstroke swimmers start in the water, using hand grips. In the other strokes the start is made by a dive from starting

blocks. Once the competitors are on their blocks (or ready in the water) there is one command 'Take your marks' before the starting signal is given, normally by gun or klaxon.

starter The official responsible for starting the race.

starting block The raised platform from which a swimmer starts his/her race, being from 20in to 30in above surface. Blocks normally incorporate grips for backstroke starts.

symmetrical strokes Shorthand term for breaststroke and butterfly.

synchronized swimming The art of swimming gracefully in the water. It was raised to the level of a competitive event in the 1960s. There are three forms of competition, all for women only: solo, duet, and team (4-8 members). A competition has two parts: a stunt competition in which each swimmer must perform five stunts, and a free routine competition performed to music and in appropriate costume.

timed final In some longer events only heats are held, with no final, the result being declared on heat times. In such events, the competitors should be graded, with the fastest swimmers going together in the final heat.

timekeeper The official responsible for timing a swimmer. In major meets three timekeepers are assigned to each lane, with a chief timekeeper organizing them.

timing system The electronic equipment used in major competitions, incorporating the starting klaxon for each lane, finishing touch pads, and automatic digital readout of finishing times and positions of all competitors.

touch Act of completing a length or race by touching the end of the pool with the appropriate part of the anatomy (a hand touch is not obligatory in freestyle).

Trudgen The first style of swimming in which both arms were recovered (*qv*) above the water. It was named after John Trudgen,

who made history in 1873 by using a breaststroke kick and recovering his arms above the water alternately.

turn The act of changing direction at the end of the pool in order to start another length. In breaststroke and butterfly the touch must be made with both hands simultaneously and at the same level; turns in these strokes are made *open*, with the head above water. In backstroke (in which a touch with the hand is required) and front crawl a somersault or spin (or a combination of both) is fastest. Such turns are called *tumble* turns.

underwater swimming Group of pastimes and activities mainly performed underwater. There are two main branches: *snorkelling*, in which respiration is maintained through a breathing tube (and is therefore a surface sport); and *aqualung* or *scuba* (self-contained underwater breathing apparatus) diving, in which compressed air is carried in cylinders.

151

Water Polo

No team game makes more demands on its participants than this tough and fast water sport. A sort of water-borne handball, water polo has been the only water-based team game to claim any kind of popularity since it was first organised in Britain in the nineteenth century and entered the Olympic program in 1908. Success in water polo requires the player to have the highest swimming ability, refined catching and shooting ability with either hand, an instant tactical appreciation, and a considerable physical presence and resilience. Because one or two weak players can bring about a team's downfall, the most successful teams have a well-balanced squad in which all players are skilled in attack and defense.

Despite its long history, water polo is a changing game. The rudiments have remained the same: to score more goals than the opposition. But the rules have been changed regularly with various aims: to reduce the amount of gratuitous violence in a game with much man-to-man contact; to discourage teams from retaining possession of the ball for too long without attempting to score; to make refereeing more effective; above all to make the game more attractive as a spectacle.

As water polo began in Britain it is not perhaps a surprise to find that British teams won the Olympic gold medals four times (1900, 1908, 1912, 1920). The British game then went into a decline in world terms and the lead was taken up by the countries of eastern Europe, notably Hungary—Olympic champions in 1932, 1936, 1952, 1956, 1964 and 1976—the USSR and Yugoslavia. With their well-drilled, fit, and above all strong teams the European nations appear capable of continuing to lead the world in this sport.

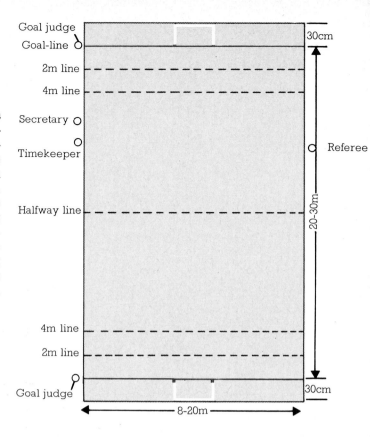

Above: The layout of the playing area. The minimum depth is 1.8m for international matches. There should be ample room round the pool for the referee to walk and goal judges to sit. The goal posts, which must be fixed rigid and perpendicular, and crossbar may be of wood, metal, or synthetic material and are painted white. The dimensions of the goals vary with the depth. All lines must be clearly visible throughout the game.

advantage A rule which allows the referee to use his discretion whether or not to stop play for a foul when a stoppage would be disadvantageous to the non-offending team. Applied properly, it speeds up the game.

bat or knuckle shot A shot (*qv*) in which the ball is flicked into the air with one hand and batted with the open hand or knuckled with the hand partially closed. It is used when swimming towards goal; also used as a pass, though less accurate than a throw.

brutality A major foul which includes deliberately striking or kicking an opponent or official.

caps *See* hats.

choice of ends The decision made by the captain winning the toss before the start of a game. In pools with one deep and one shallow end, it is said to be an advantage to attack the deep end in the last period of play.

corner A free throw taken from the 2m line by a member of the attacking team when a defending player was the last to touch the ball before it went out of play across the goal-line.

deep water Water too deep to stand or walk in. Major international tournaments are played as specifically 'deep water' events.

dry pass A pass made so that the ball may be caught.

extra man A team with a numerical advantage because the opposition has had a man excluded is said to have the extra man.

extra time Additional periods of time played after normal time when the scores are tied and a definite result is required. Played after a five-minute interval, it consists of two three-minute periods of play with a one-minute break.

field The playing area, minimum/maximum dimensions of which are: length 20-30m; width 8-20m; depth 1m (1.8m for internationals). Center, 4m, 2m, and goal-lines are marked on the poolside; goals are placed centrally at each end of the field on the goal-line.

field goal A goal scored from open play, as opposed to from a penalty.

flags The referee is equipped with two flags (on a single stick) matching the hat colors of the teams to indicate free throws. Goal (*qv*) judges also have flags.

free throw Awarded to the non-offending team after a foul. It is taken by the most convenient player from the spot where the foul was committed, except for fouls within the 2m area, which must be taken from the 2m line. The player may throw the ball or drop it in the water and dribble it. Goals may not be scored directly from a free throw.

goal A point scored when the ball completely crosses the goal-line between the uprights and under the crossbar, provided it was not punched and had been played by two players after the start, a restart, or a free throw.

goal judges The two officials each positioned at either end of the pool level with the goal-line.

goalkeeper The only player who may, within his own 4m area, stand (*qv*), punch the ball, or touch it with two hands. He may pass the ball anywhere except within the opposition's 4m area.

goals Dimensions of goals in deep water: height 0.9m; width 3.0m; width of posts and bar 0.075m.

half-screw A backhand pass or shot in which the ball is projected sideways from the player.

hats Swimming caps worn by players for identification. The goalkeeper wears a red hat with the number 1; other hats are in blue, white, or team colors and numbered 2 to 11.

hole A position directly in front of goal often taken up by a specialist goalscorer.

major fouls Serious infringements of the rules. As punishment the offending player is excluded from the water for 45 seconds actual play (or until a goal is scored). A player committing a major foul incurs a personal (*qv*) fault.

neutral throw A throw-in by the

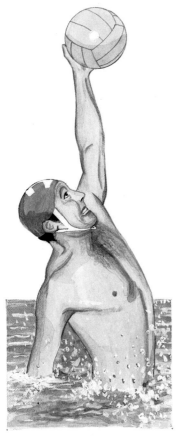

Left: A player attempting to pass the ball under pressure from an opponent. The player needs to try to rise above and away from his opponent before he can execute the pass. A strong alternate breaststroke kicking will enable him to achieve this, the piston-like leg action making it difficult for an opponent to get close.

Bottom: Three stages in the backhand shot, one of several shots in a good water polo player's repertoire. The shot is made with the wrist and elbow flexed and the ball steadied between hand and forearm. Other shots include the lob—a deceptive shot useful in deep water—the power shot, and the push and knuckle shots.

Right: The yellow spots indicate the best positions to aim for when shooting at goal, depending on the player's distance from it. They also depend on the goalie's position and his goalkeeping ability. Spots around the goalie's head are best when close in because, due to the keeper's arm action, this is the most difficult area for him to cover. From further out, say from 20ft or more, the attacker is more likely to choose one of the four corners.

Left: A player rises high to catch the ball. The water polo ball is spherical and completely waterproof. It weighs 15-17oz and has a circumference of 27-28in. With the exception of the goalkeeper, players are not permitted to touch the ball with both hands simultaneously. Once a player has possession of the ball he may not hold it for more than 35 seconds.

referee to restart play after a stoppage through illness or when players from both teams offend simultaneously and the referee cannot distinguish who committed the foul first, or when the ball strikes an overhead obstruction.

ordinary fouls Minor infringements of the rules, which are punished by the awarding of a free throw to the opposition.

penalty goal A goal scored from a penalty throw.

penalty throw A free throw at goal from any point along the 4m line with only the goalkeeper between the penalty-taker and the goal. The goalkeeper must remain on his line, while the taker must throw directly at goal. It is awarded to the non-offending team when a defender strikes or makes to strike an attacker or commits a foul within his own 4m area which prevents a goal being scored; or when a player re-enters the water after expulsion during the final minute of the game (or of any period of extra

time) incorrectly or without permission from the secretary (*qv*); or when a player leaving the water deliberately interferes with play.

personal fault Awarded against a player committing a major foul or giving away a penalty. Any player awarded three personal faults is excluded from the game, although he may be substituted.

pit Another name for a hole (*qv*).

possession A team may retain possession for only 35 seconds without shooting. To exceed this time is an ordinary foul.

punching Hitting with a clenched fist. It is an ordinary foul for a field player (but not for the goalkeeper within his own 4m area) to punch the ball. It is a major foul or brutality to punch another player.

push shot A shot or pass made by picking the ball up and propelling it by straightening the arm.

referee The official in control of the game and the players while he and they are in the precincts

of the pool. Usually there is one referee but in major games two referees may be used.

screw A backhand shot or pass projecting the ball directly behind the thrower.

secretary The official whose task is to record the score and personal faults awarded against each player. He also signals the third personal fault, controls the re-entry of players and signals improper entry.

shot Any scoring attempt in which the ball is propelled towards goal.

sling shot A shot in which the ball is thrown with a straight horizontal arm; it often begins with the player's back to goal.

standing Allowing one or both feet to rest on the floor of the pool. It is an ordinary foul for field players to take an active part in the game when standing.

substitutes Up to four substitutes per team are permitted. Substitutions may be made between periods or after a goal has been scored. A player expelled after

three personal faults may be substituted; a player expelled for brutality may not.

swim-up The start and restart of the game after the inter-period break: the ball is thrown on to the halfway line by the referee and the teams swim from the goal-line to claim possession.

timekeeper The official who keeps the time and signals the end of each period of play. He also counts the periods of possession and exclusion after a major foul, using appropriate signals in each case. A game lasts 20 minutes; four periods of five minutes each with a two-minute break between. Time is calculated on an 'actual play' basis, the timekeeper's watch being stopped when the referee stops play and restarted when the ball is put back into play.

walking Progressing by walking on the floor of the pool. It is an ordinary foul except for the goalkeeper within his own 4m area.

wet pass A pass made on the water and not in the air.

Water Skiing

A sport in which a person uses skis and propulsion from a motor boat to plane on the water, water skiing has enjoyed an increasing popularity since the end of World War II. Its origins, however, go back to the early twentieth century. But it was not until 1924, when the American Fred Waller patented his design for water skis, that the embryo sport developed its own identity. Large crowds watched the first competition at Long Island in 1935, and four years later the American Water Ski Association was founded. Elsewhere the sport was making similar progress, especially in the western Mediterranean, and in 1946 the World Water Ski Union was formed to control the sport internationally. Britain did not take to the sport until the end of the decade, but today the British federation is second only to the American body. World championships, first contested in 1949, are held every two years.

Championships feature trick skiing, slalom and jumping, plus an overall category for the best all-round performer. In tricks, the skier has a limited time within which to perform a series of freestyle movements for which points ranging from 20 to 450 are awarded according to their difficulty. Mono-ski tricks have a higher point value. In Slalom — a timed run through two lines of buoys — half a point is awarded for every buoy successfully rounded and also for returning to within the boat's wake before the next buoy. Upon completion of the course the boat speed is raised by 1⅞ mph up to a set maximum of 36 mph for men, 34 mph for women. If the course is still successfully negotiated at these speeds, then the rope is shortened by predetermined amounts, until the skier falls or misses a buoy. In jumping each skier receives three attempts over the ramp and the longest jump scores.

Jump ski   Slalom ski

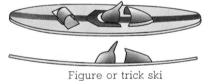

Above: Three types of grip: 1 The slalom grip, sometimes called the 'baseball' grip, used for slalom and jumping. 2 The toe hold for tricks. 3 The standard two-handed grip for general-purpose and trick skiing.

Above left: The tow handle for trick skiing features a specially adapted toe-strap between the bridle.

The competitive skier has a different type of ski for each event. Jump skis, which have wooden or alloy fins, are longer, wider and more robust than general-purpose skis. Slalom skis have a tapered tail to assist speed of turning, and a deeper fin to prevent sideslipping in tight turns. Trick skis, or 'bananas', are much shorter and have no directional fins.

Figure or trick ski

bad gate Getting off to a bad start to the slalom course by taking the wrong line through the gate (qv).

banking A way of going through the air after jumping. The body is more horizontal than upright and the skis go out to the left-hand side, although still pointing in the correct direction.

barefoot Planing on the water without skis. An American innovation, and equally popular in Australia, barefoot skiing is mainly concerned with tricks, but slalom and jumping are also practiced

beachie A barefoot start from the beach.

binding The toe and/or heel piece usually of rubber, designed to hold the foot in place on the ski. The heel binding is on a movable metal runner, whereas the toe binding is mounted on a fixed metal shoe.

cut (1) To shorten the tow rope during slalom. After the first run through the course at maximum speed, the tow rope is reduced from 59ft 10in to 52½ft and subsequently to 46ft 9in, 42ft 8in, 39ft 4in and 36ft 11in. The reductions, which are made from the boat, are called first cut, second cut, etc.
(2) A maneuver in jumping with which the skier increases his speed above that of the boat on his approach to the ramp. Having crossed the wake and swung out as far to the opposite side of the jump as possible, he pulls himself sharply back across the wake to make his diagonal attack on the ramp. It is sometimes called a double cut.

deepie A barefoot start in deep water.

deepwater start Method of starting in which the skier crouches in the water with the skis pointing out of the water and in line with the boat. As the boat accelerates, the skis rise to the surface.

dock start A method of starting in which the skier sits on a dock or pontoon with the front of the skis pointing out of the water. As the boat accelerates, he is launched on to the surface.

early buoy To take a good line around the first slalom buoys and so make a good start to the pass.

figure skiing Another name for trick skiing.

flying beachie A spectacular barefoot start off dry land. The skier runs to the water's edge, launches himself in the air, and lands on his back in the water, where he does a deepie (qv).

gassing Giving the boat more power to compensate for the sudden drag of the skier pulling on the tow-rope to make his cut (qv) prior to approaching the jumping ramp.

gate Twin marker buoys 8ft 2in apart at either end of the slalom course and through which the boat and the skier must pass. The skier has to take the gate at an angle in order to get round the first buoy of his pass.

helicopter A 360° turn, either off the ramp or off the wake.

hooking The action of a slalom skier whose ski, as he rounds the buoy, turns too far in so that he appears to be going back on himself instead of taking a line for the next buoy.

hot-dogging Performing spectacular tricks such as somersaults and helicopters (qv).

jumping One of the three main competition events in which a skier jumps from a ramp back on to the water. The ramp is set at 5ft 11in for men and 4ft 11in for women. Although the speed of the boat is approximately 35mph the skier approaches the ramp at around 50mph.

line-off An American term for shortening the tow-rope during the slalom.

mono-skiing Skiing on one ski.

observer The person in the boat who faces the skier, interprets his signals to the driver and generally has regard for his safety.

parakiting, or parasailing A branch of the sport in which a parachutist is kept aloft by being towed by a boat. As his 'chute is

154

The deep-water start on two skis

The deep-water start on one ski

A step-over turn on two skis

A mono-ski side-slide

A 360° mono-ski surface turn

The reverse foot-hold slide

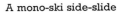

Right: A championship slalom course: 250 x 25yd.

Far right: Jumping. The ramp is coated with wax and kept wet with running water.

Path of boat

Path of skier

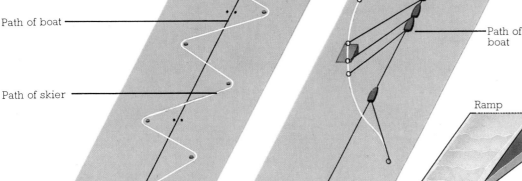

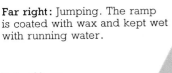

Path of skier

Path of boat

Ramp

already open, he must take off from land, but he may come down in water. How long he stays up is dependent on himself and the conditions, while the height he can attain is governed by the length of the tow-rope.

pass One length of a slalom or trick course.

pylon A tow-rope hitch more amidships than the transom hitch. Usually a pyramid of metal posts, it should be high enough for the tow-rope to clear an outboard motor.

racing An individual branch of competitive water skiing. Skiers race against themselves over set distances and, provided they do not come into contact with the boat, may restart if they fall. Speeds in excess of 100mph have been recorded.

rope on neck A barefoot trick in which the skier puts the long V-handle over his neck and skis with his arms extended.

rope on teeth A barefoot trick in which the skier is pulled along while gripping the handle be-

tween his teeth.

salute A movement in which the skier lifts one ski clear of the water and holds it straight ahead at a steep angle.

scooter start A method of starting for mono-skiers. The skier steps from the shore on to the water, propelling himself with one leg in a 'scooting' action as the boat accelerates.

side-slide A trick movement performed with the ski or skis at right-angles to the line of advance. The skier has to turn to his left or right through 90° to attain this position.

slalom One of the three main competition events. The skier must enter the course through the gate for the run to count. He or she then travels on a zigzag path through a course containing six buoys set out in an equidistant, diagonally staggered formation, and leaves through the exit gate.

step-over turn A trick movement, performed on one ski or two, in which the skier lifts his

free leg or one ski over the tow-rope while making a 180° turn.

surface tricks Tricks performed on the water, as opposed to the wake of the boat.

toe-hold slide A mono-ski movement in trick skiing, the skier placing his foot in the toe-strap (qv). Points are awarded for the basic slide and the reverse slide if each is held for at least two seconds.

toe release Used to release the tow-rope from the boat when a skier falls while performing a toe hold trick.

toe strap The special fitting within the handle of the tow-rope used in tricks.

transom hitch A connection for the tow-rope at the back of the boat.

trick skiing One of the three main competition events. The skier, using specially designed skis, has two 20-second passes to perform as many tricks as possible. These should incorporate side-slides, skiing backwards, step-over turns and turns.

using one ski or two on surface water or the wake.

tumble turn A barefoot trick in which the skier rolls forward over one shoulder on to his back and from this position makes a definite movement to twist forward and regain his original upright skiing position.

turns Movements in trick skiing. There are two basic turns:
180° A front-to-back turn, followed by a back-to-front turn through the same angle.
360° A complete turn made without any pause. The skier transfers the handle from one hand to the other while making the turn.

two-ski slide A side-slide (qv) performed on two skis.

wake The disturbed water behind the boat. It helps the skier obtain lift from the water when performing tricks.

wake tricks Tricks performed on the wake. To meet with the judges' approval, there must be daylight between the water and the bottom of the skis.

155

Wheeled Sports

Cycling

Cycling has a wide international appeal, whether as a leisure activity or as a competitive sport, indeed one which has increased in recent years with energy crises and individual desires for fitness. As a competitive sport, its popularity among participants has never waned, even if spectator appeal is more fluid. On the Continent of Europe, where cycling is the national summer sport of Belgium, France and the Netherlands, the sport flourishes for both amateur and professional riders. There are annual amateur and professional world championships, usually held concurrently at the same venues, and for amateur male riders a selection of events have been included in the Olympic Games since 1896.

Since the first recognized cycle race in Paris in 1868, the sport has developed in two principal directions: road racing and track racing. Each takes a variety of forms. For example, the road race may be a multi-stage national tour, such as the Tour de France for sponsored professional teams, or the amateur Tour of Britain; it may be a one-day classic or a *criterium*. Track racing includes sprints for individuals and tandems, individual and team pursuits, motor-paced races, time trials and madisons, the latter featuring largely in indoor six-day racing. World track records are kept at 1km, 5km, 10km, 20km, 100km, and one hour from standing starts, and from flying starts over 200m, 500m and 1000m. Linking road and track racing is the time trial, which developed in Britain in the late nineteenth century as a result of the closure of public roads for racing, while away from conventional events, the cycle is used for such varied sports as cycle polo, grass-track racing, cycle speedway and roller racing.

Right: These cross-sections show the steepness of the banking on a 250m track. The straights are banked to about 12°, but the curves to almost 45°

Banking on curve

Banking on straight

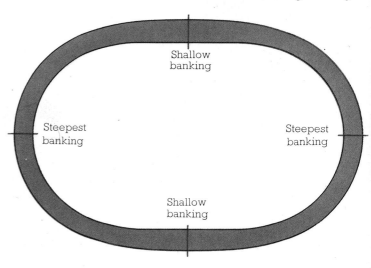

Shallow banking

Steepest banking

Steepest banking

Shallow banking

Above: The characteristically banked cycle track. Indoor tracks may be as short as 130m, but outdoor tracks are longer (up to 500m) and less sharply banked. The circumference is measured along the datum line on the inside of the track. The fastest surface is wood, but concrete, asphalt or macadam are more usual outdoors. Track racing is, with cyclo-cross, cycling's great spectator sport, and many differing forms of racing maintain the crowd's interest, from the psychological warfare of the sprint to the noise and spectacle of 6-day indoor racing. The cyclists race in a counterclockwise direction.

Australian pursuit A pursuit (*qv*) race in which a number of riders start at different, equidistant points around the track, each trying to catch the man in front. As a rider is caught, he is eliminated, the winner being the first of the remaining riders to cross the line when the distance is completed.

bidon French name for the water bottle carried by road racers in a wire carrier on the down tube.

bit and bit Term used for the action of riders who share the effort of riding at the front of a group while the others shelter.

block The assembly of sprockets and freewheelers on the back hub of a road racing cycle with *dérailleur* (*qv*) gears. The term is used also for the action of a rider, or riders, who tactically obstructs another rider or group of riders.

blow up To be overcome with exhaustion during a tiring part of a race.

bonk A colloquialism for extreme fatigue resulting from a combin-ation of over-exertion and a lack of blood sugar.

bonk bag See *musette*.

box To ride just behind and to the outside of another rider so that any rider wishing to over-take must swing wide to do so.

break To get clear of the main bunch (*qv*) of riders in a road or track race. The term is also used for the group of riders who have made a break and are ahead of the bunch.

bunch The main group of riders in a road or track race.

category The term used to denote a rider's status according to his or her age and standard.

chain gang A line of riders in training who exchange the lead as in bit (*qv*) and bit.

circuit races Road races that comprise a number of laps of a course which has been closed to normal traffic. It may even be a course specially marked out on an airport, or motor racing circuit.

classics A select group of one-day races in Europe from one town to another. They are famous for their lucrative prizes and high-quality fields.

close passing Overtaking an-other rider without leaving the greatest practicable space be-tween the two cycles. It is not recommended as safe riding.

cowboy A rider well known for his erratic style of riding.

criterium A road race, or series of road races, through the closed streets of a town or the roads linking a group of towns.

cyclo-cross Cycle racing in winter over cross-country cour-ses which vary in length from 15-25km and are usually over laps of a circuit up to 3km long. Competitors either cycle or run carrying their cycles depending on the nature of the terrain, which should include woodland, plowed pasture land, paths and roads, walls and stiles, and streams.

demi-fond Literally middle-dist-ance; the French name for motor-paced (*qv*) racing. It is so named because motor-paced events were longer originally than they are today.

dérailleur A gear-changing mechanism of Continental origin in which the chain can be moved on to sprockets of differing sizes that are fitted to the rear hub of the cycle. It is operated by levers on either the handlebars or the down tube. Any slack in the chain length caused by the use of smaller sprockets is automati-cally adjusted by a spring-fitted cage.

Derny A small moped-like motor-cycle used in some forms of motor pacing.

devil-take-the-hindmost A track event in which, every so many laps, the last rider in the field to pass the finish line is eliminated until there are only two riders remaining to contest the final sprint.

domestiques Members of a road racing team whose job is to sup-port the leader and any other 'protected' riders.

drop To leave a rider or group of riders behind in a road or

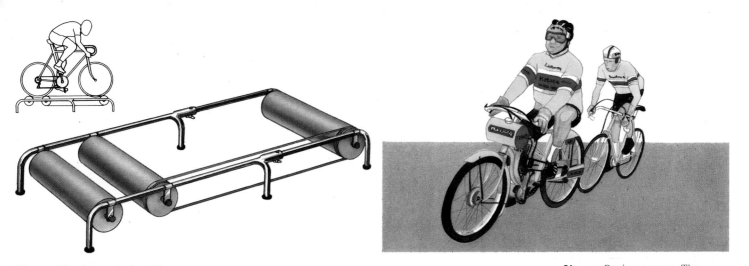

Above: The 'home trainer' is a useful adjunct to the serious competitive cyclist. It provides pedalling practice if weather or other factors make training outside impracticable. Some are adjustable to give varying degrees of resistance, simulating hills or adverse conditions.

Right: Track cycling requires enormous exertion and a high degree of discipline and technique. The trackman, more than any other competitive cyclist, needs a warm-up for the race. Unfortunately many of the great tracks have now disappeared, victims of urban development and of the general enthusiasm for road racing.

Above: Pacing a race. The Bordeaux-Paris race used the old Derny motorized bike for 40 years until it was replaced in 1976 with lightweight motorbikes. Pacing is used in both track and road events, and success in this branch of cycling depends very much on understanding between rider and pacer.

Stayers line

Sprinters line

track race; as in a break (qv).

echelon A diagonal line of riders positioned across a road to shelter from a crosswind. Also the formation at the start of a track handicap event where the riders are positioned higher and higher up the banking towards the limit (qv) man.

freewheeler Sprocket that drives the rear wheel, but if the rider so desires will run free without the pedals being turned.

general classification The overall ranking of riders in a stage race, based on the total time taken to cover the stages completed. The classification is published after each stage and is separate from the results of that day's stage.

handicap Races in which lesser riders are given the advantage of so many metres start or perhaps a time allowance.

hill-climbs Events in which the riders aim to be the fastest up the course. Distances vary in length according to the gradient but do not generally exceed 5km.

homewards In time trials, the journey from the halfway turn (qv) to the finish.

honk To ride off the saddle, standing on the pedals to obtain more power.

individual pursuit A track race in which the two riders start on the opposite sides of the track to race over a specified distance. The winner is the rider who catches the other, or in the event of this not happening, the rider with the faster time.

Italian pursuit A form of team pursuit in which each of two or more teams drops a rider at the completion of every lap until only one rider per team is left to contest the final lap. The result is determined by the finishing time of the last riders.

jump To sprint suddenly in an attempt to break away from the main part of the field.

kermesse A form of circuit road racing. Competitors ride as individuals.

king of the mountains The title bestowed on a road racing

cyclist with the best overall performance on certain designated hill and mountain sections of a one-day or a stage race.

limit man The rider with the most advantage in a handicap race.

line-out A string of riders lined out behind the leader, whose pace is preventing them from bunching.

madison A track race between teams of two riders, only one of whom actually races at any one time. The others either leave the track to eat and rest, or circle slowly around the track above the stayers line, resting, until it is time to relieve the racing partner. The new rider is pushed or slung into the race by his racing team-mate, who then goes up the banking for his rest period. The object is to ride as many laps as possible in an allotted time.

maillot jaune The yellow jersey worn by the overall leader in a stage race. It is most commonly associated with the Tour de France, where the leader is known as the *maillot jaune*.

massed-start racing Another name for road racing.

minute-man The person starting in a time trial a minute ahead of or behind another rider.

motor-paced A track race in which the cyclists are paced by motor-cyclists who also provide them with shelter from the wind and take them along in their slipstream. Championship distances are 100km for professionals and up to 1 hour for amateurs.

mountain classification The distribution of points on certain mountain sections of a road race or tour according to the severity of the gradient. The mountain prize, and usually the title of 'king of the mountains', goes to the rider with the most points.

musette A light satchel containing food and drink which a rider picks up as he passes through a special feeding station during a race. Once he has transferred the food into the pockets of his racing jersey and the *bidon* (qv) into the wire carrier, he throws

Left: The touring bike is never as light as a racing bicycle, but it combines efficiency and speed with maximum comfort on long distances. Some of its weight is due to the sturdier frame, but other major extras add to it—such as lights, water bottle, carriers, full-wheel mud guards and heavier wheels. The three-sprocket front-chain wheel allows a wide range of gearing.

Right: The Tour de France route of 1976. Every year cyclists from all over the world compete for the yellow jersey. The race began as a curiosity, the first-ever tour beginning at Villeneuve-Saint-Georges, a southeastern suburb of Paris, in July 1903. It was organized by Géo Lefèvre, the cycling editor of *L'Auto*. It was the first professional race to be broken into stages, day by day. The route of the race changes every year, but it is always planned to include as varied a terrain as possible. The mountainous regions are an important test of stamina and there is a special mountain classification, in addition to the points and general classifications, to determine the 'king of the mountains'.

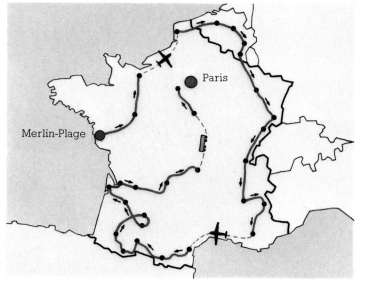

The 1976 Tour de France took 25 days. It began at Merlin-Plage on June 24 and ended at Paris on July 18. Included were two transfers by air and one by train. Strenuous riding through the Ardennes, Alps and Pyrénées mountains, as well as an onslaught on the daunting Puy-de-Dôme, were highlights.

the *musette* away. Also called a bonk bag.

oil A warning shout to notify cyclists of the approach of a car.

omnium A track contest which comprises a series of different kinds of races, such as sprints, devil-take-the-hindmost, pursuit, motor-paced, etc. Points are awarded for places in each form, with the overall placings determined on an aggregation of points won.

pacing Setting a speed for, and giving cover against the wind to, another cyclist so that he or she can make better progress. Pacing may come from another solo rider, a tandem pair, or a motorcycle.

pack To stop racing. The term is also used, though not strictly correctly, for the bunch (*qv*).

peloton French term for the main bunch of riders in a road race.

point–to–point A track race in which the riders gain points at regular intervals according to their positions. The overall winner is the rider who collects

most points by the end of the race, regardless of his actual position in the final sprint.

points classification A feature of stage races and held in addition to the general (*qv*) classification. Points are awarded to competitors according to their finishing position in each stage, regardless of the time factor, and the rider with the most points (or least depending on the system being used) at the end of the race wins the prize for the points classification. Points may be distributed in ascending order so that the stage winner receives one, second place two, etc, or in descending order with the winner receiving, say 15, second place 14, etc. A points classification list is drawn up daily and attracts as much interest as the general and mountain classifications.

pressures The conventional, high pressure wired-on tires.

prime An intermediate prize or bonus awarded to the first rider to pass a certain point during a race. It may be the summit of a

mountain stage, a town boundary, a notable landmark, or the finishing line after so many laps of a track.

pursuit Track races in which individuals or teams start equidistant from each other and try to catch the other. Such races are usually fast, furious affairs. Distances are 5km for professionals, 4km for amateurs and 3km for women.

repêchage An extra heat in a sprint or motor-paced race to give those who have been eliminated during the qualifying rounds a second chance of reaching the next stage of the competition.

road racing Racing over a route other than that specially constructed for cycle racing, and generally of a kind suitable for other road traffic. It may take the form of a stage race over a number of days, a one-day race over a circuit, or from one town to another.

roller race A 'race' in which the riders use stationary cycles

mounted on three rollers which turn to record the 'distance' travelled during an allotted time. In some instances the rider may be supported by an attendant for all or part of the race.

safety line A distinctively colored line 90cm from the inside of a cycle track, inside which overtaking is not allowed if the forward cycle is itself on or inside the line. Also called the sprinters line.

scratch races Track races in which all the competitors start on equal terms.

scratch winner The rider in a time trial who returns the fastest time.

selection from behind Term used to describe the tactics of a rider who, rather than trying to break from the field at a later stage of the race, sets such a severe pace that riders behind him are forced to drop back.

sit in To stay in a bunch of riders and not accept the responsibility of setting the pace.

sit up To stop making an effort

Below: Cyclo-cross is practiced during the winter months. Ideal terrain for this sport includes fields, woods, banks, paths, narrow gaps and bridges. Although agility and nimbleness are assets, the best cyclo-cross performers are those who can use their bikes while lesser men are forced on to their feet. Races usually last just over an hour.

Above: A typical cyclo-cross bike. The type needed for this pursuit is of a special standard, combining aspects of both the touring and racing versions. The frame is basically similar to that used for road racing, but the increased fork and clearance are designed to avoid mud-clogging. The brake stirrups are wider for the same reason, and the bottom bracket is higher. The toe clips are double-thickness to prevent damage. The tires themselves are specially dotted with 'knobs' to ensure a firm grip on icy or muddy roads. Since cyclo-cross is a winter sport and demands that the cyclist also be a hardy runner, the bike must be kept as light as possible to enable him to carry it uphill and especially sturdy to enable him to take a running jump on it to sprint down dale. Gears are usually much lower than those on racing cycles.

during a race by adopting the sit-up position rather than the crouched racing position.

six-day race An indoor track event in which two-man teams race over a period of time on six days, usually in the evenings and perhaps for a matinee or two. Included in the event are a variety of races such as sprints, madisons, time trials and elimination races.

sprint A track race between two, three or more riders over a variety of circuits but with only the final 200m being timed. A feature of sprinting is the maneuvering that goes on in the first part of the race, the riders slowing down, switching position up and down the bank, and sometimes virtually stopping in an effort to avoid being at the front when the timed sprint starts. Sprint competitions are on a knock-out basis. Races are held for tandems (*qv*) as well as for individual riders.

sprinters line *See* safety line.

stack up When a rider falls off his cycle in spectacular fashion.

stage race A long-distance road race, such as a national tour, in which the distance is divided into sections to be ridden over a number of days, the winner being the rider who covers the overall distance in the fastest time. Prizes and bonus points are awarded along the route, and there are points (*qv*) and mountain (*qv*) classifications in addition to (and irrespective of) the general (*qv*) classification.

station The point on a track from which cyclists start. Used only in pursuit races.

stayer A motor-pace rider.

stoker Name given to the rider who sits behind on a tandem and provides extra power.

tandem A bicycle for two riders, one seated behind the other and both pedalling. Only the front rider steers.

team pursuit A track event between teams of four riders. Each rider leads the team for one lap, or perhaps half a lap, and then swings up the banking and slots in at the back of the team. The result is determined on the time of the third rider of the team to cross the finish line.

tester A time triallist.

time trial A road event over a set distance, or a track event over 1km, in which an unpaced rider is individually timed. Each rider starts at a regular interval, usually a minute, and has to judge his or her own pace from previous experience. When overtaking or being overtaken, riders are not permitted to use the other rider as a pacemaker. Known in France as *course contre la montre* (the race against the watch).

toeclip A light metal frame secured to the pedal and fitted with a strap to prevent the foot from slipping off while pedalling.

track racing Racing on a specially made track. This is usually oval in shape with back and finishing straights, and is banked all round with steeper banking at the corners to allow riders to keep up their speed. Tracks may be in-doors or outdoors with surfaces of concrete, asphalt, or wood. Racing, which is in a counter-clockwise direction, takes the form of sprints, pursuits, motor-paced events, time trials, madisons and six-day races.

turn In a time trial, the point where the rider completes the outward half and begins the homeward part of his race.

UCI Union Cycliste Internationale, the world governing body of cycling since 1900.

unknown distance A form of track race in which the riders do not know the distance they are to ride until the bell sounds for the last lap.

up the banking A position near the top of the corner banking on a track. From here, a sprinter is able to develop a powerful attack.

whip An official at a race whose duty it is to ensure that all the riders are at the starting place in time.

work To help in making the pace of a race.

161

Motorcycling

Two-wheeled motor sport, like the four-wheeled variety, took root in late nineteenth-century Europe, notably in France, where there were few restrictions on racing over public roads. The British were not so fortunate; indeed, it was because of government prohibitions on the mainland that the now world-famous Isle of Man TT races were inaugurated in 1907. Ironically, the success of the TT—and of British riders and machines there—brought the British motorcycle industry pre-eminence in the years up to World War II. Nor was interest in the sport limited to road racing. Lack of roads for racing merely sent the enthusiasts off the roads to develop new events: trials, scrambles, grass-track, sand-track, speedway, hill-climbs, sprints and drag racing. Sometimes these activities were pusued on the amateur's road machine, which would be stripped down for the day's sport and then reassembled for the journey home.

Complacency and a lack of economic foresight were to cost the British motorcycle industry dearly after 1950 as first the Italians and Germans, and later the eastern Europeans and Japanese provided the machines which the champions—and soon everyone—raced. The Japanese campaign to conquer world markets with competition success was phenomenal: in most branches of the sport—speedway was a notable exception—the names of Honda, Yamaha, Suzuki, and later Kawasaki, topped the leader-boards. In road racing, which today draws larger crowds to its major meetings than four-wheeled motor sports world championship events are contested annually at 50cc, 125cc, 250cc, 350cc, 500cc, F.750, F.1 (over 750cc), and sidecars. Dirt-track and moto-cross also have annual world championships.

broadsiding The spectacular method of cornering employed by speedway (qv) riders. It originally involved trailing the inside leg behind with the knee almost touching the ground, but this was superseded by the more efficient foot-forward technique. Also known as *power-sliding*.

bump start See push start.

capacity The measurement in cubic centimeters (cc) of the cylinders through which the pistons move. It is used to determine the class in which a machine competes.

clean Term used in observation (qv) trials for a penalty-free run.

clutch start Method of starting when the bike's engine is already running as it waits to start. The rider engages first or second gear and disengages the clutch; when the starting signal is given, he slips (and abuses) the clutch to achieve optimum revs.

dab Term used in observation trials for touching the ground once with any part of the body—usually the foot. Such an action

incurs one penalty point.

dirt-track racing Practiced in the United States on mile-long (1.6km) unpaved oval tracks, often on powerful machines. Racing is from a massed start with the first rider to cross the finish line winning. The term was once used in Britain for speedway (qv).

drag racing A form of racing in which two riders race specially prepared road or competition machines over a straight quarter-mile (400m) strip. Racing is on an elimination basis, with the first rider to reach the finish going on to the next round, although elapsed times and terminal speeds are recorded.

dustbin Colloquial name for the fuller type of fairing that completely covers the front wheel as well as the steering head and engine. It is no longer permitted on road racing machines except for sidecar outfits.

enduro Form of time trial (qv).

fairing Streamlining fitted to the front of a machine to lower the

drag coefficient from wind resistance. In road racing, only the dolphin kind of stream-lining is permitted.

FIM Fédération Internationale Motocycliste, the governing body of world motorcycle sport since 1947.

footing Term used in observation trials for touching the ground twice or more with any part of the body. It incurs three penalty points.

four-stroke The standard principle of engine design in which every fourth stroke of the piston produces power.

grass-track racing Racing around short, speedway-style oval tracks on fields containing such natural hazards as dust, flying stones and bumps. Most grass-track racing is for speedway-style machines and riding, but some variants are more akin to road racing. Events are for solo and sidecar machines.

ice racing A form of racing similar to speedway. The machines are fitted with spiked tyres

to provide a suitable grip on the ice.

leathers The close-fitting one- or two-piece protective clothing worn by riders.

Le Mans start A method of starting in which the riders run across the track to their machines, start the engines and accelerate away. So called because a similar method was used at Le Mans for the 24-hour sports car race.

long-track racing Racing over sand, shale or grass oval tracks used for horse trotting races. Practiced mostly in Europe by grass-track and speedway riders, it is also known as 1000m racing on account of the circumference of the track.

moto-cross Racing from a massed start over rough, undulating cross-country circuits featuring such natural hazards as mud, water, gravel, stones and/or grass. Most events are for 125cc, 250cc and 500cc, specially prepared machines, and sidecars of 500 and up to 1000cc, the winner being the first rider to cross the

Left: The familiar shape of the competition motorcycle, which differs little over the full range of racing. The fairing, which has become almost universal in recent years, gives the bike cleaner lines than its forerunners. Other refinements include more efficient braking, better suspension, and of course a vastly improved engine performance.

Above: A sidecar partnership off to a flying start. In this kind of racing the bike rider is close to the ground, but not as close as his partner in the sidecar. Well co-ordinated teamwork is vital.

Right: The moto-cross and scrambling machines, with their distinctive wide handlebars and high seat, have been so developed to master the extremes of terrain encountered,

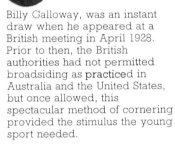

Left: A feature of speedway riding is the rider's use of his left leg and foot as a pivot to corner in a deliberate broadside known as power sliding. The forerunner of the modern foot-forward technique, in which the rider trailed his inside leg with his knee almost touching the ground, was pioneered by daredevil Australian riders, one of whom,

Billy Galloway, was an instant draw when he appeared at a British meeting in April 1928. Prior to then, the British authorities had not permitted broadsiding as **practiced** in Australia and the United States, but once allowed, this spectacular method of cornering provided the stimulus the young sport needed.

finish at the end of the set course or after a set time.

observation trial An event in which riders try to negotiate a formidable cross-country course without touching the ground. The course is divided into a number of hazard-filled *observed sections* with penalties incurred for dabs (*qv*), footings (*qv*), and failure to complete (5 points). The aim is to clean (*qv*) as many sections as possible. The riders set off at intervals, the winner is the rider with fewest penalty points at the end of the course.

outfit A motorcycle and sidecar combination. It is specially constructed to allow the passenger freedom of movement over the whole machine in order to distribute his weight to the best advantage. Latest types do not allow the passenger any movement.

production A road racing class for road machines.

push start Method of starting road racing machines when the rules of an event exclude clutch starts (*qv*), or insist on the use of means fitted to the machine, as in production racing. The rider pushes his bike with the fuel and ignition circuits on, and in gear with the clutch engaged. When the engine fires, he jumps onto the saddle and settles into a proper riding position, so providing a spectacular start to the race. Originally known as a *bump start*.

road racing Racing over closed public roads or on specially built circuits incorporating some of the features found on public roads. Riders start together or at intervals from a grid to race a required number of laps of the circuit, the first to cross the finish line being the winner. Classes of racing are for solo and sidecar machines.

scrambling A sport similar to moto-cross.

scratching Colloquialism for the fast, often hair-raising style of riding practiced on short road-racing circuits where cornering

and acceleration are as important as out-and-out speed.

senior Term used for the 500cc road racing class.

sidecar racing Racing in a motorcycle sidecar outfit (*qv*) with a passenger as well as a rider. In addition to its being a road racing class, it features in sprints, grass-track and moto-cross.

speedway Racing lightweight specially built machines which have no brakes around an oval track with a cinder or shale surface. A race is between a maximum of four riders over four counter clockwise laps of the track, the first to cross the finish line winning. Points are awarded for the first three placings and count towards a rider's, or his team's, score for the meeting.

sprints A timed run against the clock over a straight course up to a mile (1.6km) in length. The usual distance is a quarter-mile (400m). Classes are for solo machines and sidecars.

superbikes Road racing machines of 750cc or above.

tapes The starting tapes stretched across the track before a speedway race. Riders must remain behind them until they are lifted.

time trial A cross-country event over terrain similar to that for observation trials. Riders are issued with route- and time-cards which are stamped at control points along the way. A penalty point is incurred for every two minutes a rider is late in reporting at the control points, the standard time being set by the fastest rider to complete the course. The winner is the rider with fewest penalty points.

trials See observation trial; time trial.

TT Tourist Trophy A designation given to some major road racing meetings such as the Isle of Man TT and Dutch TT.

two-stroke The principle of engine design in which every second stroke of the piston produces power.

wheelies Riding on the back wheel of a machine with the front wheel in the air.

Motor Racing

Given man's competitiveness, it was perhaps inevitable that he would waste little opportunity to use the motor car for racing. Within a decade of the development of the internal-combustion engine in 1885, motoring events had been organized. In 1894 came the first of any significance, the Paris to Rouen trial, and this in turn led to the first true race, the Paris-Bordeaux-Paris of 1895: a journey of 700 miles and several days that accounted for all but nine of its 22 starters. Since then, the sport has branched out in various directions, the principal international form being road racing under the aegis of what is now the FIA. This controlling body classifies cars as single-seater racers, prototype, or production, dividing these by homologation into specific groups according to the number made, any modifications and, in the case of single-seaters, a formula. Within these groups are further subdivisions into capacity classes; Formula One grand prix cars, for example, are limited at present to 3 litres (3000cc) or 1.5 litres supercharged.

Formula One racing provides the basis for the annual World Championship for Drivers and the accompanying International Cup for Manufacturers, points being awarded to the first six finishers in selected grands prix held worldwide throughout the year. Much prestige and enormous rewards are attached to winning the world championship. In terms of prize money, though, motor sport's richest event is not a Formula One grand prix. This distinction belongs to the Indianapolis 500, raced annually in the United States.

In the United States popularity for motor racing is divided between single-seater and stock car racing on superfast speedways, drag racing and, to a lesser degree, road racing. Nevertheless—as elsewhere in the world—there are clubs to cater for the sport's adherents, no matter in which areas their interests lie.

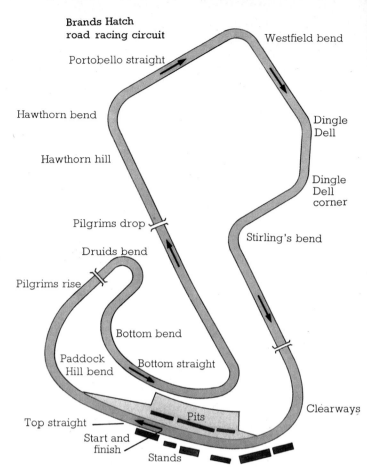

Above: Brands Hatch racing circuit. Starting with Brooklands in 1906, closed circuits were built in many countries, solely for racing and testing cars. All types of races are held on these circuits, which vary considerably in size and shape. Races last for a set length of time or fixed number of laps. Brands Hatch is one of the two major circuits in Britain. The most important race in any country's calender is its grand prix. However in the US, the Indianapolis 500, which has been run since 1911, is probably most famous.

A-frame Name given to a chassis component which vaguely resembles a letter A in shape. The A-arm suspension link is sometimes known as a wishbone.

airfoils 'Downthrust' aids fitted to single-seater (qv) cars and some sports (qv) cars to provide negative lift at high speeds. At one time mounted on struts, they are now limited to being wings on either side of the nose cone with a larger wing mounted 3ft above the rear wheels.

anti-roll bar A torsion bar mounted transversely from the front or rear axles to the suspension links on the wheels to regulate the amount of body roll when cornering.

aquaplaning Travelling on a wet track or road without the tires gripping the surface.

Armco The brand name of the corrugated steel crash barrier used on many racing circuits; now used to mean any steel crash barrier.

autocross Two, sometimes four, modified cars racing against the clock around a short, closed circuit. Results are determined on times.

back marker A driver at the tail of the field who is likely to be lapped (qv).

black flag When accompanied by a number, it means the car bearing that number must stop immediately at its pits (qv).

blow up To experience engine failure.

blower Colloquial name for a supercharger (qv).

blue flag When held stationary it indicates to a driver that another driver is close behind; when waved it indicates that another driver is trying to overtake.

capacity The measurement, expressed in cubic centimeters (cc) or cubic inches (ci), of the cylinders through which the pistons move.

champ or Indianapolis car Wedge-shaped, open-wheeled single-seater, resembling the Formula One Grand Prix cars but set-up (qv) to run on the Indianapolis-type oval track circuit. Engines are limited to 161 ci, developing over 700 horsepower and speeds in excess of 200mph.

checkered flag Shown to drivers to signal the end of the race. In theory it should be waved for only the winner and held stationary for all the other cars.

chicane A diversion, such as an S-bend, built into a circuit; often as a safety feature to slow down cars before difficult sections or to prevent continuous drafting (qv).

christmas tree The electronic starting device of vertical yellow, green and red lights used in drag (qv) racing.

CSI Commission Sportive Internationale, the sub-committee of the FIA (qv) that controls the rules of motor racing and draws up the various classes of racing held at international level.

drafting To follow so closely behind another car as to be 'dragged' along in its wake as a result of reduced wind resist-ance.

drag racing Two matched machines accelerating from a standing start over a quarter-mile strip (qv). Both elapsed and terminal times are recorded, but the winner is the first to cross the finish line, regardless of times. He then moves into the next round of the competition.

dragster A hot-rod racer used in drag racing.

drift A controlled four-wheel slide through a corner, using the throttle to balance against the effects of the slide.

dummy grid An assembly area behind the grid proper where the cars assemble and start before moving forward on to the grid (qv).

elapsed time The time taken between two points, usually the start and finish of a strip (qv), lap (qv), or race. Sometimes referred to as ET.

eliminator The long, narrow 'rail' chassis dragsters with soft-tire rear wheels and smaller 'bicycle' wheels up front. Fired

Right: An example of a Formula One car, the Brabham Alfa BT46. Top-class motor racing is strictly governed by regulations laid down by the FIA. The major forms of single-seater racing are divided into different classes prefixed by the term 'Formula'. The maximum engine capacity for Formula One is 3000cc, or 1500cc supercharged or turbocharged, limited to 12 cylinders. Design in many respects is fairly free, but there are an increasing number of regulations concerning safety. These cars take part in grands prix races, which determine the World Drivers' Championship and the Manufacturers' World Championship. It is these competitions which attract the widest international interest in motor racing today.

Left: The Porsche 935 sports car. As with single-seaters, cars in this class must conform to the relevant FIA regulations, true sports cars being classified as Group 6. Although these cars developed from mass-produced touring cars, they bear little relation to what the public buy. The two-seat specification remains but there is no longer any minimum production number. Manufacturers promote these cars as a means of proving and developing features for their production models.

by engines of over 400ci capacity, they may be fuelled by exotic substances such as nitromethane (*top-fuelers*) or pump gasoline (*qv*) (*top gas*).

FIA Fédération Internationale de l'Automobile, the governing body of world motor sport since 1947.

flat Term used to describe an engine in which the opposing banks of cylinders are set at 180 degrees to each other. It is also known as a *horizontally opposed* engine or a *boxer*.

forest rally A rally in which the majority of special (*qv*) stages are run on forest roads.

formula racing Single-seater racing to FIA-approved specifications which determine engine capacity, number of cylinders, minimum weight without ballast, and other essential requirements.

ftd Fastest time of day. Also called *best time of day*.

funny cars Dragsters which are plastic- or fiberglass bodied replicas of late-model produc-

tion cars powered by modified and supercharged engines.

GPDA The Grand Prix Drivers' Association.

go into the country To leave the circuit while racing; also known as *farming*.

graded drivers The select list of drivers drawn up by the FIA on the basis of results in Formula One world championship events, sports car events and the European Formula Two trophy. World champion drivers of the previous five years are automatically included.

grand prix, or grande épreuve A title given to the most important international race in a country's racing calendar. It is usually a Formula One world championship event.

green flag Indicates that the road is clear of an earlier danger.

grid The area in road racing where cars are lined up in starting (grid) positions determined by lap times set in practice. The position of the cars is staggered so that none is directly behind

the one in front.

hill–climbing Racing against the clock over closed mountain roads or over short, twisting courses of varying gradients. Drivers have two attempts in which to record their best time.

homologation Recognition by the CSI that a car in one of the authorized FIA categories conforms to their requirements for that group.

intercom A microphone and earphone attachment fitted to crash helmets by rally (*qv*) drivers and their navigators/co-drivers to effect communication.

jump-start A driver's anticipating the fall of the starting flag and so stealing an advantage over his rivals. It is penalized by a time penalty.

karting Racing with karts powered by homologated two-stroke engines with capacities from 100-270cc and chain driven. Chassis dimensions are standardized, with constructions varying from ladder-shaped frames to multi-tubular construc-

tions. Also known as *go-karting*.

lap (1) The distance to be raced around a circuit. (2) To establish a lead of a lap over a rival by getting so far ahead that it has become possible to close up from behind and overtake.

limit The fastest possible speed, taking into account the car, the track, and weather conditions, at which a driver can travel. Anything in excess would precipitate loss of control.

line The path a racing car takes through a corner.

monocoque A method of construction which uses a 'single-shell' frame instead of a chassis or a multi-tubular spaceframe (*qv*). The car's body strength comes from the combination of the body's components themselves.

monoposto Italian word meaning single-seat; applies to the early single-seater grand prix cars.

NASCAR National Association for Stock Car Auto Racing, the controlling body for stock car racing in the USA.

Left: An eliminator AA dragster A drag race covers only a straight quarter-mile (402m) strip. Cars compete in pairs. There are various classes, but all cars have highly tuned engines and are capable of speeds over 230mph within the distance. Competitions involve a series of elimination rounds. Originally, the driver sat at the rear of the dragster, perched behind or even above the engine, but as in other forms of racing the rear-engined dragster has become more accepted. From the 'burn out' of the slicks before the drag to the billowing of the parachute which brings the dragster to a halt, drag racing provides one of motor sport's most dramatic spectacles.

Right: A US stock car, the CAMC Matador. US stock car racing is for cars that have the same outward appearance as mass-produced cars, but are highly modified with virtually all the car reworked or replaced to increase performance and safety. Pride of place in stock car racing goes to the NASCAR Grand National type which race on fast, banked oval speedways and superspeedways over distances of 250-600 miles Tracks can be banked in excess of 30° to counter the centrifugal force of the cars. NASCAR also sanctions smaller events, as does USAC.

off-the-road A mainly American sport in which a variety of vehicles including four-wheel drives, beach buggies and motorcycles race over unpaved, pot-holed, boulder-strewn routes.

oversteer Occurs in cornering when the back of the car leaves the chosen line and threatens to swing round ahead of the front.

pace notes Notes used by a rally crew so that the co-driver can advise his driver on the surfaces, gradients, crests and cambers to be encountered, distances to be driven and speeds at which corners can be taken. In a shorthand unique to each crew, these instructions are relayed, usually in monosyllables, through the intercom (*qv*).

paddock The area where cars are kept and prepared at a motor racing meeting.

pit board An information board held out during a race so that a driver can see his position in the race, the laps remaining and his standing in relation to drivers ahead or behind.

pits The area set alongside the track where cars can be worked on while the race is in progress.

pole position The prime position on the front line of the grid. It is awarded to the driver with the fastest lap time in practice.

push start A method of starting in which the engine is fired by pushing the car with the clutch engaged.

rallycross A sport, specially devised for television, in which four cars race over a variety of surfaces similar to those experienced on the special (*qv*) stages of a rally. First past the post wins, with heat winners going on to a final.

rallying A sport in which specially prepared cars from FIA groups 1-4 compete over a set route which is divided into stages which may include selectives (*qv*) and/or special (*qv*) stages. Each car has a driver and a co-driver/navigator. Penalty points are deducted for each stage of the rally completed, with penalties incurred for offences against the rules of the event and late arrival at control points. The winner is the car with least penalty points.

red flag Flag which indicates that all cars must stop at once.

road racing Racing over public roads which have been closed to normal use for the duration of a meeting, or on specially prepared circuits incorporating some of the features found on public roads. Racing may be from point-to-point—though this is rare nowadays—or over a series of laps of a closed circuit. The winner is the first car to finish the full distance.

rolling start A method of starting a race. The cars, arranged in grid formation, follow a pace car carrying the starter, who flags them off as they approach the starting line. The pace car peels off into the pit lane.

sedan car racing Racing production cars homologated to FIA groups 1-2 on the road racing circuits. Modifications are allowed within the regulations of the group.

SCCA Sports Car Club of America, a controlling body for road racing in the USA.

selective In rallying, a section of public road which has not been closed to normal traffic but over which a target time has to be met.

set up To prepare the suspension, tires and steering to obtain the best road holding on a particular circuit.

shunt Colloquialism for an accident which damages the car.

single-seater racing Events for cars built to Formula specifications with uncovered wheels and a cockpit for only one driver.

slicks The thick, treadless tires used on racing cars. Made of a variety of special rubber mixes, they have a high level of traction up to a certain breakaway point —and then the car goes into a high-speed slide. They are useless in wet conditions.

spaceframe A form of multi-tubular chassis construction.

Right: The Fiat 131 Abarth, a successful rally car. Rallying is permitted on public roads and features cars which are or have been developed from models produced for public use. This form of motor sport has continued to grow in popularity, encouraged by the large sums that manufacturers are prepared to spend on promotion. Cars compete over a course made up of a number of stages. Each car has a driver and a navigator. Rallies take place throughout the world, often in adverse conditions specially chosen to prove the quality of the cars and their crews.

Most of the rectangular bays are cross-braced, or *triangulated*.

special stage A section of a rally route over which cars are timed to the second and penalties incurred on the basis of a set target time. It may be a public road closed to traffic or a private road, but wherever possible it is routed over demanding terrain.

speedway A race track, oval in shape or with two long and two short straights between four banked corners. Racing is counterclockwise, the cars being set up for the left-hand cornering and the banking.

spin To lose control of the car and go into rotational movement.

spoiler An airfoil (*qv*).

sports car Under the regulations for FIA Group 6 racing, an open car with two-seater all-enveloping bodywork and some road equipment such as lights.

spyder An open-topped two-seater sports car.

squirt A short, sharp burst of speed. Often used in reference to drag racing.

starting flag The national flag of the country in which the race is being run.

stock car Highly modified production sedans (*qv*) which race around speedways (*qv*) and occasionally on road racing circuits. In Britain a stock car is a stripped down, modified and or specially built car for racing around small, usually quarter-mile oval circuits with cinder or equivalent surfaces. Racing is divided into classes, with massed starts placing the novices ahead of the more experienced drivers; the color of the car roof denotes the drivers' status. Some contact is permitted during the racing.

strip A drag-racing track.

supercharger A device capable of augmenting atmospheric pressure to increase the induction of air or fuel/air mixture into the combustion chamber.

ten-tenths Driving on the limit.

thermo-probe An instrument for checking tire temperatures.

ton Colloquialism for driving at a speed of 100mph.

trials An event in which the aim is to drive a specially built trial car up a rough, hilly course. Penalty points are incurred according to the numbered flags lining the route: the highest number at the bottom and zero at the top. Time is immaterial, the winner being the driver with least penalty points at the end of the day. A feature of trials is the role of the compulsory passenger who bounces up and down in his seat or leans out at corners to help gain extra traction.

tune To prepare the engine so that it performs with maximum power and efficiency and to set (*qv*) up the suspension and steering.

turbocharger A supercharger (*qv*) which is a turbine system driven by the exhaust gases being fed to it.

unblown Without a supercharger (*qv*).

understeer Occurs sometimes in cornering when the front tires lose their traction and so fail to respond fully to the steering.

USAC United States Auto Club, which organizes championship racing such as the Indianapolis 500, stock car, midget, and sprint racing on oval, dirt-track and road racing circuits.

veteran Cars built up to and including 1918.

vintage Cars built between 1919 and 1930.

wash out To lose control of the front end of the car.

white flag Indicates that a service car is on the circuit.

wishbone *See* A-frame.

yellow and red striped flag When stationary it indicates oil on the track ahead; when waved it indicates oil in the immediate vicinity.

yellow flag When stationary it indicates danger and vetoes passing; when waved it indicates there is even greater danger and that drivers must be prepared to stop.

yump A bump which can cause a fast-moving car to become airborne.

Roller Skating

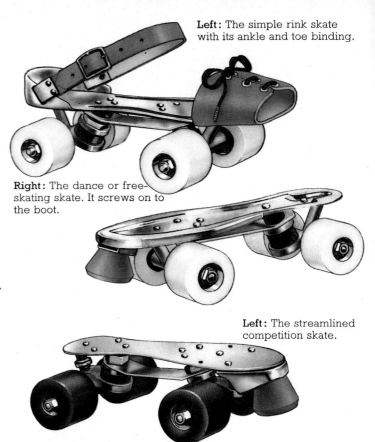

Left: The simple rink skate with its ankle and toe binding.

Right: The dance or free-skating skate. It screws on to the boot.

Left: The streamlined competition skate.

As a pastime, roller skating has enormous appeal. Yet as a skillful, competitive sport for skaters of both sexes it rarely receives the attention or publicity it deserves. Indeed, it would appear destined to remain overshadowed by ice skating, the sport which prompted the development of the four-wheeled roller skate as an alternative for when ice was not available. Not surprisingly, then, roller skating takes similar forms to its parent sport, with figure skating, dancing, speed skating and hockey being practised by roller enthusiasts. World and continental championships are held under the auspices of the FIRS. Although recognized by the Olympic Committee, it is not included in the Games.

Figure skating, performed solo or in pairs on indoor rinks, uses similar compulsory figures and free skating routines as ice skating. The main difference is that the figure circles are already marked on the rink floor. Judging is based on the execution of the figures and on the technical merit and artistic impression of the free skating program. Roller dancing, too, is similar to its ice counterpart, with dances such as the waltz, tango, fourteen step and fox trot being performed. Roller hockey is played mostly indoors between teams of five using flat-bladed sticks and a ball slightly smaller than a field hockey ball. Play continues around and behind the goal cages, but if the ball leaves the skating surface a free hit is awarded against the team responsible. Speed skating is principally a track or road pursuit because of the distance of the events. The recognized distances for speed skating are ⅝mi, 3⅛mi, 6¼mi and 12⅜mi for men; ⁵⁄₁₆mi, 1⅞mi and 3⅛mi for women.

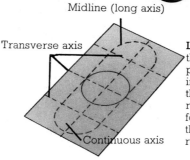

Midline (long axis)

Transverse axis

Continuous axis

Left: To help skaters perform the movements of dance patterns, the rink is divided by imaginary axes. The circle in the centre of the illustration represents the continuous axis for circular dances. For figures, the circles are painted on the rink.

arabesque A form of spiral (*qv*) skated with the body bent forwards from the waist and the free (*qv*) leg stretched out high behind.

bracket A one-foot turn (*qv*) made in reverse (*qv*) rotation of the curve (*qv*) and with the character (*qv*) of the edges (*qv*) changing.

character The type of edge skated on; either inside or outside.

chassé A step made by bringing the free foot on to the floor alongside the skating foot, lifting the skating foot for a moment, replacing it, and extending the other foot to its former free position.

choctaw A two-foot turn from one foot to another on edges of a different character. There are five types: closed, open, crossed, uncrossed and swing.

circle eights Figure eights performed through two circles on either foot. The four basic circle eight figures are forward and back inside eight and forward

and back outside eight.

compulsory figures Figure skating movements performed by solo skaters on the two or three circles marked on the rink surface. Each figure must be repeated three times in succession with the skaters starting where the circles intersect.

compulsory program A short program of compulsory movements in both free skating and pair skating.

counter A one-foot turn made in reverse rotation of the curve but then continued in natural rotation. The skater moves on to a second circle traveling in a reverse direction to his first curve. The character of the edges remains the same.

continuous axis Imaginary line running around the rink.

cross-over The method used for going round corners. The skater, traveling on the outside edge of the inside leg, brings the free foot over and in front of the skating foot, transfers to the inside edge of that skate, and

then brings the original skating foot back alongside to continue stroking (*qv*) on the outside edge. The push is made off the inside leg.

crossed chassé A step made by placing the free foot on the rink behind the skating foot (so that the feet are crossed) and then lifting the original skating foot ahead and to the side of the other foot so that it again becomes the skating foot.

curve The arc described by a skater. It is also called an *edge*.

curve eight A figure eight in which the first circle is skated on the outside edge of the right foot and the second circle on the outside edge of the left foot.

edges Term used for the way a skater moves in curves. As weight is applied to the side, or edge, of a roller skate, the wheels turn to that side. There are inside and outside edges for skating forwards and backwards.

FIRS Fédération Internationale de Roller Skating, founded in 1928.

footplate The part of the skate to

which the boot is attached.

free foot Refers initially to the foot which is off the skating surface, but it also applies to any part of the body on the same side. It is also known as the *unemployed* side.

free skating A figure skating program incorporating such movements as jumps, steps and spins performed in harmony with music.

inside edge The side of the skate corresponding to the inside of the foot. Curves skated off this side, whether forwards or backwards, are called inside edges and are denoted in abbreviated form as RFI, RBI, LFI, or LBI according to the skating foot and the direction of travel.

kilian hold A dance hold in which the partners face in the same direction, the lady's left shoulder resting on the man's right shoulder.

midline An imaginary line bisecting the length of the rink.

mohawk A two-foot turn from one foot to another on edges of

Chassé

Arabesque spiral

Spreadeagle and layback

Above: A skater executes a forward cross-over preliminary to a turn. Whereas the ice skater uses the inside and outside edges of the skate to shift position, the roller skater uses the inside and outside wheels. Cross-overs are used in both figure and free skating schedules.

Above: A backwards cross-over. Skating backwards requires a fine sense of balance and the ability to create and control a seemingly unnatural momentum. The arms are an essential part of this impetus.

Below: A backwards cross-over seen in sequence.

Above: The initial stance – toes in, knees bent – which is adopted when skating backwards. Impulsion is made by pushing with the inside of the foot.

Below: A skater comes to a toe stop. Figures may not be executed with the toe stop in pure figure skating, but in dance skating such figures are allowed limited usage to interpret certain music.

Lift

the same character. There are five types: closed, open, crossed, uncrossed and swing.

natural rotation Moving in the same direction as that of the curve being traced.

outside edge The side of the skate corresponding to the outside of the foot. Curves skated off this side, whether forwards or backwards, are called outside edges and are denoted in abbreviated form as RFO, RBO, LFO, or LBO, according to the skating foot and the direction of travel.

progressive or run A movement in which the free foot is brought ahead of the skating foot and placed on the rink so that it becomes the skating foot while the other trails behind to become the free foot. The movement is then repeated.

reverse rotation Moving in a direction contrary to that of the curve being traced.

rink The hall or arena where skating is practised and competition skating performed. The

skating surface should be hard, maple floors with polyurethane surfaces having proved the most satisfactory.

rocker A one-foot turn made with the natural rotation of the curve but then continued in reverse rotation. The skater moves out of the turn on to a second circle traveling in a reverse direction to his first curve. The character of the edges remains the same.

roller derby A sport in which two teams of five men or five women race around an oval track, winning points for lapping opponents. Physical contact is permitted, although tripping is not, and the contestants are not restricted to any set lanes. Men and women do not compete in the same races.

run Another name for a progressive.

school figures Another name for compulsory (qv) figures.

spin A series of fast-moving rotations on one foot or both depending on the movement.

spiral An edge skated on one foot at a constant speed and held for at least one circle.

spreadeagle A position in which the raised heel of the non-skating foot is placed alongside the heel of the skating foot. A spreadeagle is also a free skating movement in which the skater glides sideways on both feet with the heels turned in towards and the toes pointing away from each other.

strokes The skater's gliding movements on one or both feet. The impulsion for each stroke is made by pushing with the side of the foot from the T position.

T position The skating position where the heel of one foot is at right-angles to the middle of the other foot, so making a T shape.

teapot A movement in which the skater bends the skating leg to achieve a squatting position and then bends forward from the hips while keeping the free leg extended to the front.

toe stop A rubber mounting on the front of skates for braking.

three jump In which the skater takes off from an outside edge, turns in mid-air, and lands on the inside edge of the same foot.

three turn A one-foot turn with which the skater changes the character of the edges while following the natural rotation of the curve. It is so called because the pattern skated is that of a figure three.

tracing The path of the employed skate on the surface.

tracing foot The foot which is skating, or tracing, a figure. It is also called the employed foot, and either term is used for parts of the body on the same side.

transverse axis An imaginary line bisecting the midline of the rink.

turns The movements with which a skater changes from skating forwards to skating backwards (or vice versa) without stopping. They may be performed on one foot or two and may keep the skater on the same curve, as in a three turn, or take him into a second curve, as in a rocker.

Skateboarding

In the mid-1960s, a short, charming film, made in the USA, introduced to an unsuspecting world at large a new phenomenon, and in doing so won itself an Academy award. The film was *Skater-Dater*; the phenomenon was skateboarding, a new sport which took surfing on to dry land by means of roller skate wheels fitted to short, surfboard-shaped decks. For a time the new sensation thrived in the US. National championships were held; the public marveled at the skateboarders' antics as they performed wheelies and handstands, zigzagged down hills, or wove in and out down slalom runs. But skateboarding flourished only while it retained the attention of the media. Without it, there was a decline. One reason for the loss of support was the quality of the wheels used to propel the boards. Made of hard rubber, clay composition, or even metal, they were so susceptible to rough, uneven surfaces that wipe-outs became almost a way of life. All but the most faithful sought a less painful way of expressing themselves.

What saved the sport was the urethane (plastic composition) wheel. Allied to a further 1970s' innovation, the truck that would allow directional changes when weight was applied to the sides of the board, the urethane wheel opened new horizons to skateboarders; by the second half of the 1970s the craze had rekindled. Primarily it is an individual pursuit, but there are always those who seek a competitive outlet, whether it is in performing tricks with the ultimate style, going through slalom paths, or recording the fastest time on a downhill course. The majority, no doubt, are happiest tic-tacking along their neighborhood pavement.

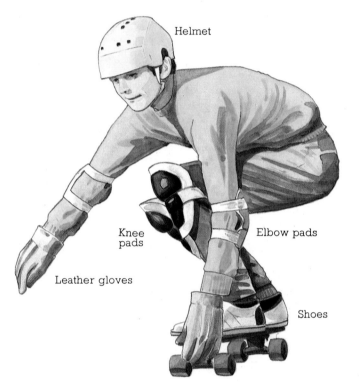

Below: Skateboarding the safe way. To avoid street pizzas such as bongos and hamburgers, skateboarders should wear knee and elbow pads, strong leather gloves, helmets, and strong but thin-soled shoes at all times.

Helmet

Knee pads

Leather gloves

Elbow pads

Shoes

backsiding A board turn made in the direction the rider's back is pointing: a left turn for a natural (*qv*); right for a goofy (*qv*).
barrel jumping Jumping from one skateboard, over a length of obstacles such as miniature barrels or an area marked by two cones, and then landing on another skateboard.
bearing The steel mechanism around which the wheel revolves. There are basically two kinds: open (or loose), in which the ball-bearings are visible, and sealed (or shielded). Sealed bearings give a quieter ride and do not require the same amount of cleaning as the open variety. In addition, sealed bearings can be removed from the wheel.
blank The flat deck of a skateboard.
blue tile fever The 'high' experienced by skateboarders who climb to the blue tiles around the edge of swimming pools.
body cranking Moving the arms and shoulders backwards and forwards to increase momentum.

bongo A head injury resulting from a skateboarding accident.
bowl riding Skateboarding at a skatepark with a bowl for performing freestyle tricks.
bunny hop Lifting the board off the ground by crouching down, holding each end with the hands and making small jumps.
carving Making a wide turn without the wheels sliding sideways.
catamaran A movement involving two skateboarders who sit sideways on their boards facing each other, holding the nose and tail of their own boards and placing their feet on their partner's board.
cerbie Riding up and down the cerb of the pavement.
christie Riding in a crouched position with one leg extended to the side.
coffin Riding while lying with one's back to the board and the arms crossed over the chest.
coned Said of the wheels when they wear to a taper as a result of over-tightening of the trucks (*qv*).

cushion The small rubber or urethane ring, which absorbs vibrations and helps with steering.
daffy Riding two boards with the front foot on the front of one, doing a nose wheelie (*qv*), and the rear foot on the tail of the other, doing a tail wheelie.
deck The riding surface of the skateboard.
double decker Riding two boards, one of which is placed on top of the other.
downweighting Sinking down on to the deck to apply bodyweight to the board.
drop-in An unconventional method of entry into a bowl or pool from a high point on the lip (*qv*).
eating it Falling off the board.
endover Taking the board through several 180° pivots alternately at the nose and tail wheels while continuing to move forward.
flex A flexible deck.
flex memory The amount a board returns to its original shape after

bending and the time it takes to do it.
frontsiding A turn made in the direction the rider's chest is pointing: a right turn for a natural; left for a goofy-footer.
goofy, or goofy-footer A skateboarder who rides with his right foot forward.
gorilla grip Gripping each end of the board with bare toes and jumping in the air.
gremlin A bad board rider.
grip tape Anti-slip self-adhesive tape applied to the surface of a deck for firm foothold.
hamburger Graze from falling off a moving board.
hanging ten Riding with the bare toes of both feet curled over the front edge of the board.
hardware All-embracing term used for components of a board.
helicopter Spinning through 360° in the air with the board.
high jumping Jumping over a bar while the board travels under it and then landing on the board.
hot-dogging Freestyle riding incorporating tricks.

170

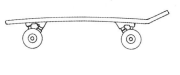

Left: A skateboard with a kick-tail. This type of board is suitable for bowl riding and freestyle. Slalom riders use flat or slightly upward cambered boards while downhill racers use long, flat stiff-decked boards which are more stable.

Kick-tail

Deck

Trucks

Wheels

Right: A handstand on two boards, one on top of the other, with the skateboarder's hands gripping the ends of the top board. Handstands are usually performed on a slight slope.

Below right: Riding the bowl or bank, a breathtaking aspect of a spectacular sport.

Left: A skateboarder weaving along a slalom course. Slalom courses are marked out on a hill, anything from a gentle slope to a steep incline; competition slopes are usually 1-in-10. The cones are placed 11½ft to 14¾ft apart either in a straight line or set apart widthways to open out the course.

kick-tail The raised end of a deck.

kick turn A method of turning by lifting the front wheels and pivoting on the back of the board until it points in the new direction.

lip The curved top edge of a bowl, bank or pool on which various maneuvers (eg lip slides) can be performed.

natural A skateboarder who rides with his left foot forward.

nose wheelie Riding with one or both feet over the front wheels and the rear wheels off the ground.

one-eighty A kick turn through 180°.

pavement pizza Scars caused by a fall while skateboarding.

pipe A half pipe (semi-circular) or full pipe (circular)—course feature found in most skateparks.

pirouette A 360° turn made while jumping off a moving board and then landing on it again.

pool riding Skateboarding in empty swimming pools.

power slide Changing direction sharply by leaning into a turn, touching the ground with one or both hands and spinning the board around with the feet so that the back wheels slide sideways across the surface.

pumping Downweighting and unweighting rapidly to the left and right so that the movement of the bodyweight on the board increases its speed; often used when turning the board between slalom gates.

radical Difficult, exciting skateboarding.

riser pad A rubber, urethane, wood or plastic pad between the truck and the underside of the deck.

road rash Skin burns from falling off a moving board.

rocker A one-piece deck curved up at either end so that the center of gravity is close to the ground. It is used mostly for bowl riding.

seven-twenty Two 360° turns on the back wheels of the board.

shoot the duck Riding in a crouch position on one leg with the other extended to the front and the arms stretched out to either side.

slalom Riding in and out of a row of cones or similar obstacles.

slide stop Stopping by sliding the tail of the board sideways at an angle to the forward movement.

space walk Riding with the nose of the board off the ground and waving from side to side.

speed wobble Losing control of the board by traveling too fast, or because the trucks are loose.

stoked Getting high on skateboarding.

tail saver An attachment fitted to the tail of the board to prevent damage resulting from dragging. Also called a *skid plate*.

tail wheelie Riding with the feet over the back wheels so that the nose lifts off the ground.

terrain An area suitable for skateboarding.

three-sixty A 360° turn on the back wheels of the board.

tic-tacking Alternating front side and back side kick turns to provide momentum while skateboarding along a flat surface, or even uphill. The fast rhythm of the kick turns builds up the forward movement.

traversing Riding across a hill.

truck The steering unit to which the wheels are attached and which is itself attached to the deck. By adjusting a central kingpin, the skateboarder adjusts his board's maneuverability according to the kind of riding.

tuck A crouching position.

unweighting Springing upwards from the deck to release bodyweight from the board.

walking the board Taking small steps along the deck while riding the board.

walking the dog Performing a continuous series of 180° turns, lifting the nose and tail alternately for each turn. One foot remains anchored to the deck to act as the pivot foot while the other lifts the relevant end.

wedeling Rapid, rhythmic small turns.

wipe-out A fall off a board.

wired Under control, or perfected; used in relation to riding methods or tricks.

Winter Sports

Curling

Known as the 'roaring game' on account of the noise made by the curling stone running over the ice on an outdoor rink, curling bears considerable resemblance to bowls. The major difference—playing surface aside—is the absence of the moving jack. The target area is the circular house at either end of the rink, with points being scored for each stone therein which is closer to the tee than any of the opposing team's stones. Each team, or rink, comprises four curlers, who each deliver two stones: first the leads alternate their stones, then the number twos and threes, and finally the skips. The delivery is from the hack or crampit on the foot scores. The duration of the match may be a number of ends, or a length of time. Curling is played in North America, central Europe, Scandinavia and New Zealand, as well as its native Scotland.

A feature of curling is the practice of using brooms or brushes to sweep ahead of the running stone. By clearing its path, reducing forward resistance, and even raising the surface temperature, this lengthens the stone's travel before the draw takes effect. Any member of the team may sweep, but the areas are strictly defined. All members of the playing team may sweep from the sweeping score at one end, to the sweeping score at the other end, while the skip, and the opposing skip, may also sweep behind the sweeping line. In addition, players of either side may sweep if one of their stones is moved by another stone. Sweepers must beware, however, not to touch a running stone, for if one of their own, it is removed from the rink, and if an opponent's, the stone may be placed where the skip of that side estimates it would have come to rest.

Right: The layout of one end of a curling rink. The rink is an area of ice which measures 46yd from foot score to foot score. The houses are normally marked by blue outer circles and red inner circles. Behind these are the hack or crampit—metal or rubber-covered footholds—from which the curlers deliver their stones. The distance between the two hog score lines is 24yd.

Below: Curling stones are circular in shape, having smooth polished surfaces with reflected shades of blue, red or grey. The maximum weight of a stone is 44lb, including the bolt and handle. It has a circumference of no more than 36in and a minimum height of one-eighth its greatest circumference.

House
Foot score
Center line
Back score
Sweeping score
Hog score

apartments to let Rarely used term for an empty circle.

birl The twist a curler gives the handle of the stone on delivery to obtain draw (*qv*).

biting Said of a stone just touching the outside circle.

bonspiel Matches with a large gathering of curlers participating.

borrow The width a stone draws to the left or right.

broom The broom carried by each curler for sweeping the ice ahead of a moving stone (*qv*). The skip (*qv*) holds his in a vertical position in the circle as a target for his players. There are two main types: the brush used in Scotland and Europe, and the corn or whisk broom in North America.

burnt Term used for a stone which is touched by mistake, usually while curlers are sweeping.

button Name given to the tee (*qv*) in North America.

check To lay a stone by, and at an angle to, another stone.

counter Any stone which is within or touching the house (*qv*) and therefore is potentially a shot (*qv*).

crampit A narrow sheet of metal on which a curler stands to deliver the stone.

dead guard A guard (*qv*) which stops directly in front of the stone it is protecting.

dolly A squat wooden marker, in shape resembling a chess pawn, used in some countries by skips to mark the tee.

double take-out A strike (*qv*) which removes two opposition stones.

draw (1) The controlled line along which the stone runs to the left or right as a result of the turn given to the handle at the moment of delivery. (2) A stone given just enough weight to reach the house (*qv*).

end The delivery of all 16 stones to one end of the rink (*qv*). When the scores have been taken, the next end is played on the same sheet of ice but in the opposite direction. *See* take the end.

every inch A skip's command to his sweepers to sweep hard all the way.

ewe lamb A solitary scoring stone surrounded by opposition stones.

fill the port To lay a stone in the port (*qv*) so that the opposition cannot play a stone through it to the tee.

fled the tee Said of a stone that goes past the tee.

freeze To draw right up to another stone without actually moving it.

Game of Points A version of curling. Each player scores for himself only. As it excludes sweeping, it is not regarded as true curling by many purists.

guard A stone laid in front of the shot, or in front of a stone which could be promoted to a winning position, to prevent the opposition from taking it out.

hack A metal or rubber-covered ridge on which a curler places the sole of his foot when delivering the stone. As the name suggests, it was originally a hole cut

in the ice, and a variation of this method is used in Canada and the United States.

hack-weight The force imparted to a stone on delivery so that it travels to the hack behind the house.

hand, or handle The in-turn or out-turn given to the stone as requested by the skip.

head An end (*qv*).

heavy A stone played with too much force which carries past the required mark. The term is also used for dull ice.

hog Any stone that fails to cross the hog score. Unless it has struck another stone lying in position, it is removed from the ice.

hold The skip's command to stop sweeping.

house The circle or circles cut or painted on the ice at either end of the rink. The diameter of the outer circle is 12ft; inner circles, if drawn, are at 2ft intervals. Stones have to be within or touching the house to stand a chance of being shots.

Above: A curler releases his stone in the last stage of the delivery action. The stone is thrown rather than pushed or slid. There are two main styles of delivery: the standing and the long-sliding delivery. In the latter, the curler slides far out on the ice before releasing the stone.

Below: Three of the nine shots played in the Game of Points. (a) Striking. A stone is placed on the tee. One point is scored if it is struck by the played stone and two if the placed stone is struck out of the outer circle. (b) Inwicking. Two stones are placed, one on the tee and the other on the edge at 45° to the central line. If the latter is struck on the inside by the played stone, one point is scored; if the played stone moves both stones, two points are scored. (c) Chap and lie. A stone is placed on the tee. One point is scored if it is struck out of the outer circle so that the played stone comes to lie within or on the same circle; two points if the placed stone is struck out of the outer circle so that the played stone lies within or on the 4ft circle. The black discs represent the placed stones and the yellow discs the played stones.

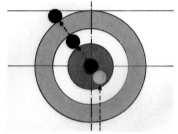

Striking

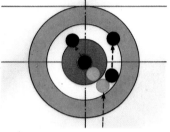

Inwicking

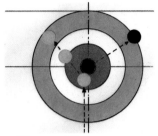

Chap and lie

Above: The skip directs a member of his rink to play a shot. (1) An in-hand shot is asked for; the stone is aimed at the broom to curl into the stone on the tee. (2) The signal for an out-hand shot. (3) The signal to guard a winner or a stone which could be promoted to a winning position. (4) A full strike is called for.

Right: Wielding a Canadian corn broom. The other type of broom used for sweeping is the Scots brush. Many curlers believe the latter to be more effective though it is less spectacular in action than the Canadian broom. Good sweeping is a match-winning factor—the main requirements are rhythm and power.

in-hand/turn The stone's curl to the right at the end of its draw.
keen ice Term used for fast ice.
kiggle-caggle The rocking movement of a stone that has not been thrown squarely on to the ice.
lead The first player on a rink (*qv*).
narrow A stone which is thrown inside the line of the skip's broom and so will not draw in to the required target.
out-hand/turn The stone's curl to the left at the end of its draw.
peels When both rinks have the same number of shots.
pinching the broom An American term for a narrow (*qv*) stone.
port A space between two stones through which another stone could pass.
pot-lid A stone which is lying on the tee.
promote To strike another stone so that it moves forward. Also known as *raising*.
read To study the ice and know what influence it will have on a stone. Ability to read the ice accurately is essential for a skip.
rink (1) An area of ice on which curling is played. Two target areas, 38yd apart from center to center, are cut or painted on the ice at either end, each with four lateral lines: the foot score, back score, sweeping score and hog score. A center line, in alignment with the tees, may be drawn 12ft back from the centre of each tee. (2) A team of four players.
rock North American term for the stone.
roll The rolling of a stone on to its side after it has struck another stone. Any stone which rolls over or comes to rest on its side is removed from the rink.
rub A light touch on another stone.
run The path of a stone from delivery until it comes to rest, its movement being subject to conditions on the ice and the effect of the sweepers.
runner A fast-moving stone.
shot A winning stone, ie one that is inside the house and nearer the tee than any opposition stone.
skip The captain of a rink.
sole (1) The concave top and bottom surfaces of the stone. The sole may be changed simply by detaching and refitting the metal handle and the bolt to which it is secured. (2) To deliver the stone so that its sole runs smoothly and squarely on the ice. It is said to be *well-soled*.
soop To sweep.
spiel A bonspiel (*qv*).
stone The smoothly curved granite curling stone which is of circular shape and, including handle and bolt, must not weigh more than 44lb nor have a circumference larger than 36in. The top and bottom surfaces are concave with a bolt to be screwed through the center and a gooseneck handle attached to it. In Scotland, colored discs are put on the stones for identification, although other countries still favor colored tassels of wool attached to the handles.
strike A fast-running stone, or runner, which is intended to hit and move another stone.
take out To remove an opposition stone from the circle.
take the end A skip's decision not to play his last stone lest he disturb the head. Instead he decides to take the head as it lies with only 15 stones.
tee The center of the circles.
tee high A stone which comes to rest in line with the tee.
thin, or tight A narrow (*qv*) stone.
toucher A stone which is just touching the outer circle and so qualifies as a counter (*qv*).
turn The in-hand and out-hand movement of the stone.
up The skip's command to his sweepers to stop sweeping. A derivative of 'holdup'.
well-laid A delivery that follows the skip's instructions perfectly.
wick A stone which hits another stone and rebounds off at an angle.
wick and roll A stone that rolls (*qv*) after wicking.
wide A stone which is thrown outside the line of the skip's broom.

175

Ice Hockey

Speed comes readily to mind when thinking of ice hockey. Nor is this association confined to the flash of the small, hard rubber puck over the ice or the lightning bursts of skaters around the rink. Attacks and goals come fast and furiously; violence can erupt in an instant; and just as quickly offenders find themselves off the ice serving a suspension on the penalty bench. Referees, like the heavily padded players, are uncompromising; penalties are strictly enforced. Little wonder, then, that teams carry as many as 20 players, although only six may be on the ice at any one time: goalkeeper, two defensemen and three forwards.

Play commences at the beginning of each period with a face-off, there being three periods of 20 minutes actual playing time each. Generally, stoppages are few because the boards keep the puck in play. Passing between zones is controlled by the offside law, while players entering the attacking zone must be in line with or behind the puck. Goals may be scored from anywhere on the rink except within the opposing team's goal crease, the aim of the game being to score more goals than the opposing team. Players, in addition to being credited with the goals they score, are credited with assists in the scoring statistics.

Although the actual site is disputed, Canada has rightful claim to giving birth to the game and, in 1879, to formulating its first rules; by the turn of the century, the sport's growth had spread from North America to Europe. Ice hockey has been an Olympic sport since 1920, with world championships held annually since 1930. For the North American NHL professional players, the Stanley Cup is the sport's most coveted annual prize.

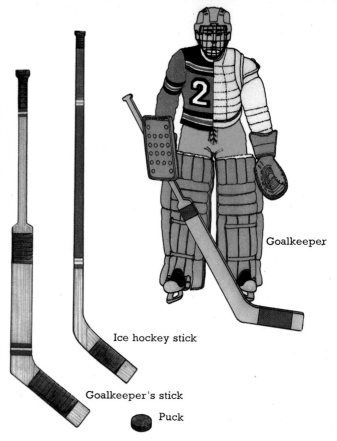

Goalkeeper

Ice hockey stick

Goalkeeper's stick

Puck

Above: The goalkeeper's stick is wider and longer in the blade and part of the shaft than that used by the other players. The puck is a hard-rubber disc. Goalies wear protective equipment, as any part of the body may be used to stop the puck. Skates are exceptionally robust and are designed for high speed and maneuverability.

Ice hockey boot and skate

alternate captain In addition to a captain, a team must have up to two alternate captains, one of whom takes over the captain's responsibilities when he is off the ice. Alternate captains wear a letter A on their sweaters.

assist A point credited in the scoring records to the player or players taking part in the play immediately preceding a goal; it does not include the goalscorer. No more than two assists may be given on any one goal.

awarded goal A point awarded to the attacking side when, with their opponents' goalie (qv) off the ice, an attacker in possession of the puck in the opposition half and with no defender between himself and the goal is fouled from behind or interfered with by an opponent illegally entering the game. An awarded goal is also given when the goalkeeper throws his stick at the puck or at an attacker taking a penalty shot.

bench The rink-side area where the coaches, managers, trainers,

players in uniform and team doctors sit during a game. There is a bench for each team.

board – checking Deliberately forcing an opponent on to the boards (qv). Also called boarding.

boards The barrier surrounding the rink which keeps the puck in play.

body checking The use of the body to block an opponent's progress. It is legal if practised by any player against another in possession of the puck.

butt-ending Pushing the top of the handle into an opponent. It incurs a minor (qv) penalty; a major (qv) penalty if against the goalkeeper in his crease (qv) or in the event of injury.

center The central attacking player.

clipping Falling and/or sliding into the path of an opponent with the puck to make him lose possession. It incurs a minor penalty; a major penalty in the event of injury.

crease The area in front of the

goals. Under IIHF (qv) rules, it is a semicircle with a 6ft radius; under NHL (qv) rules it is a rectangle 8ft wide by 4ft deep.

cross-checking Using the stick, while holding it off the ice in both hands, to obstruct the progress of an opponent. Penalties are incurred as for butt-ending (qv).

dead Said of the puck when it is hit over the boards or becomes lodged in the side netting of the goal. It is also dead when a goal is scored, or when the whistle is blown. The official clock is stopped until play restarts, usually with a face-off (qv).

defensemen The right and left defenses.

delayed penalty Imposed on a player who is sent off the ice while two team-mates are already serving suspensions.

face-off The method of starting play at the beginning of each period, after a goal, or after stoppages for infringements when there is no penalty shot awarded. The referee drops the puck on the ice between two opposing

players, each standing approximately a stick-length from the face-off spot and facing their opponents' end of the rink with the full blades of their sticks on the ice; they may not touch the puck until it hits the ice.

face-off spot The blue spot in the center circle and the six red spots, four of which are inside circles in the goal zones and two in the center zone 50ft from the middle of the blue dividing lines. Under NHL rules, there are four center-zone red spots, in line with the goal zone spots and 5ft from the blue lines.

forwards The attacking unit, comprising the center and the right and left wings.

game misconduct penalty Dismissal from the ice for the remainder of the game. It is incurred by a player committing his second misconduct (qv) penalty offense.

goal A point scored by the attacking side when the puck legally and completely crosses the defending team's goal-line

176

Right: A rink marked for play under IIHF rules. Surrounded by boards 4ft high, it must be 180-200ft long and 83-100ft wide. The corners are curved. The markings lines are laid down over the base ice and then covered by another layer of ice.

Below: Although the ordinary player is not as highly protected as his goalkeeper, his equipment is considerable: ankle guards, shin pads, thigh and hip pads, a padded jersey, shoulder pads, elbow pads and huge padded gloves, all surmounted by a plastic-padded helmet. Underneath, the player wears perspiration-absorbing underwear and footless socks.

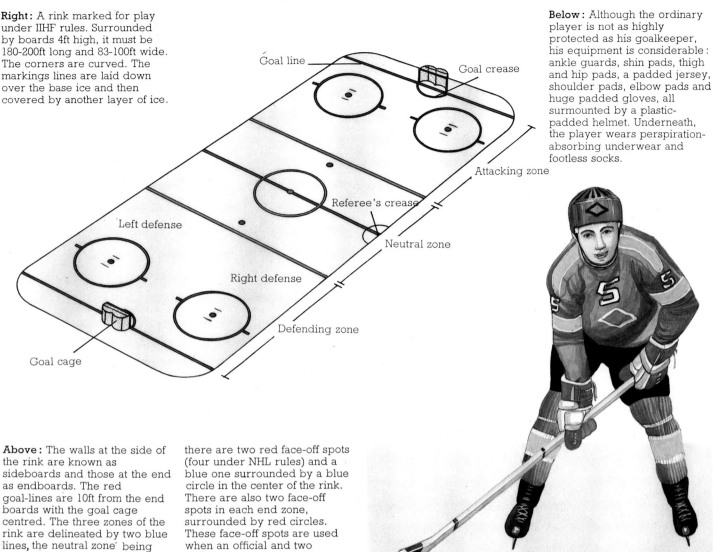

Goal line — Goal crease

Attacking zone

Referee's crease

Neutral zone

Left defense

Right defense

Defending zone

Goal cage

Above: The walls at the side of the rink are known as sideboards and those at the end as endboards. The red goal-lines are 10ft from the end boards with the goal cage centred. The three zones of the rink are delineated by two blue lines, the neutral zone' being divided in half by the center red line. Inside the neutral zone there are two red face-off spots (four under NHL rules) and a blue one surrounded by a blue circle in the center of the rink. There are also two face-off spots in each end zone, surrounded by red circles. These face-off spots are used when an official and two players hold a face-off to begin or resume the action\game.

between the goalposts and under the crossbar.

goalie The goalkeeper. Also called a goalminder.

high sticking Carrying or using the stick above shoulder height. It may incur a minor penalty.

holding Using the stick or hands to impede an opponent's progress. It incurs a minor penalty.

hooking Using the blade end of the stick to impede an opponent's progress. It incurs a minor penalty; a major penalty in the event of injury.

icing Said of the puck when it is hit by a player from behind the center line and crosses his opponent's goal-line without making contact with another player. It is not 'iced' if a goal is scored from the hit, if the hit is from a face-off, or if, in the referee's opinion, a defender other than the goalkeeper could have, but did not, play the puck before it crossed the goal-line.

IIHF The International Ice Hockey Federation. It has been the world governing body for amateur ice hockey since 1908.

kick shot An illegal shot made by placing the blade of the stick against the puck and then kicking the stick to propel the puck.

lie The angle between the blade and the handle of a stick.

major penalty Incurred for such offenses as fighting or unintentionally causing injury to an opponent. The offending player receives a five minute suspension for his first major penalty, 15 minutes for his second and match suspension for his third. A substitute is allowed after 5 minutes for a player serving a major penalty.

match penalty A match suspension and exclusion from further games until the player's case is heard. It is incurred for such offenses as kicking, deliberately injuring or attempting to injure an opponent and starting a fight.

minor penalty A two minute suspension, during which the offending player may not be replaced by a substitute. A goalminder's suspension is usually taken by another team-mate on the ice. In the event of a team, while short-handed, conceding a goal, except from a penalty shot, a minor penalty (or the first if there are several) automatically ends.

misconduct penalty A ten minutes' suspension for such offenses as abusive language. The suspended player may be replaced immediately by a substitute.

NHL National Hockey League, the North American professional league competition involving 18 clubs in four divisions.

offside An infringement of the rules governing passing, which, in simplified form, state that a player may pass only to a team-mate in the same zone or, if he is in the defensive zone, to anyone in his own half.

penalty bench, or box The rink-side area where players sit to serve their penalty suspensions.

penalty shot A clear run and shot at the opposing team's goal awarded to a player who has been fouled when in a scoring position in front of goal.

power play A sustained attack by one side, especially when their opponents are short-handed.

puck Vulcanized rubber playing disc. It is 3in in diameter and 1in thick.

short-handed Said of a team which has fewer players on the ice than its opponents.

shut-out A goalkeeper's achievement in not conceding a goal during a period of play, a game, or a number of games.

sin-bin Colloquialism for the penalty bench.

slashing Swinging the stick to impede or intimidate an opponent. It may incur a major penalty.

spearing Poking the point of the blade into an opponent. Penalties are incurred as for butt-ending (*qv*).

stick-handling Controlled possession of the puck while skating.

suspension A period of time spent on the penalty bench as the result of an infringement.

177

Ice Skating

The art of moving over a frozen surface on the blades of skates, ice skating is thought to have been practiced for almost 2000 years. However, it was only in the nineteenth century that it became an organized, competitive sport. As such, it today takes three individual forms: figure skating for solo and pair skaters, ice dancing, and speed skating. Of these, the last is held on closed, outdoor tracks, while figure and dance skating, which call for much precision from their exponents, are performed on artificial indoor rinks so that competitors are not disturbed by the vagaries of the elements. All three are included in the Winter Olympic Games, dancing gaining admittance to the Olympic arena as recently as 1976. In addition each has its own world championships: figure skating since 1896 (men), 1906 (women), and 1908 (pairs); dancing since 1952; and speed skating since 1893 (men) and 1936 (women).

The basic necessity for speed skating is fitness and stamina; the essence of figure and dance skating being the ability to perform a program of movements based on edges, steps and spins. Equally as important as style and interpretation is technical excellence, which is why figure and dance skating competitions comprise compulsory movements as well as freestyle. For the solo skater there is also the additional test of the compulsory figures. In major championships these consist of three prescribed figures to be skated in order of ascending difficulty, each figure being skated three times. They may be skated on either foot, or on a combination of both, and on either a forward or backward inside or outside edge. Up to six points are awarded for each figure. Free-skating movements are marked on artistic impression and technical merit.

Right: The ice skating boot and blade are the most important part of a skater's equipment. The boot should fit the ankle tightly enough to give support, but the two flaps should not meet. This boot is shown fitted with a figure-skating blade.

Toe rake

Right: Two types of blade. The top is the school figure-skating version, designed specifically for cutting circles—the usual training figure—into the ice. The lower blade is for free-skating, which combines figures with spins, jumps and steps.

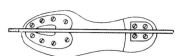

Above: A detail of the bottom of a skate. The blades are screwed into the sole and heel of the boot and are changeable. They should be polished with chamois and sharpened regularly by a professional. To protect the edges when walking on the skates off the ice, special skate guards should be clipped over the blades. After use, the blades should be wiped dry and stored in a dry place to prevent rust.

arabesque A sustained edge (*qv*), not necessarily curved, with the free foot extended to form a line or upward curve with the body.

armbands Worn by speed skaters to indicate which lane (*qv*) they started in. The skater drawing the inside lane wears a white armband, the one on the outside a red armband.

artistic impression One half of a judge's assessment of a free-skating or freestyle dance program. Points to six are awarded for deportment, flow of movement, harmonious composition, conformity to music and use of the rink.

axel A free-skating jump (*qv*) in which the skater rotates one and a half times in the air. Take-off is from a forward outside edge (*qv*) and landing is on the backward outside edge of the other skate. In pairs (*qv*), the woman is turned one and a half times above the head of the man, who rotates beneath her throughout the movement. In a variation she is thrown forwards and rotates

before landing. It is named after the Norwegian Axel Paulsen.

blade The metal runner on which the skater glides over the ice. It is usually screwed to the skater's boot. The blade for figure and dance skating is slightly curved from heel to toe and has a hollow ridge along its center. The speed skating blade is straight, thinner and longer, and its use is forbidden during public sessions on rinks.

bracket A turn (*qv*) from one edge to the other edge of the same skate, the turn being made inside and against the rotation of the lobe (*qv*).

camel spin A one-foot spin (*qv*) executed with the body in a continuous line with the free leg extended behind so that both are parallel to the ice. It is skated on the flat of the blade.

catch-waist camel A camel performed in pairs skating: bodies close together, arms around each other's waist and their free legs pointing in the opposite direction parallel to the ice.

center In compulsory (*qv*) figures, the point where two circles touch.

change-foot spin A spin during which a change of foot is performed.

character The kind of edge skated on; either inside or outside.

chassé A movement in which the free (*qv*) foot is placed on the ice beside the skating foot, which in turn is lifted slightly ahead of or alongside the new skating foot to become the free foot momentarily before being returned to the ice. It is used mostly in a dance sequence.

choctaw A turn from the inside or outside edge of one skate to the edge of opposite character of the other skate.

clean An unmarked ice surface.

clean figures Compulsory figures in which all edges are skated cleanly without any flats (*qv*).

clean jump One in which neither the take-off nor landing edge shows any sign of turn on the ice.

compulsory, or schools, figures

Traced (*qv*) by solo skaters as the first part of their figure skating competition. They include the eight, three, loop, rocker and counter.

counter A turn, made on the same edge, composed of two symmetrical curves, the first following the reverse and the second the natural sense of rotation.

cross-foot spin A spin executed with the legs crossed, the toes together and the heels apart. It is performed on the flat of both blades.

crossing controller The official who ensures that speed skaters cross lanes in accordance with the rules of the competition.

crossing line That part of an outdoor speed skating track within which the two skaters change lanes each lap. It comprises the whole length of the back straight from the end of the curve.

crossovers Transferring from the outside edge of one skate to the inside edge of the other by crossing the free leg over and in front

Figure and dance skating

Right: Lifts are among the most spectacular steps in pair skating. The strength of the male skater and the graceful balance of his female partner must be based on a secure trust in each other's ability and a sureness of shared technique.

Below: A free-skater executes a stag jump.

RFO

RFO

RFO

Start

Finish

LFO

LFO

Above: A forward outside figure eight showing the direction and position of the body. It is one of the basic figures a skater practices to improve balance and control.

of the skating foot, placing it on the ice, withdrawing the original skating foot and then replacing it ahead of the new skating foot. As this, in turn, is withdrawn, it strokes the ice to give the glide propulsion.

curves The corners of a speed skating track.

dancing *See* ice dancing.

death spiral A pairs movement in which the woman, while leaning back with her head almost on the ice, is swung around at speed by the man, who maintains his upright position throughout.

double When used in reference to jumps, it means twice the number of complete mid-air rotations. A double axel, for example, has two and a half rotations as opposed to one and a half in an axel.

edge The sharpened side of the blade that makes contact with the ice. It is an inside or outside edge in relation to the inside or outside of the foot. An edge is also the cutting of a curved line

on the ice by use of body lean towards the center of the circle being skated. There are eight possible edges, each denoted in an abbreviated form: LFO, LFI; LBO, LBI; RFO, RFI; RBO, RBI. The first initial denotes the foot (left or right), the second denotes the direction of glide forwards or backwards, and the third denotes the character of the edge, outside or inside.

eight A figure eight skated as part of the compulsory figures program. It is made up of two adjacent circles skated in a number of prescribed ways.

figures *See* compulsory figures.

flat The simultaneous use of two blade edges when tracing figures, so making a double-line imprint in the ice. It is a fault in technique.

flat-foot spin A spin executed on the flat of one skate with the skater's weight balanced centrally over the ball of the foot.

flip jump A toe (*qv*) jump in which the skater, taking off from a back outside edge, rotates in

mid-air and lands on the back outside edge of the other foot. Also called a *toe loop* or *cherry*.

free Used to denote the skate, foot, or leg not being skated on. It also applies to parts of the body on that side.

free-skating Performing jumps, spins and turns interrelated with spirals and linking steps. In solo competition, the free-skating consists of two programs skated to music: prescribed free-skating moves and free-style. In pairs, partners must give an overall impression of unison and harmonious composition, even when they are not performing in contact.

freestyle A free expression of free-skating moves interpreted to music.

glide To move over the ice on one or both blades.

half-turn Sometimes used to mean a turn through 180°.

hockey stop A stop made by bringing both blades together and turning at right angles to the direction of the glide.

hollow ground Describes the blade of the figure skate with its concave groove between the two edges.

ice dancing An ice sport for a mixed pair, incorporating movements deriving from those learned in figures. It is, nonetheless, quite separate from pairs skating. Lifts above waist height are not permitted, and feats of strength and skating skill which bear no resemblance to the dance sequence are counted against skaters. Competitions are divided into two sections: compulsory and free dancing. For the former, each couple skates three specific dances from the international schedule plus an original set-pattern dance of their own choice to a specified rhythm. The free dancing should consist of a non-repetitive performance of dance movements, or variations, plus novel movements combined into a four-minute program of original design.

jump A movement in which the skater takes off from the ice

179

Speed skating

Below: Skaters matching gliding stride for gliding stride in a sprint event. Outdoor speed skating is a time trial rather than a race against the partner, for each is striving to record the fastest possible time. In the world championships, times are converted into penalty points to decide the overall result in the event of a tie. Lanes are decided by a draw—the skater drawn first taking the inside lane—or, in some championships, on performance in the preceding event. In the latter instance, the skater with the lower points total starts in the inside lane.

Above: The boot and blade used by an indoor, or short-track, skater. Indoor events are generally classified as short-distance (500m, 1000m, 1500m) and long-distance (3000m, 5000m) and may be contested by as many as four or six racers respectively at one time. Because of the excessive wear on the ice at the sharp corners, the indoor track may be moved to a fresh surface several times during a meeting. Outdoor skaters, not needing the ankle support required for short-track cornering, favour a lighter shoe than the indoor skater. The blade, compared with the figure skating blade, is longer and is straight with steel tubing providing extra strength—an essential factor considering that speed skaters reach speeds in the region of 30 mph. It is by rolling the blade during the stride that the speed skater achieves the swaying motion that is a characteristic of the sport.

rotates in mid-air and lands to continue gliding backwards or forwards. Most jumps entail counterclockwise rotations, the lutz (*qv*) being an exception

lane The area of an outdoor track within which a speed skater travels. It is 4-5m wide. A championship track has two lanes which, except at the crossing straight, are divided by snow, painted lines, or rubber blocks.

lasso lift A pairs skating lift (*qv*) in which the woman is lifted overhead and makes one and a half rotations with her legs in a split position. The man remains forward so that his partner completes a landing on her right backward outside edge.

layback spin A one-foot spin executed with the body bent backwards so that the trunk is parallel to the ice.

lift A movement in pairs skating in which the female is lifted off the ice by the man. She must not be carried for more than three full rotations.

lobe Part of a circular figure.

loop A school figure.

loop jump A jump with a mid-air rotation through 360°. The basis of more advanced jumps, it is made off a backward outside edge with the landing on the same edge.

lutz A toe jump in which the skater makes a clockwise rotation from a backward outside edge. Landing is on the same edge of the other foot.

mohawk A turn executed by moving from the skating foot to the free foot, retaining edges of the same character.

pairs Figure skating by a man and woman in partnership. It features, among other movements, spectacular lifts and spirals (*qv*). Competitions feature the compulsory movements and freestyle.

pre-start line Lines marked 0.75m behind the starting line for speed skating races. Skaters must stand still and upright between the pre-start line and the start line when waiting for the start.

program A selection of compulsory movements or a free-style routine in figure and dance skating.

pursuits Speed skating races in which two skaters start opposite each other in the center of the two straights. The winner is the first to overtake the other skater, or the one with the faster time at the end of ten laps.

rat's tail An imprint left on the ice following a back push-off. So called because the mark resembles the curl of a rat's tail when it is relaxed.

ready Called by the starter to warn speed skaters to take up their starting positions prior to firing his gun or blowing a whistle.

relays Speed skating races for teams of two or four. All skaters in the team must take part and may enter the race at any time except during the final two laps. The incoming skater must touch or be touched by the skater being replaced.

rest position That adopted by a figure skater preparatory to commencing his or her compulsory figures.

rink Place where skating is practiced and performed.

rocker A compulsory figure. The turn is made on one foot on edges of a different character against the natural curve of the circle.

roll A simple outside edge in the form of a lobe with the curve in the opposite direction to the preceding edge or lobe.

salchow A jump in which the skater takes off from a backward inside edge and rotates in mid-air to land on the backward outside edge of the other foot. It is named after its originator, the Swede Ulrich Salchow.

shadow skating Refers to a pairs partnership performing their movements in unison when not in contact with each other.

sit spin A spin executed on one foot. It begins as a standing spin, but then the skater sinks on to the skating knee and into a sitting position with the free leg

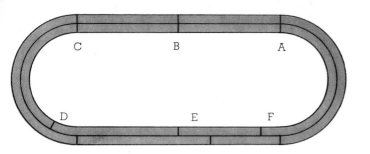

Above: The speed skating track used in outdoor international competitions is a closed, two-lane oval circuit normally 400m long. The curved ends of the track are semicircles with an inner curve radius of 25-26m. The lanes, which are a minimum of 4m wide, are usually 5m wide and are divided by snow although painted lines and rubber blocks are also used. On a standard 400m track the start (E) of the 1000m race is marked in the middle of the crossing zone (back straight) and the finishing line (B) is marked in the center of the opposite finishing straight. The other starts and finishes are (A) 500m start; (C) 10,000m start and 500m, 1500m, 3000m, 5000m and 10,000m finish; (D) 1500m start; (F) 3000m and 5000m start. Pre-start lines are marked 75cm behind the starting lines. The crossing line is the whole length of the back straight from the end of the curve. Skaters have to change lanes every time the crossing straight is reached, except in the first straight of the 1000m and 1500m race on a 400-meter track.

Changing lanes is not allowed when entering, skating on or leaving a curve. The onus is on the skater leaving the inner lane to avoid collision.

Right: A woman speed skater in action during a long-distance race. Skaters in these races usually clasp their hands behind their backs to conserve energy —thus giving the appearance of effortless movement. Women race over distances of 500, 1000, 3000 and 5000 meters in their world championship, the overall winner in these events being declared the champion. In the Olympic Games the women's distances are 500, 1000, 1500 and 3000 meters, the winner of each event receiving a gold medal—there is no combined champion. The men's world championship distances are 500, 1500, 5000 and 10,000m, the Olympic distances being the same with the addition of the 1000m. Northern European skaters—especially Russian women—have achieved the most success.

extended forwards.

skate guards Wooden, rubber, or plastic attachments to clip over the blades when they are not being skated on. They are essential to protect the edges.

snow plow A method of stopping. The toes of one or both feet are turned in at an angle resembling that of a snow plow's blade.

speed skating Racing on ice. Events are contested outdoors on a closed, two-lane oval track, usually 400m long, or indoors on a short track with sharp corners and short straights. Outdoors, only two skaters race at one time, the result being established on individual times. Indoor races have larger fields with final placings determined by finishing order. Major international competitions are held outdoors. In the Olympic Games, medals are awarded for each event, but in the world championships only an overall winner is declared.

spin More than one complete rotation of the body on, or as,

near to possible on, the one spot. Spins can be executed in an upright position on both feet, or in various sitting or camel positions on one foot.

spiral A glide on one leg, either backwards or forwards, with the body in any of various poses. It should be performed with grace, and the pose should not waver during its execution.

split jump A toe jump in which the skater, while half-turning in mid-air, does the splits by bringing both legs up into a horizontal position. Take-off is usually from a backward inside edge; landing is on the forward inside edge of the other foot and the toe-point of the original skating foot.

split lutz A jump in pairs skating. It starts with both partners skating side by side on a backward edge and ends with the man on a forward outside edge and his partner on a backward outside edge. During the clockwise rotation in mid-air, the woman assumes a splits position.

spreadeagle A two-footed glide with the feet positioned in line, heels turned inwards together and the toes pointing outwards.

spreadeagle jump A half or full rotation from, and returning to, the spreadeagle position.

stroking Rhythmical gliding strides over the ice with alternate feet providing the impulsion.

T-stop A method of stopping by placing the free foot at a right-angle behind the skating foot so that it scrapes along the ice.

technical merit One half of a judge's assessment of a free-skating or freestyle dance program. Points to six are awarded for the difficulty of the program, its variety and clearness, surety and originality.

teeth The toe rake (*qv*).

three A two-lobed figure, so called because the tracing of the turn at the extremity of each circle resembles a figure three. The turn is made on one foot by going from one edge to the opposite on the same circle.

three jump A half-rotation in mid-air from a forward outside edge to the backward outside edge of the other skate.

toe jump A jump in which take-off is assisted by the toe-point of the free foot.

toe rake The serrated points at the front of the blade. Also known as *toe picks*.

toe spin A spin executed with the weight on the toe rake.

trace To imprint the outline of figures on the ice with the edge of the blade.

travel Deviation from the center of a spin. The term is also used for any movement over the ice.

triples When used in reference to jumps, it means three times the number of complete mid-air rotations executed.

turn A movement with which a skater reverses direction from forwards to backwards, or vice versa, without stopping.

twizzle A dance step in which the skater makes a full rotation so quickly that it is performed virtually on the one spot.

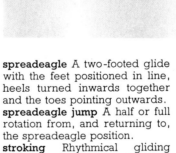

181

Skiing

A major competitive as well as recreational sport for all ages, the modern sport of skiing originated as a form of winter transport using bone skis over 4000 years ago in northern Europe. It was developed as a sport in Norway early in the nineteenth century, and has since spread rapidly through Europe and North America to become internationally popular.

Skiing is divided into three groups: Alpine, Nordic and freestyle. Alpine skiing is probably the most popular winter recreational sport, attracting thousands of new participants each winter. At its best, it demands great skill and concentration from the competitive skier, who must negotiate a descent with perfect accuracy and dexterity in order to achieve the fast time required, There are three Alpine events each for men and women contested at the Winter Olympic Games covering slalom, giant slalom and downhill. The popularity of Nordic skiing, which comprises cross country and ski jumping, is on the increase as cross country is physically less difficult for the beginner, and is also less expensive. Ski jumping, however, is more the prerogative of the experienced competitor, who skis at speeds of around 60 mph down specially prepared ramps before taking off to perform jumps reaching over 400ft in some cases. Ski jumping takes up two of the nine Olympic Nordic events. In addition to the Olympics, world championships are held biennially, and there are also the various national competitions.

The development of freestyle skiing in the USA in recent years has opened up new horizons in this sport, adding an air of individuality and freedom to the rigidly practiced disciplines required by a traditional skier.

Nordic cross country

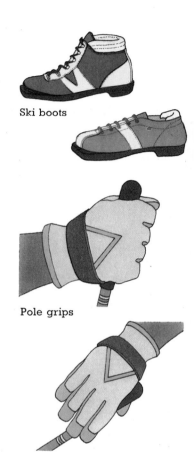

Ski

Ski boots

Pole grips

For competition Nordic skiing, the skis are light and narrow with special tension characteristics to provide the forward spring needed for cross country work. The binding is limited to the toe of the light, low-fitting boot so that the heel is free to move up and down with each stride.

---

abonnement A season ticket or pass to use lift facilities. The abonnement works either on a point system, each lift using up a certain number of points, or may be valid for a set period of time for a specified lift or lifts.

acrobatics Freestyle stunts in mid-air in which the body remains upright, as opposed to a somersault. Normally referred to as *upright aerials*.

aerials Any freestyle stunt performed in mid-air from a jump. In competitions, aerials are judged for perfection of take-off and landing, height and distance, and for the stunt itself.

après ski French term used universally to describe the night life, bars, etc found in a ski resort, and the type of clothing worn off the slopes.

Arlberg method Skiing technique developed in Austria in the early twentieth century in which emphasis was placed on the crouched position and stem skiing. It was the forerunner of modern skiing, but was later superseded by the parallel-ski method.

artificial skiing Alternative name for dry skiing (*qv*).

avalement A tight turn on a mogul (*qv*); also called a jet turn. Developed to improve control over moguls, it is started by a sinking motion with the legs. The skis are then thrust forward through the turn.

back flop A freestyle maneuver in which the skier sits back and then lies down on the skis while still moving.

back scratcher A recognized freestyle aerial maneuver in which the ski tails are brought up behind the skier to touch his back, the tips of the skis pointing downwards.

backward snowplow Simple freestyle ballet stunt in which the herringbone (*qv*) position is assumed and the skier moves backwards down the slope. By linking this to the snowplow and snowplow turn (*qv*), a series of spins through 360° may be executed.

ballet skiing Freestyle skiing to music through a sequence of linked turns and stunts. One of the three freestyle disciplines.

basket That part of a ski pole about 3in from the tip which prevents it from sinking too far into the snow.

biathlon Olympic event combining cross country skiing with rifle shooting—the competitor makes a number of stops during the course to fire shots at a target. The winner is the competitor with the lowest adjusted time after penalties have been added for inaccurate shooting. A four-man biathlon relay is also contested.

bindings The metal and plastic assembly which attaches the ski to the skier's boot. The three modern varieties of bindings – step-in, turntable heel and plate – all incorporate elaborate mechanisms to free the skier's boot in the event of a fall.

bird nesting Off-piste skiing through trees.

bunny slope Gentle ski slope suitable for the beginner.

cable car Form of transport in which skiers are carried up the mountainside in an enclosed cabin.

camber Amount of flexibility in a ski, ensuring that the skier's weight is spread along its length rather than remaining exclusively in the centre.

canting Method of building up the heel of the boots in order to compensate for the natural forward tilt of the legs, and thus ensuring that skis are perfectly flat on the ground.

chair lift Lift on which skiers sit while keeping their skis on their feet. It is not enclosed.

chattering Term used to describe the noise made by skis as a result of vibration when travelling at speed over hard snow.

christie Name derived from Christiania (now Oslo) for a parallel turn—uphill christie (*qv*), stem christie (*qv*) and parallel christie (*qv*).

citadin A class of Alpine ski races restricted to part-time skiers who are not resident in

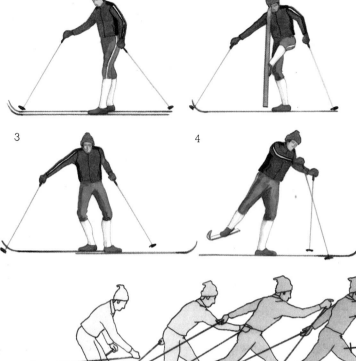

1 2

3 4

Left: Four phases of the kick turn; made from a stationary position to change direction by 180°. With the poles at either end of the skis (1), the ski on the inside of the turn is swung forwards and upwards (2), then brought down in the new direction (3). The other ski is swung around parallel to it (4).

Below: The basic, or diagonal, stride, which consists of a kick-off from one foot and a gliding step with the other, the poles being planted alternately as the opposite leg begins its kick. The grips before and after the push are illustrated on the left below the ski boots.

Above: Herringboning, a method of using a shorter diagonal stride for uphill skiing. The toes of the skis are turned outwards and the heels kept together, the edged skis preventing backsliding.
Left: Double poling, in which both poles are planted in the snow simultaneously, can be used to rest or to obtain increased speed.

an Alpine region.

climbers Attachments to the undersides of skis used to prevent backsliding during ascent. Also known as *creepers.*

combi skis Skis developed as a compromise between hard (*qv*) and soft (*qv*) skis for travelling in icy conditions as well as deep snow.

combined event Olympic Alpine skiing event in which skiers are placed according to their results in the downhill, slalom and giant slalom.

comma Skiing position with the upper body leaning slightly away from the slope and the hips curved towards it.

corn snow Granular type of snow which turns rapidly to slush in warmer weather. Also known as sugar snow.

counter rotation Twisting movement of the upper body away from the direction of a turn. Also called reverse shoulder skiing.

critical point A place or line on the landing hill of a ski jump beyond which the slope de-

creases and it is dangerous to land.

cross country turn Form of skating turn used by cross country skiers in which the weight is shifted to the outer ski (*qv*) which is then pushed outward and away as weight transfers to the inner ski (*qv*).

crossover turns Freestyle ballet stunts in which one ski is lifted across the other.

crouched traverse Body position prior to up unweighting (*qv*).

crud Colloquial term for a snow condition occurring in warmer weather which makes skiing difficult. Usually firm on the surface, but soft and deep below. Also known as crust and harsch.

crust *See* crud.

daffy A recognized freestyle aerial stunt in which the skier takes a jump and, while in midair, points one ski forwards and up, the other backwards and down, bringing them back together before landing. A *double daffy* consists of the above manoeuvre, which is then re-

versed.

diagonal stride Basic cross country movement whereby the right arm is moved forward with the left leg, and vice versa, forming a 'kick and glide' motion.

double helicopter A freestyle aerial turn performed twice through 360°. *See* helicopter.

double pole stride Used on smooth terrain by the cross country skier. Both poles are swung forward together and the skis glide along alternately. It is faster than the diagonal stride (*qv*), but more tiring.

double poling System of propelling oneself forward in cross country skiing by putting the skis together, placing both poles in front and pulling oneself through the poles. Used on gentle slopes, or to increase speed.

downhill ski Ski which is positioned lower down the slope than the other. Also called the *lower ski.*

drag lift or ski tow One by which the skier is pulled, rather than

carried, up a slope on his skis.

dry skiing Technique evolved in recent years to enable beginners and experts to practice skiing without snow. Runs are usually constructed from plastic brush matting. Dry, or artificial, skiing is becoming increasingly popular in its own right, as well as being an ideal method of learning the fundamental techniques, of snow skiing.

edge The metal edges of the ski used to grip the snow while turning.

egg position Crouching position assumed by the downhill skier in which the head is lower than the back and the elbows are kept well in to minimize wind resistance.

fall line The most direct line of descent on a slope.

fanny pack Small bag fastened on the back at waist level for carrying light articles.

fergie A double side kick (*qv*).

FIS Fédération Internationale de Ski World governing body of skiing, founded in 1924. It has

Alpine skiing

Below: The basic equipment for Alpine skiing is a pair of skis, made of a combination of wood, metal and plastic, to which the soles of specially constructed boots are fastened with clamps or bindings; a pair of ski poles; light waterproof clothing, including gloves; and goggles to protect the eyes from the glare of the snow. A crash helmet is compulsory in downhill competition.

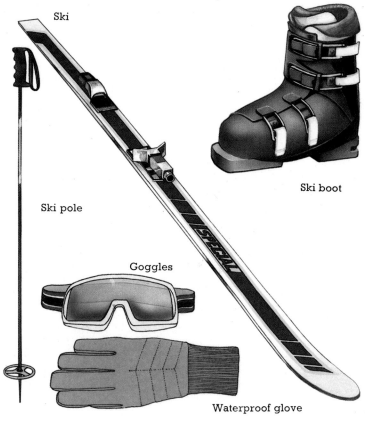

Ski

Ski pole

Goggles

Waterproof glove

Ski boot

Left: The starting gate is positioned at the top of each course in downhill, slalom and giant slalom events. Each skier prepares himself for the run behind the gate. The gate starts the clock as the racer throws himself into the course.

Right: Downhill racing is over a course ranging in length from ½-3 miles. Men's courses are longer than women's. However, descents are rarely referred to by their length but by the time taken to ski them. The course must have a specified drop, or vertical descent.

48 member nations.

floater A ramp built for freestyle aerial competitions, and used for upright jumps.

flying mile (or kilometer) A precisely measured, straight, course – often less than a mile (or kilometer) – used in speed competitions.

Föhn wind Fierce, warm, southerly wind which blows in Alpine countries and can rapidly alter the prevailing snow conditions.

gate The area bounded by two poles topped with matching colored flags through which the slalom skier must pass.

GLM Graduated length method System of ski instruction, also called *ski évolutif*, in which beginners commence with very short skis and progress through four different lengths to the longer racing skis. The system is frequently modified to use one length of short skis throughout a basic course of instruction.

godille Another name for the wedeln (*qv*) method of skiing.

gondola Small form of cable car

(*qv*) used for transporting skiers —normally four—long distances up a mountainside. Skis are strapped outside the car.

grass skiing Popular summer sport demanding similar techniques to snow skiing, and thus ideal for out-of-season practice. The 'skis' are short and on a continuous roller, similar to a caterpillar tractor.

gunbarrel A natural gully of skiable terrain with steeply banked sides.

hard skis Skis which are stiff when flexed and best suited to skiing in icy conditions.

harsch See crud.

helicopter Freestyle 360° turn performed in mid-air with the body vertical.

herringbone Method of climbing moderate slopes by facing uphill with the tails (*qv*) of the skis together, tips apart and poles behind. Steps are taken with the skis well edged (*qv*) against the slope to prevent back-sliding.

hockey stop Turn at speed from a downhill run, achieved by

flexing the knees and bringing them round to face across the fall line (*qv*). As the turn commences, weight is brought hard down on to the skis, which are thus forced away from the skier and will stop.

hot-dogging Freestyle skiing taken to its limits. A term used to describe a maneuver or action which is spectacular.

inner ski The ski which is on the inside when executing a turning circle.

inrun Downhill run made as a preliminary to a ski jump.

iron cross A recognized freestyle aerial stunt in which the skier brings both skis up behind him in mid-air to form a cross.

jet turn See avalement.

judges' tower Tall building at the end of a ski jump from which the judges watch the performance of the competitors.

jump turn Turn which is made with both skis lifted clear of the snow.

kick and glide Motion achieved in cross country. *See* diagonal

stride.

kicker A ramp specifically designed for somersault jumps in freestyle aerial competitions.

kick turn Stationary turn through 180°. One ski is moved from the parallel to a vertical position, and then down to face the opposite way; the second is then brought round to line up with the first.

langlauf German name for cross country.

layouts In freestyle, various aerial somersaults with the hands in a 'swallow' position.

leg breaker Freestyle ballet maneuver in which one ski is lifted and placed near the tail of the other, the skier's weight being transferred to it.

moebius A freestyle aerial front layout (*qv*) with a full twist.

mogul A hillock or bump on a piste (*qv*), often formed by a succession of skiers using the same point at which to turn.

mogul run One of the three freestyle disciplines where competitors ski over a bumpy mogul

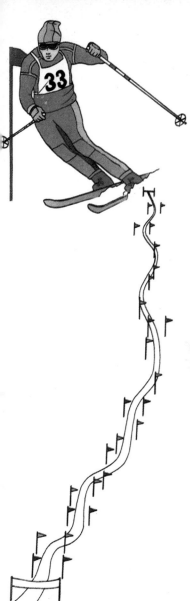

Left: The slalom consists of a downhill run over which a number of gates must be negotiated: 50-75 in men's events, less for women. Skiers may hit the poles with the body, but the skier's boots must pass a line between the two poles of the gate. No practice runs are allowed. The winner is the competitor with the fastest aggregate time over two runs.

Above: The giant slalom combines the speed of the downhill with the techniques of the slalom events. The skier must pass through marked gates as in slalom, but these are positioned further apart, allowing a higher speed to be maintained. The course is also longer than that for the slalom, but rules are similar.

course and are judged on aggression, speed and control, along with the stunts performed.

mogul turn *See* avalement.

mule kick Back scratcher (*qv*) carried out to the side of the body.

Nordic combination International event in which competitors take part in both a ski jumping contest and a 15km cross country race. Positions are based on a points system.

outer ski The ski which is on the outside when executing a turning circle.

outrigger turn Freestyle ballet turn in which the skier is well crouched down with all his weight on the inner ski; the outer ski is extended to the side off the ground.

outrun Flat terrain on which the jumper comes to a halt after a ski jump.

parablock Block which may be fitted on the tip of the ski to prevent the skis crossing. Used both for beginners and in teaching the jet turn (*qv*).

parallel christie Advanced form of the stem christie (*qv*), which has developed gradually into its present form as a parallel turn (*qv*).

parallel skiing Method of skiing in which the skis remain parallel both when running and turning.

parallel turn A turn performed with the skis parallel rather than stemmed (*qv*). The transition from stem turns (*qv*) to parallel turns can cause a skier some difficulty.

piste A ski run. Pistes are classified by color according to their degree of difficulty, with green as the simplest, progressing through blue and red to the hardest, black.

pole planting The precise placing of poles in the snow as an aid to turning control when parallel skiing. The downhill pole is brought forward until it is vertical and is then planted between the boot and ski tip. The turn is executed around the pole.

poma lift Drag lift (*qv*) or button lift for a single skier comprising

a curved aluminium bar at the end of which is a plastic disc. The bar is placed between the legs, and the skier is supported at the back by the disc.

powder Light, dry snow, usually found on the higher slopes. It is ideal for skiing.

pre-jumping A method of reducing flight through the air in downhill racing by jumping into the air before a point that would naturally throw the racer into the air.

reverse shoulder skiing *See* counter rotation.

rotation Movement of the upper body in the direction of a turn.

royal christie Freestyle ballet turn executed on the downhill ski, the other leg being extended behind the skier.

ruade Technique of jumping slightly before a parallel turn (*qv*) in order to help the skier unweight (*qv*).

rut A depression carved out of the snow on a piste by skis running constantly down the same line or track.

safety strap The small strap connecting skier and ski which prevents the ski running away if it becomes loose.

salopettes A dungaree style waterproof clothing worn by some skiers.

scaffold Construction at the top of a ramp in ski jumping from which the competitor commences his downhill run. Also called a tower.

schuss A straight downhill run at speed.

schussboomer A person who skis wildly or at speeds beyond his ability to control.

seelos In slalom, a series of three gates (*qv*) in which the second is at right angles to the other two elements of the obstacle.

short swing Rhythmic series of linked christies (*qv*) carried out on a downhill run, enabling the skier to take the slope at a steeper angle. The short swing relies on rapid re-edging of the skis at each turn.

shoulder roll A forward head roll performed in freestyle ballet

Ski jumping

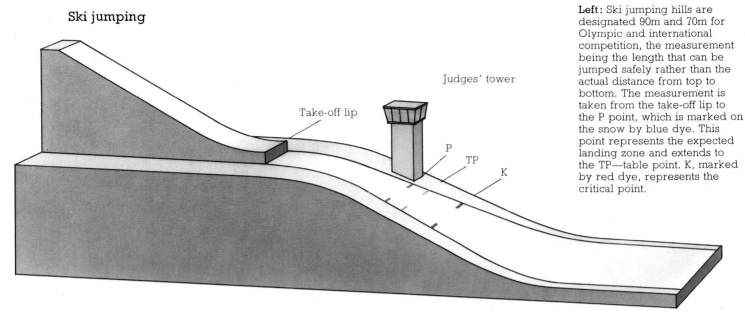

Judges' tower

Take-off lip

P
TP
K

Left: Ski jumping hills are designated 90m and 70m for Olympic and international competition, the measurement being the length that can be jumped safely rather than the actual distance from top to bottom. The measurement is taken from the take-off lip to the P point, which is marked on the snow by blue dye. This point represents the expected landing zone and extends to the TP—table point. K, marked by red dye, represents the critical point.

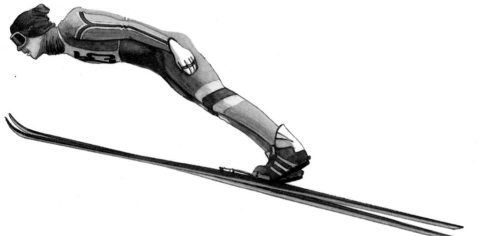

Left: The perfect posture for a ski jumper while in the air is the vorlage position, with the back and hips very slightly curved and the skis parallel. Points are awarded for distance and style, the former being taken from the take-off lip to the central point of the skis on landing. Each jumping hill has its own official table for calculating distance scores. Style, or form, is judged from the moment of take-off until the landing.

skiing.

shovel The upturn at the tip of a ski.

side hopping Extension of the tail hopping (*qv*) exercise in which the ski tails are moved to left or right during a hop.

side kick Freestyle aerial maneuver in which both skis, either parallel or crossed, are moved to one side in mid-air after a jump.

side-slip Technique of moving down a slope, either down the fall line or when traversing (*qv*), to aid negotiation of obstacles. The skis are placed together across the fall line and the edges (*qv*) released. Movement will stop if the skis are again fully edged.

side step Basic method of climbing any slope on skis. The skier stands across the fall line (*qv*) with the skis well edged to avoid slipping and, commencing with the uphill ski (*qv*), moves upwards one step at a time.

ski bum (US) Skiing enthusiast, usually working his passage from one resort to another.

ski évolutif *See* GLM.

ski flying Type of ski jumping, the distance covered being of greater importance than style or technique. As a result, jumps are more spectacular than in conventional ski jumping.

ski schools Most ski resorts have ski schools for beginners upwards with one qualified instructor per class. Classes are graded according to ability, and pupils are promoted when the instructor feels they are ready for a higher class. Private tuition is usually available which enables the skier at all levels to progress more rapidly.

sno-cat Machine used for packing snow tightly on the pistes.

snow cement A compound used to harden snow surfaces.

snowmaking Method of creating artificial snow in an area where natural resources are limited or have failed altogether. The snow is made from a mixture of compressed air and water, and is sprayed from guns to give a consistancy varying from a pow-

der to granules, depending on the air-water ratio.

snowplow Elementary way in which to brake or stop. The tips of the skis are placed together, heels wide apart, and the skis edged (*qv*) inwards. As the knees are more fully flexed and edging (*qv*) increased, braking power improves.

snowplow turn Simple turn carried out from the snowplow position by putting pressure on the outer (*qv*) ski.

soft ski A type of ski which bend easily under pressure and is best suited to skiing in deep or powder snow.

somersault In freestyle aerial skiing, a wide variety of somersaults are performed according to the skill of the skier.

spread eagle Recognized freestyle aerial jump in which the arms and legs are spread out wide.

stem christie A development of the stem turn (*qv*) executed on a downhill run.

stemming Movement of one ski

away from the other at the tail as a prelude to turning or to reduce speed.

stem turn Method of changing direction when parallel skiing on a traverse. The uphill or outer ski is stemmed and pressure applied to it as in a snowplow (*qv*) turn.

step turn Elementary turn from a stationary position. The tips of the skis are moved alternately in the direction required to form a 'star' pattern if a full circle is completed.

stick An alternative name for a ski pole.

straight running Downhill skiing in a straight line with the skis parallel and knees slightly bent.

sugar snow Another name for corn snow (*qv*).

swing A high-speed turn made with the skis parallel.

tail The squared-off back of the skis. Also called the *heel*.

tail hopping Parallel ski exercise in which a hop lifts the tails of the skis off the ground; it is completed by flexing the knees

Freestyle

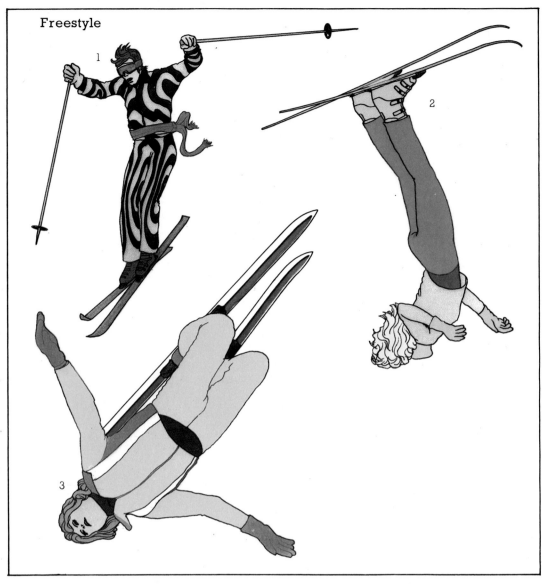

Left: Freestyle skiing, or hot-dogging, developed from man's desire to attempt the seemingly impossible and graduated to become a competitive sport. In competitions, marks are awarded for almost any aspects of a skier's performance, including originality, speed of execution and dress. The zebra suit (1) is a typical example of the less-conventional clothing favoured by hot-doggers, while the straightforward somersault (2), performed after a jump, is one of the basic stunts. The more adventurous freestyle skier will combine his or her somersault with other tricks, such as the back scratcher (3). The heels of the skis should actually touch the skier's back. In addition to such aerial acrobatics, freestyle skiing includes dancing on skis to music, a popular pursuit known to its devotees as ballet.

into a crouching position.

T-bar Type of drag lift (*qv*) for one or two skiers on which the skier is supported at the back by a crossbar (half of the 'T'), and holds on to a central bar.

team relay Nordic skiing event for men and women. The men's relay is 4 x 10km, and the women's 3 x 5km.

telemark First method ever used for turning in downhill skiing in which one ski is moved forward until the tip of the other ski is touching the boot. The other leg by this time should be kneeling on the other ski at a slight angle to the other. A rather precarious turn is then executed. Also used by jumpers on landing.

timing Alpine ski events are timed electronically to 1/100th of a second, while Nordic events are timed to within 1/10th of a second.

tip roll A 360° freestyle ballet turn in which the skier, supported by his poles, raises himself on to the ski tips and swings right round.

tip stand Freestyle stunt in which the skier 'stands' on the tips of the skis with the heels crossed behind his back and supports himself in the front on the ski poles.

tornado Freestyle ballet maneuver with a combination of linked jump-overs —movements in which the uphill ski is lifted and is jumped over the downhill ski. The weight of the body is supported by the ski poles.

tower *See* scaffold.

tramlines Ruts in the snow made by the skis.

traverse Technique of running across the fall line (*qv*). The body is in the comma (*qv*) position with most of the weight on the lower ski; the skis are pointed downhill and edged to avoid side-slipping (*qv*).

twister A freestyle upright aerial (*qv*) which incorporates a combination turn.

United States Ski Association The national governing body responsible for skiing in the U.S. In addition to setting standards

it is also responsible for the nation's Olympic and national ski teams in both the Nordic and Alpine events.

unweighting Term used to describe the momentary reduction of weight on the skis prior to a turn, achieved by rapidly straightening the body and throwing the weight forward (up unweighting) or suddenly flexing the knees while throwing the weight forward (down unweighting).

uphill christie A parallel turn which is continued until the skis point uphill and the skier comes to a halt. Weight is placed on the outside ski, the body bending as the knees 'drive' in the direction of the turn.

uphill ski Ski which is placed higher up a slope when running.

vorlage The classic ski jumping position in which the jumper leans well forward from the ankles, keeping the knees straight and arms by his side.

walking Walking on skis over flat terrain is a simple way for

beginners to accustom themselves to the feel of the skis before attempting to ski downhill.

waxing The art of waxing the soles of skis for both Alpine and Nordic events is highly skilled; the make-up of the wax used is determined according to the prevailing conditions and is of vital importance to help the competitive skier complete a course in the fastest possible time.

wedeln Smoother, more elegant form of the short swing (*qv*) in which the re-edging is much slighter. Literally, wedeln means 'tail wag'

wellen Technique employed when skiing and turning around moguls (*qv*).

window frame A 180° turn, similar to the tip roll (*qv*), in which the skier goes through his sticks and twists round to face in the opposite direction. It is a freestyle maneuver.

windslab A surface crust of snow formed by wind action.

Snow Vehicles

Man has for centuries employed the sledge as a means of transport, although sledding in general underwent a revival towards the end of the last century. Bobsledding, luge and skeleton tobogganing are the three principal fields of competitive sledding today. The most direct modern descendant of the early sledge is the luge which, although it is the more popular participant sport, was not represented at the Olympic Games until 1964, when it replaced skeleton tobogganing. There are three international luge events: men's single seaters, women's single seaters and double seaters for men only. The luge was for long overshadowed in competitions by the sport of bobsledding, which originated in Switzerland in 1890 and received Olympic recognition in 1924. Bobsledding is essentially a team sport, with both two-man boblet and four-man bobsled events contested. The four-man bobsled has been known to attain speeds over 75mph, while the boblet travels only slightly slower.

The most recent addition to this field of winter sports is the skibob, a bicycle-like apparatus for single riders, mounted on skis, and on which speeds of over 75mph are possible. Skibobbing first rose to popularity in Europe early in the 1960s, and has had its own world championships biennially since 1967. World championships are held annually for both luge and bobsled except in Olympic years. The championship events comprise four descents unless bad weather prevents competition on one of the two days. The jury then decides what constitutes the race; there must be a minimum of two runs, but a third run can be taken into account. Timing is crucial, and is electronically controlled to give results to within 1/100th of a second.

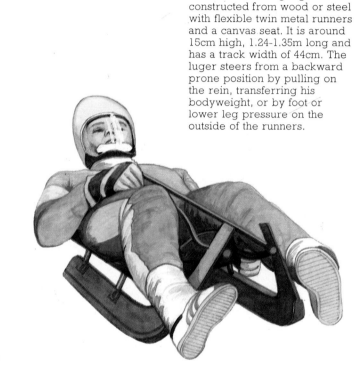

Left: A cross-section through an artificial luge course showing the curve at the base. The foundation is of cement or stone, which is then filled with snow or ice and frozen, sometimes with the aid of refrigeration. To lower construction costs, a combined luge/bobsled course is now built for international events, as specifications are similar.

Below: The racing luge is constructed from wood or steel with flexible twin metal runners and a canvas seat. It is around 15cm high, 1.24-1.35m long and has a track width of 44cm. The luger steers from a backward prone position by pulling on the rein, transferring his bodyweight, or by foot or lower leg pressure on the outside of the runners.

artificial luge course Used exclusively in international events as against the natural track (qv). A luge course varies in length from 1000–1500m and is 140cm-160cm wide at the bottom with 12 or more banked curves. Luge courses are often used for bobsled events; however some luge tracks such as Imst (Austria) are neither safe nor suitable for bobsleds.

ballast Extra weight which is added to a bobsled or luge as weight compensation (qv).

bob Colloquial name for the bobsled.

boblet A two-man bobsled.

bobsled course Natural (qv) tracks are at least 1500m long with a gradient of 8-15%. Artificial tracks must be at least 1200m long with a gradient of 8-15%.

brakeman Member of a bobsled team who is primarily responsible for starting the sled. He assists with balancing the sled and stops it at the end of the run.

cowling Streamlined fiberglass hood covering the front of a bobsled to reduce wind resistance.

control stations Points along a course from which the condition of the track and competitors' progress may be monitored.

Cresta run Famous skeleton tobogganing run at St Moritz.

double seater (1) Two-seater luge with a maximum weight of 24kg. A short strap around the driver is held by the crew to maintain close contact. The second seat is lower than the driver's, who lies back over his crew, thus decreasing wind resistance. (2) Luge event for men held over two runs (qv). The men's doubles always starts from the women's start which is usually about three-quarters of the way up from the finish to the men's start.

driving track The shortest negotiable distance from start to finish of a race track is known as the best driving track.

false start A team which, through no fault of its own, has a false start is permitted to complete the course and then start again.

FIBT Fédération Internationale de Bobsleigh et Tobogganing The official world administrator of bobsled and skeleton, founded in 1957, when luge and bobsled became independent sports.

FIL Fédération Internationale de Luge de Course. World body responsible for the administration of luge.

flexible runner Inward sloping runner, the front of which is independently controlled either by leg pressure or by means of a hand rope or rein. Used as an aid to steering.

flexible sled Any sled with flexible runners.

International Skibob Federation Organization formed in Austria in 1962 to administer skibobbing.

jury Committee of three, four or five members set up to adjudicate any problems which may arise during a race. In the event of a tie, the chairman of the race organizing committee has the casting vote.

luger Driver of a luge.

middle men The two members of a four-man bobsled team in addition to the driver and brakeman. They push the bob at the start of a race, act as ballast and give crucial help when cornering by weight transference.

natural track Tracks through natural terrain over varying ground conditions. The toboggans and techniques used are similar to those used on artificial tracks, though more improvisation is required over the rougher surface. Some luge tracks such as Kufstein (Austria) and Hammarstrand (Sweden) are partly 'natural'. A natural track is made from packed snow and ice blocks, reinforced where necessary by concrete, wood or metal. They represent the ultimate challenge to bobsleighers and are faster and more dangerous than all artificial tracks except the artificial track at Oberhof, East Germany.

night run Race carried out under floodlights after dark.

Above: The bobsled is of steel and aluminium construction with a fiberglass cowling and four steel runners. Handles on each side aid push starting. Steering is controlled with a rope and toggle system although occasionally a steering wheel is used. The brake is fitted for emergency use only as it could damage the track.

Maximum dimensions for both classes of bobsled are laid down by the FIBT. Width for both is limited to 67cm. The two-man sled, or boblet, must not exceed 2.7m in length and 375kg in total weight (weight of team and bob) while the maximum length and total weight for the four-man bob are 3.8m and 630kg.

Below: The skibob is a bicycle-like apparatus made of wood, metal or plastic, and mounted on skis. The rider wears short skis with metal claws at the heel which he uses for braking; steering is effected by means of the handlebars. The rider wears protective clothing, including a crash helmet (compulsory) and goggles.

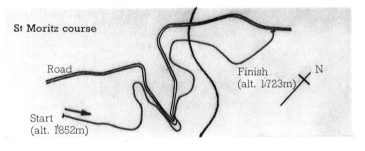

St Moritz course

Road

Start (alt. 1852m)

Finish (alt. 1723m)

N

Left: A 'terrifying, spaghetti-shaped chute of solid ice' is how one writer described a bobsled course, and it is an apt description of the world championship course at St Moritz (illustrated by the red line). Championship courses must be at least 1500m long, contain a minimum of 15 banked turns, and have a gradient of 8

to 15 per cent. At St Moritz, for example, the course drops 130m over a distance of 1575m from start to finish. Beyond the finish point is an area where the bob can come to a halt without recourse to the brake.

one-and-a-half seater Luge used in single-seater events by an above-average sized male competitor.

practice run Four or five days prior to an international event are allotted for competitors to accustom themselves to a course. A number of practice runs are obligatory before a team may take part in an event; insufficient practice may result in disqualification, as may practicing outside the given times.

rein Rope or thong attached to a luge. By pulling on the rein, the runner on the inside of a corner is lifted, thus causing the luge to turn.

run Part of a race. In a four-run event, which is the norm, two runs are made on each of two consecutive days, weather permitting.

runner deflection Area of a flexible toboggan runner which is in contact with the track surface. Maximum speed is attained when the middle thirds of the sharp inner edges of the runners

are in contact with the ice. The runners are sharpened or rounded depending on the temperature of the ice and the condition of the track.

single seater (1) Luge with a maximum weight of 22kg, usually used by women in single-seater events. (2) Men's and women's races over four runs (qv), the men's course being longer than the women's.

skeleton riding Form of tobogganing in which the rider lies in a forward prone position, rather than back as on the luge. Riders have spiked toe caps on their shoes which are used for steering and braking.

sled Any vehicle mounted on runners for transport over snow or ice.

start (1) Luge start. Luge riders sit on the luge between two metal hoops which are set in the ground, holding one hoop in each hand. Upon the signal that the track is clear, the rider pulls himself or herself forward, using the hoops to gain the maximum

acceleration which is an essential part of a fast descent. (2) In bobsled, the bob is usually positioned 15m before the starting line (qv) and pushed by the team to gather speed. There is no limit to the distance over which a team may push the bob before jumping in.

starting block Piece of wood at the back of the start box on which the brakeman (qv) braces his feet before the start.

starting line A notional line between the electronic timing devices either side of the track 15m from the starting block.

starting succession Method of determining the order in which competitors start a race. After an initial draw, the starting order is varied for each run (qv) in an event so as to give equal opportunity to all competitors.

timekeepers Officials who work the electronic timing mechanisms and check the electronic timing of a race with stopwatches.

toboggan Long light sled curved upwards at the front.

track width Distance between the inside edges of a sled's runners.

warming of runners Technique of heating the runners to give increased speed. In competitions the temperature of the runners of each luge is checked just before the rider starts his descent. It must be within 0.5°C of the ambient air temperature at the time of measuring.

waxing Application of wax to the bottom of the runners of a sled to increase their gliding ability. Waxing is a specialized art on which the result of a competition could rest. It is not allowed in bobsledding.

weight compensation In order to lessen any disadvantage held by a light rider, ballast (qv) may be added to a luge or bobsleigh. The optimum weight of a male luge rider is taken to be 95kg. A rider who weighs less is allowed to wear a weight belt equivalent to 50% of the difference between the weight of himself plus his clothing, and 95kg. Riders weighing over 95kg are permitted.